Praise for The Devil at Genesee Junction

"Veteran crime writer Michael Benson embarks on a deeply personal and thought-provoking investigative journey into the murders of two young female neighbors nearly a half-century ago. Along with one of the victim's mothers and a private investigator, they leave no stone unturned in identifying suspects and linking them to other grisly killings throughout the United States. It's a page-turner."

—**Robert Mladinich**, author of *From the Mouth of the Monster: The Joel Rifkin Story*; coauthor of *Lethal Embrace* and *Hooked Up For Murder*

"Benson has written an unusual combination of memoir and true crime that is as affecting as it is compelling. The upstate New York location becomes a unique setting for the haunting and personal story that he unfolds, like the born storyteller he is."

—**Fred Rosen**, author of *Lobster Boy*

THE DEVIL AT GENESEE JUNCTION

THE DEVIL AT GENESEE JUNCTION

The Murders of Kathy Bernhard and George-Ann Formicola, 6/66

Michael Benson

ROWMAN & LITTLEFIELD
Lanham • Boulder • New York • London

Published by Rowman & Littlefield
A wholly owned subsidiary of The Rowman & Littlefield Publishing Group, Inc.
4501 Forbes Boulevard, Suite 200, Lanham, Maryland 20706
www.rowman.com

Unit A, Whitacre Mews, 26-34 Stannary Street, London SE11 4AB

British Library Cataloguing in Publication Information Available

Library of Congress Cataloging-in-Publication Data

Benson, Michael.
The devil at Genesee Junction : the murders of Kathy Bernhard and George-Ann Formicola, 6/66 / Michael Benson.
pages cm
Includes bibliographical references and index.
ISBN 978-1-4422-5233-2 (cloth : alk. paper) — ISBN 978-1-4422-5234-9 (electronic)
1. Murder—New York (State) 2. Cold cases (Criminal investigation)—New York (State) I. Title.
HV6533.N7B46 2015
364.152'30974788—dc23
2015018321

∞ ™ The paper used in this publication meets the minimum requirements of American National Standard for Information Sciences Permanence of Paper for Printed Library Materials, ANSI/NISO Z39.48-1992.

Printed in the United States of America

For Alice

CONTENTS

AUTHOR'S NOTE

This book is 49 years in the making. Some of it was first written when I was a kid. I was already chronicling the nightmare, even when it was fresh. Big chunks were written in the 1980s, then again in the 1990s, with the remainder written between 2011 and 2015.

Although this is a true story, some names and locations have been changed to protect the privacy of the innocent. Pseudonyms will be noted upon their first usage with an asterisk (*). When possible, the spoken word has been quoted verbatim. However, when that is not possible, conversations have been reconstructed as closely as possible to reality based on the recollections of those who spoke and heard the words.

In places, there has been a slight editing of spoken words, but only to improve readability. The denotations and connotations of the words remain unaltered. In some cases, witnesses are credited with verbal quotes that in reality only occurred in written form. Some characters may be composites.

Information based on a published source is endnoted. In some cases, articles have survived the years only in clippings, and original page numbers may be missing from those endnotes.

FOREWORD

The Curious Farmer

Satanic ages last 1,458 years. The last one, where God was on top and Satan was cast down, started in A.D. 508. Consequently, the new satanic age began in 1966 and this time Satan is on top. 1966 was "Year one, Anno Satanas—the first year of the reign of Satan."[1] — Anton Szandor LaVey, founder, Church of Satan

It was a sunny summer Wednesday around noon, and the Mortons* of Lester Street couldn't find their dog. The dog had run off to do its duty and hadn't returned. The Mortons lived in one of the houses that backed against the Pennsylvania Railroad tracks, between Ballantyne Road and the swimming hole. Francine Morton Wilson led a search party made up of her and her two much younger brothers. Crossing the tracks, they looked north toward the stone trestle and saw the poor dog's cadaver lying on the tracks.

"You two run home," Francine said. She would investigate alone. At first she thought a train had hit him, but as she got closer she realized that the reality was much worse. Someone had neatly slit the dog down the middle, opened him up, and pulled out the innards. Who would want to do that to a little dog? It was just the sort of sick thing her husband Clint Wilson* would do, she thought—if he had the guts.

Three hours later and two miles to the west, 43-year-old farmer Vincent Zuber was on his spinach-green John Deere tractor cutting hay along a dirt service road that ran parallel to the West Shore railroad tracks near the intersection of Archer and Beaver Roads.

That road, sometimes no more than two ruts in the weeds, was used at night as a lovers' lane. Zuber's family had been farming in Chili since 1882, and though the family recognized that teenagers getting steamy on their property was a potential problem, laissez-faire reigned, and no one yet had left the farmhouse to shoo away the passionate youngsters.

Follow those tracks a couple of miles east and you were behind my house. Go a few hundred feet further and you were at the Genesee Junction where the Pennsylvania crossed the West Shore track of the New York Central, only feet away from the swimming hole. Take those tracks even further east and you came out on Scottsville Road at the iron river trestle where my great-grandmother Mrs. Richard Watkins died at the age of 35 in October 1916, struck by a West Shore train as she crossed the Genesee River. ("How did she get hit by a train?" I asked my paternal grandma when I was little. "She didn't look both ways," she replied.)

Zuber had a great view of his surroundings from his high perch atop the tractor. The air was cooler today. It had been a hot summer, and the heat had broken. Breathing deeply in appreciation, Zuber smelled what he later described as a "very rich odor," unmistakably putrescence.

A cow must've gotten out and died, he thought. Truth was, the death smell had been there a few days before, but he'd thought it was a woodchuck and didn't investigate. He'd hoped it would dissipate. But the smell was getting worse. Zuber took a deep breath and drove toward the scent. He left the field and drove onto the dirt road, heading eastward. He stopped the tractor near a cluster of high bushes, south of the dirt road.

Zuber shut off the engine and climbed down. As he pushed his way through the weeds toward the bushes, he saw evidence of teenagers. There was a girl's comb, a girl's flip-flop—what they called "thongs" back in those days, a cheap rubber sandal—and then . . . well, then, searing into his memory, the nightmare, partially hidden in a thicket of elderberry bushes and high weeds, a human leg and foot, baked into brown suet.

The farmer's mind clicked right away. The missing girls.

Zuber—arms flailing, screaming, white as a ghost—forgot about his tractor and ran in a cross-lots beeline to the home of a friend and neighbor, 42-year-old sheriff's sergeant Glenn J. Saile, who would know what to do. Saile served four years in the navy during World War II and became a deputy sheriff not long after his return to civilian life in 1946. Saile lived on Beaver Road Extension, about a quarter mile south of the railroad tracks.

Zuber had only seen one body, but Saile quickly found the other only a few feet away and began the notifications at 3:30 p.m. Crime scene technicians, homicide investigators, people from the medical examiner's office, and members of the press were soon on the scene. The bodies had been butchered with a knife. The next day the story was in the *New York Times*.[2] That night, Walter Cronkite mentioned the grisly discovery. With Zuber's permission, the Monroe Tree Surgeons were called in and defoliated the Archer Road crime scene. The sun baked and reflected off the newly bare clay. It looked like an Egyptian archeological dig.

ACKNOWLEDGMENTS

The author wishes to thank the following individuals and organizations without whose help the writing of this book would have been impossible. First and foremost, Donald A. Tubman, licensed private investigator—who put the *pro* in *pro bono*. Next up, my associate investigators Donald Campbell, MaryAnne Curry Shults, Amy Minster Hudak, and Tom Wiest. And, in alphabetical order, special thanks go to Philip Albano; Terri Albee; Wesley R. Alden, assistant regional design engineer, State of New York Department of Transportation; Mitch Alepoudakis; Gary and Richard Barnes; Ed Behringer; Joe Bender; Rita Benson; Tekla Benson; Frank Berger; Alice, Corky, and Betty Bernhard; Susan Bickford; Doris, Debby, and Laura Bookman; Marcia Bors; Maggie Brooks; Suzanne M. Camarata; Kim E. Clark; Garry Coles; Richard Cooper; Mary Crane; Patrick Crough; Christine Curran; Gary Curran; Sharon Cushman, Eastland (Texas) librarian; Paul Czapranski; Gus D'April; Linda Dambra; Carol Cooper Davis; Muriel Dech; Harry De-Hollander; Cheryl Dennie; Sandra Devlin; Martin D'Olivo; Evie Douglas; Mary Wilkey Dunne; Richard Egan; Rick Erickson; Robert F. Falzone; Christine C. Fien, editor of the *Gates-Chili Post*; Anna Maria Giorgione; Gary Goldstein; Patricia Graham-Wahl; Vicky Graham; Jack and Tom Greco; Grace Green-D'Agostino; Steve Griffin; Michelle Honea, deputy district clerk, Eastland County, Texas; Karen House; Norm Jacobs, publisher, Starlog Group; Rick Jensen, executive editor, Messenger Post Media; Danny Johnson; Paul R. Johnson; Barbara Johnston; Joyce Judd; Detective Sergeant Gary Kaola of the MCSO;

Linda Kearns, librarian, Scottsville Free Library; Noah M. Lebowitz, director of the Records Access Office in the Monroe County Department of Communications; Joan Lenhard, this investigation's director of transportation; Sandra Luke-Curtin; Pat McCarthy; Maureen McGuire, Kevin Doran, and Caroline Tucker of WROC-TV news; Larry Mancuso; Tracy Howe Miceli; Donna Melideo; Jim Memmott at the *Democrat and Chronicle*; Rona Lee Merritt; NYPD retired detective Robert Mladinich; Livingston County attorney, David J. Morris; Don Mosele; Kathleen Westlake Moses; George Mulligan; Elton Brutus Murphy; Judith Naso; Jim, Pat, and Mike Newell; Lois Forrester Oas; Pam Obein; former FBI special agent and sheriff of Chemung County, New York, Pat Patterson; Lisa Pappa; George Peterson; Jean Phillips; Joseph Picciotti; Cathy Pittanaro; Michele Pollifrone-Hass; RPD officer Patrick M. Piano; Audrey Shea Rader; Paula Ritz Ralston; Wayne Randall; Larry Rath; Mary Ann Reese; Donald G. Riechel; Catherine Roberts; Johnny Rowe; John Saeva; Doris Sailes; Gertrude Saxman; Patricia Schaap, historian, County of Livingston History Research Office; Rhonda Schaefer; Stephanie Scribani; Gary H. Sedore at the Friends of Mount Hope Cemetery; photographer and lifelong friend Philip Semrau, who took the cover photographs; Marcia Shea; Ken Shero; Patricia Short; Christine Sidarsky, Rochester City historian; Terry Simmons, former deputy, Eastland County (Texas) Sheriff's Office; Gary Steinmiller; Mike Taggart; Dig Taggart; Jim Totten; Tammy at the MCSO Records Access Office; Sandra Sage Trebold; Trina Treu; Tom Tryniski; Heather Rowe Tumia; Daniel W. Van Alstine; Joseph and Nathan Versace; the Victim Services Division of the Texas Department of Criminal Justice; attorney and former teammate Chris Walrath; photographer/history teacher/friend R. Jerome Warren; investigator Gregory S. Wildman, Field Intelligence Office, and Sergeant Scott Walsh, Major Crime Unit, MCSO; Mary Wilkey; Ed Wilkins; Joyce Marks Witherow; Janice Witt; Ed Yaw; Sandy Shulmerich Yaw; David Young; Mary Young; Kim Zuber; and Dan Zupansky, host of the *True Murder* podcast.

I

COUNTRY LIFE

Today you'd call Ballantyne suburban, but back in the 1960s, it was *country*—dusty rural with just a copse of houses, some of them shacks without indoor plumbing, on or near Ballantyne Road, in the town of Chili, which was pronounced to rhyme with "jai alai."

My dad, whose hands were well scrubbed, was an insurance adjustor for the Insurance Company of North America, with offices in the Sibley Tower Building in downtown Rochester. Suit and clip-on bowtie. We'd lived in the city proper, on Campbell Street in the "Dutchtown" section, until I graduated from kindergarten in 1962, at which time—to beat the suburban rush—my dad bought a house and four acres at the end of a bumpy, potholed, L-shaped dirt road called Stallman Drive, off Ballantyne Road. The house was on Lot 5 of the Ballantyne Acres subdivision, a weed-covered field that went all the way back to Black Creek—the dark, lazy, meandering stream that contributed to the Genesee River a mile to the east and was known to the Seneca and Iroquois Indians as Chekanango.

Our house sat just west of the Pennsylvania Railroad tracks, parallel to and only yards from a large drainage ditch that we called the "runoff." Only as an adult did I look at a vintage map and realize that our runoff was the bed of the old Genesee Valley Canal. The railroad tracks followed the canal's old elevated towpath, where beasts of burden once tugged boxcar-sized barges northward. That ditch had been dug in 1836 in what started out as an attempt to connect the Alleghany River at Olean with the Erie Canal inside the city of Rochester. The idea looked good on paper, but the canal never fully functioned. The section through Chili was prone to flood damage. The southernmost portion was never dug, and to get around the Genesee River gorge at Letchworth, canal builders used an old Indian portage route that necessitated way too many locks. By the 1960s, the runoff existed without historical context. Come winter it iced over and became our hockey rink.

Dad's need was simple: to get his wife and kid away from the changing city, without leaving himself a hellish commute—and he accommodated himself well. He enjoyed his cozy yet sturdy country home, a stucco two-bedroom screaming for an addition or two. He bought a big straw hat, held beer parties on the lawn, and dug a large garden. The airport was on the other side of the creek, just prop planes at first but then the airport was enlarged, made international, and the 727s were deafening.

Our dirt road became dusty in the summer. We could see cars coming from around the bend from the telltale dust cloud billowing up from behind the Formicolas' house.

The town refused to pave the road. For years it was the only dirt public road in Monroe County. A truck did come down twice a summer to fill the potholes with crushed rock, cut the weeds on either side of the road, and spray black oil that briefly kept the dust at bay.

The other flaw in my dad's plan had to do with the nighttime. The instant the sun went down or the humidity rose, the mosquitoes came out in swarms. It turned out Ballantyne Road was once called Mosquito Point Road, but the name was changed to pump up real estate prices to suckers who never visited their prospective properties after dark.

Dad, never one to go gentle into any good night, battled the "skeeters." He tried scented candles, insect repellent, but nothing worked. He bought what we called the Zapper and hung it from the old-fashioned lamppost in front of the house at the end of the rock garden. Plugged in via two extension cords, it had a "special light" that attracted bugs, then fried them with electricity. We could hear them crackling and burning in there. It was kind of satisfying. The device didn't distinguish mosquitoes from other bugs, and the loudest pops and crackles came from exploding moths. The Zapper proved fun but ineffective when it came to reducing the number of mosquito bites we suffered. So Dad built a wall. During the spring of 1966, our outdoor patio was transformed into a screened-in porch. That summer he put a chaise longue in there and ran an extension cord through the living room window to a black-and-white portable TV set, and the mosquitoes could watch him through the screen all they wanted. He would laugh at them. If one did get inside the screen, Dad always had a flyswatter handy.

My father, the only white-collar worker within a mile, knew *nothing* of the neighborhood he lived in. He made a martini and poked around in his garden. Anything going on outside the four-acre Benson estate, he didn't care. My mom joined a housewives bowling league at Olympic Bowl on Scottsville Road, so she heard some Ballantyne gossip. I, on the other hand, being a kid, knew some troubling things about the neighbors. Some of them were scary poor, a disproportionate number goofy, living in shacks with outhouses.

It was a blue-collar, lower-middle-class neighborhood, but there were some pathetic folks. Others were life hardened and frightening. I thought that was the way the world was. Ballantyne was haunted by a clump of alcoholics, junkies, dead-eyed men who'd given up the ghost, and abused teenagers who wanted to prove they could dish it out, too.

Which isn't to say I wasn't having a great time. My world, at age six, seven, and eight, was tiny, a scattering of five houses, mostly limited to the kids who also lived on Stallman Drive—the Tylers,* the Putnams,* and the Formicolas—as well as another house of kids, the Mulligans, on Ballantyne Road. The back of the Mulligans' house faced our house, and only days after we moved in, Big George Mulligan—a strong Irish carpenter who'd married a Native American and had three good-looking kids—used an industrial-strength mower to carve a path through the field between our houses, a path that would soon be worn to bare dirt by our footsteps going to and from each other's houses. Connecting Bensons with Formicolas, Bensons with Mulligans, Mulligans with Formicolas. I didn't need a path to the Tylers', which was just beyond the bend in the road. The road *was* the beeline.

There were shortcuts everywhere, fields crisscrossed with dirt paths. The weeds contained wild strawberries, wispy timothy like an old man's hair, and an occasional tangle of burdock. At the end of June, the strawberries were ripening, growing right up out of the clay across the fields, and their almost-cloying scent filled the air. (When *Strawberry Fields Forever* came out at the end of 1966, my first thought was, "Cool, the Beatles have one, too.")

The first "kid" I met from the neighborhood was Frankie Tyler,* who insisted that people call him Rocky. He was much older, like 16 already when I arrived in 1962, wearing a Yankees cap, and the first thing he said to me was, "Could you teach me how to throw a curveball?" Rocky once went out picking strawberries in our back field, and because he didn't have a bowl, he collected them in his white T-shirt, which he held up at the bottom to form a sort of hammock, and from then on that T-shirt had a large red stain covering his belly. Rocky had a sister named Gert, 14 when we moved in. She was pretty but had trouble spitting out her words, and she braided her hair into pigtails so that there was a part running down the center of the back of her head. You could see her dirty neck. The Tylers lived in the one house on the street that had an outhouse, and in the winter they heated up the unpainted cinderblock house and cooked on the wood-burning stove. The whole family had a distinctive smoky smell.

There was no Mr. Tyler around, but mom was crazy Ol' Lady Tyler, Dorothy, who once came to our house and asked my mom if she could listen for Martians in our washing machine. My mom went into the living room and asked my dad what to do. He stopped reading the sports page. "Let her in. Let me know if she hears anything." She didn't, which comforted him. "If she'd heard something, there'd be no getting rid of her," he reasoned.

Dorothy liked to talk to my mom. "Remember that preacher years ago that was supposed to have killed his wife?" Dorothy asked.

Truth was, my mom did. The murder occurred when she worked at Neisner's, a five-and-dime in downtown Rochester. That made it about 1948.

"Well, the wife's body was dumped right back there," Dorothy said, pointing toward the "crick."

"Really," Mom said with concern in her voice. Dorothy was crazy, but that didn't mean she couldn't be correct.

"I know the preacher didn't kill that woman. You know why? Because I know who did," Dorothy said with a wink.

Nuttier than a fruitcake, my mother concluded. Professionals agreed. Dorothy was in and out of institutions.

(Years later, I looked into this. On April 23, 1949, the Reverend George Hetenyi allegedly shot his young wife Jean. She was found floating in the river near the mouth of Black Creek. After four murder trials, each reversed on appeal, Hetenyi pleaded guilty of manslaughter and was sentenced to time served, i.e., 17 years behind bars.[1])

We had only been on Stallman Drive for a year or so when there was no more Frankie. He went somewhere for good.

The Tylers had a big old sloppy black dog named Jack that everybody loved. He had never been on a leash in his life, smelled bad, and wandered Stallman Drive freely, making the rounds, being social. He would sit still and relax when you picked the burdocks out of his fur.

Old Lady Tyler seemed to me way too old to have two teenaged kids. Yet they called her Ma. Maybe the old lady, with all that bubble, bubble, toil and trouble she was into, just looked years older than she was. At age six, I had difficulty distinguishing between people age 40 and 60.

I later learned that there were older Tyler kids who attended high school in the 1950s and were long gone by 1962. Frankie and Gert were the babies. Dorothy's craziness was just humorous until about 1965. Gert had blossomed, landed a boyfriend, and could be seen walking along the shoulder of Ballantyne Road with her hand in the guy's back pocket. My mom thought it was disgusting and clucked her tongue. Gert bloomed and became well scrubbed, made-up, and with it. She had her hair cut short and bounced self-consciously down the halls of Wheatland-Chili Central School, swinging her broad hips like a new butterfly learning to fly. Getting her act together terminated Gert's residence on Stallman Drive. As soon as she could, she got out. Her days of using the outhouse were through. There was a rumor that Ol' Lady Tyler chased Gert down Stallman Drive with a carving knife in her hand, and that was what got her put away the last time. The Tyler house became vacant, and we never saw any of them again. (Years later, when I was away at college, the Tyler house was used as practice by the Chili Volunteer Fire Department, torched and extinguished, rats running in all directions. The blackened hulk they left was slowly swallowed over the years by enveloping vegetation.)

During the summer of 1962, when I was still brand new in the neighborhood, the Mulligan kids, George, who was 8, Nancy, 11, and Sue, 13, received a black pony, whom they named Benny—which also happened to be my dad's first name.

Big George Mulligan had already built a fantastic tree house for us to play in, and now he built a barn in the backyard for Benny. I used to ride that pony bareback, clinging tightly with white knuckles at the ebony mane, as he ran up and down the pathway between our houses, jumping the ditch that ran along the back of the Mulligans' yard. One time my mom opened the back door to our house, and Benny the pony ran right inside. The Mulligans eventually saddled the pony, and I remember the smell of the saddle soap as Little George rubbed it lovingly into the leather. That was the summer that Marilyn Monroe died.

Our phone was on a party line. If the phone rang two short rings, it was for us. If it rang one long ring, it was a call for a neighbor. Sometimes we'd pick up the phone to make a call, and there would be nasty-toned people on the line, crabbing at each other.

My back field, among the wild strawberries, featured a small one-stall horse barn made of tar and wood, and an eight-foot-tall wooden corncrib beside it that for me was one big four-sided ladder, still sturdy enough for a six-year-old to climb on without it even bending. In the barn I kept a blue metal tackle box in which I preserved all of my found treasures, talismans of the perfect country summer: a small bird's nest, a cocoon, a piece of petrified wood, and a set of Man in Space trading cards that came with Popsicles.

There was a mountain of sun-baked horse chips behind the barn. Each spring I would repeatedly fill the wheelbarrow with the free fertilizer and put it on my folks' increasingly complex garden. I was home from college when I shoveled the last of it.

The barn (which became the home of my dad's tumbling pigeons), corncrib, and Mt. Dung served as forts and clubhouses, and various obstacles during endless games of cowboys and Indians. George-Ann Formicola and I (in my worse-for-wear coonskin cap) were always the cowboys because the Mulligans had Indian blood. The Indians had more fun, guiding us through the woods, searching for Indian arrowheads—George found one once!—and so George-Ann and I quit being cowboys and joined in the hunt. The Mulligans knew survival techniques—in case we ever got lost in the woods, you could use the foliage as a compass.

My mom's biggest memory of George-Ann was that she was a helpful little girl. One time she came down to the end of the road to see if I could come out and play and I was somewhere else. My mom was weeding the large vegetable garden. George-Ann sat down on the ground and weeded alongside my Mom until the job was done. They chatted. George-Ann told her that her name was supposed to be

Georgianne, but a nurse misspelled it on her birth certificate so they just went with it.

I call it the Putnam house because I played with the Putnam kids, but Burton Braddock* owned it, on the inside of the bend in Stallman Drive, next door to the Formicolas and directly across the street from the Tylers.

A couple of days after we moved in, Burt came down to talk to my old man. He wanted permission to hunt and fish on our property. Dad said, "Sorry, you'll end up shooting my kid," and Burt never spoke to him again.

Now, when Burt lived alone for the first few years, he had no trouble avoiding us Bensons. Then he roped up with a bottle-blonde divorcee named Pauline Putnam, who moved in with him and brought her five kids with her: Larry, who was three years older than me; Dawn, one year older; David, a couple of years younger; and toddler twins. Say what you want about Burt, he was taking on a lot. Larry and Dawn Putnam were the two who became my friends.

Burt raced stock cars on the side, because the lot between his and our house was an eyesore of junkers with hand-painted numerals on their sides, ready for the figure-eight races and demolition derby.

One summer Saturday afternoon Burt had a motorboat parked in his side yard along with the junkers. My folks had company over, a couple of uncles and other drinking buddies. Everyone was standing around outside, sitting at picnic tables, smoking and drinking, pitching horse-shoes, and whatever. My dad was wearing Bermuda shorts and knee-high orange socks. Burt Braddock came out of his house and started screaming in our direction. I don't remember what his beef was, but he was pretty vulgar about it. "He's drunk," my mother said, embarrassed. Braddock picked up a rock and threw it in our direction, but he yanked it and it went short right, directly into the windshield of his boat, crack-ing it. There was a stunned silence, and then Braddock turned around and went back inside his house.

"I guess he showed us," my Uncle Tom said.

George-Ann Formicola and Nancy Mulligan were attached at the hip in 1962. George-Ann was 10 and Nancy was 11. In the summer of 1962 everyone was doing the twist, and few did it better than Nancy and

George-Ann. I couldn't take my eyes off them. Around and around *and* up and down. When twisting faded, they limboed the hot days away. How low could they go? They could go very, very low. Nancy went lowest, but George-Ann was more fun to watch. Sometimes I got to hold the stick.

George-Ann taught me why you can't play the Name Game (*Mike, Mike, bo-bike, banana-fanna . . .*) with the names Chuck, Mitch, and Marty. She was the best at Simon Says. I thought I was smarter than the game, and most games of Simon Says were a snap for me—but George-Ann could get me, something about the staccato in her cadence.

George-Ann had one older sister, Gina, who had a curvy figure, wore harlequin glasses, and had already been around the block a couple of times when George-Ann reached puberty. And puberty hit George-Ann hard. She went from tomboy to buxom when she was in sixth grade. (In her eighth-grade yearbook photo, George-Ann looked like a woman standing among children. You could easily imagine a cigarette hanging off her lower lip like on a gangster's moll, and the second she got out of school there probably was.)

When I got to Chili, George-Ann and Nancy were part of the gang. Gina Formicola, like Sue Mulligan and Gert Tyler, was too old to care what us brats did. Since Nancy was George Mulligan's big sister, I was in George-Ann and Nancy's vicinity a lot of the time, either doing the same thing or doing different things in the same place. They were told to keep an eye on us little boys.

Nancy, despite her Indian blood, was a pretty blonde with smooth hair. George-Ann was dark, fleshy, and liked people to think she was tough, an illusion combated without her knowledge by her pigeon-toes. You could always tell George-Ann's footprints in the snow, so turned in were her toes. In the summer she wore battered tennis shoes, with worn holes in the sides so that her pinky toes protruded.

A school friend from Morgan Road said she got along with George-Ann because they shared a rich hatred of gym class. "We goofed on everything and laughed a lot."

There were times when George-Ann did seem pretty tough. She'd scratch her mosquito bites bloody, and once when she was crossing the barbed-wire fence that separated our property from a field owned by Rochester Gas and Electric, she cut her calf so badly that the blood was running down her leg, and when I told her maybe she should wash it or get a Band-Aid or something, she just laughed at me.

During that first summer there was a lot of baseball and softball and kickball going on. Half the time we were playing, and half the time we were looking for a lost ball in the weeds.

George Mulligan dug up some clay, mashed it up, and built his own pitcher's mound where we took turns pitching and catching with a real baseball. For me, George was the voice of kid wisdom. He taught me how to whittle a slingshot, tie on a thick rubber band—the thicker the better—and use it to shoot stones at sparrows. BB guns eventually rendered the slingshots obsolete. We'd fish in Black Creek right behind my house, the current trundling as slowly as an hour hand, almost imperceptibly, left to right. Throw a leaf in the dark water, then look back later, and it had moved toward the river. We fished with worms we dug ourselves. George would hear sunfish purling near the inky surface. We'd cast to the spot and, with just the slightest commotion, a pair would strike our hooks almost simultaneously.

Nancy and George-Ann chattered about who was cuter, Dr. Kildare or Ben Casey, two popular TV shows about a handsome doctor. I don't remember who had who, but the girls disagreed. You'd think Nancy, with hair the color of the sun, would go for Kildare, whereas the darker George-Ann, olive complected, would side with the downright swarthy Casey, but it could have gone the other way. What I remembered most was that, as they argued, they executed complex exchanges of cat's cradle.

It was the time of the British Invasion, and Nancy and George-Ann went to see the groups when they came to the Rochester War Memorial downtown. Animals, Stones. It was too much to wish that the Beatles would play Rochester, but they were hopeful the Kinks might come to town. They taught me about cool music. Nancy, George-Ann, and their good friend Debby Rockow who lived on Black Creek Road. Once, when Debby was my babysitter, she let me watch *Shindig!* on TV. The Kinks sang, "Who'll Be the Next in Line?"

Once Nancy and George-Ann took George and me to the other side of the Pennsylvania Railroad tracks, to a long footpath that ran along the south bank of the "crick" from Lester Street, all the way to Tacy's bait shop behind the Ballantyne School. They told George and me that they had two friends, the Romano brothers, stationed alongside the path hidden in the bushes, and these boys were going to pull a string taut a few inches off the ground. Our job was to run bravely down the path without slowing down, even though we knew somewhere along the line we'd be tripped by the string. George and I did it, and it was really scary. Of course I now realize that there was no string, but the trick was not designed to humiliate us. We'd been brave, and George-Ann told us that meant "we had heart." They also, I might add, used the exercise as an excuse to visit with the Romano brothers.

Still, the girls were older and were capable of humiliation. The girls tried to talk me into a snipe hunt once, but I'd read too many Hardy Boys books to fall for it.

At night during the summer we could hear the whooping and hollering of rowdy teenagers back by the swimming hole. The dark water of Black Creek was 12 feet deep there, and you could jump off the ancient stone trestle without hitting bottom. In Ballantyne, it was pronounced "crick" and "trussle." Male voices barked orders. Female voices squealed and screamed—a wild party every night.

The creek back then was lined on either side by magnificent Dutch elms.

By 1965, Nancy and George-Ann were still around sometimes, but they no longer paid George and me that much attention. They told us to get lost so they could talk about something they didn't want us to hear. George and I decided to dig a hole to China behind my barn and ended up with a grave-shaped cavity about three feet deep, a good hiding place. Not that we had anyone to hide from.

I'm not sure I ever spoke to Sue Mulligan, the oldest Mulligan kid, who was a babe. I mean seriously good looking. She was runner-up for Harvest Queen, an award-winning cheerleader, and Queen of the Junior Ball. She even attended modeling school. Mrs. Mulligan griped that Sue slept all day and stayed up all night. I only saw Sue when she was sunbathing, doing the sleeping all day part, a transistor radio on WBBF playing softly next to her. As I ran the path to the Mulligans', I would wonder which side Sue would be on, back or front, happy that it didn't make much difference because both were great. Sometimes I would pause to give a scritch to the Mulligans' cat Pyewacket to elongate the moment, but I stayed quiet so as not to wake the sleeping beauty.

George broke his right arm severely one night when he fell out of his tree house. I wasn't there. I didn't see him for a long while. When the cast came off, George had one arm that didn't work well. We tried once, but our days of playing catch were through. (Which only made it more amazing when he became a star swimmer in high school, setting sectional records even with a decidedly asymmetrical crawl.) While George was healing, I began hanging around more with Larry Putnam, who was three years older than I was. Weird, he broke his arm too. He was trying to impress pretty Sandy Schiano on the Ballantyne School grounds by walking across the top of the soccer goal. He fell and broke his arm in such a way that it had to be set up over his head. After that, when we went to the Towne Theater to see a James Bond picture or maybe *Fantastic Voyage*, we had to sit in the back because nobody could sit behind Larry and the monstrous white cast he held aloft all summer.

During summers, from the time I was five, almost six, until I was nine, that was my world: Mulligans, Formicolas, Putnams, and Tylers. School was the Ballantyne School, at the southwest corner of Scottsville and Ballantyne Roads, built in 1938. Before the Mount Morris dam, the school was used as a springtime shelter for scores of families marooned by the melt. It served as a school until 1974, when it was turned into a Monroe County Sheriff's Office (MCSO) substation.

It had about 11 rooms, not counting restrooms, all on one level. There were nine classrooms, a gym/auditorium/lunchroom, and a teacher's lounge (where they all smoked). The big room had a stage with red velvet curtains and lights built into the floor. There were painted lines for a basketball court, with the skinny lane so the key looked like a key. When I started first grade there, under the stern guidance of four-foot-ten teacher Louise D'Amanda, the school accommodated K through six. I lived in a centralized school zone called Wheatland-Chili. Ballantyne area was in the town of Chili, but the other grammar school and the junior/senior high school, Wheatland-Chili Central School, were seven miles to the south in the village of Scottsville. By the time I finished at Ballantyne School, in June of 1966, only K through four went there. Fifth and sixth grades were moved south to Scottsville, opening up a couple of Ballantyne classrooms, which were used for special classes.

So, in order to become a Wheatland-Chili graduate, Ballantyne students had to get past Miss D'Amanda, who held kids back to repeat first grade like she was getting a commission. Some of the Bernhard kids, Evie Douglas, and Nancy Mulligan all took first grade twice. Miss D'Amanda threatened kids with failure all year long, and each year every kid who wet his pants or who couldn't read had to go through the whole frustrating process a second time. I remember being extremely anxious on report card day. After all, Miss D'Amanda once told me she wanted to "wring my neck." It sounded uncomfortable. When I saw "Promoted" circled, I gave a big sigh of relief. I looked at one girl, who had taken the brunt of Miss D'Amanda's venom all year, as she just sat and quietly cried.

Evie Douglas, who was in the same class as George-Ann and Nancy, remembered the Ballantyne School as the hub of local activities. "It seems like forever ago now, but there were *still air-raid drills*, duck and cover, as if we could protect ourselves from the roof falling in! Crazy."

The Ballantyne Bridge across the Genesee River at that time was a black iron monstrosity, 212 rusty feet long, built in 1913, as a twin to the iron trestle only a quarter mile downstream, two lanes wide—barely. That was the second bridge in that spot. The original was built in the 19th century sometime. Farm owner Anna Ballantine (spelled with an *i*) needed to get her goods across the river and didn't want to go all the way into the city to do it.

As a little girl, Evie was allowed to walk by herself to Coop's, the small beer and cigarettes store on the other side of the river. Now Scottsville Road is an expressway, and Ballantyne Road is a designated truck route. The latest Ballantyne Bridge is eight lanes wide. Today, walking to Coop's, if it were still there, would be treacherous and inadvisable for the quickest and most alert pedestrian.

Back then, Ballantyne Road was just a lonesome country road with mature poplar trees on either side. Shoes were optional. Future shock first rippled across Ballantyne in 1958 with the building of Rochester's first shopping mall, South Town Plaza, just a couple of miles east of the Genesee River on Jefferson Road. Now everybody and their mother needed to cross the Genesee to get to the new stores, and the rickety Ballantyne Bridge, the northernmost river crossing outside the city limits, wasn't doing the trick.

By 1964, construction on a new bridge started. Progress arrived. Evie recalled, "When New York State brought in their heavy equipment to, I think, widen Scottsville Road in preparation for the new bridge, there was a group of us hoodlums that decided to use the big orange bulldozers as target practice with rocks! Someone alerted the police, they came, and we scattered in four different directions from the scene. Too bad for me I was the slowest runner and got a police escort home! That was one of the two times I remember getting my dad's belt across my back end!"

The Douglas house was 48 Ballantyne Road, a double lot next to the little church on the north side. The second lot was in the rear and went all the way to Black Creek Road, right across the street from the Romanos. Evie said, "Because my parents never cleaned it up, our property left a lot of opportunities to make secret paths in and around old scrub trees to get to the Romanos' house." She'd never in her life been down Stallman Drive. When she was growing up, the Pennsylvania Railroad tracks were the western boundary of her world.

In 1962 and most of 1963, it didn't occur to me that things could go wrong. Country life on Stallman Drive suited me fine, with its barefoot summers and snowball-fight winters. I guess in the back of my head I knew that someday I would outgrow my miniature social scene, that I was the youngest and would be the last one left who still wanted to play kickball. But I could never have anticipated the black cloud that would cover the sky over Stallman Drive and stay forever.

Yet, looking back, there were harbingers.

On July 2, 1963, after about a week of summer vacation, I was at my grandma's in the city on Campbell Street. It was a hot and humid Friday afternoon. A monstrous thunderstorm blew across the city, sheets of rain going sideways, bending trees under a black and yellow sky. As the hail beat against Grandma's living room window, she turned off the TV set and told me to keep my face away from the window. So I stretched out on the couch and listened to the storm, which sounded unimaginably violent. At that moment, 11 minutes to four in the afternoon, out at the airport, aiming straight for Black Creek and Stallman Drive was Mohawk Airlines Martin 404, rolling bravely down the runway. The plane made it off the ground, barely, and as soon as it was aloft, a wing tilted downward and struck the runway, causing a wing-over-wing cartwheel that left the fuselage broken in two and aflame. Airport firefighters responded quickly and put out the fire. There were three crewmembers and 40 passengers aboard. Amazingly, only seven were killed, almost all of them at the front of the plane. Two crew and five passengers died. The remaining member of the crew was seriously injured, as were survivors at the front of the plane. Twenty-nine passengers were also seriously injured, while six, who sat at the back of the plane, suffered only minor injuries. Every ambulance in the city was called to the airport to move the injured to area hospitals.

Now that was bad news for everybody, but it was particularly bad news for the Bensons because the Insurance Company of North America, where my dad was a claims adjustor, insured Mohawk Airlines. He was used to dealing with people who had been seriously injured, but he wasn't prepared for this. It was like visiting an army hospital the day after a battle. Dad was late picking my mom and me up from Grandma's that Friday night because he went directly to the airport to view the crash scene. The next day he visited patients, many of whom were fresh out of surgery. The man that bothered my dad the most was a fellow who sat up front in the plane and had had his face burned completely off. (His name was Alan Jeffry Breslau, and he went on to write a book intended to be inspirational to other burn victims.[2]) My dad spoke of this guy briefly, about his bravery, and about how once he was "healed," they were going to build him a sophisticated mask attached to a pair of glasses, which the guy could put on when he received visitors.

That November, President Kennedy was shot. It was a Friday afternoon, and I was in Muriel Dech's second-grade class. We were sent home early, and when I got home my mom was crying. I spent three days watching TV. We went to church at St. Mary's in Scottsville that Sunday, and Mass was startlingly cut short. Father Hartman announced that someone had just shot suspected assassin Lee Harvey Oswald, and he sent us all home to pray that this was not the beginning of World War III.

Then, the following summer, the whole world showed signs of Armageddon. For years, white people in Rochester had been moving out of the city, just as my dad had, while the inner city filled with African Americans, many newly from the South. On July 24, 1964, a lady called the cops on an unruly block party, pointing out one drunken man as being particularly offensive. When the (white) policemen showed up with a K9 unit, the sense of overkill caused a rumor to speed along Joseph Avenue. Like any good rumor, it got better with time: a police dog attacked a child; a cop slapped a woman. Three days of rioting ensued. Four hundred people marched down Joseph Avenue, breaking store windows. Over 200 stores were damaged. By 3:30 the next morning, the crowd grew to 2,000, spreading out over both Joseph and Clinton Avenues. Governor Rockefeller called in the National Guard, the first time the Guard had ever been used in a northern city. At 10:00 that night, a white man was attacked and killed by a mob on Clarissa and Atkinson Streets. The lowlight of the riot came when a police helicopter assigned to "survey the damage" crashed into a house on Clarissa Street, killing three.[3]

After that, the trickle of white people moving out of Rochester grew into a torrent. The towns surrounding Rochester—Greece, Gates, Chili, Henrietta, Brighton, Irondequoit—quickly lost their farmland to housing tracts.

So there were signs, lug nuts loosening—but things went completely off kilter in late 1965, and this time the bad news was closer to home. My friend George-Ann Formicola, still only 13 years old, was pregnant. One morning she was at the school bus stop; the next she wasn't. As of late, I hadn't seen her that much outside of the bus stop. She was a teenager now, and I was still a kid.

One day that winter I was walking down Stallman Drive toward Ballantyne Road and saw her standing in front of her living room window, clearly pregnant. She waved happily at me, and I sensed her loneliness, but I didn't wave back. I just stared.

My brain reeled as I quizzed my mom, asking her at one point how George-Ann could have a baby if she wasn't married, and wasn't she just a child herself? How could a kid become a mother? My mom had no sufficient answers. Perhaps her brain was swirling as well. George-Ann, she said, "liked boys too much."

Freaked out, I reacted poorly. I should have waved back. In the fall of 1965 when I saw George-Ann and Nancy smoking cigarettes, I felt anxiety. It wasn't the danger of smoking that upset me, but that it was such a grown-up thing to do, way too grown up to be done by anyone

I'd played Simon Says with. So, with George-Ann getting pregnant, I was terrified.

When George-Ann returned to the bus stop near the end of the 1965–66 school year, she looked the same, but I couldn't look at her or speak to her. Throughout a long June, I couldn't wait for summer vacation so I wouldn't have to wait at the bus stop with George-Ann anymore. I wished she would just go away—forever.

Looking back on it as an adult, it's impossible to quantify the effect George-Ann's pregnancy might have had on her social life. Not everyone had trouble looking at her like I did, a confused little boy, but we can be certain that George-Ann did not reenter the same social scene she'd left.

And so, as the summer of 1966 began, George-Ann found herself with a new best buddy, Catherine (Kathy) Ann Bernhard, who lived on Names Road, just a few lots east of Lester Street, with a backyard that reached the south woods—the "Forever Wild" it was called—land untouchable according to town ordinance, and woe be to the politician who tried to change that.

According to Kathy's mom, the Ballantyne neighborhood might have been rural in 1962 when the Bensons moved onto Stallman Drive, but back in 1949 when the Bernhards moved to the area, it was pretty much nonexistent.

"There was just a big open lot south of Ballantyne Road and east of Scottsville Road. They'd driven stakes into the clay to show where you were supposed to build your house." And build they did, a $200 prefab shack from Sears.

Only a few houses were already there, one of them being the Starr* home built in 1946. Names Road, when it was built in the early 1950s, ran parallel to Ballantyne Road, one block to the south.

John and Alice Bernhard made for an odd couple. She was a sturdy woman with distinctively wide-set eyes, flat nose, and small jaw. Her husband was a small, wiry man who was never around. If Alice needed him, which wasn't often, she knew where he'd be, sitting at the Castle Inn, a blue-collar watering hole on Scottsville Road, just a quarter mile or so north of the Ballantyne School. As a kid I was in the Castle Inn all the time during the day because I was a friend of the owner's kids. Their mom would be tending bar. The customers were guys in work overalls or plaid and denim, starting early or catching their morning buzz after working the graveyard shift.

Kathy Bernhard, already 16, was older than George-Ann Formicola, although she and George-Ann were in the same class at school because Kathy had been held back—as so many were—by Miss D'Amanda.

The Bernhard kids, visually, were an odd mix. Kathy had black hair. Betty was a blonde. Four out of the six Bernhard kids had picked up Alice's distinctive facial features. The eldest, the only boy, Corky, had the eyes, as did Catherine, Patricia, and Betty, the youngest. Looking as if they'd come from a different family were Alice Jr., second oldest, and Diane, who came between Patty and Betty.

Kathy was a nice girl, but a tomboy. Evie Douglas remembered her as unpretty. Evie Douglas said, "I know that Kathy had not yet reached an age of makeup, beauty aids, or beauty tips. Kathy inherited certain facial characteristics. The family was not financially well off—one income and Alice and six children. Do the math. There was no money for braces, facial hair removal, or things like that."

Evie Douglas was a good friend of the Bernhards. For a while Kathy hung out with Evie, but Evie ended up being better friends with Alice Jr. Evie remembered a strong sibling rivalry between Alice and Kathy. They were close in age. Kathy felt that Alice had taken Evie away from her, and that made her pout for a while.

Evie and Alice once spent a whole summer together, the summer of 1965, in fact, at the Douglases' summer cottage. This was a sort of payback for a previous summer when Evie, who was 11 at the time, accompanied the Bernhards, minus Dad and Corky, on a long camping trip that took them up and down the East Coast, at one point all the way to Maine.

Evie remembered, "We camped rather than stayed in motels. Sleeping bags, tents. Alice bought the simple foods that we'd prepare ourselves. Every day was a picnic! Vacation on the cheap with a bunch of kids. Everyone pitched in and had chores to do."

No one remembers if the Bernhards planned a 1966 summer vacation trip. If they did, the plans were canceled.

2

MISSING

Up until 1966, Junes in Ballantyne were the best. Schoolwork ended a few weeks before the school year did. The last days were spent cleaning desks and playing outside. There was Field Day, during which the whole school was out on the schoolyard, competing in amazing races and games. We ran with eggs balanced on spoons. We tossed water balloons. There was a three-legged race and a flat-out 100-yard dash. The fastest kid at Ballantyne School in 1966 was Alan Myers. Mrs. Nowicki, my fourth-grade teacher, always said through her massive buckteeth, "That Alan Myers is greased lightning." Second fastest was Mike Schiano, Sandy's brother, who was later paralyzed in a car crash and spent the remainder of his life in a wheelchair.

The boring last month of school in 1966 was eased along by the June 11 Strawberry Festival, the PTA's big annual fund-raiser, held on the Ballantyne School grounds. There were more races and games, crafts, and a white elephant gift exchange, and everyone ate too much angel food cake with strawberry preserves and whipped cream on top. Betty Bernhard recalled carnival-like booths and games. Winners got very inexpensive prizes, like an eraser shaped like a dinosaur. A school band showed up and played "In the Good Old Summertime."

School went almost until the last week of June. On the last day, George-Ann and an unnamed friend (not Kathy) were waiting in front of the junior/senior high school in Scottsville for the school bus home when a red convertible pulled up with two young men in it. The driver asked if the girls wanted a ride home, and George-Ann said no, her parents wanted her to take the bus. The guys were persistent, however, and eventually the girls got in the car and they took off.

The fateful day—the fourth Saturday in June, the first after school let out, June 25—was also graduation day at Wheatland-Chili High School in Scottsville, commencement proceedings, 7:00 p.m.

Bob Mills, the Channel 8 weatherman, called for the "three H's: hazy, hot, and humid." A milky sunshine splashed heavily onto Ballantyne Road. By midday, you could see the heat rising from the softened blacktop.

That was the first year I played organized baseball, a member of the T-Shirt Senators of the Chili Youth League. My dad was the manager. I played ball at Ballantyne School that morning, Senators vs. Indians. (A weekday evening game had been rained out.) I played two innings in right field—thanks, Dad—and singled in my only at bat.

June 25 started like any other day for Alice Bernhard. She got up and went to work at R. T. French Co.—at 1 Mustard Street, Rochester, New York—as always. She left daughter Kathy in charge of the housework and taking care of her three younger sisters. Alice said, "Kathy was my housekeeper, chief cook, and bottle washer, babysitter, everything." Kathy was also the best cook in the family. "She could cook chicken like there was no other chicken in the world." Kathy took home economics at school, of course, but she started cooking long before that, picked it up herself. "She always had two or three cakes on the counter, and her cookies and bread were delicious." They'd bought a new stove a week before, and Kathy was looking forward to an opportunity to use it—but she never got that chance.

Kathy was also the seamstress in the family and made all her own clothes. She only owned one store-bought dress, and that was the one she'd be buried in.

She didn't talk too much about her future, but once she'd let it slip that she dreamed one day of being an airline stewardess. Even though she didn't like school, she worked hard. She'd been barely passing for years, but in 1966 she had gotten her average up to a C+, a feat that made her "real proud."

Kathy talked of quitting school, but Alice told her she had to stay until she was finished. Kathy was eager to get a job and have money of her own, but Alice told her she was going to be grown up and have to work for a living soon enough. She was 16; her job was to "enjoy life." If Kathy had some spending money, it was because she babysat or ironed for a neighbor.

That morning, Kathy had done the family washing and was folding clothes and matching socks in the living room during the early afternoon when Mrs. Marcia Werner* from across the street came over to borrow a garden cart. Mrs. Werner recalled, "I heard Kathy tell her sisters to get cleaned up because they were going to the movies that afternoon." The double feature *Munster, Go Home* and *The Ghost and Mr. Chicken* was playing at the Towne Theatre across Jefferson Road from South Town Plaza.

Over on Stallman Drive that morning, George-Ann was doing housework as well and had done "two weeks' worth of ironing" by the time her mother Ruth got home from her job at Conti Packing Co., 2299 Brighton Henrietta Town Line Road in Henrietta, wholesale sellers of meat and meat products. After work, Ruth and George-Ann had lunch together. Ruth then had an appointment at the hairdresser's, and George-Ann cleaned house. When Ruth got back, she and George-Ann got in the car, picked up Kathy, and went shopping at South Town Plaza.

Ruth would later recall her daughter's obsession with horses. Horses and horseback riding were "her whole life." Unlike Kathy, George-Ann did well at school. She was also, for what it was worth, an exceptional bowler. She bowled in a league up at Olympic Bowl on Scottsville Road. Like Kathy, George-Ann had been pestering her mother to let her get a job that summer. Ruth said she thought George-Ann was too young to have a full-time job, but George-Ann persisted and Ruth agreed that the following Monday she'd ask around where she worked to see if they had an appropriate opportunity for a 14-year-old.[1]

If they dropped off and picked up Kathy's three younger sisters at the movies, no one remembered to mention it. At South Town Plaza, George-Ann bought a brand new two-piece swimsuit, and when they got back, she was eager to try it out. Kathy changed into her swimsuit (also two pieces), met George-Ann at her house, and then the pair walked together to the old stone "trussle," where they were seen swimming from 5:30 to 6:30, listening to Kathy's radio tuned to WBBF 950 on the AM dial, Rochester's number-one rock-and-roll station, *pow-pow-power music*, home of the Busy Bees. Spinning the 45s on the air was the "Honeybee" Jessica Savitch, Rochester's first female deejay.

According to the hits played that day, it was a hot town, summer in the city,[2] where your baby did the hanky-panky,[3] where your wild thing made your heart sing,[4] where Li'l Red Riding Hood (perpetually lost in the woods) was looking good,[5] and you were hungry for that sweet thing, baby.[6]

The Queen Bee said stuff like, *"WBBF, home of the busy bees, Ra-cha-cha. It's another hot one out there. Hu-u-mid. Heh heh. Class of '66, nice goin'! Happy graduation to all you cap'n'gowners. Turn up the heat a li'l bit more now with some Stones. . . ."*

". . . I see a red door . . ."

As they swam, the girls listened to a series of two-and-a-half-minute reminders, explicitly nihilistic, that there were pleasures in adventure, disobedience, and experimentation.

The Pennsylvania Railroad tracks ran north and south and crossed Ballantyne Road so that they separated Stallman Drive from the rest of the neighborhood. If you followed a path that started at the dead end of Lester Street, heading north alongside the tracks, you came to the bridge crossing Black Creek, the stone trestle (technically a culvert) built in the 19th century to replace the previous wooden one. The bridge originally served the towpath for mules tugging barges, and in 1966 it was where the Pennsylvania Railroad crossed Black Creek. In the years immediately following World War II, there remained a fear of sabotage, and the New York Central railroad police kept guards posted at all bridges. The night watchman for the stone trestle from 1946 to 1948 was Beanie Wilson of Scottsville. By 1966, the guards were gone, and teenagers ruled the territory after dark. On the south bank of the creek just east of the bridge was a gradual grassy slope, where entering and exiting the creek for swimming was easy. On days when it was too cool to swim, the spot was a favorite for boys with fishing poles, pulling out sunfish as fast as they could rebait. It was here that paddlers in canoes often rested. On June 25, 1966, as George-Ann and Kathy swam, there were other people back there—a Puerto Rican group that had traveled south from the city.

From the trestle, the girls returned to the Bernhard house at dinner-time. Alice knew they were telling the truth about swimming because they were still soaking wet, and Black Creek's fecund combo of algae and silt always left a telltale odor. Mother Alice had just gotten back from work and served the girls hot dogs and milk.

With the temp still in the eighties at 7:30 that evening, the girls said they were going back to the swimming hole for one more cool down. They'd be back in an hour and have some salad.

Alice reminded them that it was graduation night at the high school and that everyone was cooking outside, and if they didn't return in an hour they might miss the barbecue. The girls said no problem. Alice wasn't worried. Kathy, she knew, was scared of the dark.

As they left, Kathy clicked on her radio.

"Follow me, I'm the Pied Piper," sang Crispian St. Peters on WBBF. *"I know where it's at."*[7] The lyrics came through loud and clear.

The Puerto Rican picnickers saw the girls again about 7:35. They walked out on the trestle, looked around, and left without going back in the water. Perhaps they were meeting someone who wasn't there. Maybe they didn't like the place still being used by "city people."

The girls were next seen on Scottsville Road heading north toward the Castle Inn. They were seen (and talked to) by friends while crossing Ballantyne Bridge to go to the store. A third eyewitness said they were seen walking south on Scottsville Road, south of the Ballantyne Bridge, near another swimming area called "the Swing," where kids had tied a rope to a tall overhanging branch and used it to swing themselves into the deeper water. Kathy still had her radio with her at that point, the witness said. The Rochester afternoon paper, the *Times-Union*, listed the Swing as "where the girls were last seen."[8] (For years there had been a swing rope at the Black Creek swimming hole near the stone trestle, but the tree branch had broken off by June 25, 1966. If a kid wanted to swing on a rope, he or she had to go to the river.)

The sun set at 9:03. By 9:30 it was so dark that, back at the swimming hole, unless there was a train coming, you couldn't see your hand in front of your face. Nightfall brought dampness but little cool. At sunset, up and down the road, graduation parties started up, beer, laughter, tears, music—and almost no one thought about George-Ann and Kathy.

At Sue Mulligan's graduation party they heard a scream, a cry in the distance disturbing enough that they turned down the poolside music for a moment. When the scream wasn't repeated, they turned the music back up. George thought the scream came from back by the creek, a ways to the west.

By the early morning hours of June 26 the moms were on the phone. Ruth Formicola called Alice Bernhard, who'd fallen asleep and was unaware that Kathy wasn't home. Minutes later she called the sheriff's office. Her daughter was missing. The girls were missing.

"Oh, they probably just ran away," folks said, trying to make the parents feel better. Bullshit, the parents thought silently. The girls were in their swimsuits. Two-piecers. They took no clothes with them. What girl ran away in her swimsuit?

Nope. Someone had them, and nothing good was happening.

On Sunday, June 26, a 17-state alarm went out. On Monday, teams from various agencies began daily searches by the trestle and along the creek and railroad tracks. Men in boats coursed the creek looking for submerged objects and eyeballing the banks. Teams of sheriff's deputies and volunteers from the Riverdale Fire Department checked out barns, buildings, and railroad cars in the vicinity. (Riverdale was a cluster of streets built south of Ballantyne Road and west of Scottsville Road.) On Tuesday the creek was dragged, and on Wednesday the Genesee River was dragged where it adjoined the creek, south of the spot where the doctor's wife was discovered almost 20 years earlier.

The confluence of Black Creek and the Genesee River moved during the 1950s. The stream had meandered its way through the lowland north of Mosquito Point/Ballantyne Road and contributed to the river at a spot just south of the iron Genesee River trestle. Then a big ditch was dug from the creek just north of Black Creek Road straight to the river. The confluence moved to its current location, a quarter mile south of where it had been, just behind Ballantyne School. The big ditch was dug to address flooding along the Black Creek watershed.

That Wednesday, June 29, the morning paper, the *Democrat & Chronicle*, reported the grim news that Kathy's radio was found on the "cinder road" that led from the area of the swimming hole to Scottsville Road. The discovery, made by a neighborhood boy, caused an "intensification" of the search. Bloodhounds were brought in. Spotlights were transported to the trestle so that the search for clues could go on after dark. Sheriff's sergeant Norman Doe flew low over the area in a helicopter, in hopes that something helpful could be seen from above. Scuba divers under the direction of State Trooper David Schwarz of the Batavia Headquarters searched the swimming area.[9]

By Thursday, investigators gave up on the notion that the girls might have drowned. Sheriff Skinner said that if they had, their bodies would have "come to the surface by now."[10]

Kathy's mom *never* thought the girls drowned. It seemed ridiculous to her. *Both* of them? "Why, they've been in that creek and river since they were in diapers," Alice said. "Swim? They're like fish!"

Kathy might have set a world record for earliest swim that year. It was around Easter when she came home soaking wet. When Alice asked her where she'd been, she said, "In the creek." During the winter, Alice took Kathy to the City Natatorium where for a quarter she could swim all evening "and have a ball."

Ruth Formicola agreed that George-Ann was unlikely to drown. "She learned to swim in the backyard pools, and I used to take her everyplace to swim—Mendon Ponds, Lake Ontario, all over."

The Riverdale Fire Department put together a search team, which included Don Mosele, one of the Bernhards' Names Road neighbors. The search covered several square miles and concentrated on sheds and barns and dirt lanes. The highlight of these searches came when, near exhaustion, the team worked its way south along Scottsville Road, as far as the Swing, where kids had been swimming in the Genesee River on Saturday evening. More or less across the street from the Swing was a long dirt lane with an abandoned old house at the end of it, known as the old Rogers house. It looked like something out of a horror movie, so the tough-guy firefighters approached it with trepidation, fear that turned to near frenzy when someone looked in a broken window and saw a pair of legs sprawled across the floor. When the door was battered open and the men entered, they were relieved to discover that it was just a mannequin that someone had left on the living room floor.

Back on Stallman Drive, there was a steady flow of official vehicles using the convenient dirt cul-de-sac in front of our house—the "circle"—to turn around and head back out toward Ballantyne Road. There was the racket of the helicopter flying low over our back fields, and the sounds of the creek being dredged and dredged again, all the way from Black Creek Park to the Genesee River—but especially, it seemed, right behind the Benson house. And they found nothing.

Investigators shifted the focus from searching the areas where the girls were last seen, where woods and scrub brush made some sites difficult to penetrate, to checking out phone tips received by the sheriff and the families.

Calls, Sheriff Skinner bragged, were coming in from all around the country. One caller said she saw the girls near the Sea Breeze amusement park at about 5:30 on Sunday morning. Another caller placed two girls in swimsuits in the town of Churchville on Sunday. The sheriff said all tips were being checked out, urging people who knew something to call and guaranteeing confidentiality.

"Sometimes people are reluctant to call," Skinner said, "because they feel their bit of information is not important. But we want to get every tip possible and we will check out every one no matter how small."[11]

On Friday, July 1, the girls had been gone six days, and a small item ran in the *D&C* called "Missing Girls Puzzle Police" that now included, for the first time, postage-stamp-sized photos of the girls.[12]

Detective Michael Cerretto told a reporter, "Frankly, it's a real puzzler." Police, he said, were searching all vacant buildings in the Black Creek area near Scottsville Road. "There was no reason for the girls to have run away. There weren't family problems or anything of that kind."

I knew better than that.

That afternoon, in the *Times-Union*, another small item ran, this time noting that a "house-to-house check" was efficiently conducted in the Scottsville Road/Ballantyne Road region.

All homes and businesses were paid a visit, Detective Lieutenant Charles Kittlinger said.[13] Whatever it was that those neighbors said during the house-to-house check, none of it made the papers.

That was it for the daily coverage. Investigators remained, but reporters were out of there, on to something else. Small items still appeared in the back pages, but days went by and nothing.

On the Fourth of July, a tiny story said that the only update was no update. "We're working in the dark at this point," an unnamed authority said. "The discarded radio is the only clue."[14]

For the rest of the summer, it was never quite quiet on Stallman Drive. Previous to all this, the only sounds I heard in bed were the planes, the trains, and the small frogs we called peepers—all predictable sounds. But now, with the girls gone, those constants were interrupted irregularly by the echoing bleats of shouting voices up around the bend and the distant softened exclamation of car doors slamming.

The girls disappeared so early in summer vacation—the first weekend—that it happened before the Douglases left for their summer cottage. One of the first to speak to the police was Evie Douglas. Deputies canvassed Ballantyne Road, and someone said he'd seen George-Ann riding around on a bicycle built for two—and that made Evie a witness. She was the girl with the tandem bike.

"George-Ann and I biked together to Scottsville not long before she disappeared," Evie told me. "I don't remember what we talked about. We didn't talk about boys, I remember that. I knew George-Ann missed some school but had no idea she'd had a baby. I didn't learn about that until later. We didn't ride the bicycle along Scottsville Road and instead took the quieter route, on the other side of the river on East River Road, through Rodney Farms. We were too pooped to ride all the way back, so we rode the bike to the T. J. Connor School" (the Scottsville grammar school on Beckwith Avenue), and Evie's dad came to pick them up.

Now, with George-Ann missing, the deputy wanted to verify that the bicycle was at the Douglas house, which it was. "Police—state cop or sheriff, I don't remember—wondered if the girls had borrowed it and gone off somewhere," Evie explained.

A couple of weeks after the girls disappeared, George Mulligan told me he had something he had to show me. He led me into my own back field, about three-quarters of the way to the creek, a hundred yards back, and there was a series of five unlit campfires, little teepees of kindling wood, all in a row, maybe 20 feet between them, running parallel to the water. It looked as if someone had planned to set a row of fires and had done everything except strike the match. If it had been someone else—Larry Putnam, for example—I would have figured that he built the little teepees and then took me out to show them to me to hopefully freak me out, but George was not the prankster type. He was a sincere guy. This was certainly something he wouldn't think was funny.

Besides, I don't remember being close to freaking out. Ask me that day what happened to George-Ann and Kathy, and I was apt to say they ran away, that they had clothes stashed someplace where their parents didn't know.

It didn't seem like a stretch at all to assume George-Ann had a secret life or two. Being a teenage girl was filled with peril and mysteries and adventure and consequences that were practically imponderable for a nine-year-old boy.

I didn't bother to tell my mom and dad about the unlit campfires, although I didn't like the idea of someone in my back field doing *anything*. Before long, I would realize how spooky those teepees were— and still I kept my mouth shut.

On July 12, with the girls gone 17 days, the morning paper reported that Kathy disappeared with a large beach towel, which had not been found.[15] Deputy Emily Manzler, the liaison between the MCSO and the families, said the towel was three-by-five feet and had on it a large drawing of a suntanned blonde wearing a two-piece swimsuit and carrying a big straw hat.

Manzler was a veteran of missing-girl cases, and she didn't like this one at all. She said, "Girls who run away almost always take two things with them: money and cosmetics. These girls had nothing. Not even a lipstick. No clothing. This is a strange case. Very strange."

By the middle of July, a *D&C* reporter, Jan Sturtevant, checked up on the parents. With just about three weeks gone, what was going through their minds? Did they still have hope?[16]

Sturdevant expected to encounter broken hearts but was not prepared to learn a horrible thing about human nature. The parents of both girls had been plagued by crank phone calls. Alice got most of them, but Ruth received a few as well.

"We started getting calls right after they disappeared," Ruth said. "At first, they just asked us if we'd heard anything about our daughters.

Those calls let up after awhile. But the last few days, we've started to get more calls, mostly from people who say that I know where George-Ann is and I'm covering up for her." During many of the calls, the caller never spoke at all. "You pick up the phone," Ruth said, "and you know someone is there because you can hear breathing. But they never say a word."

Alice Bernhard added, "They don't use obscene language, but they tell me point blank that I am a liar. We know where the girls are, they tell us, so why don't we call off the hunt? One man said he saw the girls on Genesee Street [an African-American neighborhood], and another one said they are living with colored people on Ormond Street. A woman told me the girls were picked up in the nude at a coin laundry downtown. She wouldn't believe I didn't know anything about where they are and still don't. One woman told me that Kathy was pregnant. She said I knew it and was just trying to cover up. All I can say is that this is a funny way to cover up something."

Detective Lieutenant Michael Cerretto told Sturdevant that all of the rumors were false. "No one knows where the girls are, except maybe the two girls themselves," Cerretto said.

The article ran in the next morning's newspaper without photos.

Around that same time a police "flyer," which did have photos of the girls, was sent to all police and sheriff departments in New York State.[17] A nationwide Teletype on the girls was sent to law enforcement agencies.

Phone tips had slowed but not stopped. One new one came from a woman claiming she'd seen the missing girls in the Port Bay area, on the shore of Lake Ontario about 30 miles east of Rochester. Other calls had them placed in various parts of western New York. One tip took investigators to New York City. All of the calls were unfounded.

The day before Sturdevant interviewed the Chili moms, someone tortured, raped, and knifed to death eight Filipina nurses from the South Chicago Community Hospital in Chicago, Illinois. (I didn't know what rape meant, but it always seemed to be used in conjunction with "knife," so I figured it had something to do with being stabbed, some *aspect* of it.) By July 17, bloody fingerprints identified the butcher as Richard B. Speck, 6'1", 160 pounds, brownish blonde hair, slightly longer than a crew cut. He matched perfectly a description given to police by the lone survivor, a 23-year-old nurse who played dead and prayed that the man would forget how many women he'd killed. Thirty-two of Speck's fingerprints were found at the crime scene. He had a "Born to Raise Hell" tattoo. After the murders, Speck "hid out" in a series of bars and motels. Tired of fleeing, on July 19, he drank a bottle of wine in his room at the Starr Hotel in South Chicago and then broke the bottle so that he could cut his wrists. As soon as he started bleeding he had a change of heart and called for help. An ambulance arrived and took Speck to Cook County Hospital, where his tattoo was recognized.[18] Speck was stitched up, arrested, and taken into custody. The press loved Speck and boldly proclaimed his act "The Greatest Sex Crime in History."[19]

My dad tried to recall the night the girls disappeared but remembered only watching a Glenn Ford movie on the screened-in porch. (Years later I bought a back issue of that week's *TV Guide*, and sure enough, NBC's Saturday Night at the Movies that night was *Fate Is the Hunter*, about a man who investigates a plane crash. What caused it? Everyone seemed to think it was pilot error, but Glenn Ford had other ideas.) Dad's memory wasn't perfect, though. He insisted that the girls disappeared on his birthday, when in reality his birthday had been a few days earlier.

Monroe County sheriff Albert W. Skinner had held the job since 1938. A bachelor who lived in the jailhouse, he was reelected 12 times. He was a lifelong cop and had grown into a big man, 5'10", 280 pounds. The man could hurt a guy just by leaning on him—and he'd leaned on a few. The sheriff was a big man, all right—54-inch waist, size 8⅔ hat— but he was old, 73 in 1966.[20]

Skinner's record as a leader appeared progressive enough on the surface. During his tenure he founded the mounted patrol, the bomb squad, and the airport division. But in many ways the MCSO had developed into a staid organization under his leadership. (Skinner lost the 1973 election to William Lombard and died on October 27, 1975, at 81.)

On July 21, 1966, the *Gates-Chili News* ran an item in which Sheriff Skinner pleaded with citizens for information: "Has anyone seen George-Ann Formicola or Kathy Bernhard since the evening of June

25, 1966? Does anyone have even an inkling of a clue that might lead to the whereabouts of the two Chili girls?"[21]

This was followed by a summary of the girls' last hours. The paper noted how tenacious the sheriff had been since the girls disappeared. Sheriff Skinner's men had interviewed hundreds of people and had even "worked on and run down wild rumors." Sheriff's Detective Carl Knapp had mailed out circulars bearing photos and descriptions of the girls, but the *Gates-Chili News* chose not to run the photos.

Knapp tried to squelch all the chitchat: "All rumors to the contrary, the two girls are still missing." He added that George-Ann was 5'5", 107 pounds, with light brown hair and dark complexion. Kathy was 5'3" and weighed 107 pounds. She had brown eyes, black hair, and dark complexion. The paper went to bed well before its cover date. By the time the paper hit the stands, as it turned out, everyone knew where the girls were.

3

FOUND

It was Wednesday, July 20, around noon, when Francine Wilson says she found a dog butchered on the railroad tracks, and three hours later, Vincent Zuber discovered the bodies. Zuber ran cross-lots to Sergeant Saile's house. Saile lived on Beaver Road Extension, about a quarter mile south of the railroad tracks. By 4:00 that afternoon, the scene off Archer Road was a beehive of activity.

Detective Cerretto, already working the missing persons case, became the double homicide's lead investigator. He was the one who counted the choices a motorist would need to make to get from the swimming hole to the dump site by car. It seemed an unlikely navigation for an out-of-town driver.

Cerretto thought the killer was a local, someone who knew how to get from one spot to the other. Or the girls gave the driver directions to the lovers' lane off Archer Road because, for whatever reason, the swimming hole was no longer private enough for their needs.

Maybe the guy was just driving down dirt roads in general, trolling, and took this particular route only because he'd already tried many of the others in hopes of happening upon opportunities.

The commonality of the dump site and the swimming hole was that they were both just south of the same railroad tracks, but it wasn't a given that those tracks had anything to do with it. The appeal was in the dirt roads that led cars into the privacy of remote locations.

After being thoroughly photographed at the scene, the bodies were removed. Investigators seized and bagged shovels full of dirt from under the bodies. These, along with Kathy's comb, the flip-flop, some .22 caliber rifle shells and 12-gauge shotgun shells, the girls' bathing suits, and several beer cans found in the area were sent via air freight to the FBI crime lab in Washington, D.C., for analysis.

I was at my maternal grandmother's house in the Dutchtown section of Rochester that afternoon, just as I had been when the plane crashed. My mom was visiting with her mom, and my dad was at work. When he was done, he'd pick us up, and we'd all go home to Stallman Drive together.

Normally I would have been watching the *Adventures of Superman* and *Huckleberry Hound*, with all the regular commercials—Lemon Pledge very pretty . . . that peppermint flavor that hangs on hangs on hangs on to what it's got . . . I want my Maypo . . . Tang, chosen by the *Gemini* astronauts . . . Wheelie-Bar made by Wham-O—but they weren't on. Scheduled programming was scrubbed in favor of the astronauts themselves in *Gemini X* undocking from an unmanned spacecraft, the *Agena*, as both orbited the Earth.

The previous day they'd successfully docked. The day before had also featured Michael Collins's 49-minute space walk. This was an experiment that needed to be performed routinely if man hoped one day to walk on the moon. On that afternoon, the undocking went well, and the coverage ended at 6:00 so the local stations could do the news.

The local news on Channel 8, the NBC affiliate back then, used to open their show with the day's three top headlines. In terms of TV, these were primitive times, and WROC illustrated the day's top stories without so much as a superimposition. The headlines were set in white type on a blackboard, not unlike one you might see in a hotel lobby announcing the day's special events. A strip of paper inserted along a groove covered each headline.

"Here are today's headlines," newscaster Tom Decker would say. And then, one by one, the strips of paper would be pulled away, revealing the headline underneath, which Decker would read. Every once in a while, if the shot wasn't framed tightly enough, you could see fingers—possibly Tom Decker's—grabbing the paper and pulling.

That day's top headline: "Bodies of Missing Chili Girls Found."

I turned to my grandmother. "Does that mean . . . ?"

With a grim nod she confirmed that they were dead. Everything in my mind is categorized by things that happened before that moment, and things that happened after.

Dad came and got us not long after that. I was in a daze, although I remember my mom in the car saying that George-Ann was "boy crazy," only 14 and already once in trouble. My old man just grumbled about how bad the crime scene must have been, with the heat wave and all. At some point I realized that the girls were not just dead but that someone had killed them. Dad mentioned animal and insect activity, and my mom hushed him, noting the little pitcher with big ears in the backseat.

My dad wanted to drive down Archer Road, but we didn't go over there until the next day.

Years later, I learned that a sheriff's deputy had to guard the crime scene overnight, with lights out, just in case the killer wanted to return. His other job, should it come up, was to chase away couples who were unaware of the news and might contaminate the scene. The guy chosen for the task was Deputy Frank Huck.* Years later Huck wouldn't want to discuss the investigation, but he did recall how "spooky" that night was, alone in the dark with the crickets and the smell of decomposition. The stars were clear, and there was a sliver moon, just two nights past new.

By the time we drove by in Dad's AMC Rambler (with push-button transmission) the following day, crawling along Archer Road as we approached the railroad crossing so we could get a good long ogle, there were a lot of cops on the scene, some in uniform, some in suits and ties, some of them stamping around in the weeds taking baby steps, and some just gathered in small circles. Some had a walkie-talkie in one hand and a cigarette in the other.

On the night the bodies were discovered, we went straight home. We'd grown used to having extra cars parked up and down Stallman Drive. But we weren't prepared for what we saw when we pulled down our little dirt road. It suddenly had the look and feel of a major event. (It was. I later learned that the story made it into the *New York Times* the next day, and that night Walter Cronkite had mentioned it on the national CBS news, although I didn't see either one.)

Cross-legged on the rug in front of the Benson living room TV—a Muntz, model 2053A—the first show I ever watched *after* was *Batman*.

The bad guy was the Bookworm, with Roddy McDowell as "Special Guest Villain." Then *Patty Duke*, *The Beverly Hillbillies*, and *Green Acres*. A group of cowboys with mustaches called the Spahn Ranch "Marlboro Country." Actors dressed up like the Rembrandt painting sold Dutch Masters cigars, and musical chimpanzees sold Red Rose Tea. After that, I don't remember. I was troubled by the fact that I had wished George-Ann away and now she was gone. Maybe I dozed.

When the news broke, the *New York Times* reported that the bodies were discovered and promptly sent a reporter to Chili to get a bead on the terror in the community. Reporter Murray Schumach accompanied sheriff's deputies back to the swimming hole and noted the many dirt paths cutting through the weeds, beaten bare by "generations of youngsters." Now the area was quiet, so quiet you could "hear the chirp of a bird in the deep brush." The only indication that this place had once been alive with youth and fun was the smattering of litter, pop bottles, beer cans, and some cellophane wrapping.

The reporter then visited Old Man Tacy, who ran the bait shop behind Ballantyne School. Tacy complained that no one was fishing anymore. The creek had been tainted by the tragedy. They didn't even want to fish behind his shop, where the area was clear of brush and easily visible from the cars passing along Scottsville Road.

How nervous was the community? Schumach reported that when he asked questions of women at a nearby supermarket, the police were called, and for 20 minutes he had to answer questions instead of ask them.[1]

The first details I got regarding the location of the bodies came in the following morning's edition of the Rochester *Democrat & Chronicle*. The murders were the top story, but they had to share the front page with the *Gemini X* spacewalk and President Johnson's decision to bomb military targets inside North Vietnam.

The murder article featured two thumbnail photos of the girls—so tiny. George-Ann was wearing a barrette. Both looked cheerful. There was a larger photo of the site beside those. This photo showed two cops poking in the bushes. There were two arrows labeled "A" and "B" that pointed into the bushes on either side of the dirt road. "A" was the location of both bodies; "B" was the railroad tracks.[2]

"No weapon was found," the article said. Preliminary examination showed that both girls died of stab wounds to the chest area. The article didn't name the farmer who discovered the bodies, but it did identify Saile, his cop neighbor.

The bodies were found 17 feet apart, face up, in the dense elderberry 24 feet off the dirt road. The nearest house was estimated to be more than a hundred yards away. The article said, "Investigators theorized the girls were taken there by car, because of the distance from where the girls usually swam in Black Creek." George-Ann was found with only her bikini top on, the bottoms were found 16 feet from her body. Kathy still wore her bathing suit.

Without providing further details, the article noted that it was the sickest thing the deputies had ever seen.

I later learned the effect the scene had on the men. Tough-guy deputies would lie awake at night and shiver when recalling the bodies of the teen girls. Many, many years later, their hands still shook when they thought about it.

Back on Stallman Drive, I was thinking that the killer had been driving down dirt roads to see what he could see, and he probably drove down our road, using the circle in front of our house to turn around. I would try forever to remember the vehicles that went around the circle that Saturday night.

Wasn't there a pickup truck? Who could tell?

There were always pickup trucks going around the circle, and we never paid any attention. At least we didn't *before*. Now we scrutinized each car. My dad would always wave and make them wave back. It gave him a chance to look in their eyes. Dad's loaded shotgun was on the wall of the back porch.

The sheriff assigned to the case: Cerretto, Chief Deputy William Linney, Detective Lieutenant Charles Kittlinger, Detectives Donald Clark and William Jarvis, and Sergeant Saile, who'd been the first cop at the scene.

Investigating for the state police were Senior Investigators John Beck and Michael Iaculli. Assistant District Attorney Jack B. Lazarus and Medical Examiner Robert Greendyke were also investigating.[3]

The bodies had been removed from the scene in cloth bags and taken directly to the medical examiner's office. Kathy was autopsied first, and it was after the first postmortem that the ME told investigators that stab wounds were the cause of death.

Greendyke later told a wire-service reporter that, in addition to the stab wounds, "an attempt had been made to behead one of the girls. Her throat was cut." (Interestingly, this quote ran in out-of-town newspapers[4] but was not printed in either of the Rochester-area dailies.)

Another quote that ran out of town but not in the local papers was attributed to a sheriff's office representative, who said, "We've got a few suspects, and we're interviewing and interviewing several others."

Dr. Greendyke said, "I don't know how long they had been dead. It was certainly more than a week. The time they disappeared would set the other limit. They were killed somewhere in between and there probably is no way of ever determining just when. Body temperature and rigor mortis are determining factors for bodies no more than 24 to 40 hours after death. But the girls had been dead for too long for these means of pinpointing the time of death to be worthwhile." He also said that there was no way to determine where the girls were killed, either. "There was nothing obvious to determine whether they had been dragged very far because of the length of time they had been there. Any broken plants or drag marks had had a chance to grow over."[5]

Deputies Emily Manzler and Raymond Braun notified the parents in person. Father Murphy of St. Pius X Catholic Church on Chili Avenue accompanied them. The parents did not have to ID remains but merely the swimsuits found at the dump site.

Kathy's transistor radio, which she'd taken to the swimming hole with her, a fact verified by the "picnickers," had been found broken in two "near a path leading from Scottsville Rd. to the area of Black Creek frequented by the swimmers." I wanted to know more about the radio. How was it broken? Had it been left on? Were the batteries run down?

Crime scene investigators complained about the thickness of the scrub brush off Archer Road. It was up to eye level, and you couldn't even see the ground unless you used your hands to push the sharp foliage aside. They were finding stuff, but nothing pertinent. In addition to a lovers' lane, the spot was also a popular shooting and dumping site. They found a washing machine, a refrigerator riddled with bullet

holes, more beer cans, and plenty of shotgun shells. There was a possibility that the killer had dumped stuff there before.

Sheriff Skinner told the *D&C* that the killer was not a walker. A car
was needed to get the girls to the spot where they were found. Antici-
pating a fresh batch of phone tips, the sheriff said a command center
had been set up at the Monroe County Jail where incoming information
could be sifted and cross-checked.

The *Suburban News*, a weekly paper out of Spencerport, ran a story in
its July 26, 1966, issue saying that Martin W. Herbst, a Democratic
candidate for Chili justice of the peace, had suggested that the Chili
Town Board should hold a public hearing to determine the views of
Chili residents on the subject of a full-time Chili police force. It is
unknown if the hearing was ever held, but no Chili police force was
ever formed and law enforcement in Chili remained the responsibility
of the sheriff.[6]

The Bensons only knew what was in the newspapers until Pauline Putnam visited and told my parents what she'd heard from a drinking
buddy of hers who was a cop. (I liked Mrs. Putnam. She didn't treat me
like a kid. "How the hell are ya, Mike?" she'd ask me.) They were
standing out by the driveway, but Mrs. Putnam was speaking loudly, as
was her style. I could see her face as I spied on the scene from the living
room window, looking out through both the window and the screened-
in porch on the other side. I could read her lips, and I could just barely
hear her when she said, "George-Ann's tits were cut off."

Pauline told my mother that she had overheard an argument between Ruth Formicola and her daughter during George-Ann's pregnancy. The Formicolas, it seemed, were trying to keep George-Ann's condition a secret, and Ruth was yelling that George-Ann should stay away
from the windows so the neighbors couldn't see. I realized in horror
that I was the neighbor who had seen.

Now the Formicolas were in complete despair. George Formicola
was a very short man, maybe 4'11", and round in stature. He had dark
brown, almost black hair when his daughter disappeared. I saw Ruth
and Gina during that summer of 1966, but I never saw George. By the
time I next saw him, in the fall, his hair was completely white.

Over at the Douglas house on Ballantyne Road, Evie remembered when the bodies were discovered: "Life as we knew it ended. No one walked around the neighborhood any longer."

At the Douglas house the feeling was that whoever did it was still walking around among us. "Is there a word beyond petrified?" Evie asks. "There was never a time after 1966 that any of us kids did so much as walk down the street. It put the fear of God in everyone."

And Evie was luckier than a lot of the neighborhood kids. She missed out on much of the initial fear because her dad took the family to their summer cottage on a lake. She didn't find out about the murders until they returned at the end of summer.

"We camped every summer of my life there after my parents built a 24-by-24 cottage in 1963. Alice Bernhard [Kathy's sister] and I spent the summer of 1964 babysitting my two brothers and my sister at the cottage while my mom commuted to work in Rochester every day."

In 1965 Evie went with the Bernhards, who were returning the favor. "My Dad loved the lake but enjoyed his quiet time too, so he stayed alone on Ballantyne Road during the week and joined his family at the lake on weekends."

Evie loved the cottage too, and after a good fixing up, she had made it her home for the past three decades. As a teen, the cottage saved Evie's life. Every summer it gave her relief from the Fear on Ballantyne Road. The cottage was in a place where she could still cut through lawns and take beelines without worrying about being grabbed and dragged into the woods.

On Morrison Avenue, one block south of Names Road, lived seven-year-old Grace Green. I knew Grace because her mom and mine bowled on the same team in the Wednesday afternoon housewives' league at Olympic Bowl.

One night "around the time of the murders," Grace woke up in the middle of the night and looked out her bedroom window. Standing in their side lot looking up at her was a man holding a knife. Her mother tried to convince her it was just a dream, but she never believed that.

On the second day after the bodies were found, the newspapers ran more details. But for me the info was harder to get. My parents thought I was better off not knowing. But I could outwait them. After they were done with the newspaper, they put it in the burn barrel on the far side of our round, blue, aboveground pool. They threw the paper in the barrel but hadn't lit it, so after they went to sleep I bravely went out in the dark and dug it out and read it on the back porch, where snakes and mice were the Bensons' constant companions. I had the willies even before I started reading, and the contents of the articles scared me even more.

An MCSO spokesman (not named) told reporter Tom Ryan that he was convinced a "sex maniac" had committed the murders. He didn't need lab results to say that. It was *apparent*. He could tell because "of the location of the stab wounds on the girls' bodies."[7] (That was the moment when I knew I was never going to sleep again.)

Police were "scrambling for a clue" that might identify the killer. George-Ann was stabbed 13 times (later changed to 14), Kathy 7. Medical Examiner Greendyke had determined that the weapon was a large knife, perhaps a hunting knife, with a blade between one and a quarter and one and a half inches wide. The weapon was not found.

The spokesperson said that there were still investigators going over the crime scene with a fine-tooth comb but admitted that no significant discoveries were made on the second day. The crime scene might have already yielded all it would.

I stopped reading for a beat. I thought about evil and tragedy and how it left black clouds behind at the locations of the carnage. The bodies were long gone, but the dump site gave off crazy evil vibes. It was a tainted spot. No motorist could cross the railroad tracks at Archer Road without taking a quick peek down that dirt road, and those drivers and riders felt the evil each time. I resumed reading.

"Was it one man or two?" reporter Ryan asked the sheriff's spokesman.

"I'm thinking one," the guy said. "I don't think two men could do such a brutal thing. He is a misogynist or an impotent pervert."

"Did the guy show any expertise? Might he be a doctor—or a butcher—someone comfortable with cutting up flesh and meat?"

"No. No signs of training at all, the wounds were inflicted with a mad thrust of the blade."

Since the early 1960s, police forces had compiled a sex-offender list, including even those who had been convicted of the most minor offenses. Now that list was coming in handy. Pervs were being systematically hauled off the streets as quickly as deputies could find them and questioned as to their whereabouts when the teenagers went missing.

A man who sexually attacked a relative in the town of Riga in July was given the third degree. The three men who'd attacked a woman in Genesee Valley Park were grilled. Friends of the girls and the Spanish-speaking picnickers were reinterrogated. The owners of cars seen in the area were questioned.

Police thought they'd caught a break when a soldier from Rochester returned a rented car with a knife and a bloody towel in it. Undersheriff Fenton Coakley and First Assistant District Attorney John Mastrella flew to Chicago to talk to the man, but it turned out he had an innocent explanation.

The reporter verified that Kathy's radio was found on the path between the swimming hole and Scottsville Road, and he was aware that the location of the broken radio was important, perhaps revealing.

It seemed to mean that the girls struggled at that spot with their abductor. Or did the killer dispose of the radio after he dumped the bodies, or perhaps after he killed them but before he dumped them? It wasn't clear. There was no blood on the radio, and killing the girls had to have been a messy business.

"What about the early reports that on the night the girls disappeared some kind of cop was at the swimming hole hassling kids?" Ryan asked.

"We found a man who has identified himself to us as an officer looking for sex offenders in the Scottsville Road area on the night of the girls' disappearance. The man turned out to be a railroad policeman who was trying to shoo away teenagers who were parked on railroad property. We are satisfied that this was not linked with the killings," was the spokesperson's wholly unsatisfying response.

The spokesman said that among the pieces of evidence that were still being analyzed were George-Ann's swimsuit bottoms, which had possibly been removed by her killer, and bits of "soil and debris" found near the bodies. A fingerprint expert was also working on the case.

The medical examiner could only determine that the girls had been dead for "more than a week," but most likely they died on the night of their disappearance.

My eyes moved over the article more quickly now as I wearied of my subterfuge. There was a bunch of stuff I already knew. George-Ann and Kathy had just finished ninth grade at Wheatland-Chili. George-Ann had missed a lot of school recently due to an unspecified medical problem. George-Ann was the younger of two and the daughter of a New York Central Railroad car repairman. She had an older sister, Gina Wilson,* who was married. Kathy was one of six kids; her dad worked at the Ajax Auto Parts Company. (I knew that place, a junkyard of grease and rust on West Henrietta Road at Brighton-Henrietta Town Line Road next to the Starlite Drive-In, hard up against the West Shore railroad tracks. Follow those tracks westward and you crossed the Genesee at the large black iron trestle; follow them further and you passed the swimming hole and the dump site.)

The *Democrat & Chronicle* ran an editorial urging readers who might know something, even something seemingly insignificant, to call the sheriff's tip line. Young people were cautioned about the danger of "riding or even communicating on highways or anywhere else with strangers or even acquaintances about whom little is known."[8] (I thought about the teepees of kindling. Mum was the word. I was a kid. No one was going to listen to me anyway.)

That afternoon, the *Times-Union* also had extensive coverage. It quoted the medical examiner as saying that these were "the most brutal murders I've ever seen."[9]

Sheriff Skinner said that the case reminded him of the unsolved slayings of Shari Smoyer, 18, and John King, 17, who were found shot to death in the back with a .45 and bludgeoned, sprawled side by side in front of King's car on a lovers' lane along Irondequoit Creek on July 14, 1963, in the town of Pittsford. The Smoyer-King killings (for more on this case, see appendix G) occurred on the opposite side of the county from Chili. The sheriff believed the Chili murders were worse because of the "way they were murdered. It looks like our man is a sex fiend. Everybody's a suspect around here until we find out who he is." The girls, he added, were not just stabbed. They were slashed as well. Skinner added that he "knew who was responsible" for the 1963 murders, that he'd spoken to the man, and he was convinced that he was not responsible for the Chili murders.

Dr. Greendyke was not optimistic about his department's ability to determine if the girls had been raped—although he didn't say what the difficulty was, if it was because of the decomposition, the nature of the wounds, or some other reason. The tests they had already run were inconclusive. His hunch would be that there was no rape.

He said, "A horrible sex crime was committed but a person who does something like this is usually impotent. He gets his kicks in other ways. The guy was a pervert, there's no question about it—or else he was certainly acting like one at the time."

At the end of one long story about the murders was a mention that investigators had been sent to Willard State Hospital (formerly Willard Asylum for the Insane, located between Finger Lakes Seneca and Cayuga) where a man was brought after attempting suicide on July 21. The newspaper didn't give the guy's name but said he'd been a former patient at the Gowanda State Hospital in western New York State between Erie, Pennsylvania, and Buffalo. When police searched the man's residence, they found a newspaper with the pages that featured Chili murder stories folded back. The guy earned one mention in the press and was never named.

In the coming days, the sun continued to rise over the swimming hole and set over the dump site. At night, without much sleep, I couldn't look out any of my house's windows. Someone might be looking back. I listened to the planes arriving and departing from the Monroe County Airport, and I listened to the sad lonesome whistles of the trains, eerily echoing as they carried freight both on the other side of the creek and along the runoff headed north toward the city. But I didn't hear the whooping and hollering of teenagers back in the darkness. The stone trestle's perpetual party had been vanquished forever by the Fear.

Naturally there was speculation that Richard Speck, the Chicago nurse stabber, might be the Chili Slasher. When George-Ann and Kathy disappeared, the concept of mass murderers was remote in American minds; there were Jack the Ripper and the Boston Strangler and, well, that was it. Stories of a Black Dahlia murder in Los Angeles and Torso Murders in Cleveland didn't make much of an impression on Rochesterians. The terms "spree killer" and "serial killer" had yet to be coined. But, because of Speck, consciousness was raised.

The world was suffering a cluster burst of evil. I could feel it. And once the virus was out, it would be with us forever. And it all came true. Once rare, psycho killer stories became routine on TV, and it began that summer.

When Speck's photograph appeared on the front page of the *Democrat & Chronicle*, Sheriff Skinner's office was inundated by calls from persons convinced they'd seen Speck around when the girls went missing. Monroe County investigators called Chicago police to determine Speck's whereabouts around June 25.[10] The Chicago police informed Monroe County that they still hadn't interrogated Speck at that time. The Miranda ruling (or the "goddamned Miranda ruling," as the cops called it) was new, and police were still gun-shy about having evidence thrown out in court. They made especially certain that Speck was aware of his rights before they asked him anything at all. It turned out Speck was elsewhere on June 25. A nurse in Hancock, Michigan, told police that Speck visited her on June 23 and stayed until the 27th when she put him on a train bound for Sault Ste. Marie, Michigan, where Speck claimed he was going to look for a job.

At Archer Road, investigators meticulously made a grid of the area and searched it square by square. Deputies widened the search, concentrating on the railroad tracks between the trestle and the dump site, including the Genesee Junction, with its distinctive built-into-the-ground turntable. The litter—a rusty can of Standard Dry Ale, Atomic Fireball wrappers, and a Coke bottle—testified that the turntable was also a teen hangout.

I wondered, was there a railroad angle to the case? George-Ann's dad was a railroad employee. Did he have enemies at his place of work? Throw in the "railroad cop" pursuing parkers . . . was there a *reason* that the Pennsylvania and West Shore railroad tracks were featured so heavily in the murders' geography?

After the third day, I was back on the porch reading a paper dug from the burn barrel. The matter of the "cop" hunting necking couples was still in the news. One of the picnickers called Ruth Formicola and said that he and his family were from East Rochester. They were having a picnic near Black Creek when they spotted the mysterious man along that stretch. The mystery man they talked to was a young man who claimed to be a "special railroad officer looking for sex offenders." (In those days, that could have meant gay men.) The sheriff contacted the railroads, and they said it wasn't one of their men working the railroad service road near Scottsville Road, although one railroad did acknowledge that an employee had, on the night of the disappearance, talked to a couple parked at Genesee Junction, only a few feet from the swimming hole. The employee simply advised the couple that they should park elsewhere as that spot was "popular with a lot of couples." The story was all euphemism, no meaning. The story of the man interested in couples who were making out near the swimming hole kept changing, but it remained as muddy as ever.

The girls had been transported by car. Police contacted gas stations, repair garages, and seat-cover stores. Somewhere there was a bloody mess. Someone might have noticed it.

Common MCSO thinking was that there was one physically imposing killer. Friends said the girls were wiry and strong. Investigators heard stories from boys who'd been at the trestle with Kathy and George-Ann and who had thrown them in fun off the trestle into Black Creek below. The girls were fighters, and it took all of those boys' strength to toss them off the bridge.

A reporter asked Dr. Benjamin Pollack, assistant director of Rochester State Hospital, "Who'd do something like this?" Dr. Pollack reacted to the knife-as-penis angle, saying the killer was probably "past his prime of life and envious of youth and vigor."[11] The two girls in bathing suits might to him have symbolized evil. His best guess was that "he is a religious man who sought vengeance on the girls because he considered them exhibitionists." He didn't believe the killer was a young person unless it was someone who was impotent and who was having emotional and presumably sexual family or marital problems. The killer demonstrated "obvious frenzy and loss of control." Although it could be a mentally ill young person, his best guess remained that it was an older paranoid who carried a chip on his shoulder.

4

CHRISTINE WATSON AND MARSHA JEAN BEHNEY

Monroe County investigators were in touch with the FBI, who kept them abreast of similar murders in other jurisdictions. One such case involved the sex-motivated slashing murder of a ten-year-old girl in an Erie, Pennsylvania, suburb on Tuesday, July 19, 1966, just an hour down the New York State Thruway from Rochester.[1]

The victim was Christine Watson of Love Road in Millcreek. Her body was found less than 300 yards from her converted schoolhouse home. The discovery was made only 45 minutes after Christine was reported missing by her parents at 1:30 in the afternoon. The body was lying on its right side, fully clothed, with a deeply slashed throat, left in a heavy growth of trees and bushes. The ground was bloodstained, plant life trampled down, with no evidence of a struggle other than at the exact spot where the body was found.[2]

The best eyewitness was six-year-old neighbor Tom Levis, who was playing with Christine in some woods near their homes. At 12:45 p.m. a man appeared, a stranger, and enticed Christine deeper into the woods by promising to show her some minnows in Walnut Creek. "Want to see small fish in the water?" the man asked. The boy refused to go along. "I'll give you some chewing gum," the man said. The boy held his ground, but Christine said OK. Tom waited for an hour for Christine to return before he went to Christine's mother and told her what happened, describing the man as having dark hair, a small mustache, and wearing a red shirt and black trousers.

Coroner Merle Wood performed the autopsy with a team of Hamot Hospital pathologists. The postmortem failed to determine definitively if the girl had been sexually assaulted. The little girl had bled out through her neck wound. Regarding the sex-crime investigation, more tests were scheduled for the remains. As police combed the woods near the crime scene, they encountered local men, armed with rifles, walking those same woods, hoping to bring the killer in dead or alive. One man was detained but released following a brief questioning. The National Guard allowed searching police to use a mine detector.

There was a flood of public interest. A press conference was called, and Millcreek police explained that there were details of Christine's murder that could never be made public—so if any tenacious reporter happened upon those details, discretion would be appreciated. Details that only the killer would know were helpful both for weeding out false confessors and when nailing the guy.

Police questioned two 11-year-old girls, Mary Curry and Sherry Alward, who'd been upstream swimming in Walnut Creek when Christine was attacked. As a result of those interviews, a search went out across Pennsylvania, New York, and Ohio for a suspicious vehicle described only as a "shiny black car."

Known sex criminals within 50 miles were rounded up and questioned, and all were released. On Tuesday night, a pair of graduate students found a man's red shirt on Sterrettania Road as it ran alongside Laurel Hill Cemetery. Police checked out the discovery, and it turned out to be a false alarm. The clothing item was a well-worn woman's blouse that had been converted into a painting rag.

What the public didn't know was that the police had a very good suspect in the Watson murder. His name was Eugene Patterson, and he'd been identified by the six-year-old boy as the man who led Christine to Walnut Creek.[3]

The thing about the crime scene that police hadn't told the public, the clue that only the investigators and the killer would know about, was that, under the small body, investigators found a shiny silver star badge, such as a kid might wear to pretend he was Marshal Dillon from *Gunsmoke*.[4]

At age nine, I wasn't the keen observer of social cues that I later became, but during those first days and weeks after the Chili murders, I was picking up on a troubling vibe. Adults blamed George-Ann's demise on her perceived promiscuity. The sentiment wasn't nearly enough "what kind of monster or monsters would do this sort of thing?" The feeling was more "George-Ann's brains were between her legs. She would walk off with anybody."

They blamed the victim. At almost 10, I have to admit I struggled with those kinds of thoughts, too. I didn't know what Kathy Bernhard had done to deserve such a fate, but I knew that, on at least one occasion, George-Ann had done some stuff that she wasn't supposed to, and I wondered if God hadn't punished her for her sins.

On July 27, a week after the bodies were discovered, Monroe County manager Gordon A. Howe ordered a cleanup of 400 county-owned building lots in Chili.[5] Many of them were overgrown with weeds, and Howe hoped that one might contain an important clue regarding the Chili murders. He also hoped the clearing of the lots would help ease tensions in the Ballantyne area, where every bush meant a place behind which a killer could be hiding.

Tensions, Howe explained, were particularly high on Morrison Avenue, which ran parallel to Names Road east of Theron, one block to the south. A Peeping Tom had plagued that street for two months—a spree of voyeurism that began well before the girls disappeared. Seven-year-old Grace Green had not been the only one on that street to see a man out her bedroom window.

Many of the lots had abandoned houses on them, shacks some of them, and the county came to own them after foreclosure proceedings for unpaid taxes. The lots were being sold to a developer, and some were consolidated to meet new zoning requirements. Chili supervisor Samuel Kent said that the town would do the labor to clear out the 400 lots, with an agreement that it would be reimbursed by the county. The Monroe Tree Surgeons defoliated the Archer Road crime scene and made it look like an Egyptian archeological dig. The Town of Chili also hired them to clean out the foliage north of Morrison Avenue and back at the stone trestle. Deputies supervised, ready to photograph and process any evidence that might be unearthed. All they found were bits of clothes not belonging to the girls, "discarded articles, and other debris."[6]

A Chili "reward fund" asked for contributions. The fund already had more than \$3,000 and would go to anyone whose info resulted in an arrest. Rochesterians were urged to donate their money through WHEC-TV, Channel 10.

Senseless violence continued to make the news. On August 1, 1966, a student at the University of Texas at Austin, former Marine Charles Whitman, went to the 28th-floor observation deck of the university's tower-like administrative building and, using a sniper rifle, killed 16 people and wounded another 32 during a 90-minute shooting spree. Whitman was shot and killed when police ambushed his sniper's nest. The autopsy revealed amphetamine abuse and an aggressive brain tumor.[7]

About two weeks after the bodies were discovered, Sheriff Skinner received an anonymous letter from a teenage girl who said she'd been with her boyfriend at the Archer Road lovers' lane on June 26, the night *after* the girls disappeared, and she'd seen something she thought the sheriff should know about. But she didn't say what it was.[8]

In response, Skinner placed items in the Rochester daily newspapers and made announcements on TV asking that the girl come forward, assuring her that her identity would remain confidential. The witness called Skinner at 5:30 p.m. on Tuesday, August 9, and told him that she saw a suspicious man on the lane where the girls were found. He was sitting alone in his car for about an hour, removing rubbish and cleaning the interior with a can and a rag. The vehicle, she said, was tan and white. When done cleaning, the man "just sat there mumbling to himself." She added, "I am 17 and I wouldn't want it to happen to me." She described the man as in his forties, heavyset, and wearing a dark, dirty shirt and a light straw hat.[9]

On August 25, 1966, the *Canandaigua Daily Messenger* (Canandaigua being just 30 miles southeast of the murder site) ran a story about a "logical suspect" in the Chili murders: unemployed used car salesman Ellis Kennedy Douthit of Abilene, Texas, who was "being held today as the prime suspect in the brutal sex slaying of two Town of Chili teenagers last June."[10] Douthit was arrested on the afternoon of Tuesday, August 23, on second-degree assault charges in connection with an "unrelated incident." That incident involved a 26-year-old Henrietta woman (Henrietta being the town just east of Chili, on the other side of the Genesee River). Douthit, the woman said, tried to force his way into her car and attempted to rape her during the early morning hours of Saturday, August 20. Douthit wore yellow surgical gloves and was allegedly armed with a knife during the attack. The victim suffered a cut hand. Sheriff Skinner said that "certain evidence and other clues"— Saturday night, a sex attack, the knife—pointed to him as a logical suspect in the Chili murders. He remained a suspect until MCSO investigators were informed by authorities in Texas that Douthit didn't leave Abilene until July 11, 1966.[11] In 1984, Douthit escaped from a Lubbock, Texas, jail where he was being held for aggravated robbery. The escape came when Douthit was taken to the dentist. As it turned out, Douthit's partner in crime, Jorita Hagens, 40, had guns hidden in the dentist's office, and Douthit alone knew where they were. Douthit shot his way out of there, critically wounding a deputy. Hagens had a car ready for Douthit as he came running out. Their flight ended in a Brownfield motel. Trapped like a rat, Douthit put his gun in his mouth and blew the back of his head off. Hagens was arrested and charged with attempted murder.[12]

On Saturday, September 3, 1966, at 12:30 p.m., just outside Womelsdorf, Pennsylvania, the Behney kids had just returned from the Reading mall. There was Sandra Lee, 15; her sister Marsha Jean, 12; and Samuel Jr., 7. Sandra had in her hand a new 45 (i.e., a single-song record on vinyl), "Sunshine Superman" by Donovan, and immediately put it on the record player. *"Sunshine came softly through my window today. . . ."* As the record played, once, twice, three times, their mother Ferne told them to get into their swimsuits; she was allowing them to go to the public pool at the Bethany Home in town, about two miles away, on the other side of the Lebanon-Berks county line. They could ride their bikes there.

"Be careful of traffic," Mom warned.

Changed and ready to go, Sandra decided she wanted to listen to her record one more time. Samuel stuck with his oldest sister, but Marsha was eager to get the show on the road and announced that she was going to get a head start. When the record was over and Sandra and Sam mounted Sandra's bike, Marsha had already disappeared around a bend in the Township Road 506. They saw no cars heading in either direction.

Sandra heard three screams, the first one long and terrifyingly shrill. As the trailing siblings rounded the bend, Sandra saw that there was a car stopped about 500 feet up the road, and it looked like Marsha had gotten off her bike and was lying down.

Sandra pedaled as hard as she could, but it was hard with Sam as a passenger. She later recalled, "The man was bending over my sister. He was about ten to fifteen feet away from me at the time. He glanced at me. I looked at him. For about ten seconds he looked at me. He then turned around and ran up to his car, parked with the motor running. He drove off, fast, the gravel started flying, heading towards the Bethany Home." The car was a '57 Chevy, white on top, tan or brown on the bottom. The man was heavyset, with a dark complexion, dark brown hair, and about 30. [13]

Marsha, wearing only her red, white, and blue swimsuit, lay motionless at the side of the road. Her bike was on its side, undamaged. Blood was coming out of Marsha's left side, near her heart and under her arm. "I couldn't stop the bleeding. I knew she was dying. I said the Lord's Prayer," Sandra recalled. She ordered her brother to take her bike back home for help. Moments later, a motorist stopped and took Sandra to the Bethany Home where an ambulance was called. Marsha was DOA at Reading Hospital.

The cause of death, the coroner concluded, was a "pierced heart," apparently a stab wound inflicted by a "sharp and thin" instrument. In addition to the fatal wound, slash wounds were found on the girl's left arm, wrist, shoulder, and head. There were nine wounds in all. The manner of death, the coroner said, was murder. [14]

A five-and-a-half-month manhunt ensued, covering most of eastern Pennsylvania. The break came in February when teenagers Joan Louise Tobias and Cynthia Ann DeLong walked to the local fish hatchery at around 1:30 on a Sunday and encountered a man in his car. The defendant yelled something vulgar at them. The car didn't come to a complete stop but slowed way down as it passed the girls. As the car pulled away, they tried to memorize the license plate number: it began 5438.

That turned out to be enough info for police to pick up John Irvan Miller, 31 years old, a "loner" who lived with his parents on Level Road in Lower Providence Township, about 50 miles from the crime scene.

He drove a salmon and off-white 1957 Chevy. Miller greatly resembled Sandra Behney's description. Miller worked at the Peerless Paper Products Company in the town of Oaks in Montgomery County. When hauled into the state police barracks, Miller was belligerent toward newsmen and had to be yanked into another room by Assistant District Attorney John Hoffert Jr. Miller was charged with murder and arraigned. He maintained his innocence. "I've never driven on the road where the murder occurred," he said.

Miller retained Fred I. Noch to represent him. Called in to view a lineup, Sandra took her time but confidently identified Miller as the man who stood over her slain sister.

In jail, Miller began a hunger strike.[15] He said he was protesting being falsely accused. Police suspected an ulterior motive: to make himself harder to ID as the "heavyset" man standing in the road over the dead little girl.[16]

Jury selection for Miller's trial began on September 18, 1967.[17] During voir dire, the *Reading Eagle* printed the names and addresses of every prospective juror who was dismissed following a challenge, as well as that of every juror who was seated.

At the trial, Sandra was asked to identify the killer. "That man," she said and started to point, when her emotions overcame her and she began to sob violently. She was given a moment to compose herself, and Judge Hess offered her some water.

Sandra's cross-examination lasted more than an hour. No, she didn't see the man stabbing her sister. She didn't see "an instrument" in the man's hands. But she held her ground regarding the three times she had identified Miller. No, police had *not* helped her. During the lineup, she insisted, she spent a long time, five minutes, looking at the men before choosing Miller.

Testifying on his own behalf, Miller said he spent the entire day of the murder within a half mile of his home mowing and pruning trees on a piece of ground that he owned. During cross-examination, Miller said he heard about the murder sometime prior to February 1967 on his home or car radio and admitted that he had clipped and saved all of the articles regarding the murder in the Reading newspapers. He also admitted that he might have had other papers relating to other crime stories in his room.

The only other witnesses called by the defense were Miller's two bosses, who said that he was a competent and fine worker but admitted under cross-examination that they had no idea how he behaved after hours.

During rebuttal, the prosecution attacked Miller's alibi. He said he had been working around his property, but his neighbor—68-year-old Mary Seminack—testified that Miller was nowhere around. She looked for him on September 3, 1966, and was unable to find him. It gave her the willies to think about it now, but she had wanted Miller to meet her daughter. After the murder, Seminack said, Miller used a pickup truck rather than the two-toned car he'd been driving. Under cross-examination the woman said that she did not see Miller on the 3rd or for the rest of the week. She found Miller to be "very helpful" and a "nice fellow" but had never really engaged him in conversation other than hello.

Miller was convicted, but only of second-degree murder. He showed no emotion as the jury foreman announced the verdict. The judge said that, had he been on the jury, he would have voted guilty as well, then added, "Although I might have gone to first degree. No doubt this was a difficult case. The police did a very fine job in developing the testimony."

The killer smirked as he was escorted from the courtroom, and Sandra Behney was so infuriated that she had to be restrained by state police and lawyers. Now a convicted murderer, he finally confessed en route from court to the Berks County Jail. Informed that his sentence was likely to be 10 to 20 years for second-degree murder, Miller allegedly replied, "That's not bad for killing a girl."[18] Miller, deputies reported, was in a "talkative mood" during the car ride. He said that he had intended to rape the little girl, but she screamed and he had to knife her to death to silence her.[19]

"If I'd gone to a bawdyhouse, that girl would be alive today," Miller said.

Marsha Behney's murder didn't bring an end to 1966's string of obscene violence. The Chicago area, already reeling from Richard Speck, was further stunned on September 18 when Valerie Percy, the beautiful twin daughter of up-and-coming Republican politician Charles Percy, was murdered in her bed by a killer who used a glasscutter to get in, then navigated the Percy mansion (18 rooms overlooking Lake Michigan) perfectly in the dark. Sharon Percy, Valerie's twin sister, awoke to find her twin fatally stabbed, her nightgown pulled up to expose her naked torso. [20] The case was never solved, and it so shocked America that a scheduled TV premiere of the Alfred Hitchcock movie *Psycho* was postponed and then canceled altogether by CBS. The film contained a graphic scene of a showering woman being stabbed to death by an intruder. [21]

The cancellation of the movie was a big relief as far as my mother was concerned. She didn't want me to see it. My mom's anxiety was wasted. I had already seen *Psycho* at the Rochester Drive-In on Scottsville Road, in 1960 when it came out and I was still three. With the speaker rolled up into my dad's window, I was in my PJs and sitting on my mom's lap. When the bad thing happened to the pretty blonde lady, my mom jumped out of her skin and became so upset that I was upset. "The girl just fell down! She's OK. The girl just fell down and bumped her head!" my mother said, with a strain of hysteria. I was pretty young, but I knew one thing for sure. The girl did not just fall down. And she was nowhere to be seen for the rest of the movie. My mother felt guilty for upsetting me with her reaction and for my being there in the first place with this pornography. By 1966 the movie was famous for changing people's bathing habits, and the scariness of that scene was legendary in my house.

Whitman and Miller and Speck were all piling on as far as I was concerned. I got the point. No one was safe, ever—particularly if they lived in a solitary house at the end of an L-shaped dirt road. There was a new heaviness in the air. Mostly you just had to feel it, but you could see it in my mother's jaw, which now set slightly to one side, a sign of stress. Whereas I'd previously been allowed to be anywhere within earshot of my mom's scout whistle, now my world shrunk to my house, my pool, and my yard. I wasn't even allowed to go into my own back field. I never picked wild strawberries again.

So I spent the end of July and August on my pool platform listening to WBBF. I memorized the lyrics to the Top 40 and played air guitar on the pool strainer, making the red-stained pool platform my stage. At night I had the transistor under the covers with the earplug in. As I lay awake, I tried to remember everything I could about the area back by the trestle and what I now knew was called the Genesee Junction. It wasn't a common playground, being back by the railroad tracks, but I had been there several times, both with Larry Putnam rather than George Mulligan. (George and I always fished on our side of the creek. The fish were no different on the opposite bank, so there was no reason to go there.) Larry and I used to go on treasure hunts, looking for empty pop bottles that could be exchanged at Coop's for two cents. Six bottles equaled one comic book. Our searches sometimes took us afield. The last time I'd been back there by the tracks I got in big trouble, and Larry Putnam earned his reputation with my mother as a troublemaker. We returned from playing in a freight car—in the summer it was about 150 degrees inside a freight car—and I had unknowingly stood on something so hot that the bottoms of my shoes melted. My mom had a fit. Even before the girls disappeared, she thought it a bad idea to hang around freight trains because there might be "homo hobos." Say that three times fast.

I remembered a lot from back there by the tracks, though. There was a tiny one-room house where a man might have been stationed, when there was a reason for a man to be stationed there, and there was the turntable, a perfectly round concrete structure sunk into the ground. In 1965 it was in the middle of some woods, so it was nearly impossible to imagine it in use. It was bizarre to walk through the trees and come across this paved hole with a spoke at its center. The date in the concrete read 1910. The turntable, I later learned, was meant to turn around steam engines, which meant it would have been obsolete sometime in the late 1940s or early 1950s.

As a teenager I would imagine men and women in cloaks and hoods standing along the edge of that circle, dividing it into five equal parts, forming a human pentagram like the kind they had with covens or devil-worshipping cults. It was the perfect place for clandestine meetings and casting spooky spells.

I was familiar with the stone trestle and the swimming hole as well, because it was one of the places where George Mulligan and I had gone fishing. There was a beautiful grassy area that led in a gentle slope to the water's edge, just southeast of the trestle. I thought of that spot where the north–south and east–west tracks crossed, the actual Genesee *Junction*. Facing north, you'd head directly for civilization, south, for the boondocks. I pondered the "railroad cop," the guy who did or didn't exist, who was either near Scottsville Road or near the swimming hole, who was either telling necking couples to get off railroad property or was advising them to move elsewhere because the area was too popular, the one who might have been looking for sex criminals. Even though I was just a kid, I wondered how common it was for grown men to peek into cars on lovers' lanes. And when caught, how often did they identify themselves as low-level law enforcement as a cover/excuse? How much of this was normal? And if all of it was weird, why was it weird so close to me?

Evie Douglas recalled the fall of 1966: "My Dad didn't like the fact that I spent a lot of time at 'Old Man' Frey's house. He had a little bicycle repair shop at the end of Lester Street. He was retired, and his bicycles found their way into a lot of neighborhood families. I think it was because to get there you had to walk past other homes that had older boys living in them. Richie Barnes* had an older brother, but I don't remember his name. Dad didn't like me going to Hunter's house, as it was at the dead end of Lester Street by the creek."

I remembered Richard Barnes as well, although I didn't know he'd had an older brother. He'd been our paperboy and had the perfect 1966 hair, very long and swept across in the front where it appeared to be held up by his eyebrows, but neat at the sides and back. Guys with hair like that always had it falling down onto their eyes, so they had to flip their head to get it back atop the eyebrows where it belonged.

Evie didn't want to give the impression that she was afraid of the older boys in the neighborhood. It was actually her dad who was worried. Evie thought very highly of Richard Barnes and certainly harbored no anxiety about his older brother either.

By January of 1967, the dozens of men and women from the county and state who'd been working the Chili murders had dwindled to two. They were MCSO Detective Sergeant Donald Clark and Detective Michael Iaculli of the State Police Bureau of Criminal Investigation. Both men had families and children approximately the same age as Kathy and George-Ann. Over the seven months since the murders, they'd worked 3,000 hours on the case and investigated more than a thousand suspects. They'd contacted law enforcement in almost every state and had quizzed the victims' families countless times in hopes of unearthing the one clue that might break the case. Clark and Iaculli allowed reporter Carol Rubright of the Rochester newspapers to be part of their world for a day.[22] The investigators ran their operation out of a small office at the back of the Monroe County Jail, the "command center" that had been set up during the first days after the bodies were discovered. The day began at the office, planning. Who would they visit? Who would they follow? Perhaps they spent the day checking a person, trying to clear him or connect him with the crime. Each suspect needed to be located and, with cooperation from Albany and Washington, checked for a criminal record. Although they almost always confronted the suspect in person at some point, they did not notify the suspects' employers. Clark said that even at this late stage of the investigation, they were still receiving two or three phone tips per week.

"Most of the leads are submitted by cranks," Clark explained, trying to "get back at" an enemy or a neighbor with whom they were having a dispute.

"Cranks are the biggest waste of time we face," Iaculli said, "because we have to check out each and every one thoroughly."

The single lead that had led to the most man-hours wasn't a crank, however. That was from the 17-year-old girl who'd seen a car at the lovers' lane on the night after the girls disappeared. The investigators indicated that the description of the car by the lovers' lane witness was more complete than had been previously revealed in the papers and had included not just the colors (tan and white), but the make, model, and year as well.

Both men believed the car was what was going to convict the killer: "Bloodstains on fabric can never be cleaned out," Clark explained.

The investigators kept tabs on similar crimes committed elsewhere. Of these, the Behney murder in Pennsylvania was the most interesting because of the swimsuit angle, but there were others in Florida, Ohio, Rhode Island, and Wisconsin.

On July 23, 1966, 20-year-old Lynda Moore was found murdered with a knife in a car on a lonesome road south of Jefferson, Ohio.[23]

The Wisconsin murders were the most noteworthy, taking place in and around Milwaukee. On September 3, 1966, the same day as the Behney murder, 10-year-old Julia Beckwith was raped, beaten, and stabbed to death in a Milwaukee vacant lot.[24] In October, 18-year-old Sherryl Thompson was found by her altar-boy brother behind a Catholic Church, stabbed 22 times, mutilated, and half clothed. The church was nine blocks west of the spot where Julia Beckwith's body had been found six weeks earlier.[25] Exactly a month after the Thompson murder, on November 4, 19-year-old Diane Olkwitz was found stabbed more than 100 times at the factory where she worked in Menomonee Falls.[26] That serial killer turned out to be Michael Lee Herrington, a 23-year-old Milwaukee shipping clerk. His wife was expecting their first child during his killing spree. He also admitted that he had stabbed 11-year-old Kathleen Dreyer and left her bleeding in the street one week after the Thompson murder, escaping in a 1957 Chevrolet. When caught, he blamed his anger on his mother, by whom he said he was regularly beaten. He was convicted in 1967 and sentenced to several lifetimes behind bars.[27]

The Monroe County investigators told Rubright that they were "confident" the Chili murders would be solved one day, and when that happened, Clark would go back to investigating burglaries and Iaculli would return to the Henrietta State Police substation.

Back in school, starting fifth grade, my first in Scottsville, the murders were rarely discussed, but I do remember one exchange. Someone said those girls were killed by Jack the Ripper, and another kid said no, he took off their clothes before he killed them, so he should be called Jack the Stripper,[28] and everyone laughed.

By spring 1967, media coverage of the Chili murders was sparse. When there was an article, it always featured a reassuring quote from the sheriff, explaining that his office was still on the job.

"We will never close the files," Skinner said. "We'll check any lead, go any place, and talk to any person if we think it would help."[29]

And the guy the MCSO wanted to talk to most of all was John I. Miller.[30] The similarities between the Behney murder in Pennsylvania and the Chili murders were impressive. Identical weapons were used. All of the victims were young, petite females wearing only swimsuits—and the suspected "souvenir" in the Chili case was a towel with a picture of a girl in a bathing suit on it. (Plus, we later learned, Miller's car resembled the one seen on the Archer Road lovers' lane on June 26, 1966.) The problem was that Miller was "in a state of mental health that prevented investigators from quizzing him."

On April 13, Detectives John Kennerson and Michael Iaculli went to Reading, but Miller clammed up. In a separate visit, Michael Cerretto tried talking to him. Again, nothing. All Miller did was curse them out. Then came the trial, the conviction, and Miller's confession. Monroe County tried again. Now that Miller had confessed, Cerretto hoped he would be more forthright about all of his criminal activities. Cerretto told the press that Miller was the *only* suspect in the Chili murders, and he thought he was a good one. The *Lebanon Daily News* reported on September 27, 1967, "Miller reportedly admitted having been in Rochester at the time of the deaths of the two girls."[31] (Although, according to an MCSO written report, Miller later withdrew this statement, replacing it with "I was away from home at that time but not in Rochester.") During the first week in October 1967, Cerretto and Iaculli were back in Reading, trying once again to find out what Miller knew.

On October 14, 1967, the *D&C* published a photo of Miller under the headline, "Did Murderer Stop in Area?"[32] The paper did this at the request of the MCSO. An unnamed investigator said, "Our investigation indicates Miller very well could have been in Rochester then." That disclosure was based not just on Miller's earlier statement, but on "other information obtained" while MCSO investigators were in Pennsylvania, info that "they didn't want to make public at this time." Over the next four days, 20 people called the MCSO saying they'd seen the guy. The "strongest" of these phone tips came from a "former bartender" at a "Scottsville Road restaurant." The bartender said Miller was at the bar on the night of June 25, 1966. None of the 20 calls placed Miller in a motel or hotel, and none placed him in a car.[33]

Twenty sounded like a lot. But that was less than the number of Rochesterians who "saw Richard Speck" when Speck was hundreds of miles away. It was the power of suggestion, and you couldn't trust those eyewitnesses. Everyone wanted so badly to be helpful.

Dawn Putnam and I were allowed to ride our bikes up and down Stallman Drive, but no further. I had my transistor radio on the handlebars, and we listened to WBBF and talked about stuff. One day she told me that she'd been "raked." I had no idea what that meant and told her so.

"It's like attacked," she said.

"Who did it?" I asked.

"It was Keith's brother Clint."

I went home and asked my mom what "raked" meant. "You know, like attacked," I said. Her jaw pushed to one side and she didn't answer.

The first anniversary of the murders came and went, and the Fear remained strong. In August 1967, two teenage girls were walking along Ballantyne Road at 5:20 p.m. when a brown panel truck passed them, stopped about 100 feet in front of them, and began to back up. The truck had no license plate, and they never saw the driver. It backed up until it was almost next to them, and then a couple of other cars came along and it sped away. The girls immediately called the sheriff's office. Deputies searched for but never found the brown truck with no plates. [34]

In Chili, the Fear got a boost on December 20, 1967, when a man's body was discovered just off Ballantyne Road, at the end of the Bookmans' driveway, about a fifth of a mile south of the Ballantyne Road/ Beaver Road junction. My mom was a friend of Doris Bookman, and I went to school with several of the Bookman girls. The school bus went by the next day, and I saw a red mud puddle. It turned out the guy was just a few days out of jail and had been shot through the head. [35] The sheriff suspected revenge, not robbery, and the case was never solved.

5

THE DOUBLE INITIALS MURDERS

In 1971, there began in Rochester a series of murders so heinous that they obscured in many minds the 1966 crimes. The three victims were little girls, and—reminiscent of an Agatha Christie novel[1]—each had the same first and last initials. Their bodies were all found raped (by this time I knew what it meant) by a roadside, strangled by ligature. Some believed they were also found dumped in a town that started with the same initial as their names—although that theory required some creative uses of the map.

Long before anyone caught on to the initials angle, the case wormed its way into the Rochester area's collective nightmare. The bad dream started on November 16, 1971, when 10-year-old Carmen Colon disappeared from the Bull's Head section of Rochester, southwest of downtown.[2]

Carmen had been running an errand for her grandmother, going to the Jax Drugstore on West Main Street. According to eyewitnesses, she made it to the drugstore all right, but somewhere between the store and her home on Brown Street, she vanished.

Then came the nightmare part: Carmen wriggled free from her captor at one point and jumped out of his car. Naked from the waist down, she ran hysterically down the shoulder of Interstate 490, screaming for help. She was seen by *dozens of motorists* as she ran toward traffic, an adult male running after her, a dark Pinto hatchback parked alongside the road. It was rush hour, and scores of cars drove by, observing the child in distress. No one stopped. Carmen's killer caught her and dragged her back to the car.

Her body—severely scratched by fingernails, strangled, and sexually assaulted—was found two days later in a gully against a rock in a wooded area off Stearns Road, outside the village of Churchville.

The murder dominated the news for weeks, but the commotion had died down by April 2, 1973, a rainy Monday, when 11-year-old Wanda Walkowicz disappeared while running an errand for her mother.[3] Wanda went by herself to the Hillside Deli on Conkey Avenue, on the east side of Rochester. As was true in the Colon case, it was late afternoon, about 5:00. Wanda made it to the store, purchased groceries for that evening's dinner, and vanished on her return trip to her Avenue D home.

Wanda's body, sexually assaulted and strangled, perhaps with a belt, was found on the morning of April 4, just west of Irondequoit Bay, on a hillside next to a Route 104 access road in the town of Webster. She was last seen talking to someone in a car outside the deli where she had shopped, but no one saw the driver.

The similarities in Carmen and Wanda's murders were obvious. The initials motif was noticed at this point. Instant infamy. It was like Rochester had its own Zodiac Killer. Local girls with alliterative names became terrified. They looked at maps and guessed where their own lifeless bodies would be dumped.

Terror turned to panic on November 26, 1973, the Monday after Thanksgiving, when ten-year-old Michelle Maenza disappeared. Michelle lived on Webster Crescent on Rochester's east side. As had the others, she disappeared while on an errand for her mother.[4]

Mom had left her purse at a store in the Goodman Plaza near their home, and she sent Michelle by herself to retrieve it. The somewhat portly Michelle made it to the store, retrieved the purse, and was returning home. At that point, she was seen by her uncle who offered her a ride, but she declined.

She was next seen in the suburban town of Penfield, outside a fast-food restaurant. Michelle's abductor had fed her. She was last seen in a car that was parked on the shoulder of Route 350 in the town of Walworth. The car had a flat tire but had not yet been jacked up. Several passersby, one of whom stopped and offered to help, noticed the car and the girl sitting inside. The driver of the disabled car made it clear that he wanted no help, so the Good Samaritan went on his way.

Michelle's body, raped and strangled, was found two days later in a ditch about eight feet from the shoulder of Eddy Road in the town of Macedon in Wayne County. Michelle Maenza in Macedon. The autopsy tended to verify the sighting at the restaurant. Her final meal was a hamburger. The Route 350 witnesses came forward, and, working with a composite artist, they produced drawings of the suspect.[5]

Despite a huge task force assigned to the case, the murders remained unsolved.

The best clue the police had was the dark Pinto hatchback seen on 490 as the seminude Carmen Colon ran for help. Interestingly, one of the fellows driving a dark Pinto hatchback in 1971 in the Rochester area was Kenneth Bianchi, who lived in the nearby town of Gates and later became one of the Hillside Stranglers, killer of eight girls and women in the Los Angeles, California, area in 1977–78, and two more in the state of Washington before his arrest.[6]

At the time of the Chili murders, Kenny was in 10th grade and lived one town over. Kenny Bianchi and I went to the same school for one year. For the 1961–62 school year, Bianchi was in the fifth grade and I was in kindergarten at Holy Family School at the corner of Jay and Ames.[7]

He moved to Gates, and I moved to Chili. Bianchi was born to a prostitute in Rochester in May 1951 and was given up for adoption. By age 11, his age when we attended the same school, Kenny was already a discipline problem, having furious tantrums. He was married briefly at age 18. At age 20, he bragged to a girlfriend that he had killed a man from Rochester. In 1973, Bianchi became convinced that the Rochester police suspected that he was the city's Double Initials Killer (DIK).

As it turned out, the Rochester authorities made no connection between Bianchi and the DIK until after he had been arrested as the Hillside Strangler—so he had nothing to worry about. Everyone in the county who drove the correct make of car had been spoken to. Authorities had in no way singled him out. Besides the similarity in cars, there was no evidence to link Bianchi to the initials murders. The crimes stopped in 1973. Bianchi stayed in the Rochester area until 1976.

While it was true that the police were not specifically looking at Bianchi during their search for the DIK, there were other suspects— one was a fireman, an alleged rapist who committed suicide in 1974 while fleeing from the police. The fireman hid in a parked car outside a home on Fieldwood Drive, on the city's far east side, and shot himself. (In 2007, with a warrant from the MCSO, the fireman's body was exhumed from Holy Sepulchre Cemetery. His DNA did not match that found at one of the DIK crime scenes. Coincidentally, all three initials victims were also buried in Holy Sepulchre.)

Long before Wanda and Michelle were murdered, Carmen Colon's uncle was a suspect. He committed suicide in 1991, not long after shooting and wounding his wife and brother-in-law. After begging police to kill him, he turned his gun on himself.[8]

Also under suspicion in the Colon case was a known child molester who worked in the Bull's Head area where she disappeared. The man, now dead, couldn't account for his whereabouts on the day Carmen disappeared.

Some theorize that there was no serial killer, that two or three different killers were at work here, copycats misdirecting police. There were differences in the murders. The first victim was strangled manually from in front. The other two were strangled with a belt from behind.

The most stunning consistency in the three cases was the victims' actions before each abduction. All three were running errands for Mom involving going to a store, picking something up, and returning. All three had been to the store, accomplished their task, and were returning home when abducted. That was so specific. That seemed to me to be even more indicative of an MO than the fact that all three had alliterative names.

Police have tried for years to find a connection between the three victims that would point to the killer. It was the kind of case that used up detectives. What was a pattern and what was a coincidence? Who knew? Some believed the initials motif to be a media construct, one that betrayed itself by bending geographical borders. Carmen Colon had not been dumped in Churchville at all, but rather in the town of Riga. This was countered with, yes, but the location was very close to the Chili border. Maybe the killer thought he was in Chili. All three victims were poor and Catholic. They all lived with single moms and had learning disabilities. The Walkowiczes and the Colons once lived two doors apart. All were abducted in the late afternoon, picked up urban and dumped rural.

Bianchi committed many of his West Coast crimes in league with his adopted cousin Angelo Buono. Buono, too, came from Rochester, but he had left the East many years before. He could have visited.

Buono was 31 at the time of the Chili murders. Kenny was 15. In Los Angeles, they would abduct girls by claiming they were cops. Might they claim to be "railroad police"?

Still, Angelo and Kenny were stranglers—and the Chili guy was a knife-as-penis butcher.

Detective Cerretto had the misfortune of being obsessed with catching both the DIK and the Chili killer(s). His day never came. Up until the late 1980s, the DIK was hands down the most famous serial killer to strike the region. (His deadly exploits were later the subject of a 2001 Discovery Channel documentary and were heavily fictionalized in the movie *The Alphabet Killer*, filmed in Rochester, starring Eliza Dushku and Timothy Hutton.[9])

6

ZODIAC AND OTHER CONSPIRACY THEORIES

If there was satanic significance to the month and year of the Chili murders, if 6/66 had meaning, then the proximity to the summer solstice had meaning. The next black holiday would feature Satan's encore. The black holiday following the summer solstice is Lammas Day, August 1, 1966, which was the day Charles Whitman climbed to the top of the University of Texas tower in Austin and killed 16 people, wounding 32 others, with a sniper rifle.[1] After that came All Hallow's Eve '66, when beautiful co-ed Cheri Jo Bates was murdered in Riverside, California.[2]

Cheri Jo was 18 and a freshman at Riverside Community College. In high school she'd made the dean's list and was a varsity cheerleader. Now she lay dead in an alley next to a storage facility on a remote edge of campus, found at dawn by a janitor. The coroner said she put up quite a struggle and received many stab wounds before she succumbed, slash and stab wounds to the chest, throat, and face. She was found wearing the same clothes she'd last been seen in, the previous evening, in the school library. Cheri Jo's yellow car was still parked where she'd left it, about a hundred yards from her body. The key was in the ignition, and the ignition wiring had been pulled loose so that the car wouldn't start. Later a note, apparently from the killer, was found written on a desk in the college library. Today, because of compelling handwriting comparisons and a letter received by the press years later in which the purported killer referred to "doing his thing" in Riverside, the murder of Cheri Jo Bates is thought by many to have been one of the first murders committed by Northern California's notorious Zodiac Killer.[3] Year one, *Anno Satanas*, indeed.

The guy who proclaimed 1966 to be year one of Satan's reign was Anton LaVey, whose biography raised goose bumps. LaVey was the one who first publically listed the satanic holidays, including Summer Solstice, and acknowledged that the days were taken from Wicca. LaVey understood that many of his Church of Satan followers would already be Wicca practitioners, and Wicca stole the holidays from ancient pagan calendars anyway. LaVey's motto was "Do as Thou Wilt," and he wrote his teachings in a published book called *The Satanic Bible*. Halloween, or Samhain, as he called it, was the night during which the wall between our perceivable world and the astral plane was absolutely at its thinnest.

No one accused LaVey of participating in ritual abuse or human sacrifices, but his followers were a different story. Were there those who read his book and took the symbolism to heart? Some of LaVey's disciples might have been just youthful experimenters, rebels against everything, contrarians who stood up when told to sit down—for them the upside-down crosses and anything-goes attitude of the Satanists were most appealing. Some Satanists were vain and used the goth fashion as a mask to hide behind. Outlaw motorcycle clubs latched on to LaVey's symbolism. All fine and good. But there were other followers who used the Church of Satan as a justification for their own sociopathic inclinations. Fact: hundreds of American homicides each year can be deemed satanically or ritually inspired, and yet, in the cases that are solved, the perps have *rarely* turned out to be members of an organized devil-worshipping cult. Richard Ramirez, for example, drew pentagrams and the words "Hail, Satan!" at the scenes of his murders, but he turned out to be a lone nut, not a member of any satanic group.[4]

Satanists do not believe that Satan is God, but rather a messenger of God who brought Eve the knowledge of God. They believe restrictions on human behavior should be, for the most part, eliminated.

The closest link—that is, with the least degrees of separation—between LaVey and actual mayhem came in San Francisco during the summer of 1966, even as MCSO deputies were searching for George-Ann and Kathy.

LaVey produced a Witch's Review that summer, a sort of vaudeville/cabaret show for the devil-worshipping set. Performing as a topless vampire in the show was Susan Atkins, who later became notorious as "Sexy Sadie" of the Charles Manson Family. Atkins was the murderer of movie star Sharon Tate. Bobby Beausoleil, another Manson Family member, also costarred with LaVey in a theater production of *Invocation of My Demon Brother* written by Kenneth Anger, author of the scandal-sheet-as-art masterwork, *Hollywood Babylon*.

Certainly the vicinity of the summer solstice has always been a popular time period for unusually bizarre murders. Some quick examples:

On June 22, 1958, in El Monte, California, 37-year-old Mrs. Jean Ellroy was found strangled with a cotton cord and one of her stockings. Her body was dumped on a lane leading to Arroyo High School. Police suspected she was killed elsewhere and left on the lane, which was called King's Row. The victim was seen earlier that night, in a cocktail lounge and at a drive-in restaurant, accompanied by what witnesses called a "swarthy man." Years later, the case got a fresh airing out due to the efforts of Ellroy's son, James Ellroy, who grew up to be a famous writer of crime novels, including *The Black Dahlia* and *L.A. Confidential*. The murder was never solved.[5]

On June 22, 1990, the mangled corpse of 21-year-old Ron Baker, a UCLA student, was found at the mouth of the Manson Tunnel, seriously, in a park in Chatsworth, California. Baker, a small-in-stature astrophysics major, was found wearing a strong necklace with a pentagram pendant. He'd been stabbed 18 times, and his throat was slashed so deeply that he was nearly decapitated. Despite the tunnel's reputation for occult activities and animal sacrifices, Baker chose the tunnel as a regular site for meditation. Although he grew up Methodist, the victim allegedly was a believer in Wicca, which is against bloodletting. Investigation led police to the victim's roommates, who apparently bungled a kidnap-for-ransom scheme.[6]

In June 1991, Despina Magioudis traveled to Redding, California, to attend a summer solstice event on Mount Shasta, but met a grim end. It wasn't until August that Magioudis's body was found bludgeoned and strangled in a field. The case remained unsolved until July of 2011 when a convicted rapist in Iowa, 43-year-old Eric Norton, confessed to the murder while being interrogated by police after DNA evidence linked him to a 2007 rape.[7]

At three in the morning on June 26, 1977, David Berkowitz, or possibly another member of the Son of Sam cult, fired into a parked car occupied by 20-year-old Sal Lupo and 17-year-old Judy Placido. The couple had just left the Elephas disco in the Bayside section of Queens, New York. Of all the Son of Sam shootings, thankfully, this did the least damage. Both victims received only minor injuries. Berkowitz, who was convicted of all the Son of Sam killings, claimed that members of the cult had long wanted to shoot someone outside the Elephas because the cult studied the writings of 19th-century occultist Eliphas Levi. Two men were spotted fleeing the scene, a stocky black-haired man and a thin blonde man with a mustache. The dark-haired man was running, and the blonde was driving a car without its lights on. Berkowitz, who was stocky and had black hair, later said that the Elephas shootings were done by a cult member who was thin, blonde, and had a mustache.[8]

On June 25, 2008, the 42nd anniversary of the Chili murders, in Vermont, 43-year-old Michael Jacques kidnapped and murdered 12-year-old Brooke Bennett. The murder uncovered a ring of men who had sex with young girls and exchanged video child pornography via the Internet. Jacques and his cohorts allegedly seduced the girls by telling them they'd been chosen for initiation into the ways of sex by a powerful organization called "Breckinridge," which now totally controlled their lives and was known to "terminate" girls in the program who were not deemed appropriately cooperative. Because of this brainwashing, Jacques was able to use another young girl as an accomplice to draw the murder victim into his deadly trap.[9] During the summer of 2013, Jacques pleaded guilty to kidnapping and murder and was sentenced to life in prison.[10]

In 2011, after I initially outlined for him my intention of writing about the Chili murders, my agent, Jake Elwell of the Harold Ober Associates literary agency, suggested that I read a book called *Dogtown* by Elyssa East. Only after I began reading it did I realize that it was about a bludgeoning murder in a godforsaken section of Massachusetts that took place on June 25, 1984.[11]

7

A GENERATION LATER . . .

Along with the Fear, for me anyway, came illness. My allergies worsened after the murders until I was allergic to everything and suffered suffocating asthma attacks. No more riding Benny the pony. No more helping George Mulligan muck out the barn. I took hellish speed-freak antiasthma medication that aggravated my insomnia. Nights were spent listening to the grinding of my bedroom machinery, air purifier and humidifier. Of the solitary pursuits available to me, writing struck me as the most fulfilling, and even then, at 10 years old, I was filling tablets with stuff I found interesting. Space exploration. Scary movies. Baseball.

And that was the way it was for a few years.

When I came out of my cocoon, not long after puberty, nobody spoke of the murders anymore. And when I tentatively mentioned George-Ann, folks became quiet and looked at their shoes. So thinking about it remained for alone time.

As I grew into adulthood, the ecology around Stallman Drive was changing. The magnificent Dutch elms that lined Black Creek died of Dutch elm disease. The Monroe Tree Surgeons came through and got rid of all the deadwood, but the change in the natural order turned the creek banks into a jungle land of thick growth. Places that hadn't seen sun in 30 years, where the earth was open and cool and mossy, were now baked, and much photosynthesis ensued.

Fast-forwarding now, I happily graduated from Wheatland-Chili High School in 1974 and four years later nailed down a BA in communication arts at Hofstra University on Long Island. I wanted to become a writer and was willing to suffer to do it, and so I bummed across the country with no money to write the great American novel, a pretty good one. But hippies-finding-America manuscripts were a dime a dozen. Nobody cared.

I don't know how other people felt in the late 1970s when they first saw the movie *Halloween*. I noticed that others viewed the boogeyman-comes-to-town scenario somewhat in the abstract. I took it very personally, and it delivered me right back there, giving me the same stomach anxiety that I felt in 1966. *Halloween* was like a flashback. The Fear now had a wicked soundtrack. Thank goodness for special effects. I was getting to see the kind of violence that until then I had only imagined. I became addicted to the modern horror film—splatter films. I was a couple of years out of college already and looking to publish my first book, which I decided would be a comprehensive encyclopedia about hip movies, like splatter films and 1950s black-and-white sci-fi. I'd include movies that were good, and movies that were so bad they were good. This project changed over the years and ended up being my first published book, *Vintage Science Fiction Films 1896–1949*, a scholarly work published in hardcover with no dust jacket by McFarland in North Carolina. For a couple of years I saw every horror picture. I went to multiplex cinemas, big movie palaces that had been divided up, and made friends with the (mostly) girls who worked the ticket windows. Sometimes there were two, three horror movies playing simultaneously, so for one price I'd switch from theater to theater and see them all. One time, to my delight, I saw a movie called *Deadly Spawn*, and one of the victims was a woman I knew from college, Jean Tafler. She got her head lopped off, and they had made, for the scene, a mannequin head that somewhat resembled Jean.

The 1966 Fear had not left me yearning for no fear, but rather for synthetic fear, for Fear's Lovely Counterfeit.

The real thing returned to Rochester on November 22, 1984, when the beaten and raped body of Wendy Jerome was found lying in an alcove of School 33 by a man who said he found her body as he was walking by that evening. She lived on Denver Street on the city's east side and had left home at 7:00 that evening to visit a friend a few blocks away, but she never arrived. The location of her body was not on the route between the two homes. Her throat had been cut. Her pink hoodie had been removed and placed over her beaten face. Between the rape and the murder, she'd been allowed to get dressed.[1] If she'd had the same first and last initial, she'd be famous.

During my first postcollege years I worked a job in social research and at night wrote my movie book, which when published made me about 50 bucks. After that, I worked for five years on another encyclopedia, this one covering baseball parks in America, major and minor league, dating back to the Civil War. I didn't get all of them in there, but I got most of them.

The ballpark book made me a little more money, maybe a hundred bucks. After two books and no scratch, I decided to make my big move. For years I'd been researching the JFK assassination and considered myself an expert. So, with the help of friend and editor Gary Goldstein, I acquired an agent at the William Morris Agency, Matt Bialer, and wrote *Who's Who in the JFK Assassination*. While promoting the book I found myself on the grassy knoll speaking privately with Oleg Nechiporenko, a retired KGB operative. Later we toasted friendship, with shots of vodka of course, and for a few years he sent me a postcard every Fourth of July.

I still get a kick reading new baseball histories and conspiracy theory books and finding myself in the footnotes.

Again, I made a move. I quit social research and went to work for a newsstand publisher, Norm Jacobs and his Starlog Group. I was editing a boxing magazine at the end of the 20th century when I met my current agent, Jake Elwell, who kept me busy. With Jake, I had more than 50 books published. I wrote a bunch of *Complete Idiot's Guides*, paired up with experts. I worked with an astronaut, a spy, a pro wrestler, a biker, and an FBI agent. Not all of my books were thick volumes; there were books for kids, presidential and sports bios. I ghostwrote. I book-doctored. At any given time I was working on two or three books. I once finished 10 books in 10 months.

I was married with two kids by this time, and during our periodic visits to Stallman Drive to visit Grandma and Grandpa Benson, I walked over to the trestle. It was such a beautiful spot, and I made a conscious effort to exorcise it. I went there one August with my cousin and daughter, and I photographed them by the edge as if looking at something in the water, with Black Creek and the stone bridge as their backdrop. That winter we went back to the spot, and I took the same photo from the same angle with everything covered in snow and ice. I loved those photos. I had the summer version made into a jigsaw puzzle and gave it to my cousin as a gift. When my daughter gave me a water-color set one Christmas, the first thing I did was paint the scene twice, one summer, one winter. Those paintings are framed and hanging in my living room. One winter, my family and our friends the Semraus went to the trestle and had the greatest snowball fight ever, splitting into two teams, one on the bridge and the other by the bank of the creek. It went on for hours, and I couldn't lift my arm higher than my waist the next day.

And, like the last olive in a jar, I shook the devil out of that spot.

But there was no chasing the demons from the dump site. I visited Archer and Beaver as well, and it made me shiver. I half expected to smell the lingering putrefaction.

During the late 1990s, I began asking longtime Ballantyners what they remembered about the 1966 murders. Memories varied wildly. But everyone I talked to initially agreed on one thing: Jack Starr* killed those girls.

Jack Starr? Who? What did I know about Jack Starr? Nothing.

I quickly learned that the original Starr clan had lived—some of them, anyway—in a house on Names Road, about a block away from the Bernhards. My first source was my mom's friend Doris Bookman who lived down on the country end of Ballantyne Road, near the WHAM radio tower. (That was the family that had the corpse of an ex-con dumped at the end of their lengthy driveway in 1967.) Doris was up on the gossip, and she had the story on the murders. Jack Starr did it. Everyone knew it was he because before the murders he was "paying George-Ann too much attention." Jack had a thing for little girls and traded drugs or alcohol or something for sex. He was dead now. She didn't remember the cause of death. There might have been a second man as well, and he was in a prison in Pennsylvania. George-Ann and

Kathy had been seen talking to Jack that afternoon, and this was perhaps why they returned to that spot.

I knew nothing about Jack, and apparently to know him was to consider him a suspect. But the little I knew about criminal profiling told me that Jack was far from the perfect fit. The biggest thing in his defense was modus operandi. A Jack-the-Ripper-style murder was unlikely to be spontaneous. Historically, these types of murders ("sex mutilation murders," "lust murders"[2]) are not committed by men who have a social or legal problem that murder can fix, or by men who murder professionally. *These crimes are committed by men who find this sort of murder fun, by men who thought of mere rape as small-time or unfinished business.*[3] That could all change if it turned out that Starr and another man had enticed the girls to return to the swimming hole. Two men in combo can have a personality more reckless and sociopathic than either could muster alone.[4]

Some things I learned about Jack Starr were verifiable and true. He was the brother of Jean Starr, later Jean Owens,* who had become a local politician.

I mentioned my interest in the case on a pre-Facebook Internet site of Wheatland-Chili alumni and was told by Kathy Bernhard's next-door neighbor, Gary Curran, that Jack Starr was killed in Vietnam. That was what they did back then when they had killers that they couldn't convict: they'd scare the shit out of them and tell them it was either Vietnam or the electric chair, it was up to them.

I forged on to the cavernous main Manhattan library, the one with the lions, and excavated some old newspaper stories I'd read as a boy. I found weather reports on the key days. At 5:00 p.m., June 25, 1966, it was 91 degrees, no breeze, only six degrees off the all-time record for that date. It was no wonder kids were swimming in the creek and up and down the river. By 8:00, the temperature had only fallen to 85 degrees. If the sky had been clear, there would have been a waxing crescent moon, but it had clouded over, and later that evening it began to drizzle, sprinkling on and off until two the following afternoon. The light rain cooled things off to 74 degrees by 11:00 that night. On Sunday, when the rain stopped and the sun came back out, the temp shot back up past 90.

The weather for the day the bodies were found: clear skies, 73 degrees, wind 11 miles per hour out of the north-northwest. A perfect day.

In March 1999, from my home office in Brooklyn, I telephoned Wayne Randall in the Outer Banks of North Carolina, not far from Kitty Hawk. Randall was two years retired from the MCSO, for whom he started working in 1969. He said he was familiar with the case and wanted to get it wiped off the books.

I asked if he knew about the railroad cop or employee who had been shooing picnickers away from the swimming hole on the night of the crime. He said he did not know about that but thought it was an interesting twist. I asked him to describe the condition in which the bodies were discovered.

"The girls had their pussies cut out," he said. "It looked as if it had been surgically done, by someone who knew what they were doing."

"Oh shit . . ."

"Not hacking like someone just stabbing and slashing. It was surgical."

That contradicted what the unnamed sheriff's office spokesman had said in 1966, that there was no expertise indicated by the wounds, which had apparently been caused by a "mad thrust of the blade."

Wayne had been told that the prime suspect was a fellow who lived down the road who had later gone on and gotten himself killed in Vietnam. I asked him what made the suspect a suspect. Was he seen in the area? Did he have a past with these girls?

"I think he had a past with other girls," Wayne said. "Exposing himself and things like that."

"Neighborhood creep," I said.

"Right," he replied. "One of those guys that when he died people said, 'Good, he won't be coming back.'"

Neither of us mentioned George-Ann's pregnancy.

I went on the web and found a site that had an obit for every American killed in Vietnam.[5] I found this

> Nicholas William Starr, Jr.,° born February 1947, killed in action in Vietnam February 1968. He'd just turned 21 years old, killed by hostile gunshot or small arms fire. Rank: Specialist fourth class. Lived on Names Road with his parents Mr. and Mrs. Nicholas Starr Sr. Spouse: Mary Lou Starr, Garner Trailer Park, Linden Ave., Penfield NY. Had six brothers: Alfred, Harvey, Howard, Jack, David and

Gerald. Had three sisters: Jean, Carol, and Christine. Was drafted on his 20th birthday and sent to Vietnam in August 1967. Completed course at the Manpower Center as a cook.

I found old issues of the *Scottsville News* that offered the sad tidings.[6] Nicky's parents were notified of his status at the beginning of March 1968. Three weeks later, the family was notified that he had been killed.[7] Posthumously Nicky Starr was awarded the Bronze Star Medal for heroism.[8] He'd been felled by an initial burst of enemy fire, wounds that would eventually kill him, but he continued to lay down cover fire for his band of brothers and refused evacuation.

There went that theory. The kid killed in Vietnam was Jack's brother.

Because of the sexual mutilation, I thought there was a good chance that the Genesee Junction killer was a psycho who was passing through. I had burned out on watching splatter movies and was now hungrily reading every "true crime" book I could get my hands on, not just for the entertainment value, but in hopes of gaining insight into what had occurred back home when I was nine. The true-crime genre was relatively new, dating back no further than *In Cold Blood* by Truman Capote, which wasn't published until 1965. It was during this reading binge that I read two books about the serial killer Arthur Shawcross.[9] I had a particular interest in Shawcross because he was a Rochester serial killer, and I remembered the case well. Plus, as I was to learn, there were aspects of his story that made the little hairs at the back of my neck stand on end.

During the late 1980s, Rochester had *several* serial killers slaying streetwalkers. When I was on Stallman Drive visiting, after my wife and I had just had our first child, on the local TV news there were interviews with crack-damaged hookers on Lyell Avenue bragging of fearlessness: They only went with guys they knew. They were working in teams. Despite this, they continued to drop like flies.

Then, later, we were also visiting the folks for Christmas when the serial killer Arthur J. Shawcross was arrested, so I got to see the breaking news reports in real time.

Shawcross's capture had been cleverly done. Sheriff's deputies had found one of his victims' blue jeans frozen in the snow off a rural road but hadn't announced the discovery. Sex killers, they knew, were particularly prone to returning to the scene of a crime. A few days later a helicopter spotted a man standing over the corpse with his penis in his hand.[10]

Shawcross's murder trial was telecast live on Rochester TV, to spectacular ratings. Rochesterians heard unprecedented talk from their TVs—talk of murder, rape, sodomy, pedophilia, mutilation, and cannibalism. The killer's insanity defense, like almost all insanity defenses, was rejected angrily by the jury. He was convicted and sentenced to 250 years to life at the Sullivan County Correctional Facility in New York State.

As a youth, Shawcross established a pattern of traveling back roads by car, setting fires, and spending lengthy times alone in the woods. Shawcross turned 21 years old on 6/6/66. During that all-important month of June 1966, he was floating around Upstate New York "looking for a job." As was his lifelong habit when free, he liked to park his car and wander along streams and rivers looking for secluded places to "fish." (In 1972, around the time of his first two known murders, Shawcross's then-wife Penny said he had gone on dozens of fishing trips during their time together, but she'd never once known him to bring home any fish.)

He was sexually dysfunctional. He wanted a divorce from his first wife because she either wouldn't give him oral sex or wouldn't allow him to give oral sex to her. He was already experiencing impotency problems that would plague him for the rest of his life.

He had been to prison once for arson, having torched a factory on Watertown's Factory Street, creating more than a quarter million dollars' worth of damage, and had been on parole for just over a year. He bragged of setting a brushfire near his barracks while in the army. "I flipped a match into the weeds. I didn't mean to start a fire. It just caught—whoosh!" There was a glint in his eyes when he said it. One of his wives once said that setting fires for Shawcross was a way of achieving sexual excitement.

Stress hit Shawcross hard. He ran away from it and became violent. And so, with his marriage falling apart, he was feeling stress in June 1966 as he ran away from his marital difficulties, doing what he'd done since he was a boy, wandering alone in the woods and along waterways, every once in a while stopping to build a campfire and think sadistic thoughts.

Throughout his killing career, Shawcross's violence was triggered by arguments with his mother or one of his wives, and his first marriage was crumbling. The most casual slight from a woman could trigger a murderous rage in him if he was already in an angry mood because of problems with a key woman in his life. (I thought of George-Ann's way with a verbal barb.)

Shawcross was an expert with a knife. He'd hunted deer and could dress game. Later, Shawcross would talk about wanting to kill a doe so that he could use his hunting knife to remove the animal's vagina. He said he was going to give the deer's genitals to his girlfriend's youngest son. The trouble was he bagged a buck, so he had to give the kid a deer's penis instead.

He bragged of his bestial escapades—sheep, cows, and once a chicken. For the previous two years he'd had a series of short-lived unskilled jobs, including one in Watertown, New York, at which, as an apprentice butcher, he eviscerated animals at the Adams Meat Market in Adams, New York. That was where, he later boasted, for $85 a week he learned to "slaughter 19 cows and bulls a day." He sickened his wife with tales of his workday, and he once told his cousin, "At the end of the day that crick runs red!"

That summer, due to his domestic woes, Shawcross thought of himself as a bachelor again and "rambled." According to Shawcross's own words, he did "strange things" that summer, driving around in a hot-looking 1958 Pontiac.

"I was picking up girls and having sex with them," he boasted. "I couldn't stop myself."

The Chili girls disappeared in June 1966, their bodies were found in July, and in August 1966 Shawcross and his wife separated for good. That summer Shawcross lived in the town of Sandy Creek, New York, which was well south of Watertown and only about 90 miles northeast of Rochester.

On April 6, 1967, about nine months after the Chili murders, Shawcross was inducted into the army. He went to Vietnam and came back telling horrific stories in which he killed young females. But, since they were "Viet Cong chicks," they weren't really murders at all. This was war, and by taking out those enemy girls, he was doing his duty for America.

He claimed that he would go off on his own into the jungles of South Vietnam and would stay for two, three days at a time. "I'd look for the enemy by myself," he boasted.

In one story, he was wandering around the jungles of South Vietnam, a lone rogue warrior, when he happened upon two teenage girls bathing nude in a stream, waist deep in water. "They were both VC [Viet Cong]. I mutilated them," Shawcross later told a forensic psychologist. He claimed he had cut off one of the girls' heads and placed it on a pole. He further described his Vietnam "experience": "I took her and butchered her like a steer, neck down. I cut the body down the middle, then cleaved the backbone to wash the blood out."

It was the same thing he would have done, he explained, if he'd killed a deer. During one version of the story, he then cut a breast off the girl and roasted it over a fire before eating it. It was like eating "charco-broiled pork," he said. After his Rochester arrest, Shawcross complained that the mutilation murder of the two girls in Vietnam haunted him the most. He would dream about it and wake up crying.

His narratives changed with each telling, and later the body part he ate would shift from a breast to a "chunk of her hip." He described how the sweat was pouring off the girls. He said he raped one of them after tying her down on the ground.

Talking to cops and shrinks after his Rochester arrest, he engaged freely in rewriting his biography to his advantage, and it would have been perfectly in keeping for him to transpose his earliest murders onto the rogue warrior actions of a self-proclaimed war hero.

And he didn't always keep his stories straight, such as the time he started to talk about how he had killed a woman in Vietnam and then stopped and admitted that he was actually discussing "the ones here."

After Shawcross's killing career ended, he increasingly leaned on his "Rambo" stories to boost his ego. He considered his Nam kills his "accomplishments," his "achievements." He used posttraumatic stress syndrome from the war as an excuse for his later murders.

Those war stories were horrific, sure—and they were also apparently untrue. According to his military records, he served two six-month tours as a supply and parts specialist and was honorably discharged in April 1969. Shawcross's Vietnam stories were apparently made up out of whole cloth, as he never made a jungle patrol. Revealingly, none of Shawcross's Vietnam tales involved him killing men. All of his claimed battle kills were of females. So Shawcross's war stories were fiction.

In the summer of 1972, Shawcross committed his first two known murders in his hometown of Watertown, in the Adirondack Mountains, 200 miles from Rochester.[11] The victims were kids, 9 and 12, a young boy, then a girl.[12] The girl was from Rochester, and he killed her under a bridge over the Black River. (The Chili victims had gone swimming near a bridge over Black Creek.) The boy was sexually mutilated after death, perhaps for cannibalistic reasons. After his arrest for killing the girl, Shawcross told his interrogators that the stuff he did in Watertown was nothing compared to what he'd done in Vietnam.

Before Shawcross's actual military career was known, psychiatrists took his Vietnam stories at face value and commented that Shawcross had blurred borders of what was appropriate in Vietnam compared to what was appropriate in Watertown.

Shawcross's childhood history demonstrated that Shawcross never had a firm grip on what was and wasn't appropriate.

Slowly, under psychiatric examination, Shawcross revealed himself to be an obvious sexual sadist from childhood. There were still people in the area who knew Shawcross when he was a boy and described him as evil even then.

"There was talk that he was Satan," said one former schoolmate. Shawcross was a violent bully who spent long stretches alone in the woods with a loaded .22 at his side.[13]

Shawcross got out of prison for the Watertown murders in 1987. Because of an incredible plea bargain after which he pleaded guilty to manslaughter for the death of the girl and was never officially charged with the murder of the boy,[14] he served only 15 years.

He was relocated to Rochester against his wishes. "Why Rochester?" he asked officials. He told them he'd been in Rochester as a young man and was not happy to return. At one point he said that, as a young truck driver, he'd visited Rochester and didn't like it.

At another point he said that, after acquiring money in a robbery, he took a bus to Rochester and lived there on the money he had. He said that he did not want to live in the same city as Karen Ann Hill's parents, who wanted to see him dead. He told a psychiatrist that Rochester was where he went fishing once and was *attacked by five men*.[15]

The corrections system had previously tried to place him in small Upstate New York towns—Binghamton, Vestal, Delhi, Fleishmanns—but he was repeatedly drummed out by angry townsfolk, including at least one lynch mob.

Eventually, despite his complaints, he was relocated in Rochester where officials hoped he would be better able to establish himself in anonymity. The corrections people, however, did not inform local law enforcement that a convicted child killer had been given an apartment in Rochester.

In Rochester, Shawcross murdered prostitutes and other vulnerable women of the street by strangulation and dumped many of their bodies near or in the Genesee River. Several victims had had their vaginas removed.

One of the last prostitute murders was strangled, but Shawcross came back later to play with the body. He used a saw to remove the entire crotch. "I ate it," he later boasted.

A comparison of Shawcross's behavior and that of the Chili killer was compelling, so much so that on March 22, 1999, armed with my knowledge of Shawcross and the Chili murders information that I'd gotten from Wayne Randall, I sent a written summary of my findings to the MCSO's Captain Maureen Chisholm of the Criminal Investigation Division. On April 19, Detective Sergeant Gary Kaola called me at work. He said it was regarding Shawcross and that I should call him. After a couple of days of phone tag, I spoke with him on April 21. He told me that they had sent a team of interrogators to the Sullivan County Correctional Institute and that they had asked Shawcross if he knew anything about Black Creek or the Chili girls. Shawcross put his chin on his chest, closed his eyes, balled his hands into fists, and refused to discuss it. Tellingly, it was the same reaction his interrogators got when they asked him questions about his mother. It was his standard response to what he considered a tough question.

"So, that's about all we can do, and I can't really talk to you about it because it's an active investigation," he said. I thanked him and he hung up. I felt great. I had, by proxy anyway, gotten into Shawcross's face and confronted his entire ego system. He'd had a chance to deny he was the Chili killer and refused.

At the time, I was editing a magazine called *Untold Stories of Vietnam*. On April 29, 1999, I sent Shawcross a letter. I explained that I was a magazine editor and wrote, "I have read about you and your experiences in Vietnam. I was wondering if you'd like to write a story about your experiences for my magazine. One of the things we like to emphasize is the trouble Vietnam veterans have readjusting to life in the United States after their return from the war. Perhaps, down the road, you could write about that aspect of your life as well." I enclosed a self-addressed stamped envelope, but he didn't get back to me.

In 1999, and again in 2001, Shawcross made headlines when he sold his artwork for fantastic prices. Newspapers called him "the real-life Hannibal Lecter."[16] There was much criticism of the sale, as Shawcross was being allowed to use his infamy for profit.

On November 11, 2008, Shawcross complained of leg pain and was checked into an Albany hospital. He died hours later at the age of 63.[17]

8

I DON'T KNOW JACK

During the first decade of the 21st century, I ghostwrote a true-crime book about a serial killer in the nation's heartland. The book was a bestseller (#4, *New York Times*, paperback nonfiction) and was made by Sony Pictures into a TV movie on CBS. For about a year I was rich. I decided to spend half, save half. So I spent half, and the other half was paid in taxes. The saving part never got done. But for a while there I was having a great time. My wife got jewelry and sterling silver tea sets, my daughter went to Paris, and I, along with a few college buddies, became a thoroughbred racehorse owner, occasionally visiting the winner's circle at Belmont Park and Aqueduct Racetrack. The horse biz being what it is, I won some and lost some, breaking about even, but I had a hell of a time.

I wrote a true-crimer under my own name, *Betrayal in Blood*, about a cuckolded lawyer in Rochester, a small man who had his much younger blonde wife murdered in the middle of the night in their home by an "intruder" that he'd hired. The twist was that the hit man was the wife's brother! It was published by Pinnacle Books and sold well.

After *BIB*, I wrote a pair of books with former NYPD cop of the year, retired detective Bob Mladinich. I knew Bob through boxing. I edited *Fight Game* magazine, and he wrote for *The Ring*. He and I sat in the ringside press corral for many championship bouts in Madison Square Garden, Atlantic City, and the casinos of Connecticut. He was drafted into the true-crime world when a photographer he covered the fights with while still in college grew up to be Joel Rifkin, the Long

Island serial killer. The first book we did together was about a wife accused of hiring her boyfriend to kill her abusive ex-husband. The twist was the goon shot the wrong guy, accidentally murdering the husband's lookalike buddy. Our second collaboration was about a New Jersey college freshman, a football player, who visited Manhattan for the first time unchaperoned, met a girl, and ended up lying shot dead in the street a block away from a house party near the Parade Grounds in Brooklyn.

I went back on my own and wrote *The Burn Farm* about a sociopathic dominatrix widow who recruited mentally slow men onto her New Hampshire horse farm, killed them, and then incinerated their bodies in her oven and in a bonfire on her front lawn.

Then came *Killer Twins* about identical twins who grew up in Elmira and independently became murderers. In at least one case, they murdered identically. One twin became yet another Rochester serial killer—pretty much picking up where Arthur Shawcross had left off.

And so it was while working on another notorious Rochester murder case that my mind turned again to George-Ann and Kathy. My dad had passed away a few years earlier but my mom still lived on Stallman Drive, so I again revisited the locations. There were many swimming pools now. The swimming hole hadn't been a swimming hole for many years. Looking at the murky, algae-filled water, it was hard to believe it ever had been. But the spot, featuring its 19th-century stone bridge, was still well trafficked by kids fishing, and the peaceful grassy slope was still a tranquil spot to sit and watch the creek and stone trestle. I walked over the trestle and then westward along the far side of the creek until I found the turntable. I checked carefully for signs of satanic rituals, but I didn't see any. The satanic celebrants in hoods and cloaks were only in my imagination. There was still litter, but nothing fresh. The beer cans were rusted and had been opened with a "garage key" can opener. That dated them as pre-1970.

I went to the dump site, which was remarkably unchanged. Wispy weeds covered the sun-scorched land. It looked more like it had on the night of the murders than it had during most of my childhood, when the area was shaved down to the clay and kept that way.

My mom stayed on Stallman Drive alone for a few years, but the isolation got to her and the winters were very hard, so she moved into an apartment.

Following the publication of *Killer Twins*, the publisher gave me a series of multiple-book contracts, and I wrote true crime as a full-time job. I cranked them out: *Mommy Deadliest* about a woman who poisoned her husband with antifreeze, *Watch Mommy Die* was about an attractive and charming gentleman who claimed to be researching a book about serial killers when he was actually learning to be one, *A Killer's Touch* about a dirtbag who kidnapped, raped, and murdered a young mother, and *A Knife in the Heart* about a lethal teenage love triangle. Finally, there was *Evil Season*, about a man named Elton Brutus Murphy who murdered a middle-aged art gallery owner, cut away her vagina, and took it home with him. Although the killer denied being a cannibal, he did cook for the only time ever just after the murder and served one rooming house neighbor "pork stew." I asked Murphy what had happened at the crime scene. He maintained that he had entered the art gallery with only rape and murder on his mind. The mutilation was spur of the moment. He'd gone to the art gallery twice that Friday afternoon. He'd come to the crime scene from a nearby bar where he drank too much courage, couldn't complete the postmortem rape, and in his fury cut out her vagina with his best knife. "The old knife/penis cliché," he said, a truly postmodern psycho.

On June 25, 2011, I changed my Facebook status to "45 years ago today Kathy Bernhard and George-Ann Formicola disappeared while swimming in Black Creek." The status received a voluminous response. It was through Facebook that I contacted Evie Douglas, the girl who'd ridden with George-Ann all the way to Scottsville, seven miles, on a tandem bike only days before the murder.

The girls must have known their killers. That was the Ballantyne consensus. That's why they got in the car with them and went to the lovers' lane.

I thought for a time that the argument against this was the radio. Kathy had been separated from her radio. Wasn't that an indication that the girls had left the swimming hole under duress? I realized the answer was maybe. There was also a chance the killer put the radio where it was found, and he could have done it after he dumped the bodies. It seemed like a lot of back and forth, but it was possible.

Evie told me she'd heard that Jack Starr died of AIDS and that he'd made a deathbed confession to the Chili murders. Evie's father rented a room from Alice Bernhard before his passing in 1989, and Alice was a close family friend anyway, which was why she confided to Evie's dad that she knew the truth about Jack's confession and death.

"Jack was much older than us, five or six years older," Evie said. "Girls at 14 or 15 back in the day did not hang out with 20-something guys." George-Ann did.

Evie was never allowed to hang around back by the trestle, but she had talked to Debbie Rockow and others who had gone back there, or had older siblings who went back there, and there were stories about "all manner of people who hung out partying. Drugs, alcohol, and sex." She was in awe of "those parties," the same rowdy parties the Bensons heard from the screened-in porch, cries from the trestle riding the night wind.

She knew another family on Lester Street, the Mortons—Francine and Ruthie Morton. The two oldest girls babysat Evie and her siblings. She knew the Starrs but was unaware that there were three older brothers. She only knew Jack, who she thought was the oldest but was actually fourth in line. She also knew Jerry and "Little Chrissy," who was the youngest of the brood. Carol, who later married and became Carol Kane,* was born in 1950 and fell between Jerry and Chrissy in age. Since we know that Alfred, the oldest, was born in 1930 and Chrissy was born sometime after 1950, there was more than a 20-year span between the oldest and the youngest. It's no wonder that Evie didn't know about the four oldest. It was as if the Starrs had two families. Maybe there were two moms, I guessed. Evie knew Jean Owens as the mother of her friends Mitch and Earl Owens, but she had no idea that Jean was formerly Jean Starr, with kids about the age of her youngest sister.

Evie said that she had also recently gotten back in touch with a Ballantyne local named Steve Frazier,* who'd hung out with her little brothers, Roy and Marty. Evie and Steve had a long talk about the neighborhood, and they agreed that there was a before and an after, that Ballantyne experienced a great *innocence loss*, at which time the Fear crept in and Ballantyne became a smaller and colder place.

Evie and Steve remembered how before the murders "all of us kids growing up in that corner of Chili ran around from Black Creek to Riverdale, through front yards, backyards, up and down streets from the early morning until well after dark."

On a personal note, Evie added, "I remember having nightmares about the girls after their remains were found. I felt it deeply because I was close to Kathy and her older sister Alice. "Alice and I were inseparable for a couple of years before she discovered 'men,'" Evie said. It was from Alice that Evie got all of her crime scene info: bodies mutilated, breasts cut off, sexual organs cut up. Getting back to her conversation with Steve Frazier, Evie said Frazier didn't know about Jack Starr being a suspect, but Steve was a "wild child" and might know what he was talking about. And what Frazier did know was that, back then, Jack Starr was involved with a tough crowd, young men who drank at the Castle Inn on Scottsville Road; the Suburban Inn on Jefferson Road, just on the other side of the Ballantyne Bridge; and the Genesee Park Inn on East River Road. Evie's friend said that if Jack Starr killed the girls, he must have done it with that badass friend of his, the loser who married Francine Morton. Frazier didn't know the guy's name, but he grew up a neighbor of the Mortons and so again was in a position to know. The Mortons lived on Lester Street, directly across the tracks from us. There were two older Morton girls, Ruth and Francine. Those were the girls who babysat for the Douglases. Then there were two much younger boys, Ray, a year older than I was, and Dave, who was my age. (Ray and his wife Cindy moved into the Putnam house* at the bend on Stallman Drive and raised a bunch of kids, and I had friendly visits with them in the 1980s and 1990s when I went home to see my folks.)

This information gave Evie the willies. If Jack Starr and John Bernhard were both doing their drinking at the Castle Inn, then they must have known each other—the suspected killer and the father of the victim, drinking side by side at adjacent stools. "It creeps the living hell out of me," Evie said. "What a line for communication."

Frazier called Francine Morton's husband a "total loser." Evie said that she agreed that it was probably Jack Starr and his loser friend from Lester Street because she'd talked with Kathy's mom about it, and they'd agreed that they didn't think a single man could pull it off.

Alice Bernhard remembered that Kathy and George-Ann were tomboys. They weren't princesses, that was for sure. They were rough and tough, and if there had been a lone killer, Alice was convinced that one of them would have been able to escape, and Evie was inclined to agree.

Evie said, "If the killer knew George-Ann and Kathy, they would have to know that it was impossible to lure one away without the other, because they were always together."

I knew better. I knew that an armed man could take down a whole family. See BTK. Richard Speck by himself controlled *nine* nurses.

Evie first learned that one of the Starrs was a suspect when her father told her that if she went to the Bernhards', she should go the long way around. He didn't want her walking past the Starr house.

"Jerry and Chrissy Starr were not in anyone's circle of friends, either," Evie said. Before the murders, Chrissy was on what Evie called "the outskirts of my gang." Evie's group, a bunch of tomboys, got bored quickly at Chrissy's house because all she ever wanted to do was "princess girl stuff." That was before the murders. After, there was no gang, "no more gatherings in the streets."

To sum up, Alice Bernhard was convinced it had to be two men, Jack Starr and another. And Steve Frazier said that if someone helped Jack Starr kill the girls, it must have been the "loser" married to Francine Morton.

Evie added, "Did you know Alice lost a second daughter in a deep sea diving accident in the 1970s? That woman has been to hell and back two times in her life." Evie concluded, "I'm a parent. How do you deal with the loss of a child to a murder that is never resolved? And what about Jack's chum, Francine's husband? Where did he go? I don't consider myself a sleuth by any means, but I found Steve Frazier's information chilling and very credible."

I was inclined to agree.

Frazier's theory was that the murders were a natural residue of the depraved scene that had taken root after dark by the trestle—a scene, I thought, for which a demonic code like 6/66 might be irresistible.

I still had next to no reason to believe that Jack Starr was the Chili killer. Talk, talk, talk. He seemed more the stuff of legend, about which stories grew upon stories. Had anyone seen him on the day the girls disappeared? Was his behavior odd—or particularly odd—immediately following the murders? Was he *really* the father of George-Ann's baby?

I located other possibly pertinent obits. Nick Starr Sr., the dad, lived to be 85. He died in 1993. A robust old age was attained by the man whose eldest was born more than 20 years before his youngest. Two of the older sons were twins, born in 1933. Howard died in 1978 at age 44, and Harvey lived until 1999, age 65. Harvey's widow was named Jacqui. Alfred, born 1929, died in 2002, was married to Naomi, and was predeceased by Jack and Nick. *There!* Confirmation that the suspect was dead. But who had the correct story of Jack's death? It wasn't Wayne Randall or Gary Curran. It wasn't Vietnam. Doris Bookman said he died in a car crash. Alice Bernhard said he died of AIDS because he took needle drugs. The Starr daughters, as well as Jerry and David, were still alive. David lived on Black Creek Road, while Jerry lived on a rural road in southernmost Monroe County.

Evie told me about Kathy's mother, Alice Bernhard, who was an old and dear friend of hers. "She would love to talk to you about it," Evie assured me. It was time to give the June 1966 murders another shot. When I told my mom, she said, "Alice is a sweetheart. Everyone loves her."

Alice, I learned from my mom, had mentioned me in a comment. During a party on Names Road, my mom and Alice had discussed my true-crime career.

"It's too bad your Michael couldn't write a book about my Kathy," Alice said.

So I sent Alice a letter explaining who I was, what I wanted to do, and warning her that I would be calling.

9

ALICE AND CORKY

On the morning of August 2, 2011, Alice answered the phone and said she'd received my letter and was willing to talk to me. Her son Corky was there. He was curious as to who was on the phone, and when she explained he took the phone.

"Corky! I'm Mike Benson. I grew up at the end of Stallman Drive, just on the other side of the railroad tracks."

"Okay," Corky said brightly. He didn't remember me—he had never met me—but that was no reason not to be neighborly.

"And now I'm a crime writer, and I want to write about what happened in 1966."

"Mm-hmmm," he said, just acknowledging, not disapproving.

I stopped the pitch for approval and started interviewing: "What do you remember from back then?" Long pause. "I know it's hard," I said.

Corky said he was in the service at the time. He remembered very little. "I couldn't get away in time to really hear anything," he said, almost apologetically. "I don't remember. That was a couple of days ago."

"Quick question: It was Catherine with a C, but Kathy with a K?"

"Yes."

"Do you know when your parents moved to Names Road?"

"I was, what? Five or six? They built the house here before they built the Mount Morris dam. Before the dam, the whole front yard would flood out," Corky recalled. Corky had a quick conversation with his mother and came back with, "It was 1949 when we first moved here."

I later looked it up. The dam was completed three years later.

I told Corky that flooding wasn't much of a problem for us. For one thing, we didn't move in until 1962, and for another the house was on a little bit of a hill back there behind the Mulligans.

"Yup," Corky said. He knew what I was talking about. "We were swimming in our front yard for a few years," he said with a laugh.

"It sounds fun. Corky, could you put your mom back on?"

"Sure."

I told Alice that I wanted to start out by talking about her. She told me she grew up Alice Dunigan in Rochester, on Azalea Road, near Elmwood. It was nice, with beautiful Highland Park and Cobbs Hill to the north and Mount Hope Cemetery, where Kathy was now, to the west.

She met her husband while "working for the White Tower." (Not to be confused with White Castle.)

"That little restaurant downtown?"

"Yes, but it was on Alexander Street back then."

"In what years were your children born?"

"You've got to be kidding me," she said with a laugh. "Corky was born in '46. The youngest one was born in '56. And all the ones in between, I have no idea."

"That's from Corky to Betty, right?"

"Yes. From the tallest to the smallest."

I tried to get her to talk about Kathy. What made her special? What did she like to do?

"They used to just run wild around here," Alice said. "There weren't any houses or nothin'."

Corky at that point took the phone from his mother: "Hey, Mike, you said you're writing a book?"

"Yes. That is, I want to write a book. I'm writing a book proposal."

"Is it going to be about just our family?" Corky asked.

"No, it's going to be about the effect that what happened had on the whole neighborhood." I told Corky about the paths that cut through the fields and how they all grew over. Then I abruptly shifted gears. "I also want to talk a little bit about Jack Starr. Did you know him?"

"Yeah."

"Do you believe he killed your sister?"

"The signs were pointing that way. But I honestly don't know."

"I've only seen one picture of him, and I didn't know him. What was he like? Was he a creepy guy?"

"To tell you the truth, Mike, the whole neighborhood was crawling with creepy guys back then," Corky said. "It's what I grew up with. A majority of them were in and out of jail."

I asked who he was talking about, and he gave me a couple of family names, which I recognized as families notorious for their badass brothers. Not necessarily families of psycho killers, but maybe families of guys who knocked off liquor stores. I later looked up one set of brothers in the New York State Department of Corrections database and learned that one brother did five years for manslaughter, while another did a year for burglary, both in the 1970s.

Corky added, "There were a couple of others, too, who went to jail for odd things."

"Did the bad kids hang out back by the trestle?"

"Oh, we all did. That was our favorite swimming hole. We used to hang around there quite a bit."

"Why do you think so many people think Jack Starr did it?"

"Well, my mother said he admitted to it. Jack was a drug user, too."

"Did he know the girls?"

"Oh, yeah. He knew both of them."

"How well? I mean, because he's quite a bit older . . ."

"You know, all us kids ran the neighborhood quite a bit back then. So we all knew each other."

"Had you ever heard that Jack Starr was the father of George-Ann's baby?"

"No."

Corky said the Bernhards and the Formicolas didn't know one another. From what he understood, George-Ann had just started hanging around, and although she was accepted like everyone else, she wasn't familiar.

I told Corky that I had felt confident that calling Alice would be okay because Evie Douglas said that Alice liked talking about it, liked to get it off her chest. He said he knew Evie, knew her father even better.

"The last time your mom put you on the phone, was she upset about something?"

"No. I questioned things," Corky said. "When I hear someone asking personal questions like that, it kind of raises red flags with me."

"Well, this is what I do for a living. I have written eight true-crime books, and if this becomes a book, it will be the first time I ever knew anyone who was in the book. Those other books were about recent cases that took place somewhere else. If my questions are a little more personal this time, it's because George-Ann was my friend. My intent is not to embarrass anyone," I said.

I didn't say that people were not going to be embarrassed. There was an indignity to being the victim in a crime book, and the surviving family shared it. But there was no shame in it, either. No one ever volunteered for the job. Readers, I believed, were hip to that and were more apt to credit a family's strengths rather than nitpick at any perceived weaknesses.

I was learning that the Bernhards were a resilient lot and that their matriarch was a character.

I told Corky that I hoped to sell the book idea to a publisher and eventually make some money. Unfortunately, in order to do that, I had to get people to dredge up unpleasant memories that perhaps they'd rather leave buried.

"I can tell you that, in other cases, when I've talked to victims' family members, they often find it a pleasant experience," I said to Corky. "They feel better afterward, like they've gotten something off their chests that they'd been holding inside. Evie Douglas told me that your mom seemed eager to talk about it and urged me to call her. If there's a book, Jack Starr might have something to worry about, but the Bernhards are going to be okay."

"Well, Jack Starr is no longer living."

"Do you know how he died?"

"I believe it was with drugs."

"Was he a heroin user? Was that what you had heard?"

The leading questions were an indication of impatience, but who knew how much time I had?

"Yeah."

"I had heard AIDS, which could be from dirty needles."

"I had heard that also," Corky said. I wasn't surprised. According to Evie Douglas, it was Alice's version. Corky had no idea what year, or what decade, that might have been.

"Well, do you have any more concerns about me? I'm a good guy. I'm not here to upset anyone. I want, at least in part, for the book to be a tribute to Kathy and George-Ann. The cops didn't try hard enough to figure out who did it."

"They didn't," Corky concurred. "They had the Double Initials Murders right after that, and this got kind of pushed under the table."

I told him about my failed attempts to get the sheriff's department to open their files to me. Even though it was 45 years later, it was an open case, and so the files were not for the public.

"I figure a new look at the files can't hurt anything. It can only help, and maybe give a little closure," I said.

Corky agreed with that.

"I'd like to make up my own mind about whether or not this guy did it," I said.

"Yup," Corky said.

"Okay, let me speak to your mother again. Thanks, Corky."

With Alice back on the line, I said, "When we left off, there were kids running wild . . ."

"Yes," she said. "There were no houses, and it was a free run for the kids."

"Your house is older than the other houses on Names Road?"

"Not all of them. The Starrs was here before me. And also the Howards down there at the end. At this end of the road there was no houses." She laughed. "There was no road! It was just a big empty lot. It was a field, you know? A farmer's field. We had to walk down from Ballantyne Road, and the guy said, 'You got a post here, here, here, and here. That's where you live.'"

Alice didn't get her driver's license until after her third child. Back in those days, she said, she usually had a car, but it was always a junker. Her husband worked in a junkyard, and he would bring home some old vehicle that had a few miles left on it, and Alice would drive that. When that one stopped running, John would bring her another one. One time the switch was made right in the middle of the street, right where the old car died. John would switch the license plate onto the new vehicle, and Alice would be mobile again, for a while. The family's financial situation actually improved when she kicked John out and got a job.

"How well did you know George-Ann?"

Alice sighed deeply. "I had to work for a living," she said. "I went to work in the morning, came home, cooked, did laundry, and everything, and I never really got to know any of the neighborhood kids."

"What was your job back then?"

"I worked at French's."

"Making mustard!"

"Yeah, yeah."

After the girls were murdered, Alice took a job at Gleason Works in Rochester, and then worked as a food preparer at the Rochester Institute of Technology (RIT) until she retired at the age of 73.

"You must have been pretty used to having George-Ann in your house?"

"I don't remember."

"And you didn't know her parents, George and Ruth?"

"No."

"Did you know that George-Ann had a baby?"

"Yes, and I knew that they gave it away. And we all figured that was why she was killed. Because it was Jack's baby."

"Ahhhh. Now how do you know that?"

Pause, then, "I think it was Jack's sister that told my kids, and my kids told me."

"That would be Jean or Carol or Chrissy?"

"Chrissy. It was Chrissy. My girls hung around with Chrissy all the time."

"Okay, let's talk a little bit about Kathy's last day. I've read all of the newspaper articles, so I know what you said at the time. The girls had gone to the swimming hole and came home from dinner, so you made them hot dogs and milk and then they returned to the swimming hole. Is that correct?"

"Umm-hmmm."

"Do you remember what time they were supposed to be home? Was it before dark?"

"I never had to make a rule like that. My girls were always home before dark because most of them was afraid of the dark."

"Plus, I would guess that the mosquitoes would come out, too."

"Yes, yes. But I really think it was being afraid of the dark. The only place where they'd be in the dark was out in the backyard here, and that was because I was right there."

"When did you know something was wrong?"

"I cooked supper and fed them. After they left, I sat down and fell asleep, and I got woke up at 3:00 in the morning by Mrs. Formicola.

She says the girls weren't home. So I checked to see if Kathy was in her bed, and she wasn't. And then we called the police."

"You called the sheriff?"

"Yeah."

"Did they come right over?"

"Some bozo did. He says, 'Don't worry about it. We don't check on 'em for two weeks. She probably ran off with some guy.' He was a smart aleck. I'll never forget him—heavyset, ugly face, and all that. I wanted to punch him out, but he was the law and I didn't dare. And he never did nothin', and I kept calling to see if there was any news, and they kept saying, 'It's not two weeks yet.' So I called the state police, and they came right over and started right in investigating. And that's when they found Kathy's radio that was on that road that led down to the crick."

"Where exactly was Kathy's radio found?"

"You know the road that comes out of where the swimming hole is? It runs along the railroad tracks. It goes to the railroad bridge on Scottsville Road. It was there. That's where they found her radio, between Scottsville Road and the swimming hole."

"Any theories as to how it got there?"

"If they were being taken out by car, she threw it out the window maybe. I don't know. Nobody ever found out. Nobody even cared, really."

"Because they still thought she just ran away," I said. "I did read that the radio was found broken, so tossing it out a car window might explain that. When they told you that Kathy had run away, did you think she'd run away?"

"No. She was in her bathing suit. She was afraid of the dark. She had no clothes with her. I checked to make sure. All of her clothes were home."

"Can you tell me about the crank phone calls?"

"Ohhhhhh, we were *always* getting those."

Even after the summer was over and the bodies had been found, the calls continued. Poor Betty, Alice's youngest, was the last one out of the house in the morning for school, and she would be home alone and the phone would ring.

"I remember one call. He told Betty that he knew where she lived and he was going to get her just like he did Kathy. And later they found

Betty hiding in the girls' room at Ballantyne School. And they called me to come get her. She told me what happened, and that was when I had my phone changed."

Alice had no use for the sheriff's department, but there was a detective from the state police that she liked, Detective Manzler, a woman, over six feet tall and maybe 300 pounds (actually Emily Manzler, an MCSO deputy who'd been assigned as liaison with the families). "And you'd better do what she said," Alice remembered with a laugh. "She was a sweetheart." Alice told "Detective Manzler" about the phone calls, and she took over from there.

"And what did she do?"

"I don't know."

"You got phone calls from people saying that Kathy was pregnant and that the girls had been spotted on Genesee Street. Do you remember any of that?"

"No. Just the ones where they said they were going to get us, too."

"That's horrible."

"Yeah, well, there are a lot of sick minds out there."

"Do you remember when you found out that the girls had been found?"

"Yeah. It wasn't a surprise, really." She'd been mopping a floor when Manzler arrived and delivered the bad news.

Alice stepped away from the phone for a moment. Corky was leaving. When she got back, I asked, "How many grandchildren do you have, Alice? Can you count them all?"

"I think I got 12—12 or 13."

"Wow."

"Great-grandchildren, I got a dozen of those, too."

"Nice going! Getting back to the sad time, do you remember being shown Kathy's swimsuit?"

"No. [Law enforcement] hardly ever showed their face here. Nobody ever came by to tell me nothing."

"Did you tell investigators that Kathy's towel was missing?"

"I don't remember. It must have been. It was with her when she left."

"How well did you know the Starr family?"

"Well, better than I knew the Formicolas. Jack and my husband were a matched pair. And Chrissy. And Mr. Starr. I don't know where I met him, but I knew that bunch really well."

"Jack hung out with your husband?"

"Yes."

"They were drinking buddies?"

"Yes, at the Castle Inn."

"Did Jack Starr have a friend who might also have been involved?"

"I have no idea. But I often thought that there had to be more than one because my Kathy was a toughie. We were fooling around one day, and I'm no weakling, and we tried to stick her in a tub of cold water, just foolin' around, you know, just playin', and we couldn't get her in the tub. She could really take care of herself. I kept saying to myself that there had to be more than one. Jack was a drunk and a druggie. I don't think he had any more muscles than a two-year-old. In my mind there was more than one. There had to be—in order to get both of them. They kept telling me that maybe it was shock, that maybe he killed George-Ann first—but Kathy would've run."

I was thinking that he killed Kathy first because he knew George-Ann *couldn't* run. I'd seen her pigeon-toe her way toward first base enough times to know she was easy to catch.

Alice's narrative moved to her lousy marriage. "You see, Johnny and I didn't quite get along," she said. "I don't mean quite. I mean we didn't get along. I don't think he was even living here when Kathy died. I think he was living in the junkyard over there on West Henrietta Road. He told the police that this was nothing new, that Kathy always had guys over—which was a lie. But Johnny was a drunk, and in his mind that's the way it was. Those kids were always home for supper, always home before dark. I didn't even have to whistle or nothing. They knew what time it was, and they were always here for supper. "

"What I don't understand is, if Jack Starr is a drunk and a druggie, how does he get a 13-year-old girl pregnant?"

Alice laughed at me. "You know about the birds and the bees?" she asked.

I laughed too. "Yes, Alice," I said, "but I'm talking in terms of seduction."

"They were going together," Alice said, referring to Jack and George-Ann.

"Really?" I said, incredulous. "She was 13."

"So? When you're drunk, you don't care how old they are."

"I'm not wondering why he found her attractive. I'm wondering why she found him attractive."

"He was nice looking and he had charm," Alice said.

"Okay, see, that I didn't know."

"And George-Ann, 13-year-olds, they're not like four- and five-year-olds. I have a 13-year-old great-grandchild who would pass for 20! She's got a pair on her that shocked me!"

"I know. They grow up quick."

"Yeah! And 13, nowadays . . . . When I had my last baby in the room with me was a nine-year-old who'd just had a baby. So, 13, they're ready, willing, and able."

"How did Jack Starr die?"

"AIDS"

"And where did you hear that?"

"It was common knowledge."

"You don't remember who told you?"

"Well, he had AIDS for quite a while, and everybody knew it, and he wasn't afraid to tell anybody."

"Do you remember about when that was?"

"No. Wait, I remember where I heard it, from Johnny! When he would come home drunk and he would throw all of that stuff in my face. If any of our girls come up with AIDS, we'd know that she'd been spending time with Jack."

"When did your husband pass away?"

"I don't know. Don't care. He wasn't living here. I was divorced and happy right here by myself. And no, I did not go to his funeral. We didn't get along, I think, from the day we got married."

"I don't want to bring up the birds and the bees again, but you must've gotten along sometimes."

"You'd think."

"How would you rate the job the state police did investigating your daughter's murder? Do you think they did a good job?"

"Yes. But not the sheriff's department. Let me tell you a story about the sheriff's department. They were going to check out my backyard, to see if they could find any evidence, a place where the girls might've stashed clothes or whatever. Our property lines up against the Forever

Wild there. So, my God, there had to be 12, 15 sheriff cars lined up on the street. There was a woman down the street who was selling her whatdoyoucallits."

"She was a prostitute?"

"Yes. I sat on my steps and I watched them deputies. They'd come through my yard and went out into the trees, and they didn't even bother to go far enough so I couldn't see. And they went down to this woman's house, and I could see them there waiting in line for their turn. And when one got done, the car would go, and when another got done, their car would go, and they never got around to checking my backyard for evidence. They all knew where this woman lived apparently, and they all lined up—and my sister and I sat here and witnessed that."

"How long was it before you realized there wasn't going to be an arrest?"

"Oh, I always knew that. Because I was here, and Johnny never had nothing nice to say about me. And Johnny had more influence with those people than I ever would. I had no contact with them, but he did. He drank with them. I guess he was a little bit afraid of me because he'd go out the side door, piddle around in the backyard until he figured I wasn't watching him no more. Then he'd sneak out through the trees and wind up at the Castle Inn."

"Now, you lost a second daughter in a swimming accident?"

"Yeah."

"What happened?"

"She went to the Bahamas with the Gleason Scuba Club." By this time Alice had quit French's mustard and worked for Gleason Works, one of the largest manufacturing plants in Rochester. They made machine parts, mostly gears. "She failed the test, and the director of the scuba club said that he would watch over her like she was his own daughter. But him and another guy wanted to take pictures, so they left her alone, which was a no-no to begin with. They went down to take pictures of the deeper fish, and they left her. And then when they came back looking for her, they couldn't find her."

"This was Patty?"

"Yeah."

"Do you remember about when that happened?"

Silence.

"Do you remember how old she was when it happened?"

"Twenty-one."

"Patty was two grades ahead of me, so her accident would have been in 1975 or 1976."

(According to her obituary, Patty died March 10, 1975, in the West Indies.)

"Yeah, that's when I was working at Gleason's, which was why she got to go with the Gleason Scuba Club."

I asked about the rest of her kids, Alice, Diane, and Betty. How were they doing?

Big Alice told me her daughter Alice was estranged, a sad story about how she didn't approve of something one of her siblings did. The Alices had not spoken to one another in more than 30 years.

Diane and Alice both lived down in North Carolina. Diane came home to visit once a year during the holidays, but Alice didn't get to see much of her, either.

I asked Alice if she had photos of Kathy that I could borrow briefly. She explained that, when Alice left home, she took all of the photos she could find and all of the newspaper clippings, but she missed one, so Alice still had one photo of Kathy. Needless to say, she didn't want to part with it, not even briefly. She had a computer and a scanner and she could receive e-mail, but for some reason she couldn't send e-mail. Her grandson was supposed to come around and figure out what was wrong, but he hadn't gotten around to it. I told Alice that I would stop by and make a copy of the photo myself the next time I was around.

Alice told me to be sure to call ahead because she was very involved with the Town of Chili Senior Center, a volunteer, and she sometimes traveled with them.

"The Senior Center saved my life," Alice explained. Husband gone, kids gone, and it was dark—very dark—on Names Road. The Chili Senior Center gave her a place to go. I said I understood exactly what she was talking about, that my mom had lasted a few years at the end of Stallman Drive after my dad passed in 1999, but now she lived in an apartment building with others her age and had a sense of community again.

Alice said if I knocked on her door and got no answer, I should look in the backyard because she was outside all the time in the summer.

She assured me that I had her blessing and that if I needed she would even sign a form so that the cops knew that she was completely in favor of my new investigation. Her idea.

"Because I have no use for the sheriff's department and . . . no, retract that. That was a long time ago. I'm sure it's all different now."

I pointed out that back in 1966 there had only been one sheriff for many years, so things were done in a very old-fashioned way. The Monroe County Sheriff's Department of 2011 was a thoroughly modern crime-fighting, peacekeeping force.

"Did you hear that whoever done it cut them all up bad?" Alice asked me.

"Yeah, I wasn't going to talk about that."

"And then the guy put their bathing suits back on! He had to be a sick man, right?"

"Yup."

"And he had to have help to get those bathing suits back on."

"Maybe. Evie Douglas told me that you said Jack Starr confessed on his deathbed."

"Yeah. To a girl."

"Who was the girl?"

"I don't know. She told the vicious old lady across the road, and the witch come over and told me and I called the detective. And they went over and the girl refused to come forward. I'll bet that witch told her not to come forward. I heard that Jack Starr said that he was the one who killed Kathy, and he never said nothing about a partner."

I asked how things were these days, and Alice said there were still challenges. Betty had survived a series of health crises. Alice said Betty's first husband was a guy I knew from Names Road, a guy I remembered as a bully, and he too had turned out to be abusive.

Alice had very little memory of the time immediately following the discovery of the bodies, the time when the investigation, if one occurred, would have taken place. After they found the girls, someone—she didn't remember who—insisted that she take tranquilizers, and she was out of it for a long time.

"The story went away in the papers very quickly," I said.

"I blame my husband, John," she said. "He told reporters I was a whore."

On August 15 and 16, 2011, I wrote a "Declaration and Authorization" for Alice to sign before a notary public. It read, "Declarant hereby authorizes Agent to conduct a new investigation, including fresh interviews of witnesses, and to access the files maintained by various governmental and private agencies, including, but not limited to, the Monroe County Sheriff's Office, the Monroe County Medical Examiner's Office, the Rochester Police Department (RPD), and the New York State Police, pertaining to all previous investigations into my daughter's murder. Declarant requests that Agent follow the clues wherever they may lead and to shed as much light on this horrible event as possible. Declarant realizes that, after 45 years, there can be no real justice, but this still-grieving mother needs whatever closure this new investigation may provide. I grant this authority in full knowledge that the result of this investigation may result in a published book, the royalties from which will go solely to Agent, his heirs or assigns."

That same day I wrote a letter to the Monroe County sheriff Patrick O'Flynn explaining what I was up to and sent a copy of the letter to the lovely Maureen McGuire, one of the news anchors of the evening news on WROC, Channel 8 in Rochester. She was my favorite, and I had earlier asked her to be my Facebook friend. "If you like, I'll keep you posted," I added.

She replied in minutes, "Michael, thank you very much. I can't imagine the pain Alice Bernhard must be carrying in her heart. I am off work this week, but with your permission will be sharing this with my executive producer and assignment editor. When will you be in town?"

I gave her my schedule and contact info. "Thanks for your interest, Maureen," I wrote. "Alice wants me to stir the pot. The girls were missing for 25 days before their bodies were found, and the newspapers didn't even run their photos. They weren't girls of pure reputation (George-Ann had only recently had a baby), and it was assumed that they'd run off with guys. . . . Btw, my photographer is Jerry Warren, my old Wheatland-Chili High School teacher, who says that, as a Re/MAX agent, he sold you your house. Looking forward to speaking with you."

"Oh my goodness!!" Maureen said. "Please say hi to Jerry! I've completely redone the house—restored floors, new kitchen, etc. He'd be proud. ☺ Ok—I'm sharing this with the desk and will get back to you."

The next day, I wanted to clear up the loose ends from the information that Steve Frazier gave to Evie Douglas, that Jack Starr's partner in crime was a guy who married Francine Morton on Lester Street. Unaware of what familial scabs I might be picking, I contacted Ray Morton, whom I'd known since 1962. He was George-Ann's cousin. I knew him from Scouts, and I can remember him being over there when we were little and playing at the Formicolas. As an adult, he and his wife Cindy moved into the Braddock/Putnam house on the bend of Stallman Drive and had lived there ever since. I sent Ray a Facebook message explaining that I was working for Alice and asked him if he had a brother-in-law who resembled the guy Frazier mentioned. Ray got right back to me, writing on August 17: "Mike, I remember it quite well as George-Ann was my first cousin once removed and she and I spent a lot of time together. I have many happy memories of the Formicola house. I used to go over there when my aunt would play cards with George and Ruth. I was even allowed to spend the night a few times."

Regarding the search for the missing girls and the homicide investigation, Ray said, "They interviewed my brother-in-law, Clint Wilson."

"Is he still around?" I asked.

"Unfortunately he passed away several years ago."

Ray said Ruth Formicola and Burt Braddock's mother, Dolly, was Ray's aunt, his dad's sister. Clint Wilson was the brother of Keith Wilson, who married Gina Formicola.

Tight little group. "My sister introduced Keith and Gina," Ray wrote.

That got me thinking about the other Stallman Drive unpleasantness that occurred in the 1980s. Bizarrely, George-Ann's big sister, Gina, lost both her sister and her husband to lovers' lane homicides. Gina married Keith Wilson, and they lived in the Formicola house on Stallman Drive, both before and after George and Ruth Formicola, along with their newly adopted son William, moved to Florida.

Keith was a powerful man, a guy who could pound stakes into brick-hard clay with just a couple of swings of his sledgehammer. He combed his hair into a Brylcreem duck's ass and had a startlingly high voice, almost a helium voice.

We mostly saw Keith from a distance, but he radiated benevolence. We always thought he was a nice guy, but the contrast between his brawn and his childlike testosterone-challenged voice was comical. No one laughed in his face, of course.

Keith did not come to a humorous end, however.

Gina and Keith were in their mid-thirties, during the early 1980s, when—the story went—Keith learned that Gina was having an affair with a much younger man, a teenager named David Young. Gina and the guy ran away to Florida and lived together down there for a while. But now they were back, and Gina had moved back in with Keith. She said that it was over between her and the youngster, but Keith didn't believe her. On a night during spring 1985, Keith reportedly searched for and found Gina parked with her boyfriend on a lovers' lane in a park in Henrietta.

Gina and Young were in a pickup truck at the end of the lane, near the park's restrooms. Keith was out of control, ax handle in hand, charging his wife and her boyfriend. He screamed in his high-pitched voice that he was going to rip off the doors of the kid's truck when Young grabbed his shotgun and twice blasted away. Keith was struck in the arm and then the stomach. He dropped to his hands and knees but kept moving forward. Young, now determined to finish the job, got out of the truck and bludgeoned Keith with the butt end of the shotgun. He struck Keith so many times that the shotgun broke. The massive trauma to Keith's head killed him. Young and Gina fled the scene, drove to a pond in Rush, and threw the broken shotgun into the water. David Young, 20, was arrested and charged with murder. After the gun was retrieved by the sheriff's scuba divers, Gina was also arrested and charged with obstruction of justice.[1]

His obituary in the *Finger Lakes Times* said Keith worked for Conrail and had two sisters and five brothers, all living. There was no mention of Gina, and no mention of the cause of death.[2]

"It was murder, all right," prosecutor Richard A. Keenan argued at the 1986 trial.

David's mother, Nevin Young, told the papers that there was no way this was murder. It was self-defense all the way.

"I know he was very much afraid of the man," she said. "He told me that he warned the guy to stop but he kept coming at him. My son was protecting himself."

As the "victim's family" haunted the Monroe County courthouse menacingly, Young claimed self-defense, and it was presented in an engaging fashion by popular defense attorney Felix Lepine. Keith came at him like an animal, a powerful Paul Bunyan of a man, arms like Popeye, blind with fury, an ax handle in his hand. If Young hadn't responded with deadly force, he would have been mincemeat.

Young testified on his own behalf. He'd been so scared. The jury listened and, to some extent, believed. It was hard to fathom that Young was completely innocent. Keeping a .22 in the car was one thing; a 12-gauge shotgun was another. Young was prepared to dish some out. The jury acquitted Young of the major charges and convicted him only of criminally negligent homicide.

The judge told Young he'd gotten a "tremendous break" and that the jury had "erred."

The prosecutor said the verdict was an "insult to the family."

Young was sentenced to one to four years in jail and served 18 months. Gina and son Dean moved to Florida to be closer to Ruth, George, and William—and we hadn't seen any of them since.

Ray Morton wasn't sure why cops talked to Clint Wilson after the 1966 murders, but he knew Clint to be a "mean SOB." He was a Hells Angel and beat Ray's sister when he was high or drunk, but that was most of the time. Clint and Ray's sister were married about 15 years. As for the Starr connection, Ray couldn't be helpful.

"I don't know if Clint knew Jack, but he might have," Ray said. "They both lived on the same street." Names Road.

He impressively and concisely summed up the events of 1966: "The police left no stone unturned, but there wasn't a lot of evidence because of the era."

It wasn't like Clint Wilson was the only guy being interviewed by police.

"My dad was in a full body cast that summer because of back surgery, and they interviewed him, too," Ray noted.

I asked where the Wilson brothers lived. "Where did they grow up?"

"As far as I recall, Keshequa,* New York." Down by the Finger Lakes.

"Well, why were they in Ballantyne, marrying cousins who lived a few hundred yards apart?"

"I don't know. I do remember that it was just Clint for a time, and then Keith joined him later."

Ray said that George-Ann was buried in the cemetery south of Scottsville, New York, which is where his mom and dad were buried. When he was there, he always stopped by to pay George-Ann his respects.

"The cemetery is past Dirty Dave's up the hill," Ray explained. "George-Ann's grave is by the old windmill frame toward the back."

"Burt Braddock and my old man didn't get along," I said. "Was he a mean man?"

"He was a mean person to most people," Ray said. "He was pissed when my uncle sold me the house instead of him. He hated me for a long time after that."

Thanks to Dawn Putnam, Burt's stepdaughter, I had Burt Braddock's phone number. It wasn't a phone call I was looking forward to, and it kept slipping to the bottom of my things-to-do list. Instead, I thought about what Ray Morton said regarding Clint Wilson's motorcycle affiliation. I didn't remember there being a Hells Angels chapter in Rochester. I remembered the motorcycle gang being named the Hackers. Luckily for me, the Rochester Angels had a website.[3] I was right and wrong. There had been an Angels chapter in Rochester since 1969, and just about all the charter members were former Hackers. So, if he was already a member of a motorcycle club, Clint would have been a Hacker in 1966.

I Googled obituaries and scratched a few more names off my witness list. Assistant District Attorney Jack B. Lazarus had worked the case. He later became the Monroe County DA from 1969 to 1975, but unfortunately he passed away in April 2000, just shy of his 70th birthday. Michael Iaculli, lead state investigator, another guy who worked both the Chili murders and the Double Initials case, retired as a cop in 1974 and passed away in 1995.

The best part of my day came during the evening when I finally talked to a retired deputy who had worked the case. His name was Garry Coles, and though he currently lived in St. Petersburg, Florida, he'd grown up in Scottsville and had served as the Wheatland town supervisor during the mid-1980s. I got his number from Jerry Warren, my old high school teacher, who had been the mayor of Scottsville during that same period and apparently had had a conversation with Coles about the Chili murders years back.

I explained who I was and what I was up to. Maybe I was writing a book, but certainly I was trying to get an old lady some closure. I told him that George-Ann was my friend. He was sympathetic, complimented the purity of my motives, and told me he was reticent to talk without first getting permission from the sheriff's office. He said that he was not a spokesman for the MCSO and didn't feel comfortable speaking in that capacity.

Then a lightbulb went on over my head. Scottsville had a town landmark on its southern border, an old black trestle that crossed the Oatka Creek. Back in the early 1960s someone had painted, in huge white letters that went across the side of the bridge facing the road, george. It became forevermore known as the George Bridge, a great place for a teenager to hang out, best of all in the summer. The Oatka below the bridge was deep enough for jumping. Who was George? There were different theories, one of which was that it had been a guy named George Coles.

Now, back to me with the lightbulb over my head: "Garry, are you related to the guy who painted the George Bridge?"

"That was my baby brother!" He laughed for 30 seconds, and when he stopped he was my friend. He began to talk. He told me about how proud he was of working for the sheriff's office, that he had always tried to treat citizens as he would want his own family treated. "I can't say enough nice things about it, and if I had it all to do again, I'd do it all again." He'd retired in 1990.

Back then, in 1966, it had been a different world, he recalled. Nobody locked their doors. The worst thing that happened was you'd catch a kid doing something he wasn't supposed to be doing, and you'd drive them home to get a whuppin' from his old man. I told him that I wasn't going to get into details, but I knew that to be true. He said he knew, too—and he meant when he was a kid. "It was a wonderful time," he concluded.

"What was your personal involvement with the case?" I asked.

"They had me out pounding the bushes along the railroad tracks, all the way from Archer Road to Scottsville Road."

"Find anything?"

"I'm going to have to talk to somebody before I answer that."

"Were you familiar with the suspect Jack Starr?"

That one he decided to answer: "I knew all about the Starrs. They were quite a colorful family over there off Ballantyne Road. I was at the house many times, executing numerous arrest warrants."

He wouldn't give details, needed to talk to somebody. He told me he thought I was a great guy and he admired what I was doing, and he was going to make a few phone calls to see how much he could help me. Apparently he was hoping I wouldn't call back. When I did get back to him, about a week later, to ask if he'd made any phone calls, he said no. And that was that. (It had been my intention to reinterview Coles, but I never had the opportunity. He passed away in December 2014.)

The next day I heard from Philip Albano, who was in my class at Ballantyne School for a few years and now lived in California. He said he remembered that time well, and it still gave him the creeps when he thought about it.

"I heard they were looking for a heavyset man with bright red hair," Albano said, his memory vivid. "If you remember the bait shop at the creek, Tacy's, I was there one day counting worms when a man came in that matched the description to a T. I went into the back room and made a call, but by the time the police got there this person was gone, and I swear, Mike, I never seen him again."

Albano said there was no way one man could do what was done. "I do know that on the day the girls came up missing, they went to the trussle. I was supposed to go with them, but my father said no. I had to cut the grass first."

Then Albano got my attention. He said, "I had also found a beach towel when the girls were still missing and that the police took, along with an AM/FM radio." He specifically said, "*We* found the radio" on the road that went from the swimming hole to Scottsville Road, about halfway down. He now wasn't sure if he was the one who found the towel, which he thought was white. Someone else might've found the towel, but there was definitely a towel found, and he believed it was white.

I asked him if he knew of any creepy characters in the neighborhood that had struck him as suspect when he was a kid. He said yeah, there was a guy named Werner who lived near the Bernhards on Names Road. Werner—that was the only name he knew—was a peculiar man.

He had a dollhouse in his backyard, and Albano recalled that one time Werner somehow locked himself inside it.

10

MAKING PEOPLE REMEMBER

On August 21, 2011, Jerry Warren picked me up outside my mom's apartment house. We pulled into the Bernhard driveway right behind Alice who was returning from her volunteer job at the Chili Senior Center. Her bumper stickers read, "Wandering Witches" and "I Believe in Magic."

Alice was a spry 85, wearing glasses and a sweat suit. If she was nervous about meeting us, it didn't show. Jerry and I piled into her house, which was busily decorated with oil paintings, souvenirs, and mementos, as well as pictures of her kids, grandkids, and great-grandkids. The paintings were by her friend Joanne, who was Wiccan. Alice and Joanne went to psychic conventions together. At one convention a psychic saw the spirit of a man standing beside Alice, with a Russian hat and an unusual mustache and a walking stick that he'd whittled. Alice recognized the description as that of Mr. Douglas, Evie's father, who had rented a room from Alice for a number of years.

She made a call on a landline. There was a pause, then she said, "They're nice. I didn't get beat up, so you can stop worrying now. Okay."

As she called, I took the opportunity to look around. The walls were paneled in a blonde wood, not that you could see much wall. Just about every surface was occupied by artistic expression. The painting that hung above Alice's head as she sat in her favorite chair showed a pair of bathing nymphs, their slender naked forms and pert breasts protruding from a small pool of water as magic mushrooms grew all around. Many of the paintings, all seemingly by the same hand, showed alert tiger cats and hovering birds engaging in Disneyesque mischief. A small pumpkin served as a paperweight. There were Raggedy Ann dolls, brightly painted knickknacks, and wooden soldiers mounted on the wall. Orange dominated, giving the entire house a warm glow of impending autumn.

She hung up and turned toward us with a big smile. "People worry about me," she said.

"That's a good thing," I said.

Warren took photos of Alice, Alice and me, an oil painting of Kathy, and a photograph of Kathy when she was a child. I gave her a copy of my book, *Killer Twins*, because part of it took place in Rochester and she would recognize many of the locations. Although I hated the cover, which I found unnecessarily gruesome, I'd always considered it my best true-crime work, and I wanted to impress her.

I also gave her a copy of the front page of the Rochester *Democrat & Chronicle* from the day after the girls were found and another of the memorial page in what would have been the girls' senior yearbook. I showed her a picture of Miss D'Amanda, the first-grade teacher at Ballantyne School, and Alice growled at it.

"That woman," Alice said. "I almost came to blows with her."

I learned that Old Man Werner's first name was Joseph, and his painting of Kathy impressed me. There was caricature in Kathy's features, hairdo, and clothing. He had painted Kathy's face onto *That Girl*. There is nothing suspicious about either a good memory for faces or artistic talent, I concluded. He painted Patty too, giving both portraits to Alice after the girls were gone. Alice acknowledged that the man was odd. The story about the dollhouse might have been true, but she did not think he was a bad man.

I also learned that it was Werner's wife who was feuding with Alice, something about years ago Mrs. Werner calling the cops about the treatment of one of Alice's grandchildren. It was Mrs. Werner who had told Alice she'd heard from an unnamed girl who refused to come forward that Jack Starr had confessed to the murders on his deathbed.

When Jerry Warren was finished taking photos, we went outside. Alice pointed out the storage shed behind her house. She said that, back in 1966, that *was* the house. I tried to imagine Alice, John, and six kids in that building, about the size of the average garage.

We piled into Warren's car and headed toward the town hall. As we drove along Beaver Road—not turning onto Archer to visit "the spot"— I asked her if she could drive down Archer Road without looking down the dirt road. She said she could not and that, funny, after all these years it still hurt.

"Everyone who remembers looks down the dirt road," I said.

In the town hall parking lot, Warren pulled into a handicap spot. I jokingly told Alice that if they came to arrest us, she should walk with a limp.

We went inside and had the documents out and ready to be notarized when Alice frowned. Uh-oh. The notary needed her photo ID.

"I knew I should have brought my purse," she said.

She was embarrassed now. We returned to Names Road, and she went in the house. She came out with her purse, and boom, she fell *hard* coming down her front porch steps. Warren and I exploded out of the car and were at her side in a flash. We each took an arm and helped her to her feet.

"Don't worry, I bounce," she said.

She said she had merely skinned her knee, but as Warren and I helped her to her feet and held her up, her first attempt to take a step resulted in a completely buckling knee. After a few more baby steps, she was steadier and said that she was good to go.

"As long as there's not blood dripping down my leg, I'm okay," she said—and for a moment I thought of George-Ann, catching herself on the barbed-wire fence and laughing at her torn flesh. Ballantyne girls were tough that way.

We once again parked in the handicap spot, and this time Alice didn't have to fake walking with a limp, making my earlier joke seem like a painful omen. Warren and I each took an arm. She liked that. We escorted her in this fashion all the way back to the notary's office where Alice signed both documents.

"Alice, where was Kathy's funeral held?" I asked.

"I don't remember the name of the place," she replied. "I remember it was on Mt. Hope Avenue and they turned it into a beer joint."

Alice said Kathy was buried in Mount Hope Cemetery. You went in the side entrance near the new Strong (Memorial Hospital) building and took the cemetery road around a bend to a spot where there was a pair of evergreens, and she was right there.

Between Alice and the cemetery, Jerry and I drove to the dump site, and we kicked around in the weeds a little. I don't know why. Maybe to pick up vibes. At one spot beside the dirt road, the weeds were knocked down, and there were tire ruts. Apparently an SUV driver had recently used the spot to turn around.

Driving north on Scottsville Road we checked and saw that the dirt road alongside the railroad tracks, although still visible in the weeds, was no longer accessible via Scottsville Road. The guardrail installed after the road's most recent widening blocked the entrance.

The next stop was Mount Hope Cemetery, where we tried to find Kathy's grave. No luck. We went into the cemetery's side entrance, and there were over a hundred evergreen trees. I would have to get in touch with the cemetery and get a precise plot location.

On August 24, I returned to Alice's house briefly, accompanied by my lifelong friend and photographer Philip Semrau, who—being a good Rochesterian—was going to use a 35 mm camera and real film. Where to get the photos developed was another question. We'd wanted to use Kodak film, Eastman Kodak being the former backbone of Rochester's economy, but the Rite-Aid drugstore only sold Fuji, so that was going to have to do.

I talked to Alice at the door. She didn't give me a chance to see how she was getting around. I asked her how her skinned knee was. She said that one was good. The other one was the problem. Betty was taking her to be X-rayed later. I told her I was putting together a TV interview and verified that she was up to that. She assured me she was in for the ride.

Philip and I went back to the swimming hole to photograph the trestle and grassy slope. We walked the 100 feet north to the former site of the Genesee Junction. The little house that used to serve as a one-man station for the railroad was gone, long gone apparently, as there were tall bushes and a tree where it used to stand. The turntable was similarly protected by foliage. We would have needed a machete to get to it.

Philip took several photos looking east. You could see the rust-collared steel of the trestle across the river, and the cars crossing the tracks on Scottsville Road.

From there we went to Scottsville to look for George-Ann's grave. I wasn't optimistic. After the previous day's experience in Mount Hope Cemetery, I was wary of cemetery directions, which in George-Ann's case I'd gotten from Ray Morton. But I was pleasantly surprised. Ray's directions—"past Dirty Dave's on the left, up the hill, near the old windmill"—led me directly to George-Ann's grave.

I paid my respects.

It was a pretty spot, atop a little hill under the windmill. Look to the south and there was a cornfield. You had to really squint to see that directly across Scottsville-Caledonia Road was a strip joint called Foxy's, which at the time of George-Ann's burial had been a bar called the Top Hat.

On August 25, I played 18 holes at the Chili Country Club with my old friend, inventor Paul Johnson, in the morning, and in the afternoon, after a quick burger—eaten at the former site of Tacy's bait and marina where Phil Albano saw the red-haired man—we convened at Alice's house with the WROC TV crew, a pretty reporter named Caroline Tucker and her cameraman Bob.

Betty met us at the side of the house, the first time I'd seen her since the 1970s. Betty gave off the same vibes as her mother, a woman with a serene nervous system even in the face of Job-like miseries.

"Hi, Betty." I was pleased to see she looked healthy and well.

"Hi, Mike. She's in the backyard."

Alice was sitting on a bench beneath an apple tree in her backyard.

"How's the knee?" I asked gently.

"At least nothing's broken," she replied.

I was disrupting the peace. Beside the little house was a water feature that tinkled and bubbled lightly. It was a quiet and beautiful spot, every bit as serene as the women, an extension of them, Alice's lovely nest. And you could see to the back of her backyard, a surprisingly deep yard, and the Forever Wild beyond it. Because of the Forever Wild, Alice's backyard paradise received frequent wildlife visitors. Deer could be seen nibbling. A wild turkey and its babies strutted by one day. I knew just what that was like, living at the end of Stallman Drive.

Also insistently breaking the serenity was the Bernhards' dog, Troy, a vicious-looking slobber hound about the same size as the Mulligans' pony, Benny. Betty was calming the dog down, and of course the dog was completely gentle with her. Alice did not have to worry about intruders. Troy had it covered.

I introduced Alice to Caroline. Sympathy emanated from the reporter. She locked in on Alice, and they sat down to chat, with Bob pointing the camera at them.

Alice told the reporter about the little house in back being the only house in those days.

"I bought it from Sears for $200," she said. "Ten dollars down and the rest when they caught up with me."

Caroline asked, "You had *six* children?" She genuinely seemed impressed by the quantity.

"Yeah," Alice said with a blissful smile. "Back in those days you were expected to keep having babies as long as you were healthy. Have six kids, feel good, have six more." Alice laughed. Alice often laughed when she made statements; she had a knack for the ironic, like when she said it was so unfair that a gentle soul like Kathy would be taken by such savagery.

"Did you have a husband, Alice?" Caroline asked.

"With six kids, I should hope so."

Caroline looked at the photos of Kathy and asked if she did well in school. Alice said she did. "I never had no problems with her," Alice said.

"What was Kathy like? What did she like to do?"

After a pause, Alice said, "She liked to clean the house."

When Caroline asked her how she managed to keep going when her daughter was missing, Alice explained that she had to work. "I still had five kids to take care of," she said.

Caroline asked for directions to the swimming hole, told Alice what a pleasant experience it had been meeting her, and she and Bob split to record an establishing shot in front of Black Creek.

Just as the TV crew was leaving, Alice blurted out, "The guy took off their bathing suits, cut them up, and put the bathing suits back on. A guy would have to be sick to do something like that, right?"

The others were stunned into silence, so I quickly concurred. "Yes."

With the TV people gone, I told Alice what a good job she'd done and kissed her on the forehead. Paul and I sat down in lawn chairs and chatted with Alice and Betty for the better part of two hours, just shooting the breeze on an August afternoon. I asked whatever became of the characters that used to live up and down the street, and the Bernhards inevitably knew the answer. The Fosters, they said, owned a beer joint in the city.

Alice told Paul and me that women were stronger, that she had only recently gone sky diving and was continuing to live a full life. I remembered a story my mom told me about Alice going to a costume party as Dolly Parton, with a blonde wig and two huge balloons inside her shirt. Near the end of the party, when she had everyone's attention, she pulled out a pair of pins, one in each hand, and simultaneously popped her "boobs." "Ah, that feels so much better," Alice had said, and everyone laughed.

I mentioned that I was going to be talking again in a few days with Philip Albano who said he was the one who'd found Kathy's radio.

"I had always been under the impression that Mary Crane* found the radio," Betty said.

I remembered Mary Crane, straight hair and knobby knees. She had a brother James who wore a hearing aid. Betty said the Crane kids had all been adopted; the Cranes had taken on kids with special needs.

Before Paul and I left, Alice said she looked at the book I'd given her and wouldn't mind one "just like that" about Kathy. She said she wanted me to find out what happened, of course, but also, "See if you can get people to think about my Kathy, on account of she was forgotten way too soon." I told her it would be my pleasure.

I watched the news that night with my mom, who'd been calling her friends to make sure everyone would know I was on.

Maureen McGuire introduced the piece: "A new spotlight on a very old murder case. In July 1966 [she got the month wrong] two teens from Chili were killed. Their case has never been solved. Caroline Tucker reports on a writer's new mission to bring the victims' families closure."[1]

And there was Alice, sitting on her bench under the apple tree. "Something should have been done, something could have been done," she said.

Caroline said, "85-year-old Alice Bernhard has never forgotten Catherine Ann. She was one of six kids."

"She was a gentle soul," Alice said.

Caroline: "It was June 1966. Sixteen-year-old Catherine and her 14-year-old friend George-Ann Formicola never returned home."

Alice: "We had supper and Kathy asked if she and George-Ann could go back to the crick, but I said be home before dark."

Caroline: "Witnesses saw George-Ann and Kathy swimming in the Black Creek. It was the last place they were seen alive. Their bodies were found near the railroad tracks in Chili."

Alice: "Once it was all over with and no details, that was it. I never heard anything more, and I have been feeling cheated."

Caroline: "Today Alice is sharing her story with a crime writer. Michael Benson was friends with the girls. He was nine years old at the time."

And there I was, looking like I'd come straight from the golf course, my collared shirt the color of a Creamsicle.

"I had to go to sleep at night knowing the boogeyman had walked across my back field," I said.

Caroline: "He is now trying to heat up an old case."

Me: "I think we can find out who did it. Forty-five years later, law enforcement is forty-five years smarter."

Caroline: "Benson is trying to dig up information and old files from the Monroe County Sheriff's Department. He wants to work on the case."

Me: "We may not be able to prove what happened, but we can come up with a solid theory that may give Alice closure."

Caroline: "At 85, Alice is hoping for answers."

Alice: "I go one day at a time. I survive one day and then go on to the next."

Caroline: "Benson says he may try to write a book on the case depending on what new information can be revealed."

Channel 8 returned to Maureen McGuire at the anchor desk, and she said, "WROC has been unable to reach the Monroe County Sheriff's Department for comment."

And that was it. The news went on to the next thing.

The story appeared twice, once on the CBS affiliate at 6, and then on the FOX affiliate at 10. The stations shared a local news team. The message regarding Alice and her *need to know* came off note perfect.

They didn't mention the e-mail account I'd opened in order to field tips, so that was disappointing. Maybe they would wish they had. Between the two showings I received a call from Kevin Doran, Maureen McGuire's coanchor on Channel 8.

He told me that after the six o'clock news a woman named Mary Crane had called the station and reported a tip. Mary's name had come up earlier that day. Betty Bernhard said she thought Mary was the one who had found Kathy's radio.

Doran said, "She left a number and asked that you give her a call."

"I'll do that. Thanks."

That same day I received several tips from Don Campbell, who graduated from Wheatland-Chili in 1970, putting him one grade behind George-Ann and Kathy. "I didn't really know the girls, but I remember them from the cafeteria at school," he said. He reported having spoken to two men—Donald Burns and Donald Cameron, a farmer and an undertaker—who had worked as grave diggers at Oatka Cemetery and said that George-Ann's body had been exhumed in the early 1970s and that hairs were removed from her remains. Campbell told me to talk to a guy named Larry Rath who was acquainted with a couple of deputies who worked the case. Campbell said he'd heard from an old Wheatland-Chili classmate named Wayne Morrison that the killer, and he didn't give a name, was from Churchville—that is where the tracks led—and that the guy committed suicide.

So I talked to Larry Rath, who said that he had no knowledge of any exhumation. He had worked in a couple of other cemeteries, but never in the Oatka Cemetery where George-Ann was buried. He couldn't say whether George-Ann or Kathy was exhumed. But yes, he did know cops. He worked with them. He'd been told that the investigation had developed a "solid suspect," but they didn't have enough to prosecute. He knew nothing about the "tracks led to Churchville" theory. He had worked, at one time or another, with three deputies who knew about the case, but two of them—Dave Steinmiller and Pete Decker—were deceased. The living deputy was Don Ezard who lived in Spencerport. His number was unlisted, Larry Rath's wife chimed in.

Luckily Don Ezard had a Facebook account and was easily contacted. He got right back to me and said he would be glad to help me in any way he could, but noted that he began working for the MCSO in 1967 and the Chili murders didn't ring a bell. I sent him a summary of the case and asked him to help in any way he could, and that was the last of that.

Wayne Morrison, the guy with the story of the Churchville suspect that committed suicide, had a reputation for being an "expert" in the case when he talked to others, but when I contacted him, he clammed up and said he knew nothing.

Campbell dug out info regarding John I. Miller on the Internet, which in turn caused me to reexamine Miller as a suspect.[2] He was the Pennsylvanian man who murdered 12-year-old Marsha Jean Behney with a knife on September 3, 1966.[3] The MCSO had taken a great interest in Miller, and there was reportedly unspecified evidence that Miller was in Rochester at the time of the Chili murders.[4]

Interestingly, Miller might have still been alive. Someone named John I. Miller (a common name but uncommon middle initial) was living in a farmhouse a short distance from the site of the Marsha Jean Behney murder. As far as I could tell, he'd paid his debt to society—like Shawcross, he'd killed a child and received a sentence of only 10 to 20 years—and then returned home without any known incident. My attempts to contact him went unanswered, and I could not get Pennsylvania law enforcement to confirm that he was the Miller who'd killed Marsha Jean or get them reinterested in looking at him as a suspect in the Chili murders.

August 28 was the day Hurricane Irene dumped close to a foot of water on Downstate New York, so I took care of some computer research. As rain beat in sheets against my window, I learned that the 1966 murders were not the first time the Genesee Junction area had been the scene of hideous violence.

In 1883, a John Kelly robbed and bludgeoned Jacob Lutz with an iron pipe until brain oozed from the cracks in Lutz's skull. The murder took place outside Lutz's "frame-dwelling house" with an adjacent pigpen alongside the Genesee Valley Canal—our "runoff." The victim worked at the glue factory owned by E. B. Chapin and Edwin A. Loder, the man who at that time owned all of the land north of Mosquito Point Road.[5]

On May 31, 1915, a 22-year-old man shot his male companion through the heart with a revolver and dumped both the body and the gun in the runoff beside the Penn Railroad, where three men who were walking along the tracks discovered them. The murderer was discovered in a shanty near the junction.[6]

In 1920, the area became the site of an infamous body dump. A Mrs. Pearl Beaver Odell, wife of James L. Odell, had an affair with an Edward J. Knelp. When Mr. Odell learned of his wife's desecration, he told her the only way for her to make it right was to assist him in murdering her seducer. The Odells killed Knelp by beating him with large metal files, removing much of his skin with the flailing. They took his pulp of a body to Mosquito Point Road, to the towpath next to the old Genesee Valley Canal, dragged the body down the path, and stashed it under the stone bridge. The body was discovered and the Odells were found out, tried, and convicted.[7] He was executed in Sing Sing, and she was sentenced to 20 years. During her separate trial, she was eight months pregnant. Her prosecutor told the press that if she got the death penalty, better she be executed before rather than after her baby was born, since no child should be born under such scandalous circumstances. The comment brought nary a ripple of controversy.

I learned why 1966 deputies might have been reluctant to arrest any of the Starr kids. Jack's dad was chairman of one of the town's most powerful governing bodies. His mom was no slouch either as director of a local historical society. They'd put a series of boys into the U.S. armed service and would soon lose one in Vietnam.

Kathy Bernhard's dad, on the other hand, was a dysfunctional alcoholic who worked in a junkyard, a disparity between the dads that might have had deputies reporting to the suspect rather than the victim, a disparity that might have occurred to Jack Starr as he sat next to John Bernhard knocking back drafts at the Castle Inn.

I learned that Glenn J. Saile, sheriff's sergeant, the first cop at the Archer Road crime scene, had passed away after a long illness on October 12, 2010, at the age of 86.

Bizarrely, I learned that in 2000 one of Jack Starr's cousins had abandoned his Ballantyne Road house, just cross-lots from where Jack grew up, and when the county official came to inspect the property, he found tombstones set up like a graveyard. The back of the house had been painted so that it looked as if flames were coming up out of the ground. There was a dark wood coffin in the backyard, along with a pit covered by a tarp. A pig carcass had been nailed to a tree, and there were plastic skulls embedded into the stucco at the back of the house. The guy had been driving a hearse, which was regularly seen parked in the driveway. At first it was thought that the cousin had stolen the gravestones, and people were wondering just how ghoulish the scene was. Then it was revealed that he'd purchased the tombstones from Trott Monuments, telling the salesman there that he wanted "reject" stones so that he could build a back patio. He bought 14 tombstones. When police learned that the tombstones were legally purchased, they closed the case. It is not against the law to be within a dark shadow, i.e., macabre. No one has suggested digging up the backyard, and there was no connection between gothic style and the 1966 murders. Still, weird.

11

THE RAGAMUFFINS

On the morning of August 29, I spoke with Mary Crane, the woman who, according to Betty Bernhard, had found Kathy's radio—and the woman who'd called WROC after Alice's TV appearance. I remembered her as a girl who could run like the wind and throw a softball 350 feet.

Mary told me that she grew up a neighbor of the Bernhards, at the far west end of Names Road, corner of Lester Street. I told her I remembered her and that I too had gone to Ballantyne School.

"Get out," she said. "Small world."

"Tell me your story," I said.

Mary explained that it happened about a month before the murders, in late May or early June 1966. She was 10 years old and was allowed to go back to the creek fishing by herself. (She knew it couldn't have been after the murders, because she wouldn't have gone back there alone. And she was 10, so that meant it had to have been in the late spring of 1966.)

Her favorite spot was not at the trestle where the wild parties took place at night, but about 100 yards east of there, on Black Creek's south shore. The location was well hidden by the woods and a row of houses on Black Creek Road to the south.

Clint Wilson, the mean biker who married the Morton girl, came up on her from behind. With Clint was his brother Keith. Clint pushed Mary to the ground and held her down with his weight. He put the blade of his fishing knife to her throat and told her she was dead meat if she tried to struggle. Mary recalled the terror as it occurred to her that she was dead meat even if she *didn't* struggle. He held the knife to her throat with one hand and tried to pull down her pants with the other. Mary was a strong girl and wriggled with all of her might.

"Give me the fishing line," Clint said. "I'm going to tie her hands to this tree trunk." Brother Keith didn't hand the fishing line to Clint. He apparently didn't want to get that close. Instead, he stayed back and tossed the line in Clint's direction. But, as fate would have it, the toss was short.

"Don't move, or you're dead," Clint said. He had to roll over, off Mary, to get the line. The second his weight was off her, athletic Mary was up and running, pulling up her pants as she went. She hid in the bushes and watched the frustrated men from a distance. She stayed down until they'd left the area. She came back onto Black Creek Road through the Hunter family's backyard and ran home via Lester Street. She remembered that life for her became terrifying even before the girls were murdered. Her anxiety was only deepened by the fact that her parents were always working and never home.

"I was too terrified to say anything. I never said anything about it to nobody," Mary recalled. "I had nightmares for years about what happened at the crick. I was scared of living in the country. I lived in the city for years because I was so afraid of the country." It wasn't until 2009 that she overcame her fear of the country and moved out of her dreary home in the city into much more desirable accommodations in the suburbs.

"I always believed it was them same guys who done in those girls," Mary concluded.

The incident ended her days of going back by the creek alone, although she did still wander back there if she was with other kids. On the evening of June 25, she saw Kathy and George-Ann heading back to the creek with their bathing suits on, towels wrapped around their waists like skirts. They asked her if she wanted to come swimming. Mary explained that she was grounded, but her dad was asleep, so maybe.

"Most times I would just've done as I pleased and faced the music later, but this time I didn't. I got scared, not scared of being attacked, but that my dad would wake up and find me gone. I got as far as the edge of the front lawn, then I ran back. That night I noticed that the girls didn't come back from the trestle, but I just figured they must've spent the night at George-Ann's like they sometimes did."

Soon thereafter, Mary did go back by the stone trestle. She wasn't alone, because she would have been afraid to go alone, but she didn't remember whom she was with. She found Kathy's radio on the far side of the trestle, on the far slope you used if you were going to go swimming from that side. She recognized the radio immediately as Kathy's. Kathy always had it with her, and Mary remembered that she was always playing really cool music.

"What did you do with the radio?" I asked.

"I gave it back."

"To the Bernhards?"

"Yeah, the mom, or someone from the family." (Perhaps Betty, I thought. She was the one who recalled Mary finding the radio.)

"Not the police?"

"No."

Moments later I recontacted Philip Albano, who had also claimed to find the radio. He told me that he lived these days in Riverside, California, and was living off disability ever since a car accident forced him to have a hip replacement. I asked him what years he'd lived on Names Road. He said that they moved in, a few houses east of the Bernhards, in 1964 and stayed until sometime in the 1970s. Mom was a waitress at Barney's, a restaurant on Scottsville Road known for its hamburgers. His dad was a foreman at Ontario Plastics where he worked for 35 years. His mom passed away at 68, his dad at 78.

"Our house on Names Road was a pile of crap," he said. "Something always needed fixing."

Eventually his dad had enough and moved. During his years on that street he remembered a seemingly nonstop domestic quarrel going on at the Bernhards'. Alice was always kicking John out, and John was always hammered.

I told him I remembered him through junior high but not after. He said he had been kicked out of school for fighting and had to finish at home. He gave me the names of a couple of his tormenters, known bullies. When he fought back, boom, he was out of school.

I asked him about the redheaded man. He said he'd heard the description of a person of interest from a deputy when "they were making their sweeps" after the bodies were found. Not long after, he was at Tacy's bait and marina, selling night crawlers to Old Man Tacy. It was noontime, the Riverdale Fire Department blew the noon alarm—the "noon whistle" we called it at the Benson house—and Tacy told Albano to watch the shop while he went out to lunch. It was while Albano was in the bait shop alone that the heavyset red-haired man, maybe five-five, came in and fit the description he'd heard from the deputy to a T. Albano slipped into the back and called the cops, but when he came back out the man was gone. The cops arrived quickly, within 10 minutes, but there was no trace of the guy by that time. The memory of that scary incident came back to him vividly only a few years back when he lived for a time near the Greece/Rochester border from 2003 to 2007. He had taken his wife to the marina area. Tacy's was gone, but a pleasant picnic area had been built there. You could still launch a boat if you wanted to.

He had fond memories of the girls who were killed. George-Ann seemed like a nice enough girl, but he'd heard rumors that she was wild. Kathy liked to tease him as being the great white hunter because he got caught shooting squirrels in their backyard. He remembered Kathy as a happy-go-lucky girl, but at the same time one who "didn't take no shit." The girls, he said, invited him to go swimming with them that afternoon, not that night. About a week after the girls disappeared, Albano and his mom went to the dirt road off Archer. His mom said this was the spot where his dad first took her. "This is where I shot my first rabbit," his mom told him.

I asked him about the radio, and he said it was one of those small radios, with the handle attached at the top corner. He said, "We found it on the dirt road on the other side of the creek, between the spot where the tracks crossed and Scottsville Road."

"Who's we?"

I was hoping he'd say Mary Crane and tie things in a neat bow, but what he did say was almost as good: "It was myself and Jimmy Crane [Mary's brother], and maybe a couple of Fosters." He remembered Mary but didn't remember her being there. I'll bet she was, though. He once again mentioned that, around the same time that "we" found the radio, "they" found a white towel. This must've been George-Ann's towel. Kathy's towel was never found.

I spoke to Donna Melideo, from Black Creek Road. She was a couple of years younger than I was, but we had been friends. She said that her two foster brothers, Roy and Paul "Bubby" Gibson, claimed that they had found the radio "back by the trussle." More evidence that everyone was telling the truth. With the girls missing, the big kids formed groups to search, and so the younger kids searched too, the ragamuffins of the neighborhood, barefoot mud larks kicking at the weeds. One found the radio, and they all took credit.

Tracy D'Arcy, younger sister of my late friend and baseball team-mate Tom D'Arcy, was eight years old and living on Ballantyne Road in 1966. She'd just finished second grade. She remembered going for a walk with her best friend when, at the corner of Names Road and Theron Street, they encountered a group of older boys—she didn't remember who they were—who said, "Go home. Don't you know they found two girls' bodies back by the trussle?"

"We ran like hell," Tracy said. "My mom never really talked about it to me. I do remember it was a very long time before I was able to go anywhere, except across the back (Names) road," Tracy recalled. She remembered that a couple of local men were questioned, including another neighbor, Mr. Kent.*

(Days later, I spoke to Informant X, who told me that Mr. Kent, a Names Road resident, was a pervert. X had dated one of the Kents' kids and said the dad liked to go to the porn movies at the Rochester Drive-In across the road from the airport. The Rochester's movie screen faced away from the road, so it could show porn films without causing accidents. According to X, the dad went all the time, and the next day he made *comments*. X had once visited the Kents with a two-year-old niece in tow. Kent looked at the little girl and said, "Nice body. She is going to make a great little stripper." The kids were all familiar to me, but I knew nothing of the old man. I asked what the dad's first name was and jotted it down. Corky Bernhard had been right. The neighborhood was crawling with creeps.) As was true of many Ballantyne residents, Tracy found that the Fear, once it came, never really went away. "I know that I only went down to the trestle once in all my teen years, and I was scared to death."

Tracy said that, like Alice Bernhard, she believed Jack Starr did it. She remembered that police talked to a man named Cleary* who lived nearby. "Mr. Cleary was a perv, and I know that for a fact," she said.

Regarding Clint Wilson, she said, "I was good friends with both of his daughters. Still am with one of them, Joni. I knew him. He's dead now. He belonged to the Hells Angels and was a scary guy. He was married to Francine Morton. He was always nice to me, though."

A woman named Susan Bickford responded to the investigation's e-mail address, writing that she knew the girls from school. "We were friendly, not friends." She wrote. "George-Ann struck me as smart but not focused. She was quick and flirty and always laughing. She got pregnant during our freshman year. She never looked embarrassed or ashamed during that time or after. If it was an act, it was a good one. I was kind of horrified and mystified that she would be like that. She disappeared for several months but then came back, sassy as ever. It seems odd now, but I never once wondered who the father was.

"Kathy seemed self-conscious. After eighth grade she was always absent. During summer '66, I went off on a Girl Scout camping trip, and when we came back everyone was whispering that George-Ann and Kathy were missing. At least amongst the girls, there were several who suggested—nudge, nudge—that they had run away. I think we were in Vermont at our family summer place when their bodies were found. I read all the stories when I got back. When school started again, it was as though they never existed. No memorial service, nothing. I went on to get a great education (Hamilton, then Pratt), jumped into the high-tech revolution in Silicon Valley, and have had a blessed life. I now do consulting in high tech. I'm dedicating my first novel to them. It's a thriller."

On August 31, I received a response from Gary H. Sedore with the Friends of Mount Hope Cemetery regarding the location of Kathy's grave. He wrote, "Interred on July 23, 1966 at 16 years of age. The cause of death is listed as 'multiple incised wounds of the body.'"

The next morning I spoke with Tom Wiest, who was responding to Alice's TV appearance. Tom said that he shared Alice's feelings: "It seemed to my wife and I that the whole thing got swept under the rug." He lived near Geneseo now, but grew up in Henrietta, just on the other side of the river from Ballantyne. Eighteen at the time of the murders, a typical summer day involved stopping at Coop's store on the east end of the Ballantyne Bridge and then going to Black Creek to swim. On

Sunday, June 26, 1966, however, Tom and his friends swam instead at "the Swing" on the Genesee River, on the Scottsville Road side, 300 yards south of Greyson Road.

That afternoon, Sheriff's Deputy Frank Hall pulled up and asked them about the missing girls. Yeah, they knew them, but they didn't know where they were. The deputy sought volunteers for a search team, and everyone was in.

They went home, changed clothes, and met up at the Castle Inn. In Tom's search group were Deputy Hall, Mitch Owens, Ted Callaghan, and Alice Bernhard, the sister, not the mom. They searched from Genesee Junction almost all the way to Archer Road.

Tom recalled that you could get from Scottsville Road to the swimming hole—trestle to trestle—by car, but you couldn't get from the swimming hole to Archer Road. That westward trek demanded knowledge of the area. Sure, the girls could have been giving the driver directions, but if privacy was the only thing they were seeking, they didn't need to move far, if at all. They were already in a secluded and private spot. If they wanted to smoke pot or drink beer or have sex, they could have done it right there, or just a few feet into the woods. They didn't have to go two miles west to Archer Road.

During that initial search, Tom's group saw no one else and found nothing. He now realized that they came within 100 yards of the spot where the bodies were later found. Tom was just as glad that they didn't make the discovery, with sister Alice being there and all. That was the sort of thing that could scar a person forever.

I asked if he had any ideas as to what happened to the girls. He said, like everyone else, "I heard that Jack did it." No need for a last name. Unlike some of the other Jack-did-it people I'd talked to, however, Tom actually knew Jack.

"I knew him to talk to. He was different. Tried to be a tough guy. Jack was a bad boy, and he could have been a rapist, but I don't think he was learned enough to commit a pair of murders in that way."

"In what way?" I asked.

"Well, you know. The guy mutilated Kathy, cut off her breasts, and he gave George-Ann, I guess you'd say he gave her a hysterectomy. I heard that, after the murders, the cops were leaning on Jack so much that he lost his temper at the Red Creek [a bar on Jefferson Road] and beat up a couple of cops."

Wiest described the victims. "Kathy was quiet but nice," he said. He couldn't be positive, of course, but he didn't think Kathy was sexually active. Tom's girlfriend, later his wife, was Sharon Luke, who lived on Charles Avenue, a couple of blocks south of Names Road. He and Sharon were friends forever with sister Alice.

George-Ann was kind of smart-alecky, Wiest thought, but she didn't give off whore vibes. People said she was wild because she had a baby, but he wasn't sure he believed that.

"For all I know," Tom said, "Jack raped her, and that was her only sexual experience." A benefit of the doubt, I thought, that few were willing to give her.

Wiest said that Jack died in the early 1990s of AIDS. Six people died of AIDS from the old neighborhood, some friends of his. They all died at about the same time. It could have been one contaminated needle that wiped them all out, Wiest figured.

How did he know that Jack was the father of George-Ann's baby? Common knowledge. His wife's sister Sandy, who was now married and lived in Massachusetts, was in the same class with the girls and knew them well.

Wiest worked for 27 years for the Town of Henrietta, and also as a "sort of private investigator" helping adoptees find their natural parents. He had many friends in the RPD and had "over 100 finds." He told me that it would not have been necessary for George and Ruth to adopt George-Ann's son, if that was what anyone thought they did, because as grandparents they could just assume custody.

He was a friend of Gus D'April, who had worked the case. He volunteered his services to help with the investigation and said he would try to get me an interview with Gus.

I told him that, with the Formicolas all long gone from Ballantyne, I hadn't been able to find a photo of George-Ann. I asked if his wife had a 1965 or 1966 Wheatland-Chili yearbook, as George-Ann had her photo in one or both of them. He said he'd try the school and the town library to see if they had copies.

The next time I spoke to him he had the photos of the girls, but his scanner was on the fritz, so he needed my snail mail address to send the hard copy to me. While we were talking, he dislodged a couple of other nuggets. They were both in the 1965 yearbook, and neither was in the 1966.

Sandy Luke, he said, saw the girls on the evening they disappeared, although nothing suspicious was going on. They encountered each other on the Ballantyne Bridge. The girls said they were on their way to Coop's. The cops didn't know about that because no cop ever spoke with Sandy.

The other: "Did I tell you about the time me and a buddy of mine almost shot John Bernhard?"

"I think you forgot."

"He worked at the junkyard on West Henrietta Road. The place was called Ajax Auto Parts, owned by brothers, Sam and Ollie Stein. One time Dave Burnetti* and I went there to target shoot. We found an old abandoned school bus and shot it up until it looked like Swiss cheese. Then the door opened and out staggered John Bernhard, drunk; he'd been sleeping in the bus. How he didn't get shot I'll never know."

Just how much of a ghost town was the Genesee Junction? We knew that it had been, even in my lifetime, a busy railroad hub. It looked like a town on old maps, but had there been residents? Exactly how did the turntable work? And when did it all go away?

On September 2, I found a website that traced the history of the location from the railroad standpoint, but it was light on dates.[1] The Genesee Junction, it said, was the junction of the east–west tracks, originally used by the New York, Westshore, and Buffalo Railroad, which later changed its name to the New York Central, and the north–south tracks were built on the old Genesee Valley Canal towpath and were used by the Pennsylvania Railroad. Those tracks, of course, had been inactive since 1973 and gone since 1977. The path atop a flood-proof ridge was now part of the Genesee Valley Greenway hiking trail. Today, the New York Central tracks are still used by the Livonia, Avon, and Lakeville Railroad.[2]

A blogger named Charles Woolever interviewed a New York Central historian about the turntable and learned that it was used for trains that were traveling back and forth between Rochester and Syracuse. The historian said the turntable had stopped being used by World War II because new larger engines made it obsolete.[3]

Internet maps recognized Genesee Junction as a place, a town even. Call up Chili on Google Maps, and Genesee Junction is labeled as if it were a village. The Internet will tell you where the nearest hotels to

Genesee Junction are. I could see it on the old maps, when it was still a functioning train station. But today? It's a dirt road through the weeds.

An examination of a 1902 Chili map showed that just about everything we today consider "Ballantyne" was part of the Edwin Loder Estate.[4] His glue factory was on the east bank of the Genesee River about a mile south of the city line. And he was elected in 1889 to the New York State Assembly representing Monroe County's third district. He owned all of the land from the river westward, to about halfway between the Pennsylvania and B&O Railroads, from Black Creek all the way south to well below Names Road. The map showed Ballantyne Road as Mosquito Point Road, but the car-and-carriage bridge across the river was already known as the "Ballantine Bridge," named after Anna Ballantine, who owned a large piece of land off the River Road (now Scottsville Road) about a mile south of Mosquito Point Road.

George Formicola repaired cars for the New York Central Railroad. The job was convenient for George, as he could report to work just a few hundred yards from his home, and only feet away from where his daughter had last gone swimming. When his daughter Gina married Keith Wilson, George got Keith a job working on the railroad as well. Gina used to brag to my mom that Keith would blow the whistle when he passed Genesee Junction to say hi to her.

On September 12, 2011, I spoke with my second-grade teacher, Muriel Dech—who had also been the second-grade teacher of Kathy and George-Ann, as well as "Jackie" Starr. We chatted about me in second grade—not her favorite, she joked, I think—and the previous day's ceremonies remembering the tenth anniversary of 9/11. Then we settled back to 1966. Muriel had a chronology of the girls' last hours that disagreed with what anyone had told me before. She said that, after their hot dogs and milk, the girls didn't go back to the creek but decided to go to the Castle Inn to ask Kathy's dad for money. The last anyone saw them, they were on Scottsville Road headed toward the Castle Inn.

"Where did you hear this story, Muriel?" I asked.

"Joyce Judd told me. She must've gotten it from Alice."

This piece fit. The newspapers had reported that the girls were last seen walking on Scottsville Road. Tom Wiest's sister-in-law saw the girls crossing the Ballantyne Bridge on the way to Coop's store. It would

rise from the ashes like a phoenix, so to speak. Many people use journals or use other forms of expressive art to release some of their feelings."

I was cool with that.

When 20 workdays had passed, I called the Records Access Office of the MCSO and asked when I could expect a yea or nay regarding my Freedom of Information request. A lady said she would look into that for me, and more time passed.

It was October before I could once again feel optimistic. I received a call from Marilyn Randall, mother of my schoolmate MaryAnne Curry and the former wife of Wayne Randall, the MCSO employee I interviewed years ago on this subject. She was also a friend of Muriel Dech, my second-grade teacher. Marilyn told me that she knew a guy who was retired from the MCSO, and he was sympathetic to Alice's plight and wanted to help. On his own initiative, he had "contacted the sheriff's historian." I was to expect a package. The historian was Bill Clemens (or Clements—she wasn't sure of the spelling), and the informant was Bill's neighbor.

While waiting for my package, I made some progress on the Internet. I learned that Clint Wilson Jr., born 1941, lived in Avon, New York, in 1959 when he was arrested for third-degree burglary for twice entering the home of George Rhode in Livonia. This same Clint Wilson, now listed as living on Tuscarora-Groveland Road in Mount Morris, still 18, was arrested for reckless driving in May of 1960. This individual, now listed as living in Leroy, New York, and Rochester, died at the age of 49 on January 29, 1991.

Hours later I learned that Jack Starr died on June 26, 1992, the day after the 26th anniversary of the Chili murders. Jack's dad died in 1994, his mom a year later.

Don Campbell, volunteering for Alice's cause, traveled with his wife from his home in Buffalo to the Rundel Library in Rochester, where he found and copied newspaper articles from the period when the girls were missing. He found Jack's obit but not Clint's, then visited Mount Hope Cemetery, where he located and photographed Kathy's grave. Jack's obit said his daughter, son, and grandson survived him, and he was an army veteran.

12

PAT PATTERSON

I sent a copy of my notes on the Genesee Junction murders to Pat Patterson, with whom I'd worked on my book *Killer Twins*. Pat had been an investigator for the Chemung County Sheriff's Office in the early 1970s. He worked there for 11 years, and then for 4 more years as an investigator in the Chemung County District Attorney's Office. Going to school the whole time, he earned an MS degree in education at Elmira College. In 1975, while a county cop, he attended the FBI's National Academy for a law enforcement training program. He was elected sheriff of Chemung County for two years, and then the FBI recruited him. He became an FBI special agent in 1983 and worked for the Buffalo, Pittsburgh, and Baltimore divisions. After 9/11, he worked a few "hairy gigs" in Europe and South America and was eventually named agent in charge in San Antonio where he stayed until he retired.

On September 21, I heard back from Patterson, who, as expected, told me that, for all my fussing around, I hadn't learned much of value. He said my primary problem was that "there are a good number of suspects who could have committed the murders but little evidence you can talk about. Unfortunately, you don't have access to the evidence or the investigative reports. That's like a blind man riding a horse at full speed—almost anything can trip you up. I also suspect the investigative reports may be a little sparse considering the time and the level of sophistication of the Monroe County Sheriff's Office of the 1960s, which may be a reason for their reluctance to release any information. If this were truly an open case, I would suspect they have someone working other angles of the investigation, which is doubtful. I also suspect they have concluded that Shawcross committed the crime but don't want to make any official termination of the case on that fact. It would be embarrassing if someone popped up and confessed to the crime. In that he is dead, the case will just sit on the shelf forever, with no attention or official termination. I would suspect they have terminated other cases they attribute to Shawcross but were unable to prosecute for various reasons."

Then he zoned in on my attempts to "document rumors." Too many conclusions based on rumors, sometimes conclusions based on rumors based on other rumors. The most egregious of this guilt-by-assumption was the rumor that Jack Starr had confessed on his deathbed. Leaving it as something Alice's neighbor told her because she'd heard it from a girl who was there "wouldn't do." I moved talking to Mrs. Werner up on my priority list.

What I didn't say to Pat was that I found the neighborhood's ability to create its own myths fascinating, even though I realized it was mostly valueless from an investigatory viewpoint. You asked a Ballantyner who killed the girls, and they all had an answer. No one yet had shrugged and said, "Who knows?" Everyone had a face connected to that mystery, the face of a person now dead.

Pat continued, "You may not have certain facts which would control your direction. For instance, were the breasts of the victims removed or was there vaginal mutilation? Was the victim's vagina removed? What were the specifics beyond the chest and neck wounds? Were there apparent human bite marks on the victims? Considering the time between the period when the children went missing and when they were found, there may have been significant bloating. That might give the appearance of wounds to the skin, which may just be a result of swelling and bloating. The medical examiner's report would clarify these facts. This was a summer case that extended over several weeks. The bodies were in the advanced stages of decomposition. Just a few days in the summer can cause significant decomposition. Was there evidence the children were held elsewhere for a period of time and then brought back and dumped? It sounds as if this may have been an assault that happened quickly, with the suspect leaving the area close to the termination of the crime. There was some indication that one of the victims' bathing suits may have been put back on. Have the victims' clothing been sufficiently preserved to accommodate present DNA testing? Did it appear that the victims were staged or just dumped where they were found? Crime scene photographs may shed light on this question. Were there 13 to 14 stab wounds to the chest, and was one of the throats cut almost to decapitation? That would indicate a person with a significant amount of rage and hatred toward the victim, violence beyond controlling or killing."

Patterson brought up one point I hadn't considered, that wounds presumed to have been part of the crime might actually have been part of the decomposition, or even animal activity.

Patterson concluded that the killer was likely sexually sadistic: "If this is the case, there may be one or more common traits you might want to look for in your various possible suspects' other crimes for commonalities to this case, such as a style and pattern to their killings that involved domination, control, humiliation, and sadistic sexual violence; the attack is methodical and repeated from one victim to another; victims are chosen at random and the murders carried out in almost an obsessive or compulsive manner; souvenirs of the crime may be taken (organs, articles of clothing, etc.); the suspect has complex sexual fantasies; may impersonate law enforcement (exercising control over the victim); abduction of victim to a predetermined location; victims are most likely strangers; often use binding to control the victim; the offender displayed aggressive and antisocial behaviors during their childhood, like torturing and killing small animals, fire starting, or attacks on other children; bed wetting into adolescence or sexual molestation or dysfunction in the family; little or no remorse for the act; and type of weapon used, just to name a few traits.

"The question is: What other motives would fit the fact pattern other than that of a sexual assault? Who is the father of the one victim's child? Did they follow up on possible incest in the families? There had to be a vehicle involved. One killer or two?

"I don't think you can draw any conclusions on the number of attackers based on what you have described. The attacker could have subdued the girls in other ways—intimidation, law enforcement impersonation, a ruse, binding the victims, display of a firearm, etc."

Patterson suggested that I should be concentrating on learning all I could about the Shawcross crime scenes. "Match your suspect's other crimes to the physical evidence or MO in this case, and I think you'll find your most likely killer." Stating an absolute, he concluded, "Multiple sexually motivated crimes committed by the same person always have similarities."

And so I set out to do a systematic analysis of Shawcross's MO and homicidal signatures.[1] The Chili murders had some things in common with the Shawcross methodology: quick kills, sexual mutilation, all the victims killed in a car or outdoors, proximity to waterways, bridges, and railroad tracks.

There were also key differences. All but one of Shawcross's were by manual strangulation (he killed one by hitting her with a log), whereas police believed George-Ann and Kathy were killed with a knife. The girls' murders would have preceded the others by five years, and when serial killers do change their method of killing, the evolution usually goes from the messy to the neat, as would be the case here. Also, it should be noted that Shawcross's description of his first murders, which he said occurred in Vietnam, involved young girls bathing and being killed with a knife. There is also the possibility that the killer used a soft strangulation method on the Chili victims, asphyxiating them without breaking their hyoid bones. The knife wounds could have been administered postmortem, and because of decomposition the medical examiner couldn't tell. I wouldn't know until I got inside the initial investigation.

Also, Shawcross's other murders were all singles. If Shawcross was the killer, he never again took on two victims at once. Again, this could merely be a sign of learning, evolving as a killer. Two victims, especially scrappy ones, might have presented unanticipated problems.

Not only was there no evidence that Shawcross was even in Monroe County on the night the girls disappeared, but maybe the best argument *against* Shawcross as the Chili killer is that serial killers as a rule start killing close to home and commit their crimes further away as they go along. In that sense, the Watertown murders resembled the start of a killing career. But a look at the big picture reveals that none of his known killings involved encountering a victim more than two or three miles from home. In that sense, the Chili murders would have been very different, but he was much younger as well, 21 and driving a hot car, a souped-up 1958 Pontiac that had once belonged to the county sheriff's department. According to his own scenario for the time period, he was trying to avoid his wife, with whom he was breaking up, and "searching" for girls to "pick up and have sex with," and wanderlust may have taken him to the Genesee River and its attractively remote tributaries. It is not a new concept to suppose Shawcross killed before his Watertown murders. His wife in the 1970s told police that she'd often wondered if Shawcross hadn't been a killing machine for some time, not just the horrific stories he told about Vietnam, but when he was stationed in Oklahoma after returning from overseas as well (September 1968–spring 1969).

He had a few methods for finding prey. When his victims were prostitutes, he picked them up on the street, usually in a car, then led them to a secluded place, often near water and a bridge, to kill them and dispose of their bodies. His Watertown murders, however, involved camping out in a secluded place and waiting for victims to wander onto the scene, in one case in a woods and in another by a bridge at the bank of a river. Certainly the Chili killer could have been lying in wait somewhere in the Genesee Junction area when George-Ann and Kathy were wandering around. Killers who sought out their victims in this manner often referred to the process as they would if they'd climbed a tree awaiting a wandering buck. Shawcross liked victims he could physically dominate. Check. And he liked brunettes. Check. Kathy may have earned bonus points. Her hair was black.

Criminal profilers divide murder into four components of killer behavior: (1) antecedent behavior and planning, (2) the act of murder, (3) body disposal, and (4) postcrime behavior.[2] Regarding component 1, profilers have come to believe that a serial killer's victims are rarely chosen at random, and even those that seem random may fall into a clear pattern if investigators only had the key to the killer's criteria. It appeared on the surface that, based on victim choice, the Chili murders were drastically different from the Watertown murders, which in turn differed from the Rochester murders. Shawcross shifted from a little boy to a little girl to hookers. But gender and age may have been secondary characteristics as far as he was concerned. The victims had something in common: they were all small in stature and easy to physically control. There were large prostitutes in Rochester, and we know by his choices in wives and girlfriends that he was sexually attracted to large women, but all of his victims were under 5'6". None weighed more than 120 pounds. There were blonde and redheaded prostitutes in Rochester, as well, but Shawcross only chose the ones with dark hair.

The antecedent behavior most likely to lead to murder was conflict with a female, parental conflict, and financial, employment, and marital problems. Shawcross's wife wouldn't allow him to give her oral sex. What more symbolic response than to kill a girl and steal her vagina, which could be eaten—figuratively or literally—at his leisure?

Every detail of a killer's crime reveals personality. Sociopathic killers have a warped view of dominion. Because the world has been unfair to them, they feel they deserve the right to do as they please, regardless of the senselessness of it or the damage it causes. As children, killers as a rule do not recall ever fantasizing about happy things. When their imaginations were at work, they traveled to the darkest places. These children, when they do play with others, will tend to take charge of the play and "cast" playmates as extensions of their sick fantasies. Playmates don't last long under those circumstances. FBI studies verify our intuitive conclusion that these future killers, when they run out of people to play with, turn to animals. Childhood cruelty to animals—along with abuse of other children, destructive play patterns, disregard for others, fire setting, and stealing and destroying property—is considered a primary indicator that a person may one day become a murderer.

Killers are found to be more likely than nonkillers to have fetishes. They may eroticize objects like women's shoes, underwear, and rope. In these cases, the fetish items tend to be included in their crime scenes.

Sex killers as a rule have problems with normal sexual relationships. It is not uncommon for a sex killer's first rape to also be his first real sexual act.

One way in which Shawcross distinguished himself from other killers was that he did not drink or use drugs. More than half of sex killers had been drinking at the time of the crime. Others were taking drugs instead of or in addition to alcohol. If Shawcross committed the Chili murders, we can be fairly certain he was sober. Jack Starr, on the other hand, often drank at the Castle Inn near where the girls had been seen earlier that evening. Clint Wilson was drunk all the time according to witnesses, and he became meaner as he drank.

Not all of the killers studied by the FBI mutilated their victims after the murders, but those that did considered the mutilation the "ultimate expression of their perversion." In almost all cases, the mutilation occurred postmortem. Once the victim was dead, the killer felt that he had "ultimate control." The mutilation sometimes occurred just after the murder, but in other cases, the killer returned to the scene of the crime to further play with the corpse. Genital mutilation and breast amputation accounted for most of the mutilation, which were also the wounds that, according to unofficial sources, were inflicted on the Chili victims. Psychologists believe that genital mutilation is an attempt by the killer to remove gender identification from the victims and render them nonfemale. Of course, Shawcross said that he mutilated the genitals of his only known male victim as well.

Profilers find insight into a killer's personality by the means of body disposal. What state is the body in? What is the location of the dump site? We didn't know all of the details regarding the Chili dump site, but we knew it resembled other Shawcross dump sites. The bodies were hidden in bushes. That was very Shawcross-like. He always sought to put time between the disposal of his victims and the discovery of their remains. Because the dump site was so far from home, it is likely that, if he was the killer, all of the postmortem mutilations occurred immediately following the murders.

Can we link Shawcross to the Chili murders based on their similarity to Shawcross's Vietnam fantasies? It's a theory with a shaky foundation. Experience tells us that all sex mutilation cases and fantasies have certain things in common. Any sex mutilator—they are rare but not unique—would have cut the vagina and breasts. Many would practice or fantasize cannibalism. The prototypical mutilation killer, Jack the Ripper, left behind crime scenes with much in common to the Archer Road dump site.

Alice was convinced that the killer undressed the girls, cut them up, and then put the bathing suits back on. If true, this might indicate that the bathing suit itself had something to do with the killer's fantasy and might point an investigation more in the direction of John I. Miller than toward Shawcross. Many (but not all) of Shawcross's victims were found face down.

Did the Chili killer take souvenirs with him after the murders? George-Ann's bathing suit bottoms would have been a prime candidate for a souvenir, yet they were found near her remains. Discounting body parts, as far as I knew the only item never found was Kathy's towel with a picture of a woman in a bathing suit on it.

I learned that the father of John I. Miller's murder victim, Samuel R. Behney Sr., died on January 10, 2003, at the age of 76. He had three surviving children, Samuel, Sandra, and Susan. I located addresses for Samuel Jr. and Sandra and wrote them letters. On October 24, Sandra called me. She said she didn't know if Miller was still alive. I told her about the Miller I found near where she grew up, and it was the first she'd heard of it. She said she'd made an attempt to locate him three or four years earlier and had reached a dead end. She had long wanted to write about "the most horrible day of her life." She remembered every detail of that day, but she wasn't sure yet if she wanted to say it all out loud.

In October, I spoke to Mrs. Marcia Werner, Alice Bernhard's neighbor and reported archenemy. According to Alice, Mrs. Werner had said that Jack Starr confessed to the murders on his deathbed. Mrs. Werner had a slight European accent, and she said Alice got the story all wrong. It had nothing to do with Jack Starr. She was friends with a Mrs. Steinmiller who lived on Archer Road—very close to the dump site—and had a dress shop in her garage. Her husband was an MCSO deputy. Mrs. Steinmiller told Mrs. Werner that she had a best friend whose husband was a vice principal at a local school (she wasn't sure which), and a few years after the murders, this VP confessed to his wife that he'd killed the girls and the next day committed suicide by shooting himself.

Mrs. Steinmiller told Mrs. Werner that this guy was drinking at the Castle Inn on the evening of the murders and decided to go home "the back way," that is, on the dirt road along the tracks, and that was how he encountered the girls.

The story seemed to have a thread of truth to it. I determined, for example, that the Steinmillers really did live on Archer Road and that, though both had passed away, their son Douglas C. Steinmiller had owned the house until 2004. The house had been sold three times in the past 10 years.

This was not the first time the name Steinmiller had come up. Larry Rath told me that one of the cops he knew who had worked the case was Dave Steinmiller. Rath also said he knew nothing about a suspect committing suicide. Was the story Mrs. Steinmiller's fabrication, just so she'd have something to say when people asked her? Or had Dave Steinmiller confided inside info to his wife?

Mrs. Werner did not remember telling the reporter in 1966 that she'd been over to the Bernhards' on the afternoon of June 25 and that Kathy was telling her younger sisters that they were going to go to the movies that day. She *did* remember seeing Kathy walking out of her driveway and onto Names Road wearing her bathing suit with a towel wrapped around her waist. Mrs. Werner asked her where she was going, and Kathy said she was going swimming back by the trestle.

On a Saturday night I spoke to Johnny Rowe, who was born in 1949 and lived at the corner of Names and Lester Streets, just a couple of houses away from the Bernhards, until he was 12. Johnny then moved to the other side of the river, where he became legendary as the baddest of all badasses. He and his brothers were the most feared guys around. Johnny was not only a live wire with a hair-trigger temper, but he was a seventh-degree black belt. Once, when they tried to kick him out of the Castle Inn, he did a backflip and kicked out the light above the pool table. When he was a kid the guys from the east bank of the Genesee used to fight the guys from the west bank, but when Johnny Rowe moved from one to the other, he got both banks to unite, and they fought together as the River Rats. "I learned how to fight in the Castle Inn," he said. Rowe came by his fighting skills honestly. His dad, Johnny Rowe Sr., had been a boxer who worked at the Genesee Brewery, where he was for some time a coworker of Corky Bernhard. Johnny Jr. had gotten in trouble after a bar fight. He was ashamed to say that he'd used a weapon on a guy, a broken bottle. When he got out of prison, he worked as a martial arts teacher, teaching kids to defend themselves without a weapon. That was how he made amends.

He had a brother who did time for manslaughter. "The guy jumped on my brother's knife," Johnny said. His brother only stabbed the guy once, and at the autopsy they said four stab wounds. Rowe knew the name of the guy who'd done the actual killing, the killing his brother did time for, but he'd split for Mexico and hadn't returned. Rowe once had a list of guys who were going to die before he did, but after he found the Lord he forgave them.

He'd thought about being a cop when he was a kid, but he was too short. He'd spent a lot of years thinking like a criminal, but he hadn't forgotten how to think like a cop.

Johnny told me that Alice shouldn't worry about Kathy being forgotten, that he thought about her all the time. He remembered the murders very well. In fact, who did it had been something that had puzzled him and troubled him for years. He was 17 when it happened, and now he was 62. He'd done time. He was a physically battered man with a broken neck that was supposed to have paralyzed him, but he walked out of the hospital after the Lord healed him. He'd had hepatitis C for 38 years. He'd never done needle drugs, so he knew he must've caught it when getting a tattoo at the state fair in Syracuse in 1973. Now doctors couldn't find the hepatitis in his blood anymore. That set him on the straight and narrow path. He now was a minister who married people for free, worked with homeless people, and mailed out Bibles. He'd been married four times. Now he was happily married to a beautiful woman, with four grown kids and grandkids.

Johnny said he was pretty sure that Jack Starr was behind the murders. Either he did them or he paid someone to do them. He'd raped George-Ann and—for whatever reason, something to do with her getting pregnant—now he was going to kill her. Kathy just had the misfortune of being there.

He said Jack was "insane, totally bonkers." Rowe recalled seeing him "tearing his own hair out."

I asked him if he knew Clint Wilson, and he admitted not well. He knew he'd been a Hacker and then an Angel and that his biker name was "Ace."

"He didn't fit in," Rowe said. "He didn't hang out."

The Angel he'd known the best was Blackfoot—they called him that because he was a Blackfoot Indian—who was a Ballantyne kid and died from natural causes, a hole in his heart. Rowe rode in his funeral procession, which was huge. The Angels had wanted Rowe, but he said no. He didn't need 20 guys fighting his fights for him.

Rowe said that once he'd been at a party and was messing around with a Ouija board. He asked it who killed the girls, and it spelled out the name "Ryan Hill." Rowe said he knew a Ryan Hill* but considered it unlikely that it was the guy, because he hardly seemed the type.

He told me that Jack Starr did not ride a motorcycle. Instead he drove a black Corvette that he eventually totaled at Wehle's Curve on Scottsville Road, an accident that he walked away from despite the fact that he'd been surrounded only by fiberglass when he crashed.

"I think the police knew that Jack did it," Rowe commented. "But they didn't have enough to put him away."

Exactly 24 hours later, Rowe called me back and told me he'd had a revelation. "It hit me like a rock. Nothing like this has ever happened to me before," he said. Rowe's revelation was that Jack paid off a couple of guys to do the murder for him, and that way he could make sure he had an alibi. One of those guys had to be Ricky Donahue, who was Jack's age, weighed 200 to 220 pounds, and was always chasing girls. Donahue once punched himself in the eye so he could sue somebody. He grew up on Ballantyne Road, across the street from the Owens. He lived in one of those families where all the kids were foster kids. He was the foster brother of a girl named Robin Atwell. The other was Don Riechel, who was a "stupid guy, had a plate in his head," weighed 250, also Jack's age. He owed $5,000 to Gary Barnes,* who lived in the neighborhood. Both Riechel and Donahue were fighters. (Ballantyne girl Mary Wilkey verified that Riechel had a plate in his head, stemming from a fall "either in or into" the Grand Canyon that left him with a severely cracked skull.)

After speaking with Rowe I phoned Don Riechel. He seemed of normal intelligence, and he bragged about his fighting prowess. He said that back in 1966 the neighborhood was quiet but tough, and he and his brother Butch ran the neighborhood. Guys from other areas knew better than to come in and step on Ballantyne turf because if they did they were going to get hurt. Riechel remembered Johnny Rowe well.

I asked him if Jack Starr was his friend, and he said, "Yes and no. Jackie was a weirdo, his mannerisms and so forth. He was an asshole, pardon my French. He was domineering with his women. His girlfriend had bruises and then she was dead. He was about 22 back then, and she was 13. That was considered perverted, very much so." Riechel's theory was that Jack wanted a threesome with George-Ann and Kathy and lost his temper when they said no. "He flew off the handle really easy." Riechel verified that Jack drove a series of Corvettes, the first of which might've been around 1966. It was the kind of car girls would get into even if the driver was a creep.

"Cops knew Jack did it, just couldn't prove it," Riechel said.

Riechel admitted that by the time of the murders he had moved out of his parents' house and into the city, so he couldn't comment on whether Jack's behavior changed after the murders. He said that his father, James Riechel, took Nicky Starr under his wing, and when Nicky was killed in Vietnam he was buried right next to Don's dad. He said he'd been to a lot of parties back by the trestle. The parties, he said, were not back by the dirt road but right there at the swimming hole. They usually built campfires next to the creek. That was where the teenagers would converge. He concluded by saying I should talk to Gary Barnes.

The first member of Jack Starr's extended family who cooperated with my investigation was Lisa Owens, who referred to Jack as her "step-uncle." She told me that the family had always wondered if he did it because he was mentally unstable and "George-Ann's boyfriend." She thought that George-Ann had tried to break up with him, and that might have been the motive. Like Johnny Rowe, Lisa said that Jack drove a Corvette, but she remembered it as red. "There were stories that he washed and cleaned up that car and that he had mud and cornfield stuff on his undercarriage. The way he died and lived his life afterward, a drug addict, made me always feel he was responsible. Only God knows the truth." She told me I should talk to her mom, Jean. Lisa said, "She is very open about what she knows. She may tell you a lot. She definitely had her doubts about him." I asked her what her grandfather Nicholas did for a living, and she said that, in addition to holding public office, he worked for Delco in the city, a huge facility that manufactured parts for General Motors, and that was where he met his second wife. (The huge, abandoned, and arson-scarred Delco plant still stands on Whitney Street near Lyell Avenue, looking like a perfect setting for a ghost hunt or a horror movie.) Lisa remembered her mother talking about Jack having "done it" back when she was little, probably right around the time of the murders. Lisa was seven that year. She remembered her mother and father talking about it, saying how Jack had to clean up his car, inside and out, the day after the girls disappeared. Jack's car looked like it had been "driven through a cornfield."

Lisa's mom also talked about Jack being the murderer years later when Jack had become a family problem, addicted to heroin and stealing from Lisa's grandfather Nicholas.

Then, on the morning of November 1, everything changed. The Records Access Office of the MCSO called to inform me that they'd decided to release the files regarding the Chili murders. Xeroxing had commenced, and I should expect a package.

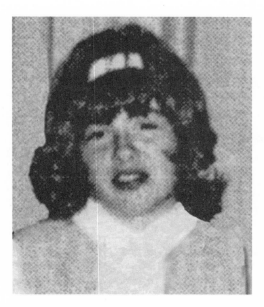

George-Ann at 13, wearing makeup and perhaps already pregnant. Was the father of her baby also her murderer? (Detail of a 1965 yearbook photo)

Kathy, looking more feminine and confident not long before her death. (Photo courtesy Alice Bernhard)

The former site of Genesee Junction, looking east toward the Genesee River. In 1966 it was still sparsely populated with railroad personnel, but not so much on a Saturday evening. (Photo by Philip Semrau)

Looking west from the Genesee Junction. One spur of track up ahead would turn left, join the B&O track before it crossed Ballantyne Road. The road turned left also. The other track continued on straight without a road to the scene of the dumpsite. (Photo by Philip Semrau)

One of the last places Kathy and George-Ann were seen was swimming in Black Creek, next to this picturesque and ancient stone trestle. A ghost town, the former site of a train station called Genesee Junction was only sixty feet away on the other side of the creek. The girls were expected home by dark, but were never seen alive again. They had with them only their bathing suits, towels, and Kathy's AM/FM transistor radio. (Photo by author)

The lovers' lane off Archer Road along the railroad tracks. The killer pulled in here to dispose of their bodies. (Photo by Philip Semrau)

Chronicle

METROPOLITAN EDITION

Sketch your world exactly as it goes.—Byron

MORNING, JULY 21, 1966

10 CENTS

'S SPACE WALK

2 Missing Girls Found Murdered

George Ann Formicola

Catherine Bernhard

By TOM RYAN

The bodies of two teen-age girls, missing from their Chili homes since June 25, were found in bushes in a lover's lane off Archer Road in Chili about 2:30 p.m. yesterday.

Sheriff Albert W. Skinner and other investigators termed the case a double homicide.

The dead girls were George Ann Formicola, 14, daughter of Mr. and Mrs. George W. Formicola of 15 Stallman Drive, and Catherine Ann (Kathy) Bernhard, 16, daughter of Mr. and Mrs. John Bernhard of 93 James Road. Both were students at Wheatland-Chili Central School.

Died of Stab Wounds

An autopsy revealed that both girls died of multiple stab wounds of the chest area.

There was no immediate report on whether the two had been sexually molested. This is expected to be made known later today when additional medical tests are completed. No weapon has yet been found.

A farmer, whose name wasn't released, made the grisly find and notified Sheriff's Sgt. Glenn Laille, who lives nearby.

An investigator said the farmer had detected an odor while working in a field several days ago and investigated when he smelled it again yesterday afternoon.

Wearing Bathing Suits

"He came across a shoe, then the bodies," the sheriff's aide said.

Both bodies were decomposed.

The girls had been last seen about 7:30 p.m. June 25 when they left the Bernhard's house to

DEATH SCENE — Detectives search for clues along dirt road near where bodies were found (arrow A). Road runs along railroad (B) toward Scottsville Road.

LBJ Assails Trial Threats, Offers Hanoi Conference

By DOUGLAS B. CORNELL

WASHINGTON (AP) — President Johnson assailed yesterday as revolting, repulsive and deplorable Hanoi's threats to try captured American fliers as war criminals. But he shied away from counter-threats and offered to talk instead.

"We are ready whenever the Hanoi government is ready," Johnson told a news conference.

"We are ready," he said, ". . . to sit down at a conference table under the sponsorship of the International Committee of the Red Cross, to discuss ways in which the Geneva Conventions of 1949 can be given fuller and more complete application in Viet Nam."

★ ★ ★ ★ ★

Johnson Highlights

WASHINGTON (AP) — President Johnson's comments, in brief, on major subjects at yesterday's White House news conference:

U.S. PRISONERS IN VIET NAM—"These men, who are military men, who are carrying out military assignments in line of duty against military targets, are not war criminals and should not be treated as such. The thought that these American boys have committed war crimes is deplorable and repulsive."

RACIAL RIOTING—"I hope that the lawfully constituted authorities of this country, as well as every citizen of this country, will obey the law, will not resort to violence, will do everything they can to cooperate with constituted authority to see that the evil conditions are remedied, that equality is given, and that progress is made."

The day after the bodies were found the girls made the front page, the only time they would do so. (Author's collection)

IN MEMORIAM

These two devoted friends, each with a unique personality would have graduated in 1969.

Those who were close to them will long remember their friendliness and great potential for success in life.

Catherine Bernhard
(1949-1966)

George Ann Formicola
(1951-1966)

It singeth low in every heart,

We hear it each and all,

A song of those who answer not,

However we may call;

They throng the silence of the breast,

We see them as of yore—

The kind, the brave, the true, the sweet,

Who walk with us no more.

John White Chadwick, Auld Lang Syne

The girls warranted a page in the 1969 Wheatland-Chili Central School yearbook, *The Genoatk*. Although it did not feature photos, Kathy's middle name was missing, and George-Ann's name was missing its hyphen, it was the only formal recognition the school ever made to their passing. (Author's collection)

There is new siding and a larger garage, but this is still identifiably the house where George-Ann Formicola lived her life. Her room was in the back on the left. (Photo by R. Jerome Warren)

Before the big house was built, the Bernhards lived in this building, which Alice now uses for storage. Alice says she bought it for $200 at Sears. "Ten dollars down and the rest when they caught up with me." (Photo by Philip Semrau)

John I. Miller, the man who confessed to the murder of Marsha Jean Behney didn't want to talk about where he was at the time of the Chili murders. (Artwork by Tekla Benson)

Many Ballantyne residents were convinced that this man killed the girls. He is Jack Starr,* shown here as he appeared at age 14, who became a drinker and drug-taker, a drinking buddy of Kathy's father and, he believed, the father of George-Ann's baby. (Artwork by Tekla Benson)

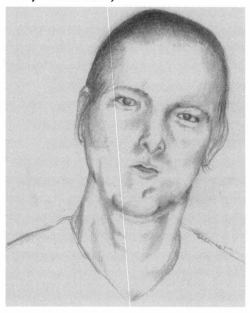

Clint Wilson*: Nothing but trouble. (Artwork by Tekla Benson)

Arthur Shawcross became known decades later as the Genesee River Killer. He claimed his killing career began in 1967 while in Vietnam when he found and butchered two teenaged "Viet Cong chicks" who were bathing in a stream. After indulging his serial-killer urges, he developed a mutilation signature and an M.O. of pretending he was a fisherman to troll for victims. (Watertown Police Department)

The Benson place as it appeared the year before the murders. The screened-in porch had yet to be built, and dirt paths through the fields connected everyone's houses. In this photo, city-boy-turned-country-homeowner Ben Benson has just killed his first snake, and it's a doozy. Check out the Rambler. It had push-button transmission. (Photo by Rita Benson)

In 2011, following the 45th anniversary of the Chili murders, Alice Bernhard and I became a team to try to find out what happened to Kathy and George-Ann. (Photo by R. Jerome Warren)

That's me at nine, photo was taken only days before the murders. I'm wearing my safety patrol belt and saying cheese outside Ballantyne School's front entrance. (Author's collection)

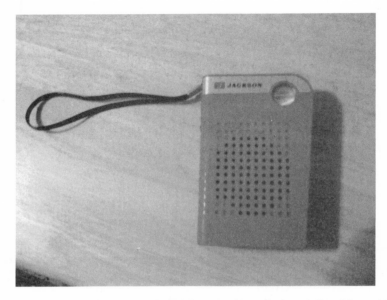

The discovery on June 26, 1966 of Kathy Bernhard's radio (much like this one) back by the swimming hole was an early and chilling indication that the girls had left the area under duress. (Photo by author)

George-Ann Formicola is buried in the Oatka Cemetery close to the base of a windmill, a beautiful setting overlooking a cornfield. (Photo by Philip Semrau)

Kathy is buried in Mount Hope Cemetery, in the City of Rochester—not far from where her mother grew up. (Photo by Don Campbell)

The pace and focus of the investigation sharpened when Private Investigator Don Tubman volunteered to help Alice Bernhard's cause. (Photo courtesy Donald A. Tubman)

13

THE FILES

On November 16, 2011, the package arrived. I read everything once—
things I now knew replacing in my mind things I had previously suspected—and called Alice to tell her the news.

"Kathy wasn't tortured," I blurted.

"Oh, thank you for telling me that."

"She went quickly. The bad stuff came after she was gone."

"I'm so relieved. Oh . . ." She said she'd been worrying about that for
45 years.

I told her I would be sending her a copy of the sheriff's report
immediately—no photos were included, so she didn't have to dread
that—but the description of what had been done to Kathy was pretty
shocking.

She made me promise that I would hold nothing back, and I said I
would send her a copy of everything I had received. I told her it had
always been my intention to treat her as a grown-up, and she said she
appreciated that.

The "files" consisted of a 29-page report, 27 pages of which—although
it wasn't strictly in chronological order—appeared to have all been
typed at once, probably sometime in 1967, as nothing in it postdated
that.

There were a handful of reports, plus a summary of the case written
in an ongoing but concise fashion. It began with the missing person

reports filed by Ruth Formicola and Alice Bernhard on Sunday morning, June 26, 1966.

The two reports agreed that the girls were last seen at the Bernhard house. Ruth wrote that George-Ann was 14 years old, 5'5", and 130 pounds, with brown eyes, light brown hair, and complexion "tan from sun."

Answering the question, "Publicity desired?" both mothers checked yes. Ruth left the "Description of Dress" section blank but wrote "None" under the heading "Money Carried."

Ruth noted that George-Ann changed clothes at the Bernhard house into a two-piece bathing suit with a red-and-white checked top and blue bottom. Both girls went swimming at the Penn Railroad bridge between Ballantyne Road and the West Shore tracks of the New York Central. Ruth wrote, "Left at 5:00 p.m."

In another hand, on Ruth's report, there was written that the parents had last seen the girls on Names Road at 7:15 p.m. There was a note to broadcast a plea on WBBF, the girls' favorite radio station, 950 on the AM dial. At that time the parents thought the girls still had a radio with them. (Next to WBBF was written the name Howard Gates, who I later learned from former WBBF DJ Larry White was a news editor and broadcaster for the station from 1962 to 1966. Gates went on to work for 25 years as the director of public relations for the Rochester Genesee Regional Transportation Authority and passed away in 2011 before I had a chance to speak with him.)

Alice's form had Kathy listed as 16 years old, 5'3", 107 pounds, with brown eyes, black hair, and "dark" complexion. Under religion, which Ruth had left blank, Alice wrote a big capital "C." Under remarks, Alice wrote, "Left house to go swimming. Left in her bathing suit, color blue, two pieces, light color blue." There was again the note in another hand that a plea would be made over WBBF. An "R. A. Walker" signed both reports at the bottom.

The first section of the summary stated that the girls had been missing since 7:30 Saturday night. They'd last been seen around a swimming hole within a mile and a half of their homes. (The actual distance was a half mile, tops.) The sheriff, at first anyway, paid no attention to witnesses who'd seen the girls up and down Scottsville Road and crossing the Ballantyne Bridge. It had occurred to me that George-Ann and

Kathy may have toured the neighborhood earlier in the day, during their first trip to the swimming hole, and this was what eyewitnesses were remembering.

The report told me that on July 20, 1966, at about 3:30 p.m., the badly decomposed bodies of the girls were found about two-tenths of a mile down a dirt road used as a lovers' lane, off Archer Road in Chili, New York, within two miles of their homes.

There was a surprise. That would have placed the bodies quite a distance further from Archer Road than I had previously believed.

The autopsy revealed that George-Ann's left breast had been cut off and that there were many stab wounds throughout the body and around her privates. Kathy's breasts were both removed, her "entire privates" removed, and her uterus had been removed. Also, there were many stab wounds about her body.

The killer, apparently, had spent more time mutilating Kathy than he had George-Ann.

Many leads, the report said, had been checked out with negative results.

Then came the details, organized by location of investigation, starting with Chili. It was again noted that the girls were "last seen at Genesee Junction, at Black Creek." At that point the girls had a transistor radio with them.

The report erroneously said that the towel and the radio were George-Ann's (although this was later corrected). Missing was a five-by-three-foot beach towel. On the towel was the figure of a girl in a swimsuit holding a large straw beach hat behind her head.

During the first days that the girls were missing, MCSO detective Lieutenant Michael Cerretto interviewed many of the girls' friends and felt that the girls had merely run off, one possible reason being that, in February 1966, George-Ann had a baby in a home for unwed mothers.

February? That was much earlier than I had thought. If the baby had gone to full term, that meant George-Ann was impregnated in May 1965. It also meant she didn't return to school for some time after giving birth.

No ifs, ands, or buts about it—the baby's father was Jack Starr. He acknowledged it. The two young people, in fact, had wanted to get married, but George-Ann's parents wouldn't hear of it.

A friend, name redacted on my copy, said George-Ann often spoke of running away and felt that she could do nothing to please her parents. The friend believed the girls ran away from home and would be located.

I'd been hoping that the police files would solve the minor mystery of who found the radio, but no such luck. The radio was found right away, during the first search of Sunday, June 26, 1966, when the girls had been gone less than 24 hours.

The nature of the search was not specified, only that the radio was found along a dirt road that led from Scottsville Road to the swimming hole, in deep grass about one foot off the road. There was no mention that it had been a neighborhood boy who found the radio, a fact found only in a newspaper report. The radio was about one and a quarter miles from where the bodies were found. Mrs. Bernhard later identified the radio as belonging to Kathy.

The report was becoming more noteworthy for the things it didn't contain. I would wait in vain for a mention of the "railroad cop" who was in the area on the night of the murders, searching for "sexual offenders" and telling "picnickers" and couples to clear out of the area.

The report described in detail the discovery of the bodies by Vincent Zuber and how quickly the dump site filled with investigatory personnel. Photographs of the scene were taken by the sheriff's identification detail.

A small white button of the type found on the sleeves of short-sleeved shirts was found under where Kathy's left hand had been. Both bodies were lying face up, 15 feet apart. They found Kathy's rubber sandals but not George-Ann's. Had the killer taken George-Ann's flip-flops as souvenirs, or had she perhaps not worn any?

The autopsy was conducted by Dr. Greendyke and attended by Detective Cerretto and Undersheriff Fenton Coakley. The bodies, it was noted, were so decomposed that they were "almost mummified."

George-Ann's left breast had been excised. She had five penetrating incised wounds of her anterior, two on her left arm, and four on her perineal area. She had incised wounds on her neck with partial transection of cervical vertebrae.

So it was George-Ann that the killer attempted to behead.

Kathy had three penetrating incised wounds of her anterior thorax, two on her left arm and hand, and two on her right arm and hand. Both girls had defensive wounds. Both had fought. That eliminated the possibility that the killer had used a soft strangulation technique to kill the girls. All mutilation wounds were postmortem—Alice was so relieved.

The report said that there was "sharp excision of breasts and perineum." I was unclear what the adjective "sharp" meant in this context. I assumed it meant "surgical," which would imply a bit of comfort with the situation and not the "mad thrusts of the blade" that had been told to a reporter by Sheriff Skinner. Also it would tend to eliminate speculation that the wounds had been caused by postmortem decomposition or animal activity.

The report noted in Kathy the absence of bladder and urethrac genitalia. Earlier in the report, it was mentioned that the uterus was removed. Here it is said that the bladder was gone. Were both correct? I reminded myself that I was not reading the coroner's report, but a summary written by a sheriff's investigator who witnessed the autopsy.

Kathy had a disarticulation and incised wound of the right ileosacrao joint. I had to look that up. An attempt had been made (with some success) to cut through the pelvis.

That was it for the autopsies. The report noted that a command post was established in the detective's office portion of the Monroe County Jail. Leads and reports from citizens were filtered through the command post for assignment to investigators. An index system was set up for the purpose of recording on cards the names and contact info of all persons interviewed or providing tips.

Cerretto was placed in charge of the investigation by orders of the sheriff. Also working the case were First Assistant District Attorney John Mastrella and Assistant District Attorney Jack B. Lazarus, both of the Monroe County district attorney's staff.

State police assigned eight men to the case.[1] The RPD assigned four unnamed detectives to the case, and the area town police departments assigned, on the average, one investigator apiece to the investigative unit. Mastrella and Cerretto were to lead the investigation.

In a joint statement, law enforcement announced that all persons to be interviewed at the jail—possible suspects or eyewitnesses—would be brought to the sheriff's private quarters, his apartment, in the front part of the jail, and there they'd be interviewed by the DA's staff with a court reporter present. All would be advised of their constitutional rights, and all that was said would be transcribed. Typists were present to make neat reports on all information obtained by the investigators, and this was then placed in book form. Much information, however, was being retained in the minds of the two ADAs and was not a matter of written record.

I had to pause and let that last sentence sink in for a moment. My assumption was that in some instances the historical record was incomplete because police did not want to create paperwork that might one day assist a killer's defense attorney. The information was now gone forever.

Tests of the soil found under the bodies failed to disclose any blood or missing body parts. The girls, they concluded, were slain somewhere else and transported to the dump site.

From the depth and width of the wounds, the medical examiner believed that the knife used was of the hunting type or a large kitchen knife, the wounds being three centimeters or one and a quarter inch in length, depth unknown.

Preliminary investigation disclosed that on that Saturday, June 25, 1966, at about 6:30 p.m., Jack Starr picked up the girls at the swimming hole in "his vehicle" and took them to Kathy's house. Starr left the Bernhard home at that time. Kathy's mom advised the girls not to eat too much as the Bernhards were having a cookout in their backyard at 9:00 p.m. and had invited neighborhood families to celebrate graduation night.

Alice later insisted that the cookout was a "family reunion" and had nothing to do with graduation. The sheriff's version didn't make sense. Who has a party to celebrate the graduation of other people's kids?

The girls said they would be gone for only an hour, but they failed to return. No report was made to the sheriff's office until about 2:30 the next morning. Then came the crux of the investigation, dealt with in great brevity: Jack Starr was fully alibied. The MCSO had checked out his activities. He had a date with an 18-year-old Ballantyne girl, Samantha Sherman.* They were together until 11:30 p.m. Starr said he was at the Bernhard residence waiting for the girls from about 7:30 to 9:00 p.m., when he left to keep his date with Sam Sherman.

Oh my. I questioned Alice about this. Alice said her memory wasn't what it used to be and she would double-check with Betty, but she was certain that Jack Starr was not at her house on the evening that the girls disappeared, and she was fairly certain that Jack Starr had *never* been to her house at any time.

I thought again of the fact that Nick Starr Sr. was a Chili politician, a man of power, and that the Bernhards lived in a shack. I thought of the fact that Alice was kept doped up during the days and weeks after the bodies were discovered, her daughters terrorized by crank phone calls.

The MCSO had a couple of sources verifying that the girls had returned to the swimming hole, just as they'd told Alice they would. First off, they were seen walking in that direction by Mr. and Mrs. John Marcille and their son Ron, who lived on the corner of Ballantyne Road and Lester Street and reported seeing the girls heading up the tracks toward the swimming hole, and once back there, they were seen by the picnickers.

The picnickers came to the jail the day the bodies were discovered. They were Felix Aquino, his wife Miriam, Albert Diaz, and Concetta Darcia. They stated they had arrived at the swimming hole for a family picnic between 5:30 and 6:00 p.m. on June 25. Upon their arrival they saw the girls swimming. At about 6:30, a "male youth," established as Jack Starr, arrived, conversed with the girls for several minutes, and then they all left in "Starr's vehicle."

I read that sentence three times. Not only was Jack Starr, a grown man, being referred to in the report as a "youth," but he was romantically linked with one of the victims and, we now know, was showing interest in the girls, getting the girls into his car, only hours before they disappeared.

At about 7:00 p.m., Felix Aquino and Albert Diaz went swimming, leaving the remainder of the party on the shore. Mrs. Aquino said that at about that time, she observed a "male [redacted], very dark." The guy was between 40 and 45 years old, 5'10", 155 to 170 pounds, wearing khaki trousers and a large straw farmer's hat, standing in the bushes looking at the Aquino party.

I ran through the possibilities for the redacted word. My best bet was that the word was "Negro." That would explain the following comment, that he was "very dark." Perhaps it was redacted simply because whoever was doing the redacting found the term potentially insensitive—although in 1966 it was not yet considered rude, certainly not by an all-white sheriff's department.

The man in the straw hat didn't have any fishing equipment in his hands. At one point he began to approach the Aquino party, aggressively enough that Mrs. Aquino reached out for a nearby machete propped up against a tree. Mrs. Aquino called for her husband, and the man disappeared into the bushes.

Mr. Diaz told investigators that, just as they were getting out of the water, he observed the same two girls who had been there previously, still wearing their bathing suits. They walked out on the stone trestle, looked around for a few seconds, and left.

And that was where that section of the written report ended. No more mention of the girls or in which direction they departed, or the man in the bushes, all of whom, we presume, were in the area at the same time. Instead of telling us when the Aquino party left, or about the movements of the parties previously described, it just ends.

The report shifted to the fact that several hundred leads had been checked with negative results. As of September 15, 1966, the major portion of the detail was secured, with Iaculli directed to remain on the detail and to work with Detective Sergeant Donald Clark of the sheriff's office. Leads continued to come in by mail and phone. All were investigated.

Investigators checked the alibis of all persons with sex perversion backgrounds.

The next section of the released files dealt with Iaculli's investigation into a list of several local men. The report noted that only the investigations that were deemed "pertinent" were written down. Again, the report began with a summary, stating that Iaculli and Clark had pursued scores of leads, all registered in a "master lead book" kept in the state police's Henrietta substation.

The first lead involved a familiar name: reported pervert Fred Kent, the Ballantyner who frightened his kids' dates with descriptions of the X-rated movies that were playing at the Rochester Drive-In. Fred Kent, the report said, had once been arrested for exposing himself. Kent, the report said, was "checked out thoroughly. Investigation disclosed that on the evening of June 25, 1966, Kent and another neighbor, Pete Crane,* chaperoned a group of neighborhood children swimming in the Genesee River." Crane was Jimmy and Mary's adoptive dad.

Another familiar name on the list was Joseph Werner, the now-deceased husband of Alice Bernhard's archenemy, the man who had painted portraits of Kathy and Patty after their deaths and who, according to one report, had once locked himself inside a dollhouse in his own backyard.

Alice told me that she knew Mr. Werner was screwy, but she also found him sweet natured and couldn't for an instant entertain the notion that he would hurt someone. Then again, he did have a temper when he refused to take his medicine. He was strong and once threw a piano through his front window. He broke that window several times, but only once with a piano. When he took his medicine, he was still goofy but in a much better mood.

The sheriff's report verified the screwy part. It said that Werner was a "mentally disturbed person," confined to the state hospital on several occasions, working days but spending nights at the hospital. Werner was home on leave on June 24, 25, and 26, returning to the hospital on the evening of June 26. His wife was interviewed and insisted that on the weekend the girls disappeared, she was with her husband at all times. A check of the neighborhood failed to produce anyone who had observed Werner away from home that weekend.

In the town of Gates, north of Chili, there lived a pervert named Alvin Lynn, who was arrested—no date given—for "carnal abuse" in the town of Greece, which was north of Gates. Lynn was employed "in the Black Creek vicinity." He'd sold his car, a 1964 Dodge sedan, not long after the murders. Investigation revealed that his vehicle had been purchased by a used car dealer named Edward Narvid. Iaculli and Clark traveled to Pennsylvania and checked out the Dodge, with "negative results." One presumes they were looking for blood. On January 26, 1967, Alvin Lynn was administered a polygraph examination by RPD detective Lieutenant Leslie Gales. The test revealed that Lynn was an "exposer," but there was no indication that he had knowledge of the Chili murders.

The MCSO report contained a long section on John I. Miller and the murder of Marsha Jean Behney. The Monroe County version of the story insisted that the killer's name was John Irving Miller—as opposed to Irvan or Irvin, which I'd previously seen from Pennsylvania sources. I guessed whoever wrote the Monroe County report was spelling phonetically.

Because of the "striking similarities" in the cases, on February 20, 1967, Sheriff Skinner requested that Iaculli and Deputy John Kennerson, his own deputy, go to Reading, Pennsylvania, to interview Miller. After receiving permission from Pennsylvania State Police chief H. F. Williams, and with the cooperation of the Miller case's lead investigator, Pennsylvania State Police sergeant Harley Smith of the state's Bureau of Criminal Investigation (BCI), the attempt to interview Miller "proved with negative results" because the subject refused and "is apparently insane." The failed mission occurred in the Berks County Jail where Miller was awaiting grand jury action.

Miller, it said, was known to take weekend trips. According to his family, he'd visited New York State. But no one could place Miller in Chili on June 25. The report gave the details of the Behney murder. Sandra Behney had been a much better witness than even the local papers had revealed. After viewing the immediate aftermath of her sister's murder, she told Sergeant Smith that the vehicle was a 1956 or 1957 Chevrolet with a light brown bottom and a light-colored top, bearing Pennsylvania registration 534, with the last three digits containing an 8 and a J.

Marsha Jean Behney's autopsy revealed that she had suffered three stab wounds on the left arm, one stab wound on the left back above the shoulder blade, and two in the left breast area, one of which severed both arteries of her heart. The wounds were $1\frac{1}{8}$ inches in length, six inches in depth.

For two months, there were no suspects.

The case broke in November 1966. A male operating a 1957 Chevrolet two-door sedan, white top, coral bottom, bearing registration 834-846, had attempted to entice a constable's 13-year-old daughter and her girlfriend, same age, into his car.

The constable immediately noted the similarities between what happened to his daughter and her friend and the Behney murder, further noting the similarities in the registration number, and contacted Sergeant Smith.

The driver of the car was John I. Miller, who perfectly matched Sandra Behney's description and whose photo was subsequently ID'd by Sandra out of an array of 20 photos.

On February 20, 1967, Sandra also picked Miller out in person from a nine-man lineup. After the lineup, Miller's only comment was, "When are you fucking guys going to feed me?"

Investigation revealed that Miller had no previous criminal record. He'd had the same job as a machine operator at the Peerless Paper Products Company in Montgomery County, Pennsylvania, since graduating from high school. He was a loner who lived with but seldom communicated with his family, confided in no one, and had no known friends. In 1958 Miller was refused entrance into the armed services for reasons that were redacted by Monroe County. After his arrest, the Pennsylvania State Police offered Miller psychiatric treatment, but he rejected the offer.

Investigation revealed that Miller, IQ 118, seldom went out at night but was habitually taking weekend trips by automobile and air travel.

Following Miller's arrest, the Pennsylvania authorities obtained a search warrant and went through his bedroom thoroughly. The search revealed a hunting knife, trademarked "Hunter's Pride," with a six-inch-long blade, 1⅛ inches in width, manufactured by the Scrade Woven Knife Company and carrying stock number 144. (The 144 had an overall length of 9¾ inches, a plain ground carbon steel clip point blade, grooved leather washer handle with plastic spacers front and rear, symmetrical upper and lower guard, and a flat metal butt plate. It listed for $4.65 in 1964.)

Also found were dozens of photographs of nude women and dozens of magazines carrying stories of murdered children. Many of these magazines had bookmarks placed at stories of murdered children. He had newspaper clippings of stories related to the Marsha Jean Behney homicide. A large quantity of contraceptives was in Miller's bureau drawer, as were many undelivered notes addressed to his mother, describing her in vile, filthy language. There was a medical book containing pictured illustrations of a human anatomy. In his suitcase he had airline ticket stubs for Los Angeles, New York City, Baltimore, Washington, D.C., Atlanta, and Seattle. Also found was a lightweight gabardine topcoat, with large dried bloodstains.

Sergeant Smith's initial interview with Miller lasted less than an hour, during which Miller admitted nothing and "heaped obscenities" on the investigator. Among Miller's antisocial tendencies was his refusal to retain a lawyer despite the fact that he had $5,000 in the bank.

On April 13, 1967, a joint force of investigators interviewed Miller's brother and sister-in-law. John, they said, was mentally disturbed and had been for some time. John preferred to be alone *all the time* and refused to communicate with his family.

They knew John took weekend trips, but if they asked him where he went, he would become hostile and abusive toward them. No, he had never mentioned being in the vicinity of Rochester—but they were convinced that from time to time he had "visited New York State."

From Paul and Martha's home, the investigators drove to the home of John's parents, Mr. and Mrs. Irving Miller, where John lived. They spoke to John's sister Mary, who said John usually stayed in his room with the door locked. He was hostile when any attempt was made to communicate with him, so hostile that her father was deathly afraid of him, couldn't even stay in the same room with him. Mary said John's job kept him busy five days a week; however he frequently left home on Saturday morning and didn't return until late Sunday night. She didn't know where he went. She asked him once and he cursed her out, went upstairs, and locked himself in his room.

John's mother told investigators that two weeks before her son's arrest, he removed from his room a large quantity of clothing, newspapers, photographs, and other personal items. Presumably these articles were destroyed.

I thought about that. What was he getting rid of?

During the visiting period at the prison, one of the investigators overheard a conversation between John Miller and his sister Mary, and when she asked, at the request of Sergeant Smith, whether or not he had ever been to Rochester, he said no. Again at the request of Sergeant Smith, Paul Miller asked his brother John if he had ever been to Rochester, and John said yes.

Investigators checked Miller's work records at Peerless, and they revealed that Miller worked the five days of June 20, 21, 22, 23, and 24, reporting back to work on Monday, June 27. (This meant that if Miller was the man spotted on the Archer Road lovers' lane cleaning his car with a can of something and a rag, he would have had to drive much of the night and report to his job on Monday morning with little or no sleep. Not impossible, but a discouraging factor.)

The week before the Chili murders, Miller had his car overhauled, telling the garage mechanic that he was going to take a long weekend trip. Miller withdrew $200 from his bank account on June 24, 1966.

On April 14, 1967, the day after the Miller family interviews, another attempt was made to interview Miller. When the investigators identified themselves, Miller stated that he didn't want to talk to anyone. He was asked if he would answer one question. Miller said he would. Had he ever been in the vicinity of Rochester, New York?

Miller shifted his gaze away from the investigator and mumbled no. When asked if he had ever been in New York State, he stated that he had never been in New York and immediately opened the door and ran into the hallway, refusing to answer any further questions.

According to his sister Mary, it was easy to tell when John was lying, as he shifted his gaze away, either turning his head to one side or bowing to look at the floor.

During this short interview, Miller appeared very frightened and backed away every time the investigator approached. The interview lasted less than five minutes.

An unsuccessful attempt was made by the Pennsylvania State Police Crime Lab to type the blood found on Miller's gabardine jacket. There was an insufficient quantity for typing. (And yet the stains were described as "large." Hmm.)

Miller's doctor was contacted to determine if his handwriting was on a pillbox found 37 feet from the bodies off Archer Road. Dr. Leber said he did not use pillboxes of the type found at the Chili dump site.

Investigators learned that the E. N. Rowell Company of Batavia, New York, manufactured the pillbox. Rowell said various distributors used the box as a standard sample box. Flyers were dispatched to all Monroe County doctors requesting handwriting comparisons. Several physicians replied, without positive ID.

The report summarized the similarities between the Pennsylvania murder and the Chili murders that made John I. Miller such a compelling suspect: (1) in both cases, the location was a rural area; (2) both murders were committed by a knife of approximately the same size; (3) in both homicides, the girls were wearing bathing suits; (4) in both homicides, the girls had defensive wounds on arms and stab wounds in the left breast; (5) in both homicides, the girls were stabbed repeatedly more than six times; and (6) both homicides occurred on a Saturday.

The New York investigators tried hard to place Miller in Chili on June 25. Miller's photo was shown to desk clerks at all Monroe County hotels and motels, as well as bars and restaurants. Nothing.

The Bernhards and Formicolas looked at Miller's mug. They'd never seen him before. What about George-Ann's visits to relatives in Pennsylvania—was there a chance she had encountered Miller at that time? No. She was always accompanied. Besides, those relatives lived 216 miles from Miller.

At some (unspecified) point either following the girls' disappearance or after the discovery of their bodies, an eyewitness named Bruce Witt came forward with an impressive story. During the early evening of June 25, 1966, Witt and his family were fishing in Black Creek under the bridge where Scottsville Road crossed Black Creek.

At 7:30 p.m., Witt and his wife saw the girls come off Scottsville Road and walk down the creek bank. One of the girls took off her sandals and put her feet in the water. The other girl sat on the rocks, talking happily.

Witt's fishing line got caught on the bridge railing, and as he went up to the bridge to free the line, he observed a 1955 or 1957 green Chevy that either had damage to the front end or was missing a bumper and grill. The vehicle stopped on the bridge. A male youth in his early twenties, with dark complexion, possibly Italian, got out of the vehicle and yelled to the two girls to come along. The girls ran up the creek bank and got into the vehicle, which made a U-turn and headed north on Scottsville Road toward the city, then made another U-turn and headed south on Scottsville Road.

The MCSO searched for a car that matched Witt's description. Negative results. Investigators' faith in Witt's report waned when it appeared the witness was "trying to be over-helpful." He remembered more and more detail each time he was interviewed, to the point where, in his last interview, the young man he saw was carrying a sheathed hunting knife at his side.

On April 19, 1967, investigators showed Witt a photo of John I. Miller mixed in with 13 other photographs. He chose two photos, one of which was Miller's photo. Despite choosing the photo, he emphasized that he was definitely not sure that Miller was the man he'd seen picking up the girls, but he did think that he'd previously seen the guy.

I pondered this part of the report as much as any other. I liked Witt's eyewitness report a lot. Perhaps he did become overly helpful as time went on, but that needn't necessarily subtract from the value of his initial statement.

The girls had been wandering rather than swimming during their second trip of the day to the swimming hole. They visited the stone trestle, perhaps the Castle Inn, Coop's, the Swing, and under the Scottsville Road bridge over Black Creek. Someone was looking for them, found them, and got them into his car. Perhaps *this* was the last sighting of the girls alive.

The report listed 34 perverts by name, a list comprised of those who either lived in or near Ballantyne or who had a history of violence. The men's addresses were redacted.

Most of the names meant nothing to me, but I did recognize a few. There was Joseph Werner, on leave from the mental hospital, and Ralph Cleary, the man Tracy D'Arcy had "known for a fact" was a pervert because her mother had said so.

There was Clint Wilson, the brother-in-law of George-Ann's sister, the man who had reportedly tried to rape 10-year-old Mary Crane back by the creek not long before the murders.

There was Fred Kent, a Ballantyne man and an exposer. He chaperoned a group of swimming children at the Genesee River on the day the girls disappeared.

There was Douglas Rockow. His cousin Debby Rockow was my former babysitter. The Rockows were cousins with the family that owned the Campbell Street bar in the Dutchtown section of Rochester that my parents frequented during their younger years. My mom was still friends with the bar owner's daughter and found out for me that Douglas Rockow was a "strange man" and had committed suicide years ago.

The other names were new to me, and I made a list for further research. Using the New York State Department of Corrections database, I learned that one was a convicted rapist, another had committed murder, and one might have been a relative of a guy who worked on the same political board as Jack's dad. Most of the names came up blank. They weren't all Ballantyne guys. West Brighton, Henrietta, and the village of Chili Center were also well represented.

Up until that point, the police summary had read with efficiency but no style, oddly picking points to make and ignoring facts of obvious relevance. Then the tone changed, and it was as if Stephen King had taken over the narration.

According to the files, in August 1966, a man named Klaus Willie Kastenholz was arrested for violation of probation on a second-degree forgery charge and sent to Attica State Prison. After a few weeks behind penitentiary bars, Kastenholz wrote a letter to the Monroe County DA, John C. Little Jr., stating that he had firsthand information regarding the Chili killers. In response to the letter, Kastenholz was transferred out of the state facility and motored back to the relative comfort of the Monroe County Jail, where he underwent "extensive interrogation."

Kastenholz said that, on the evening of June 25, at about 8:30 or 8:45 p.m., he was at the 44 Club (an illegal gambling establishment at 44 Lake Avenue in the city of Rochester, currently occupied by Iglesias Pentecostal La Vid Verdadera) and was picked up by a man named Patrick Ninnies, a man he'd known for a couple of weeks. In the car with Ninnies was a stranger introduced only as "Jack." They were in Jack's car, a black 1959 Chevy. They said they were out "looking for girls."

Together they went to the Varsity Inn, a bar/nightclub on Scottsville Road, less than a mile north of Black Creek. The relatively new hot spot was built atop what had been a dump, and the Pennsylvania Railroad tracks ran immediately behind it.

They pulled behind the place into the unpaved and pothole-filled parking lot, bumped their way to a parking spot, got out of the car, and went inside. The men were all inside briefly.

Kastenholz didn't dig the air conditioning and said he was going back to the car to get his sweater. (The temperature outdoors was still in the 80s. This guy brought a sweater with him? Did he have the sweater at the 44 Club, too? Were these guys who, perhaps, always wore long sleeves no matter what?)

When he got out to the car, he noticed that the trunk had popped open, probably as the car bounced across the bumpy parking lot. (I later verified that the Varsity Inn parking lot had "more potholes than you could shake a stick at.") He raised the lid to slam it shut, and inside the trunk were the bodies of two girls.

The bodies were covered with a blanket so that only their heads were exposed.

"Their eyes were staring wide open," Kastenholz said. In horror, he ran back into the "VI" and joined Ninnies and Jack at the bar. He tried to act cool and did not mention what he'd seen.

After having several beers each, Ninnies announced that it was time to go. They drove south on Scottsville Road to a bar at the corner of Charles Avenue, just south of Ballantyne Road, called Hokie's Place. When they got there, Ninnies reached under the front passenger seat and retrieved a knife and a gun. (Investigators asked Kastenholz to describe the weapons, but Kastenholz said it was too dark for him to see details.) Ninnies left the car with the weapons, ran across Scottsville Road, and disappeared from sight down the bank that led to the edge of the Genesee River. He reappeared after several minutes and told Jack that he had buried the knife and gun near a tree close to the water.

The report stated that sheriff's deputies had searched the area across from Hokie's thoroughly and had found no buried weapons.

That was pretty much the end of Kastenholz's story. Ninnies, "Jack," and Kastenholz never mentioned the bodies in the trunk or the weapons under the seat for the remainder of the evening. Kastenholz never saw Jack again. The next time he saw Ninnies, they were both in the Monroe County Jail, after Kastenholz was picked up for probation violation and Ninnies had been arrested by the RPD for vagrancy and possession of a dangerous weapon (zip gun).

Ninnies, at that time, asked Kastenholz to alibi for him if he was ever asked about the Chili murders. Kastenholz claimed that he refused to do so, and a day or two later Ninnies was sent to the Rochester State Hospital for psychiatric observation.

The MCSO written report noted, "Ninnies had been arrested by the RPD for vagrancy after Ninnies voluntarily turned himself in while carrying a zip gun, and was subsequently sent to the State Hospital."

By the time Kastenholz told his story to the MCSO investigators, however, Ninnies had been released from the hospital, and his whereabouts were unknown. Further interrogation broke down Kastenholz's story. He admitted that he had made up the name "Jack," as there was no such person.

He was asked to take a polygraph exam. At first he agreed—with permission of his attorney, Sidney Suher—but he changed his mind and refused. Kastenholz was sent back to Attica State Prison. But did that prove the story was false? Wasn't it possible that Kastenholz refused to take the polygraph test because he was afraid it would show that he was, at least in part, telling the truth?

And why, really, were the men together to begin with? We are asked to believe that Ninnies and Jack cared enough about Kastenholz to pick him up in Rochester's inner city only minutes after they had committed double homicide out in a desolate portion of Chili. It seemed like a moment when a couple of fellows might not want to take on a third uninvolved party. Even if Kastenholz were a drug dealer, there'd be no reason to bring him along on the night's adventures after making contact with him at the 44 Club.

What would Kastenholz's motive have been for making up the story? Was it merely a half-baked scheme to get himself out of Attica, at least temporarily? Was it an attempt to hurt Ninnies, against whom he might have had an unknown grudge?

There are compelling elements of the story. The geography is correct. There can be no doubt that Kastenholz had been to the Varsity Inn and its Burma Road parking lot, and to Hokie's, where he knew that there was a bank leading down to the Genesee River just across the road. Kastenholz may have gotten lucky, but his story correctly assumed that the girls were not dumped where they were murdered. They had to have been transported after they were murdered, and the trunk of a car seems a logical place.

He also named the second man "Jack," an admittedly common name and a cliché when it came to "ripper" crimes, yet one that correctly pointed a finger at the initial prime suspect in the case, Jack Starr. Did the Jack in Kastenholz's story drive a car that resembled Jack Starr's car? We don't know because the report contained no description of Jack Starr's car, even though it was the last car the girls were known to be in. (Later investigation revealed the strong probability that Jack Starr, part of a large family, had access to cars that weren't his Corvette, but no specific make or model was determined.)

Might Kastenholz have told his story to nudge police in the correct direction without getting himself whacked? The MCSO said no. Kastenholz was issued a summons on October 29, 1966, for "no inspection certificate" on his 1959 Oldsmobile by State Trooper Robert Avery. At the time this section of the report was written, sometime in 1967, Kastenholz was still an inmate at Attica.

Then came the really weird part: investigators, the report said, learned that a man named Horst Walter Kind—who could not have been the murderer, or have encountered the murderer, because he and his wife were attending the Policeman's Ball on the evening of June 25, 1966—once falsely claimed to be Klaus Kastenholz following a traffic stop. Despite this, the man's car, a 1959 Oldsmobile, was still thoroughly checked out with "negative results."

How had Kastenholz managed to get so many details correct? Perhaps he was just a good liar and was familiar with the environs of Scottsville Road watering holes.

On July 25, 1966, five days after the bodies were discovered, three African-American men abducted and raped a woman in Genesee Valley Park, about two miles north of Genesee Junction, on the opposite bank of the Genesee River.[2] The men used a knife to frighten away the young woman's escort—later described by police as a "milquetoast"—and to threaten her into submission. The victim was a beautiful blonde 27-year-old devout Catholic, a University of Rochester graduate student. The men, with the victim still in their car, were caught less than an hour later near the intersection of North Union Street and Ridge Road West in the town of Parma. The eagle-eyed officer who spotted them was 25-year-old rookie sheriff's deputy Robert F. Falzone, who was working off a "be-on-the-lookout" (BOLO) based on a description given by the victim's boyfriend: three black men, one white woman, brown 1960 Dodge. (I learned additional info on the arrest from Falzone himself.) The officer was parked in the elevated parking lot of a Ridge Road car dealership looking down on the thoroughfare when he saw the brown Dodge. Falzone only saw two black men in front and, ever so briefly, a white woman's head pop up in the back. Close enough. He chased them, and they sped up for a time to 75 miles per hour, but they soon pulled over and stopped. Falzone got out of his car, gun drawn, and ordered them out of the car. Sure enough, the third man was in the backseat. Amazingly, the men did not flee, and the lone officer controlled the scene. Falzone arrested the men and put the sobbing woman in the front seat of his car. She was wobbly and needed assistance. Her hair was in disarray and her dress was a mess. The men, it later came out, were taking her to an Orleans County bar called the Brick Wall, where they were going to *sell* her. They had promised to kill her if she didn't do as they said.

This wasn't the first time the sheriff had heard reference to that bar in connection with prostitution. It was a meeting place for migrant workers, 99 percent of whom were black.

The captured men—James Melvin Green, his brother Andrew Lee Green, and Ellis Thomas Clanton—refused to talk during the initial interrogation and demanded to be represented by a lawyer.

For squelching the rapacious spree, Deputy Falzone was awarded a Citation of Merit from Sheriff Skinner, who said Falzone's actions prevented a "worse crime from occurring."

The arresting deputy handed the prisoners—who were 18, 20, and 23 years old—over to the investigators at the sheriff's office, and he didn't see the three suspects again until their trial. It was Investigator Michael Cerretto who liked these guys for the Chili murders. *Kill them if they don't do what they're told.* Didn't that sound like a possible explanation for what happened to Kathy and George-Ann?

Three months later, an inmate at the Monroe County Jail named Joseph Lewis, aka Dolph Sturges, who was awaiting trial for unlawful entry, told the jail turnkey that he had info regarding the Chili murders. He claimed that he, along with another inmate, Stanley Scofield (who was incarcerated for attempted rape), had heard Andrew Green say that his brother James and Ellis Clanton had "killed those girls." Lewis and Scofield were told to keep their ears open and to try and find out more details about the murders. What type of car was used? What was the exact location of the crime? How was it committed?

On October 24, 1966, Scofield and Lewis offered investigators additional info. James Green and Ellis Clanton tried to pick up the girls in Green's 1960 Dodge. The two girls refused their advances, so they killed them with a bayonet and dumped their bodies in a field near a swamp. James Green disposed of the bayonet by throwing it into a stream under a bridge in Genesee Valley Park. (Scuba divers searched unsuccessfully for the bayonet.) James Green and Ellis Clanton then burned their bloody clothes in the rear of a house on Clarissa Street. (Deputy Robert Falzone and others checked the yard. There was no evidence of burned clothes.) Investigators secured a search warrant for the Dodge from Supreme Court judge Dominic Gabrielli. The vehicle was impounded at the Heinrich Garage at 60 Grotan Avenue in Hilton, New York. Inside the car investigators found a yellow straw hat and a pair of shoes. Those items were seized, along with a rubber floor mat found in the trunk. The car was meticulously vacuumed. Found under the backseat was a small pool of brown substance. CSI scraped up some of the matter, and this, along with the vacuumed dirt, was sent to the FBI lab. The shoes and the rubber floor mat were sent to the Monroe County lab, where tests failed to reveal bloodstains.

The straw hat was shown to Miriam Aquino, the picnicker who had reported a menacing man in a straw hat in the bushes near the trestle on the evening the girls disappeared, the one she said she scared away by grabbing a nearby machete. Mrs. Aquino said the hat was very similar, possibly identical to the one she'd seen on June 25.

That lead fell through when investigators learned that the straw hat found in the 1960 Dodge had been given to James Green by a Mrs. Dorothy Hopwood on July 7, 1966. Mrs. Hopwood's husband Stanley was president of Breton Motors Inc. and James Green's boss. Mr. Hopwood told investigators that, on July 7, he asked James Green to do some landscaping work for him. While Green was working, Mrs. Hopwood gave him the hat to keep the sun off his head. Hopwood said he paid Green by check and thus was able to pinpoint the date as July 7.

On October 27, 1966, investigators interrogated Andrew Green, who denied being a murderer. He denied talking about the murders with Lewis and Scofield. RPD detective Lieutenant Leslie Gales gave Andrew Green a polygraph. When Andrew was asked if he had discussed the Chili murders with Scofield, Lewis, his brother James, or Ellis Clanton, his answer was no, a response that the machine indicated showed deception. Did he know about the Chili murders and who had committed them? Again he said no. He didn't do it, and he didn't know who did. This time, no deception.

Andrew Green admitted that he had discussed the murders with his brother and the other men, but maintained that he had never told Scofield and Lewis that his brother and Clanton did it.

On November 2, 1966, investigators reinterviewed Andrew Green in the presence of Joseph Lewis. Lewis confronted Green. Lewis said, "You told me and Scofield that your brother James and Ellis Clanton met the two girls and after they refused their advances, they killed them by stabbing them in the chest and lower extremities, and that James

Green threw the knife in a creek or river that went through Genesee Valley Park."

Andrew Green denied ever saying any such thing.

On November 3, Ellis Clanton and James Green clammed up and asked for a lawyer. And that was the last of the investigation into the Genesee Valley Park rapists.

The rapists were tried and convicted in January 1967. (For details of the trial, see appendix C.)

Back in Chili, sometime after the investigation into the African-American rapists, Jerry Starr (younger brother of Jack) remembered something he had forgotten to mention to investigators earlier. He himself had been back by the Genesee Junction on the evening the girls disappeared, swimming in the Black Creek swimming hole with William Hunter and Earl Owens and his son. Jerry realized that it was getting late and he had to pick up his girlfriend to take her to a graduation party. He estimated that he left at 8:15 or 8:30. While he was driving east on Junction Road, the dirt road along the tracks, toward Scottsville Road, a white and gray 1959 Oldsmobile suddenly backed out of a lane on the south side of the road, directly in front of his car, forcing him to stop.

"It looked to me like there were three guys in the car, possibly colored," Jerry reportedly said.

The Olds sped to Scottsville Road and kicked up so much dust that he couldn't tell if it turned north or south when it got there. Investigators asked him why he had not mentioned this earlier, and he said he thought he had, back one time when investigators were at his house to pick up his brother Jack. The RPD ran a check on all area 1959 Oldsmobiles that were white, gray, or a combination of both. There were 243 such cars.

And on that note, the summary I had received from the sheriff's office ended.

After digesting the material, I made a list of odd and hard-to-explain things about the report, all of which seemed designed to make Jack Starr look innocent:

1. Despite the fact that Jack Starr was 20 or 21 years old at the time of the murders, and had been 19 or 20 when he impregnated 13-year-old George-Ann Formicola, he is referred in the report as a "youth." He was a grown man having sex with and impregnating a little girl, a sex crime, yet there is nothing in the report's tone to indicate this.

2. Jack Starr's alibi included spending a key 90 minutes at the Bernhards. Alice and Betty not only flatly denied that this was true, but they maintained that Jack Starr had never at any time been to their house.

3. Jack Starr's brother was possibly months late in reporting a pertinent incident.

4. No description was given of Jack Starr's car, despite the fact that it was one of the last cars the girls were known to be in. Did it resemble the Chevy that the Witts had seen the girls get into on Scottsville Road?

Former FBI special agent Pat Patterson read the summary and reported back: "With all the potentials you have as suspects, I would look at the similarities between the Chili murders and the Marsha Jean Behney case. It still looks like a sexual sadist committed this crime, and Miller certainly fits that description. His fascination with murdered children (collecting articles including one on the Behney case); significant hostility toward his mother; significant hostility and outbursts toward others and general abusive nature; antisocial behavior; possession of a weapon of a similar size to the fatal wounds in the Chili murders; possession of an anatomy book (which would help with dissection); a collection of pornography; seeming destruction of items prior to his arrest (could have been body parts or other souvenirs); a large collection of contraceptives (a little unusual for a loner who does not interact with people or have apparent relationships with anyone); and 20 separate individuals placing Miller in Rochester the weekend of the murders (as a result of his picture in the papers) would put him at the top of my list of suspects. Remember, serial killers are usually highly mobile."

Back in July 1966, the African-American rapists had referenced a bar called the Brick Wall, where people apparently could be sold. I verified that the place existed, on Ridge Road in Albion. It was raided regularly for serving drinks without a license. The owner lived in an apartment building which itself was regularly raided as a house of ill repute. The Brick Wall's parking lot was adjacent to a cluster of trailers and shanties that were part of a migrant labor camp. During the early morning hours of Saturday, October 17, 1964, there was a gunfight at the Brick Wall[3] —one dead with a small hole in the center of his forehead, one critical with lead in his gut, and three others wounded. In April 1967 a woman was wounded by a "stray bullet" while standing in the club's doorway.[4] There was more gunplay during October of that year when a 21-year-old Albion man was shot to death while walking across the Brick Wall parking lot.[5] On the night of April 15, 1972, a man met a woman in the Brick Wall, they retreated to a nearby love shack, the shack caught fire, she burned to death, and the man was convicted of arson and murder.[6] So, yeah, the Brick Wall seemed like just the sort of place where one could buy or sell a human being.

I read a December 30, 1966, memo from Captain H. F. Williams, with an attachment from Detective Inspector George E. Killen, both of the Massachusetts State Police, concerning the murder of Nancy Ann Frenier. There were similarities (breasts removed) between the Frenier murder and the Chili murders. Investigators learned that, on December 22, 1961, 19-year-old mother Nancy Ann Frenier drove her husband to work, intending to then proceed to a Laundromat. Later that day a man and woman were spotted near the local reservoir in East Providence. The woman was heard to cry out in distress, but when police arrived, only Frenier's car was still there, containing a laundry basket filled with clean clothes. Three months later, when the reservoir melted, Frenier's mutilated body was found in the water. The killer, Thomas Richard Knott Jr., a minor, confessed to the murder in January 1963 while being interrogated by police regarding another matter. He was sentenced to life in prison.[7] The lesson to be learned here: teenagers can be every bit as dangerous and depraved as adults.

At the end of November 2011, I received a second package from Monroe County. It included the written report I had submitted to the MCSO in 1999 summarizing the many ways in which the Chili murders resembled an Arthur Shawcross crime.

And there were the "morgue observations" of Frank Fontana, Edward Riley, and Frank Defede, who were sent to the morgue to get an accurate description of the clothes on or near the bodies: George-Ann was wearing a red-and-white, large-checked blouse over the top of her bathing suit. The blouse had a button-down front, short sleeves, and tears over the left breast. The top of George-Ann's bathing suit was also red and white, with smaller checks. The straps to the top went over her shoulders. A sharp instrument had twice pierced the left side of the swimsuit top. The swimsuit top was also torn at the center bottom between the breast pads. She was naked from the waist down and wore no jewelry.

Kathy wore a dark blue two-piece swimsuit, with a white stripe down the side of the bottoms and across the front of the top, and a long-sleeve button-down plaid blouse. The observers were "unable to determine" the color of the blouse. There was a possible tear on the left side of the blouse. Kathy was barefoot and also wore no jewelry.

Deputy Manzler described the scene when she, and Sergeant Norman Doe (the helicopter pilot), notified the parents that their daughters' bodies had been found. Alice was distraught, and before she left, Manzler asked a neighbor to stay with Alice. Doe went by himself to the junkyard to tell John Bernhard the bad news.

When Ruth Formicola was informed, her first words were, "Jack did it. I know he did."

Questioned on the subject, Ruth said she had "no real reason" to say it. She simply "felt it." (This document did not offer Jack's last name, although Ruth must have mentioned it.) Manzler called George Formicola at work and asked him to come home. He was informed when he arrived. Before Manzler left, Ruth Formicola's mother and Keith and Gina Wilson, already married, were both at the Stallman Drive house.

Sergeant Doe and a deputy drove along the West Shore railroad tracks to the "railroad overpass," the bridge that allowed the tracks to go over the B&O railroad. The officers checked "on both sides of the road" looking for clues.

The road system back there in the weeds was designed to accommodate fishing. There were five roadways leading from the cinder road that paralleled the tracks. All headed toward Black Creek. The area was covered with dense underbrush much like the murder scene, with several open areas and fields.

At the "railroad overpass," the men encountered a man in a 1966 Chevy convertible who was zeroing in a rifle. He told them that he had been back along the railroad tracks on a number of occasions, hunting, and several times he'd used the cinder drive along the West Shore tracks to access the area.

At 6:30 on the evening the bodies were found, Ruth Formicola and Alice Bernhard were shown pieces of bathing suits, and both identified the items as belonging to their daughters.

It was from Michael Cerretto's written report that I got my most complete crime scene details. Zuber had found one body and gone to get Saile, and the two men together discovered the second body. Cerretto said that Sheriff Skinner himself called him at 3:35 p.m. on July 20 and told him to report to the crime scene. The medical examiner's ambulance arrived at 4:45 p.m. The bodies were pronounced dead five minutes later and put into the ambulance. All ME personnel left the scene. It was Cerretto who found the white button under the spot where Kathy's left hand had been resting. The button still had some white thread attached to it. It was bagged and labeled as evidence.

As night came, according to Cerretto, three deputies were left to guard both the dump site and the entrance to the lovers' lane on Archer Road. They were told not to leave. Cerretto went from the crime scene to the morgue where Dr. Greendyke informed him of the results.[8]

Don Campbell suggested I talk to the Grecos, who for years had run an antique shop out of their house on the west side of Scottsville Road, just a few hundred feet north of the iron trestle. Campbell figured that that was one of the closest houses to where the girls were last seen. So I called Tom Greco, who was working in the shop.

Greco answered the phone and answered my questions even as he was fielding queries from customers. Tom graduated from Wheatland-Chili in 1971, which made him three years older than me, and 12 or 13 at the time of the murders. He appreciated what I was doing for Alice and mentioned that he had been on a couple of dates as a kid with Kathy's sister Patty Bernhard, including one at the Starlite Drive-In.

"We were really more friends than anything else," he said. It was clearly a pleasant memory.

He remembered that investigators came to their house and talked to Tom's dad (now deceased) during the summer of 1966 because they owned a rust-colored or silver 1957 Chevy at the time, a type of car that had caught the interest of police. Investigators said that a suspect drove a car just like that and they were checking on cars that resembled it. In retrospect, Tom came to believe that Jack Starr must have driven a '57 Chevy because he was the suspect. But I knew that John I. Miller drove a salmon and white '57 Chevy, and he might have been the suspect to whom the investigators were referring. Tom said he was always pretty sure that Jack Starr did it because he was "such a creepy person." I asked him what he meant by that, and Tom said, "He always had a strange look on his face when you looked at him."

I learned from Don Riechel that Samantha Sherman, Jack Starr's alibi girl, was the older sister of Gail and Melinda "Mindy" Sherman.* Gail was a good friend of George-Ann and Nancy Mulligan, and probably Kathy as well.

I was contacted by a Scottsvillian named Jim McNulty who said I should check into a guy named Harold "Dady" (DAY-dee) Hamilton.* According to McNulty, Hamilton once hid in the field south of Ballantyne Road, directly south of my house, and aimed a rifle at Sue Mulligan as she got off the school bus coming home. The bus driver spotted him and told Sue to go directly into her house and didn't move the bus, shielding her. The bus driver then pulled to the side of the road and waited for the police.

14

DON TUBMAN

Watson had Sherlock Holmes, I had Don Tubman, and I'm good with that. Donald A. Tubman was a 1966 graduate of Wheatland-Chili. He graduated on June 25. He worked 16 years as a Wheatland town cop, then as a criminal investigator for New York State until his retirement, and in 2011 he was a private detective.

I explained that the last time we'd spoken was in 1973. I was 16 years old, and he was rousting me from behind the railroad depot in Scottsville because I had a can of Genesee Beer in my hand.

After telling him what I'd learned, he sighed when he thought about the level of crime-busting savvy back in 1966. It was his belief that most sheriff's deputies in 1966 were ex–military police without sophisticated detecting skills.

When Tubman attended a crime scene investigation course at Monroe Community College, he was one of the first to do so. Courses like that might've been available to federal agents before 1966, but they were new to county and town cops.

He remembered the horror of the case. Back then it was his information that there was a suspect who lived on Ballantyne Road near Terry Tree Farm. He didn't remember the name.

In 1967 Tubman worked for Wehle's Farm, and there was a weirdo working there named Arthur. "Wouldn't it be something if that turned out to be Shawcross?" he said. "There was a Sammy Sherman in my class. I'll check." The reunion committee for his class might have contact information.

He said Dady Hamilton took a shot at Sue Mulligan, and when they caught him they put him straight into the psych ward.

"Hamilton tried to emasculate himself," Tubman said.

"You mean like castration?"

"That's what I heard."

I checked on Harold Hamilton and learned that he was a Riverdale kid, lived on Grayson Avenue, two blocks south of Names Road. In December 1962, Dady was rushed by ambulance from his home to St. Mary's Hospital.[1]

I checked on Terry Tree Service (actual name) and learned on Google Maps that it was the same facility that I knew as a kid as Monroe Tree Surgeons, the outfit that did the defoliating for the town and the county after the bodies were found. I remembered Donna Melideo telling me that a Monroe Tree Surgeons employee was questioned and wondered if she recalled the name.

I sent a copy of the case summary to Tubman, and after he'd read it, he called me back. "If I'd've had this case when I was a cop, I'd've solved it. In fact, I can solve it now," he said.

He wanted to talk to some old friends to see if he could pinpoint the moment when what should have been a concise and successful investigation derailed and turned into a 45-year-old cold case. After talking to ex-cops, he wanted to talk to folks inside the Starr family and find out what really happened. With Tubman now fully on board, I sent him what I thought might be helpful contact info and copies of the photos I'd collected to help him visualize scenarios and distinguish witnesses.

On December 7, I received a call from Jerry Starr, Jack's little brother, who was 17 at the time of the murders. He said he was sorry that it took him so long to get back to me but he'd been trying to get his recollections together so that he could be as helpful as possible. I asked him about Jack, who was a suspect, and he said that as far as he was concerned his brother had nothing to do with it.

"It didn't seem like something he would be involved in. He was a guy with a bad temper. We used to have drag-out fights in the house. He once bit my nose and broke it. But I never saw him being the sort of guy that would be into mutilation."

I asked him if Jack ever tortured animals, and he said that Jack and friends used to shoot frogs with a BB gun, but that was about it. He could not think of any suspects in the neighborhood. It was a tough neighborhood and there was a lot of craziness, but certainly no one he knew well was perverted enough to do something like that.

I asked him if he knew that Jack was the father of George-Ann's baby, and there was a long pause.

"I didn't know that. It wasn't, it certainly wasn't . . . I guess it was never talked about in our house." He knew that Jack got into heroin in later years and died of AIDS, but he didn't remember a single time that Jack expressed violence toward women.

I asked Jerry about his experiences on the day and evening that the girls disappeared. He said he'd been back by the trestle swimming with some other guys, he didn't remember who. I told him that the sheriff's report said it was two Owenses and a Hunter, and he said that sounded about right. He had no recollection of seeing the girls that day. The thing he did remember, and the thing he told investigators at the time, was that when he was leaving in his car, he was in a hurry to pick up his girlfriend for a date, and she lived in the city. An Oldsmobile, light colored, maybe cream colored, pulled out in front of him and made him stop. He said that he had the impression that there was more than one person in the car. The investigators weren't happy though until he said that there were three guys in the car. "I can tell you right now, I didn't then and I don't now have any idea how many guys were in that car," he said. When reporting the incident, he was repeatedly asked if the guys in the car were black, and he said a few times that he couldn't be sure. Finally, he said maybe they were black, and that made the investigators happy. "They were putting words in my mouth," he said. He remembered that the car did not slow down at Scottsville Road but turned right and headed toward Ballantyne Road. That was the last he saw it. His recollection now was that this took place around dinnertime. (He told police in 1966 that the incident took place at "8:15 or 8:30.") A few days later, when Kathy's radio was found right where that car pulled out from, he knew he had to report what he saw and that it might be important.

He said he was fairly certain that Jack had already been in the army and was out by 1966. I asked him about the Wilson brothers, and he remembered little. He thought one of them worked for the railroad. He asked me if I'd ever looked into those guys who became the Hillside Stranglers, that they might be a good fit for this. He corrected the address I sent the letter to and gave me his phone number. He told me to call him anytime and ask whatever I wanted. He was sorry he couldn't be more helpful.

On the morning of December 8, I received a phone message from Tom Greco who remembered an additional piece of info. Back in 1966, he recalled that there was another set of railroad tracks at the rear (west end) of the Greco property, a spur that enabled westbound trains to turn northward at Genesee Junction. On the other side of those tracks was a shack with no electricity or anything where a bum lived.

I called Greco Antiques to talk more about this, and Tom's older brother Jack answered. He remembered the guy in the shack, too, calling him a squatter, and said he went into the shack once and everything was moldy. I asked him about the family car back in 1966. Was it a '57 Chevy? He had no clue.

"I thought Jack Starr was a nice guy, though," Jack said.

I heard a strong female voice in the background say, "No, he wasn't. I knew his wife."

"Who's that?"

"That's my cousin Julie."

After establishing that Jack remembered nothing further, I asked if I could speak to Cousin Julie. I started by introducing myself, and she screamed.

"Mike Benson! We went to school together. I'm Julie Burnetti.* Do you still have asthma? Are you still skinny?"

That resulted in a 10-minute chat as we caught up.

She got back to Jack's wife: "We took karate classes together," Julie said. "She took the classes to protect herself from him. Sometimes she would come into class all beaten up."

"When was this?"

"I don't know. 1973. Something like that."

"Were you aware that Jack was a suspect in the murders?"

"Sure. My brother said he used to brag about it when he was drunk."

"What?"

"Oh, yeah. You know how you drink too much and all of a sudden the words start coming out."

"I've been in a lot of bars, Julie, and no one's ever confessed to murder in front of me. You think it might be okay if I talked to your brother? He's older, right?"

"Seven years older. Sure, you can call him. He's retired and bored. He'll be happy to have someone to talk to."

And she gave me his number. I sat and thought for 11 minutes and then dialed. David Burnetti° was previously known to this investigation as the guy who was target-shooting with Tom Wiest at Ajax Auto Parts when they fired upon a rusted-out school bus in which John Bernhard was sleeping. To me, Burnetti denied ever hearing Jack Starr discuss the murders in any way. I told him I would protect his identity if he was afraid to talk, and he said that made no difference. He only remembered being in the same bar with the guy a couple of times, and now, thinking back on it, he didn't think he ever saw Jack Starr after the murders, only before.

"I always suspected he was the murderer, though," he said. "Because he was gory like that."

"What do you mean?"

"Well, like the stuff he would do to animals. He'd shoot a woodchuck and chop it up and gut it for no reason."

I gave him my phone number in case he thought of anything else, but I could tell he wasn't writing it down.

David Burnetti was subsequently reinterviewed by Don Tubman, who showed up unexpectedly at Burnetti's house. Dave no longer lived in West Brighton, having moved in 2003 to a house near ground zero of this case, on Names Road at the Lester Street end.

"I'm looking for a guy I knew in school, a guy who was never afraid of anything," Tubman said.

Burnetti wasn't happy as he flashed a smile, a couple of teeth missing. He didn't recognize him yet. "Who are you?" Burnetti asked.

Tubman, who was rocking a gray beard, introduced himself, and for a moment it was old-home week.

"Sure, I remember you, Tubman. When did you stop shaving?"

They discussed a car accident Burnetti'd had that left him with a head injury.

"I'm still sharp," Burnetti said. Tubman thought he seemed the same—just 45 years older.

Tubman asked about the murders: "Did you know the girls?"

"Sure. In the year before they died, those girls were looking for anything with a pulse."

"Did you guys in West Brighton go over to the other side of the river much?"

"Not much, but sometimes. There was some interaction."

"Have any idea what happened to the girls?"

Burnetti repeated that "everyone knew" Jack Starr killed the girls.

"Who got George-Ann pregnant?"

"I never really heard who the father was."

"Did you have information directly from Jack?" Tubman asked.

"I never talked to Jack about the murders in any fashion. I did go hunting with him a few times." And he seemed like the sort of guy who could have killed the girls. Burnetti told the woodchuck story. "Removed the entrails and played with them," he detailed. "He was a sick mother who would shoot animals, then dissect."

Burnetti said the woodchuck incident occurred when he and Jack were hunting in Scottsville, although he didn't remember the precise location. It was a long time ago. He then backed off his relationship with Jack, stating that he'd seen him at parties but never talked to him for more than five minutes at a time because Jack had a very bad temper and a nasty personality. A lot of people avoided him.

"Did Jack have a hunting knife?"

"He had a knife, but it was a pocketknife."

Tubman tested his memory: "Do you remember what type of car you and Jack drove back then?"

"I drove a 1965 GTO, maroon with a black top. Jack drove a red Corvette."

Tubman called me and reported: "Burnetti was evasive and inconsistent in his answers regarding his relationship with Jack Starr." There was a disconnect in Burnetti's story: why would you go hunting a few times in Scottsville, which necessitated a car, with a foul-tempered guy you avoided at parties? That disconnect, plus stuff we heard from other West Brighton guys, indicated that Dave Burnetti and Jack Starr were pretty good friends, a part of Burnetti's social history he was trying to erase.

Marcia Shea lived in the village of Scottsville and was in Kathy and George-Ann's class at Wheatland-Chili. She told me that, until now, she had never discussed the murders. They were a nightmare, so horrible that no one mentioned it. She remembered being in a daze because she'd been friends with the girls, and there was a period of time when she "totally blanked out." She was speaking now because she wanted closure and appreciated my motives, doing it for Alice.

George-Ann, Marcia said, was tough and bossy, so much so that she "clashed" with her a couple of times. Kathy was shy and easygoing and nice. Kathy never initiated conversation, but she would talk to you if you talked to her first. George-Ann was extroverted, Kathy introverted. Marcia never knew George-Ann to date anyone at school. Marcia didn't know at first that George-Ann was pregnant. At the time, George-Ann told her she was "going to live with an aunt." Marcia told her she wished she wasn't going, and George-Ann said she wished that, too. When George-Ann returned at the end of the school year, she seemed nicer, calmer, and more mature. She admitted she'd had a child and said her sister Gina wanted to adopt the baby, but their mother wouldn't let her. The last time Marcia saw George-Ann was the "last day of testing." George-Ann and Marcia went together after school to Frances Gossen's house, which was down the street from Marcia's house.

When Marcia learned that the girls were missing, she thought right away that they'd been murdered, either by someone they knew or by more than one man. She never thought the girls had run away.

It was Marcia's recollection that Scottsville kids reacted only casually to the murders, that it was considered a "Ballantyne thing." But Marcia's sister Audrey disagreed and said that both Scottsville and Ballantyne were deeply affected by the murders.

Don Campbell found Jack's alibi witness, Samantha Sherman. She was on Facebook! According to Sherman's Facebook page, she lived in Greece (which quickly enabled us to nail down an address), worked full time for a printing company, and her sister Mindy's married name was Finnegan.* She said she had two daughters. I was sad to learn that her sister Gail had died.

On December 13, Don Tubman made first contact with Sammy Sherman. He got her home phone number from a receptionist at the printing company and called her mid-afternoon. She didn't remember Tubman, but he explained that they went to school together for six years, and she quickly became chatty.

Yes, she did go on a date with Jack Starr on the night the girls disappeared. She didn't remember the specific times, but she knew it was already dark when he picked her up in his black 1963 Corvette. She saw Jack for close to a year and, looking back on it, that car was a major reason why she dated him.

There was nothing odd about his behavior that night, she said. He seemed normal.

Tubman recalled Jack's brother Jerry Starr driving that car later on. He couldn't imagine anyone transporting dead bodies or driving through weeds in a Corvette. It was simply the wrong vehicle for the job.

Tubman asked Samantha if she thought Jack killed the girls, and there was a long pause before she said she didn't know. He could've. That night was close to the end of their relationship. She remembered dating him for a long while before the murders, but she remembered few or no dates after the bodies were found.

Tubman asked what they did on their date that night. She said they went to Shaler's, a hamburger joint up near Charlotte, the northern-most neighborhood in the city of Rochester, by Lake Ontario.

Shaler's was a good 15 miles away, the second half of it through city traffic. It was a long way to go to get a burger. The thing she remembered most about the date was that Jack had trouble with the lights on his car.

She said that it was a weird thing, but she hung out with two guys who were suspects in the murders. The other, she said, was Barney Wilson, who was the brother of Keith and Clint. (This was the first I'd heard of there being a Barney, and Tubman assured me that Barney was a third brother.) She said that she was walking somewhere with Barney once, and he told her that he was the one who killed the girls. Then he quickly took it back and said he was just joking. Ha-ha. It was the kind of joke she never forgot. She said Barney was still alive and lived in the Finger Lakes region.

Both Barney and Jack took lie detector tests, she said, and they both failed. She knew this because they both told her they failed. (Both of them said it? Separately? An organized effort to intimidate her? How much of this could we believe?)

After the bodies were found, investigators talked to her repeatedly. They talked to her at night, waiting for her to get home from work. She remembered them showing her photos of '56 or '57 Chevys and asking if any of them looked familiar.

She said the investigators told her father about the bodies being mutilated, but they didn't tell her. She said she'd heard that a uterus—she used the word "uterus"—was taken and asked Tubman if that might have been to hide the fact that the girl was pregnant.

Samantha recalled that, like Alice Bernhard Jr. and Tom Wiest, she had participated in a search for the girls during the days after they went missing. She said her group, rather than following the railroad tracks, followed the north bank of Black Creek and walked it westward as far as the spot where it went under Ballantyne Road.

During the 1980s, she lived in a house that overlooked Henrietta Park and had been home the night Keith Wilson was killed there. The whole time she lived there after that she couldn't look out the back window it was so scary. Mostly she remembered Gina's screams.

Don asked if anyone had discussed the murders with her since the initial investigation, and she said no: "Nobody's talked to me since back in the day." She and Tubman made arrangements to talk again.

The list of coincidences grew. Not only did Gina Formicola lose both a sister and a husband to lovers' lane murders, but Samantha Sherman had an uncomfortable proximity to both.

That same day I finally got in touch with Tom Wiest's friend Gus D'April, who turned out to know very little about the case. He had been RPD and had worked organized crime and narcotics. I asked him about the 44 Club that appeared in the Kastenholz/Ninnies/Jack story in the summary. I asked him what the place was like, and he said, "Just like in the movies. On any Friday or Saturday night you could go behind that place and buy any kind of stolen goods, TVs, stereos, whatever you want."

On December 15, while Don Tubman was arranging a face-to-face meeting with Samantha Sherman, I called Dawn Putnam, my next-door neighbor growing up, whose mother Pauline married Burt Braddock, George-Ann's uncle. After catching up a bit, I asked her if she knew that there was a third Wilson brother, Barney.

"I never heard of Barney," she said. "I just knew Keith and Clint. You remember Clint Wilson raped me when I was 12, right?"

"No! How did that happen?"

"I thought I told you at the time."

I felt my heart leap into my throat. Of course! She'd been "raked."

As my brain swam, I realized Dawn was still talking: "My mom and Burt were drinking at Hokie's, and I was watching my younger brothers and sister. He came into the house and raped me. He said he'd kill me if I told anyone, and I never said a word about it to a grownup until I was 18."

"Oh, Dawn, I'm so sorry."

"Yeah, well, it was a long time ago. I'm sort of over it."

I asked if, since she lived even closer to the Formicola house than I had, she knew if there had been any trouble, if George-Ann's dad had expressed anger, during George-Ann's pregnancy. She didn't. Because of her own experience, she had always thought that Clint Wilson was the father of George-Ann's baby.

"Her dad was a dirty old man, too," she said.

"Who?"

"George-Ann's dad."

"George Formicola was a dirty old man?"

"Yeah, he tried to mess around with me once when I was walking to catch the school bus. He tried to mess around with my mom, too. He gave me the creeps. Ruth was nice, though."

Don Campbell interviewed Dawn's stepfather, Burt Braddock, and not surprisingly there were some similarities between his responses and those of his stepdaughter. He, too, had believed all along that Clint Wilson was the father of George-Ann's baby. Burt told Campbell the Gina and Keith story in detail and said that, as far as he knew, Gina was in jail in Florida. He didn't say what he thought Gina was in jail for, and Campbell didn't ask.

Campbell asked about the Castle Inn, and Braddock said, "That was my hangout! My best friend went out with the barmaid there."

"Did Clint Wilson hang out there?"

"He came in now and then, but he was always abusive to the barmaid and got kicked out."

"Did you know a guy by the name of Jack Starr?"

"Jack was a pussy!" Braddock said. "I had a go-around with him once, and he backed down." He also had a few run-ins with Clint. One thing that made Burt mad was when Clint, off duty, would run his garbage truck up and down Stallman Drive. Clint and his work buddies used to all go to Hokie's and park several garbage trucks out front.

Braddock said he thought the Chili murders were committed by more than one guy because "George-Ann knew how to wrestle."

In December, Don Tubman reinterviewed Samantha Sherman. She said she couldn't remember clearly what time Jack picked her up that night, but it was after dark, and he was absolutely driving his black Corvette. He was freshly showered and smelled good. She reiterated that both Jack and Barney Wilson could've been the killer. Barney Wilson was the youngest of the Wilson brothers and was "going steady" with George-Ann. (We eventually learned that there were six Wilson brothers.) Barney made the joke about being the killer a couple of days after the bodies were found, when Barney and she were walking together, paying their respects to the families. He said he was kidding almost immediately, but it still scared her to death. Jack and Barney had separately and individually told her that they'd taken a lie detector test and failed it. Barney Wilson was still alive and lived in a small town to the south.

Sam said she didn't know if Jack had any sexual eccentricities or peculiarities, because she never had sex with him. She didn't know him to have a temper, and he was always very respectful with her. He was, however, subject to seizures. She didn't know the specific medical cause. She knew Jack had fathered George-Ann's baby, but she had no knowledge of any tensions between the Formicolas and the Starrs over it. Sam and Jack had parked and made out, but they never used the lovers' lane off Archer Road. When they parked, they did it off Brook Road, which ran off Scottsville Road south of Riverdale. She couldn't remember any of the other Starr family cars. She'd been to the Starr house a few times and thought the atmosphere inside the house was okay.

After Jack established her as his alibi, detectives came to her house in the middle of the night to question her. They followed her when she drove, so she stopped using Scottsville Road and started driving to Scottsville via the dirt road that ran along the B&O railroad tracks.

Then she told Tubman a very interesting story. She was in the Wheatland-Chili High School girls' room during the last days of her senior year, at the sinks talking to her friend Pat Stark. George-Ann walked in.

Samantha told her friend that Jack Starr was coming to see her graduate. She'd said something like, "I'm getting married to Jack for the weekend."

That made George-Ann snort and say something like, "Oh, really?"

Jack didn't show up at Sam's graduation. When he picked her up that night, he said he was coming from the Bernhards (the other part of his alibi) and that he was angry with her, telling her that she shouldn't have said what she said in front of George-Ann. Sam recalled thinking that his heart was with George-Ann.

They had a crummy Saturday night date. Jack was in a bad mood— although some of that mood was caused by car trouble. The 'Vette's lights were on the blink.

Don asked if there was a chance that Kathy Bernhard was pregnant when she died, and Sam said she thought, as did everyone else, that Kathy was not sexually active.

Don asked about the Starr family. She didn't have much to say about any of Jack's brothers but noted that Chrissy was a princess and was closer friends with Sam's sister Mindy. She gave Tubman Mindy's contact info but warned that Mindy was suffering from a kidney stone just then and was not in the best of moods.

Jack did not tell her that he'd picked up the girls at the swimming hole earlier, but he did say he'd talked to them at the Bernhards'. The only car she'd seen Jack drive was the Corvette, but she did know that sometimes he drove his brother's car, make and year unknown.

During the time when the girls were missing, Alice Sr. asked people if they'd smelled anything, that if the girls had been left nearby it was a hot summer and they'd be able to smell it.

That December, I received a Christmas card from Elton Brutus Murphy, the mutilation killer who was serving a life sentence in Florida and the subject of my true-crime book *Evil Season*. I thought of the book *The Silence of the Lambs* in which the FBI used psycho killer Hannibal Lecter as a consultant to catch a serial killer who was calling himself Buffalo Bill. Since both Murphy and the Chili killer had removed a vagina that was never found, perhaps Murphy would have some insight into our guy. I wrote up a two-page synopsis of the crime and the suspects (first names only). In about 10 days, I received a response. Murphy said that he felt "privileged and honored" that I valued his opinion.

He wrote that he'd shared my letter with some of his "convicted murder friends," asking their opinions. The prevailing belief was, of the suspects named, John [Miller] was most likely to have done the crimes, mostly because of the white-and-tan car. Murphy and his friends also believed that Clint and Jack working together might have done the crimes. Murphy never mentioned the suspect "Arthur" in his letter, but he did write, "I personally think it is possible that none of the named suspects committed the murders, that an unknown psychopath did them, then moved out of the area to a completely new hunting ground, unless he was stopped somehow either by prison or death. He would not have been happy with just two murders. He would have been driven to do it again and again. The satisfaction he derived from the first two would have only whetted his appetite, so I would be looking for other crimes in other states in the year 1966 and thereafter."

15

EVE'S ABDUCTION AND BEATING UP
A PERV

I was still receiving messages in response to Alice's TV appearance. One came from someone referring to herself only as "Eve." I spoke to her by phone on December 21, 2011. Eve, she explained, was not her real name, but she was looking to protect herself. What she had to say was difficult to say on the phone, but she'd give it a try. In 1968 she was, she wasn't sure of the word but chose "molested," by a teacher at a school in Holley. The teacher taught in Holley but lived at the time in Ogden. The incident took place at Silver Stadium, the old home of the Rochester Red Wings baseball team on Norton Street in Rochester, and it wasn't as much a molestation as it was an abduction. She told a policewoman and went to court, and she was told that she was a very lucky girl because the guy was a suspect in the "Chili murders." She didn't know what the Chili murders were. Years later she tried to figure out what that woman meant. She ran into a lot of info about the Double Initials Murders in the 1970s but found nothing about the Chili murders—that is, until she saw Alice and me on TV. She "freaked out." Eve e-mailed the state police on about August 30, 2011, a few days after the TV broadcast. A trooper, whom she didn't want to name on the phone, told her that the teacher was living in Penfield. They had a DNA sample from him, but Eve believed that it was sitting on a shelf somewhere. Eve told me that the guy, the Double Initials Killer, never stopped killing. He might or might not be both the Chili murderer and the DIK, but there had been a couple of murders since then that might have been done by this guy. There was a woman whose last name was Solie who went missing in Macedon and her purse was found in Penfield. And there was one more. The trooper she'd contacted, she said, was "the same guy" who'd worked on the Double Initials cases. She got the impression that the teacher was both a suspect in the Chili murders back in 1968 when she was abducted at the ballpark and, at the time his DNA was taken, a suspect in the Double Initials Murders as well. She had a composite sketch that had been done of the DIK and said it looked just like the teacher. She asked me if I knew anything about the Formicola girl, and I said I did. She wondered if the Formicolas in Holley were relatives of the Chili Formicolas.

"If you want to talk to someone in person about this, you could talk to Don Tubman, a private detective in Scottsville," I said. I'd said the magic word. Tubman was really convenient for her because she worked near Scottsville.

The next day, Tubman arranged to meet Eve at the Scottsville Free Library at noon. When both arrived on time and found the library closed until 1:00 p.m., they reconvened at a local coffee shop. Tubman bought, and they talked. He thought she bore a physical resemblance to George-Ann. He drank his coffee, and she took two or three sips of hers and stopped. She told him that her name was Cathy Carter.* She was 55 years old and had two kids who were 38 and 36. She said that the man who had abducted her was Vince Payne.* Actually, she spelled it for him—"P-A-Y-N-E"—and refused to say it aloud. She became anxious when she heard Tubman say it out loud. She'd gone to the 1968 Rochester Red Wings game on a school bus as part of a school trip. It was a Knot Hole game, which meant kids (members of the "Knot Hole Gang") got in at special low prices. Mr. Payne was a sixth-grade teacher at Holley. She had him for history, but he wasn't her homeroom teacher.

At some point, either during the game or just after it, he told Cathy that she shouldn't get back on the school bus, that he would take her home in his car. But he didn't take her home. He drove her instead to someplace on Lake Shore Boulevard. He parked the car in a secluded spot and began to act peculiarly. Cathy couldn't articulate what he did or said. He expressed his great affection for her, but in a nervous sweaty kind of way. He seemed to be having some sort of nervous breakdown. He got out of the car and waved his arms around.

"I can't do this," she remembered him saying.

He ranted and raved, and she remembered thinking that his anxiety had something to do with Catholicism. He did not harm her and eventually drove her back toward home, dropping her off "a few miles" from her house. She was not clear as to how she reported the incident or if he was arrested, but she remembered testifying in what she thought was a courtroom at age 13. Mr. Payne was fired as a teacher.

She'd brought with her the DIK composite drawing and a photo of Payne. As Tubman made copies, he looked at the two images and saw a resemblance, especially in the eyebrows. Chris said Payne was not a large man, that he stood only about 5'3" tall.

She told him about the Sandra Solie murder[1] and the disappearance of Brian Sullivan. Those might have been Payne as well.

Since seeing me on TV, she regularly contacted the state police, the first contact taking place on August 30 with a senior investigator named Allan M. Dombrowski, who had not been helpful. She had never met the trooper in person, and all communications were by e-mail.

(She later called me, saying that she had been contacted by the state police, not Dombrowski but another trooper, with the news that Vince Payne's DNA was not a match for the DIK. She was elated.)

After parting ways with "Eve," aka Cathy Carter, Tubman visited Henry "Dig" Taggart, a kid from the other side of the river, with older brothers known to be tough guys in the same upper echelon as the Rowe brothers. The Taggarts were bikers and musicians. Dig had a picture of Bobby "Blackfoot" Turner, the legendary Rochester biker, in his garage. Dig said that Jack Starr once had a bad fight with Dig's older brother. Jack drew a knife. Sometimes when guys fought they bonded and became friends afterward, but that didn't happen here. Drawing the knife was an asshole move, and the Taggarts steered clear of Jack. Dig didn't want to say that Jack was a bad guy. It was more the drugs than anything. Dig said his brother Mike would know a lot more about Jack.

On December 23, as Christmas preparations went on all around me, I boned up on the Sandra Solie case referenced by Cathy Carter. I ran a search for Vincent Payne, but all I learned was that he was a generous member of his Penfield church and a '62 grad of a local college. As I did that, Tubman was Christmas shopping at Marketplace Mall and ran into Patrick Crough, who had been with the MCSO since 1983 and a criminal investigator with the Major Crimes Unit since 1991. He hunted the Chili killer and the DIK as cold cases. Crough was at the mall collecting money for a camp for kids and was at first reluctant to talk shop with Tubman. But Tubman pressed the matter, and eventually Crough chatted. He remembered that the Chili case files were in disarray, probably because they had passed through a lot of hands over the years. He still thought of the Chili murders and that he had talked to Alice Bernhard as recently as six months ago. Don told me that Crough had "talked to some people" regarding the 1966 murders and that I should talk to him after the holidays.

After the mall, Tubman visited Dig Taggart's older brother Mike, who was 15 years old when George-Ann and Kathy were killed. Mike told Don that one time, earlier that year in 1966, he and a few other boys had discovered a guy back by the trestle that was exposing himself to girls at the swimming hole. The boys beat the hell out of the guy. With Taggart were Bryan Davis, who later became a member of the Pagans biker gang and was doing hard time; Billy Batrack, who died at 16 in a car crash in March 1967; and Jim Riechel, also dead and the dad of Don.

Years later, Mike said, he realized that the swimming-hole pervert was actually Arthur Shawcross. Mike said that he'd read "all three books" about Shawcross, but the only title he remembered was *The Genesee River Killer*. He remembered reading that Shawcross had, at some point, admitted that he took a bus to Rochester from Watertown and hung around Black Creek. Don asked me about this, and I said that I recalled Shawcross admitting that he had been in Rochester as a young man, but he hadn't gone into much detail. The thing Taggart came away with after his research was that Shawcross was primarily a necrophiliac. He wanted prostitutes to play dead, and when they didn't he killed them.

Tubman eventually tried to switch the subject to Jack, but Mike wouldn't budge.

"Oh, yeah, Jack was crazy, but this was Shawcross," he said.

Mike never told the authorities about the man who was exposing himself or the beating they gave him. The day the girls disappeared, he and the boys were swimming in the river on the Brighton side, north of the iron trestle. There was a swing near the end of Remington Parkway. That day at about 2:30 p.m., they saw George-Ann and Kathy on the Chili side, and Batrack, who was sweet on George-Ann, started to swim across the river toward them. When he got three-quarters of the way across, he pretended he was drowning, and the girls jumped in to save him. The last they saw of the girls, they were walking down Junction Road along the tracks toward the Black Creek swimming hole. (I later asked Evie Douglas about Batrack, and she remembered him as "gorgeous," with thick black hair. I told her the story, and she offered her opinion that the girls would have jumped in to save him even if they didn't believe he was actually drowning.)

Mike Taggart agreed that talking to Gary or Richie Barnes might be helpful but warned that it was going to be difficult to get Gary Barnes to say anything bad about the Starrs because he and Nicky Starr went off to war together, and Gary came back alone. Tubman asked Taggart what he knew of everyone's work history. Jack worked at Delco like his old man. Nicky worked at Your Host as a dishwasher before he joined the army, and Gary Barnes worked at a major Rochester corporation.

I reviewed the statements Shawcross made about Rochester before moving there following his parole, and after his arrest as the Genesee River Killer. He told two stories, one that he'd been to Rochester once as a young truck driver and wasn't impressed, and one that he lived briefly in Rochester, spending money he had acquired in a series of robberies. He never (that I knew of) made any statements about hanging around Black Creek. However, Shawcross did once talk about being jumped by five guys in an unspecified woods near Rochester.[2]

Tubman interviewed Rona Lee Merritt who grew up on Names Road in the 1950s who said that everybody thought Jack Starr had committed the murders just because the police were spending most of their time interviewing him. She also said that because of the hobos and perverts who frequented the area because of the railroads and the proximity to the city, none of the girls would hitchhike. George-Ann and Kathy might have broken out of that mold, but she was doubtful. She said that Starr was probably crazy enough to have lured them and killed them in anger. She mentioned Bugsy Yarborough as a guy who might have information, as he was apparently Jack's friend and confidant.

Tubman verified that Cathy Carter's suspect, Vince Payne, taught sixth grade in the Holley School District in 1967. The confirming source left Holley before 1968 and could only say that Payne had a classroom across the hall from his and was "a little odd." Tubman checked the state education teacher-certification unit and couldn't confirm that Payne was certified back then. Tubman theorized that Payne was disciplined by having a superintendent's hearing and was probably asked to leave. Tubman believed that Payne then took a transportation job in Penfield and got out of the classroom.

16

DEVILS DICIPLES

On January 2, 2012, Tubman talked to Danny Johnson, whose sister had been one of my best friends in school. The Johnsons had lived across Ballantyne Road from Evie Douglas. When Tubman asked about the Starr family, Danny remembered that one of them—Jack or one of his brothers, he thought—had been a Peeping Tom. I remembered Grace Green telling me of the man with a knife she saw out her bedroom window, and the deal after the murders in which Morrison Avenue had a Peeping Tom. When asked specifically about Jack, Danny could only say that Jack was "always in trouble" and "not pleasant to be around." He knew nothing of the Wilson brothers.

On January 3, Don Campbell spoke to George-Ann's uncle Burton Braddock a second time, and he said he still had copies of *WE* magazine with articles about the murders in them.

I remembered *WE*. It was printed on yellow or orange paper, a local scandal sheet. It had a soily, sleazy feel to it and usually featured sex crimes on its front page, printing the graphic details but omitting all names. I told Campbell we would love to have copies of those articles.

Braddock remembered Gina Formicola's husband Keith Wilson living with Clint and Francine Wilson at their house on Names Road. Perhaps these were occasions when Gina had given him the boot. After his job packing meat, Clint had worked for Gates-Chili Disposal, driving a garbage truck.

Campbell asked Braddock about William Formicola, the boy that George and Ruth Formicola had adopted not long after the murders. Was that George-Ann's baby? Braddock didn't know. Braddock didn't approve of the way his sister raised her girls. "She was too strict," he said. That was why they rebelled. Sure, he knew Barney Wilson. "He was probably the only normal one of the Wilsons," Braddock said.

Tubman reinterviewed George-Ann's cousin Ray Morton and came up with new and more detailed info. Clint married Francine Morton "8 to 10 years" before the murders. Ray wasn't sure, but he believed that Clint met his sister when they both worked at Conti Meatpacking (which would have made him a coworker of George-Ann's mom). Clint, Ray said, lived on Names Road about five houses from the Bernhards. Ray remembered Keith Wilson, but not Barney. He said that there could've been other brothers, but if so they didn't live nearby. He said that Clint was a Hells Angel for a while but had a falling-out with them and formed his own club called Satans Diciples (and that was how it was spelled). Ray said that Clint was "questioned repeatedly" about the murders and implied that this might've had something to do with why his sister "bailed" on the marriage. (Although he'd told me earlier that Clint was a drunken wife beater. That might have had something to do with it as well.) Ray confirmed that Clint and Jack Starr were buddies. He didn't know why Clint was considered a suspect.

Ray said Clint died of liver failure (which turned out not to be true). Francine remarried. Ray gave Don her phone number. Ray didn't know the name of Gina Formicola's boyfriend, the one who killed Keith Wilson. He grew up believing that George-Ann was promiscuous, but he didn't know she'd had a baby. Gina, as far as he knew, was still in Florida.

In search of more info about the beating up of the naked fisherman back by the swimming hole not long before the murders, I called Don Riechel. He was not in good health and could barely speak. His wife was nice enough to put me on speakerphone and relay his answers to me. According to Mike Taggart, Don's dad had been one of the guys doing the stomping. Don said he'd "heard something about a pervert" but couldn't recall details. He didn't think his dad had anything to do with it.

Any idea who the pervert might've been? The only pervert he could recall was a dimwitted neighborhood kid who'd been caught having sex with a cow, as well as masturbating in school. Mike Taggart had been clear that they beat up a stranger. (And that was my last communication with Don Riechel. In February 2012, Mrs. Riechel called to tell me that Don had passed away.)

On January 6, Tubman spoke to Jim Newell, who was an expert in the case on a couple of fronts. For one thing, he was a senior investigator for the state troopers who had worked the Chili murders as a cold case and who was currently on the security detail for Lieutenant Governor (and former Rochester mayor) Bob Duffy. Newell also grew up in the Castle Inn, as his dad owned the bar. Newell told Tubman that he had interviewed Jack Starr several times and thought Jack was the murderer. Did Jack give him an alibi? They never got that far, Newell said. Jack was sick at the time, with AIDS, and when Newell asked what happened to the girls, Jack would say, "I'll tell you before I go." But he never did.

Newell did not believe that Jack was the father of George-Ann's baby. "You ever hear of a milk-shake baby?" Newell asked. George-Ann, he believed, was so promiscuous that there was no telling who the dad was.

Ballantyne back then had its own version of "Breckinridge" working, a man/girl sex society. Newell said men used to come into the bar when he was a kid and talk about "sex parties" with adult men and young girls. He gave a couple of last names, men who lived on Names Road and who had kids I went to school with, that previously had not come up in this context.

For close to 30 years, Newell said, his dad allowed Johnny Bernhard, Kathy's dad, to drink in the bar in exchange for labor. Every night Bernhard put up the chairs and cleaned up the bar after closing.

The state cold-case officer was not working the Chili murders but was still actively seeking the DIK.

Newell had a detailed timeline of Arthur Shawcross's whereabouts, the contents of which evidently warranted no further comment.

Clint Wilson, Newell recalled, was a Hells Angel only briefly—he quit or was kicked out—and joined the Buffalo chapter of the Devils Diciples. He had not started up his own club.

If Tubman came up with something, getting the bodies exhumed would be easy enough, Newell said. Finding usable DNA from 1966 evidence, on the other hand, was mission impossible. Nothing was preserved properly back then. The notion of DNA hadn't even occurred to anyone.

Newell wanted to help more. It was a case close to his heart. But he was very busy with 2012 Rochester gang activity.

Jim's kid brother Mike "Mo" Newell tended the bar at the Castle Inn for 20 years. Mo remembered Johnny Bernhard as a "genius who, when sober, could fix anything."

On January 7, Tubman interviewed Richard Barnes, who was in George-Ann and Kathy's class. Barnes turned out to be a great witness and filled in a lot of blanks.

As far as he knew, Clint Wilson came from Avon, a town about 10 miles south of Ballantyne. Clint met Ray Morton's sister Francine at work, married her, and introduced his brother Keith to George-Ann's sister Gina. Clint and Keith had a younger brother named Barney, who was often in Ballantyne, either sleeping at Clint's, Keith's, or, on a few occasions, at the Barnes's house. He might've dated George-Ann.

Barnes knew about the beating of the pervert back by the creek. As he heard it, the guy was fishing naked. The guy could have been Shawcross. Who administered the beating? Barnes thought it was Mike and Dig Taggart, Bryan Davis, Billy Batrack, and maybe Jim Rowe, Johnny Rowe's younger brother. Billy Batrack, the kid who pretended he was drowning in the Genesee River, died soon thereafter in a car crash on an icy road. Barnes said that Batrack had sex with George-Ann but died not long after the murders.

Barnes said that he knew all about George-Ann's pregnancy. George-Ann, he said, had confided in him. She'd told her mother that Jack Starr was the father of the baby, but he really wasn't. Barnes, admittedly sweet on George-Ann, was too shy to ask who the real father was. She'd already been pregnant, Barnes said, when she inveigled her way into Jack's heart.

George-Ann had no choice but to know Clint Wilson. She didn't like him, though. Clint "bothered George-Ann." When they were swimming at the trestle, Clint would dunk her head and other stuff. On Halloween 1965, Barnes, George-Ann, and Kathy soaped Clint's windows and got caught. Clint smelled Richie's hand to make sure it smelled of soap. They tried to laugh it off and promised to wash his windows the next day, but Clint took special interest in frightening George-Ann.

Barnes believed that George-Ann was pregnant a second time when she was murdered.

During the time the girls were missing, sheriff's deputies followed Billy Batrack and the Barnes brothers. "They thought we had the girls stashed someplace," Barnes said. He recalled one time he and Samantha Sherman drove to Wolcott and Fair Haven, New York, and were followed the whole way.

Asked about the Batrack "drowning" incident, Barnes said he believed that happened earlier that year and not on the day the girls disappeared. The girls disappeared on graduation day, and there were parties going on.

Kathy and George-Ann went swimming on the afternoon of June 25, 1966, and asked if he wanted to come too, but he declined because he was helping to set up Samantha Sherman's graduation party. (Much of which, if she is to be believed, she must have missed because she was on a date with Jack Starr.)

"Kathy was tough as nails," Barnes said. "That's why the killer had to chop off her head to kill her."

"Where did you hear that Kathy was beheaded?" Tubman asked.

Barnes said he heard it from Larry Kane,* a sheriff's deputy who lived in the neighborhood, and married one of Jack Starr's sisters.

If Jack and Clint were buddies, Barnes knew nothing about it, but he did recall a time when George-Ann complained that "guys from the city come around and bother us," but he didn't have any more information than that.

More and more indicators were pointing to Clint Wilson. Clint's brother was married to George-Ann's sister. He was married to George-Ann's first cousin. He enjoyed bullying George-Ann. He'd been raping or trying to rape neighborhood girls, sometimes using a knife, threatening the girls with death if they talked. George-Ann became pregnant, lied about the paternity, admitted she lied to a neighborhood boy, and had her throat slashed with a knife.

The day after his conversation with Richard Barnes, Tubman spoke with Clint Wilson's ex-wife, the former Francine Morton, who grew up on Lester Street so that her backyard faced the Pennsylvania Railroad tracks between Ballantyne Road and the swimming hole. She said she had four daughters, and three of them were Clint's. She started out suspicious and brusque but relaxed and became friendlier as the conversation proceeded.

"He was a mean and nasty man," she said. "I eventually had to get rid of him."

She even tried to kill him once. He'd done something to piss her off, and she got in the car and tried to run him over while he was riding his motorcycle. The incident took place on Scottsville Road in the vicinity of Nordic Village Restaurant, known in 1966 as Schiano's Restaurant.

Clint, born in 1941, grew up in Avon, New York, but attended school in Scottsville because his dad worked on a farm in Scottsville and drove him to school every day. Clint and Francine met in seventh grade. This was before centralization (which caused some schools to become populated with kids not from a single town but from a geographic area that combined portions of two towns). Clint graduated from Scottsville High School. She said Clint had five brothers and sisters. There was Melvin, Paul, Barney, Bonnie, and Keith. (Francine missed two: sister Melvina and brother William.) Incredibly, three of the brothers were killed by their women. Melvin and Paul, she said, were shot by their wives, and Keith was shot by his wife's boyfriend, in what Francine referred to as a "setup murder." If she'd nailed Clint with her car, that would have made four.

The bit with Keith and Gina was a real soap opera. Gina was dating her husband's relative, eventually married him, and didn't even have to change her name because she was already Gina Wilson. As far as Francine knew, Gina and her boyfriend split for Florida and were living down there still. Tubman sought location information. Clint's brother Barney and sister Bonnie were in the Finger Lakes region, each with their own successful business.

Francine's sister Ruth was in Texas.

Her story of how she met Clint disagreed completely with her brother Ray's version of the story, in which they'd met because they worked together in a meatpacking facility. Clint, Francine said, worked for a garbage collection company. (This corroborated the info received from Burton Braddock that Clint drove a truck for Gates Chili Disposal.) His primary interest was in motorcycles. He'd been a Hacker, and briefly a

Hells Angel, but he didn't fit in and became one of the founders of the Devils Diciples chapter in Buffalo. Francine said that she was 18 when she married Clint, and they were married for 13 years, living together for most of that time. Tubman did not tell Francine that we'd developed information that Clint hurt little girls, but she did say she didn't think Clint ever molested any of their daughters. Tubman asked if she had any theories as to who might've killed Kathy and George-Ann. She said no. Tubman didn't ask if she'd been Clint's alibi witness back in 1966, but he asked if she thought he did it. "He could've," she replied, thus negating any alibi she might have once provided. She remembered police speaking to Clint a few times, but she didn't think anything of it. Cops were talking to all the men, even Francine's father, who was in a body cast at the time. Clint and Francine lived on Names Road—just a few houses away from the Bernhards on one side and the Starrs on the other—the entire time they were married. Tubman asked Francine flat out if Clint could've killed the girls, and Francine said no, he wasn't that tough. He wouldn't have had the guts. One of the reasons he quit the Angels was that those guys were into hard drugs, and Clint just liked to smoke a little weed now and again.

There was one odd thing, though, Francine recalled. On the very day the girls' bodies were found off of Archer Road, the Mortons' dog was found on the Pennsylvania Railroad tracks between Ballantyne Road and the swimming hole. It had been neatly slit down the middle and gutted. Francine shared some of her wisdom regarding bikers: "They're half crazy, and the other half don't think too good." She said she knew Jack Starr but didn't know him to be a friend of Clint's, but then again Clint spent a lot of time away from home. She also didn't remember Barney spending that much time in Ballantyne.

The info regarding the dog made Tubman wonder if the dog hadn't discovered the scene of the actual murders and had to be killed because it knew too much. I had another theory. Clint killed the dog to send a message to Francine.

Tubman said he knew the beeline to a solution. William Formicola was George-Ann's kid. His father was the killer. DNA.

During the long Martin Luther King Day holiday weekend, I learned that George Formicola, 28 years old, and Ruth Braddock, 17, applied for a marriage license on May 9, 1947—a solid 10 months before Gina was born. He was already a mechanic and lived on Myrtle Street in the city, five blocks southwest of Edgerton Park. She lived in Scottsville. In November 1950, Mr. and Mrs. Meril Braddock simultaneously gave deeds to lots on Stallman Drive to George Formicola and Burton Braddock. So brother and sister had been living next door to each other for 12 years before the Bensons moved in at the end of the dirt road. In May 1962, my dad purchased lot 11 of the Bauman Farms subdivision from the previous owner, Dallas D. Davis. Pauline Putnam would later become Burt's second wife. He was previously married on Memorial Day 1956. George Formicola died in Florida in 1994, and Ruth was apparently already dead, as his estate—which consisted of debt—went to son William. William once had a wife, but now she had an order of protection against him. Gina's drug arrest for cocaine possession, if we had the correct Gina Wilson, took place in 2001.

I discovered info on a familiar name from the distant past. In May 1966, Gert Tyler of Stallman Drive announced her engagement to a sailor named Roy Saxman, 18 years old, of the Bull's Head area in Rochester. The wedding was scheduled for July, but the couple moved up the date and married on Monday, June 27, two days after Kathy and George-Ann disappeared. Sid and Doris Bookman stood up for them.

I researched Clint Wilson and learned that he and his brother Melvin both had their fates determined by the same grand jury in Avon in October 1959. During that session, Clint, then 18, was indicted for third-degree burglary, and Melvin, 19, was exonerated of rape when a "no bill" was handed up. Clint and his brother Paul were pulled over on Route 39 north of Geneseo on May 25, 1960, and arrested for reckless driving. In 1961, Clint was involved in a two-car crash in Henrietta. The best guess is that he was already working as a truck driver for a garbage disposal company because his address was given as 1243 South Road in Wheatland, then the location of a landfill. In April 1963, Clint and Francine bought the house on Names Road. Before that, their address was listed as the Morton house on Lester Street. On June 6, 1963, Clint received a speeding ticket in Scottsville and had to pay a $10 fine. Three times Clint was in small claims court, in 1971 over a hospital bill, in 1972 over some professionally taken photographs, and in 1974 over almost $1,000 with his employer (or ex-employer), Gates-Chili Disposal Co., Inc. For the first two lawsuits, Clint was listed as living on Names Road, but his address for the 1974 lawsuit was on Sterling Street, on the west side of Rochester. In 1971, Clint's older brother Melvin listed the Names Road address as his home. In 1976, again listed as a Chili resident, Clint purchased a mobile home in Mumford, southwest of Scottsville.

In January 1974, Clint's then 30-year-old brother Paul was one of three men to be arrested for robbing a 70-year-old Penn Yan man. Paul apparently picked the man up in his car and told him they were going fishing, but instead drove him to a secluded spot and robbed him. His accomplices were a 29-year-old and a juvenile.

I found the obituary for Clint Wilson's dad, Clinton Sr. He died "unexpectedly" on November 1, 1971, at 55, at the home of his daughter Mrs. Bonnie Morrison on Main Street in Keshequa, New York. Clint's dad, a World War II vet who'd toured Europe the hard way, lived on Brandywine Road in Wayne. He belonged to the American Legion, the Moose Club, and the Keshequa Baptist Church. He was survived by eight children: Melvina of Lavonia Center, Mrs. Melvin Wilson of Fort Lauderdale, Florida (Melvin apparently was already deceased), Clint of Rochester, Paul of Keshequa, William of Wayne, Keith of Stanley, and Barney of Avon. Melvina and Bill were the siblings that Clint's ex-wife Francine had forgotten to mention, new names to this investigation.

The data bank for Jack Starr offered only four points in time over the course of more than a decade, but nonetheless conveyed a life in decline. On July 29, 1969, Jack and his wife Ann received the deed to a Names Road home a few doors down from the family house. At that time, before road crews moved Scottsville Road to put more space between it and the river, that house, at the very end of Names Road, overlooked a grassy meadow with a copse of willow trees in the center where in the 1970s there was often a cluster of youths smoking pot, the Ballantyne Bridge in the background. In March 1971, Jack, listed as a "factory worker," filed for bankruptcy, $35,000 in debt, with assets listed as "none." In May 1972, the Starrs had a baby girl.

In January and February 1980, the villages south of Rochester were plagued by a number of burglaries. Merchants had lost around $2,000. In the early morning hours of Monday, February 11, town cop William Mills arrested two men as they tried to force open the front door of a gas station. A third man escaped on foot. The men were Jack Starr and

24-year-old William Webster of Scottsville,[1] who was in my grade at
school and once, in sixth grade, socked me just for the fun of it.

Sergeant Thomas D. Torpey, head of the Caledonia police, and Investigator John M. York of the Livingston County Sheriff's Department
handled the burglary investigation. The village board of Caledonia had
agreed in January to pay overtime to fight the burglaries. They had a
cop staked out inside the gas station in the middle of the night when
Jack and Billy broke in.

Police found a 1975 Chevrolet two blocks from the station. The car,
registered in a woman's name at Starr's Names Road address, was impounded by police.

At 4:00 in the afternoon of February 11, 36-year-old factory worker
Jack Starr gave a statement to York and Torpey (a copy of which I
received after filing a Freedom of Information request). Also present
was Jack's attorney William E. Van Duser. Jack said the story started on
Sunday, January 10, when he received a phone call from Dennis J.
Callaghan, a former Ballantyne kid who now lived in Caledonia.

"You interested in doing anything?" Callaghan asked, and Starr recognized this as code for doing some sort of crime.

"I'll talk about it," Starr said, and the men agreed to meet at a late-
night sandwich joint on Scottsville Road, just on the city side of the
canal. They met just after midnight. With Callaghan was Billy Webster.
Dennis had his car, a green-and-white 1969 Ford with Florida license
plates.

Starr said, "Callaghan left his car here, and he and Billy got into my
car with me." It was a 1975 brown Chevelle. They talked in the parking
lot for a time. Callaghan's idea was to knock off an "oil company" in
Caledonia, where there were payroll receipts. Callaghan called the job
"quick and easy" and maybe worth as much as $20,000. The money was
in the office, so they'd have to break in and get it. They wanted to take
Starr's car because it was the most dependable.

"I'm low on gas," Starr said.

"I'll buy gas," Callaghan said, and they stopped at a gas station and
put five dollars' worth in the tank.

They then drove to Caledonia. Callaghan had two crowbars with
him. Starr had tools too, but they were never used. Cruising Caledonia,
they tried to locate any police. Callaghan said something about the town
cop being off duty. They scouted the oil company for a time, parked on

a side street down the block, and walked back, Callaghan carrying a crowbar. Callaghan forced open the front door, stepped inside, and motioned for Starr and Webster to join him. No sooner were all three inside when a police officer stepped out from a hiding place and said, "Freeze." Starr and Webster froze, but Callaghan pushed them both in the direction of the cop and made a run for it. "Then a lot of police came," Starr concluded.

In response to police questioning, Webster confessed to an earlier burglary that he had committed with Callaghan. On this occasion, New Year's Day, with Starr not there, they had entered the J&L Mobile station in Caledonia, and Callaghan had emptied the cigarette machine and stolen the entire safe, which they then transported to the home of Webster's mom in Scottsville on Humphrey Road. There they forced the safe open and emptied it of $1,200 in cash. They then put the empty safe back in the car and dropped it off a bridge into the Genesee River near Rodney Farms.

On the night of January 18–19, someone broke into the Olympus Restaurant in Avon. They'd come in through the back door, where there was a half-inch gap between the door and the frame, making it easy to pry open. The cigarette machine had been neatly pried as well, and $66.75 in change had been removed. The burglar knew what he was doing, opening the machine without in any way damaging it. According to Billy Webster, Callaghan and he had committed this burglary, while Jack Starr drove the getaway car.

That was the first of two burglaries that Callaghan and Webster pulled at that same diner. The second time, on January 26, instead of taking the change, they emptied the machine of cigarettes, $280 worth. They took some cigars from a nearby candy case that had been left open, all the lottery tickets they could grab (all losers, Webster later noted), and removed the "Good Luck" money that had been taped to the wall.

I couldn't find any record of Starr or Callaghan's fate, but on September 22, 1980, Judge Charles S. Willis sentenced Billy Webster to one and a half to three years in Attica.

After reading the files, I talked with a former neighbor of the Websters who said that a group, including the informant's brother, was involved back then with Billy Webster in criminal enterprises which included burglaries. The source said that Billy Webster was living in his family home's garage when he died. My source thought Billy died of a drug overdose. I did not bring up Jack's name in hopes that the source would, but he didn't.

Bottom line: Jack Starr became a criminal, but not a sex criminal.

Tubman, in search of the Mulligans, talked to Paul Czapranski, who swam with George on the Wheatland-Chili swim team. He reported that, when last seen, Nancy was in bad shape, in a wheelchair and on oxygen, suffering from cancer and emphysema. (I remembered how young Nancy and George-Ann were—12, 13—when they started smoking, and how I was frightened when I first saw them smoke.)

In the meantime, I investigated Klaus Kastenholz, who told police the intriguing tale of Patrick Ninnies and "Jack." I learned that from at least July 1965, when a 21-year-old Kastenholz married 20-year-old Delores Salasar,[2] until at least 1974, he lived at 318 Avenue B[3] in the city, which was about 100 yards from the spot on Conkey Avenue where Wanda Walkowicz, the second Double Initials victim, was last seen. His occupation was listed as "tool & die." I learned through confidential sources that Kastenholz was arrested repeatedly for possession of narcotics with intent to sell in California. If the Jack and Ninnies story was real— admittedly unlikely—they might have needed a little sump'n sump'n to calm themselves down before they decided what to do with the bodies, and Kastenholz may have been just the right guy for that.

What made the Wilson brothers so mean? The answer came when I discovered that Clint Sr., their father, had been arrested in May 1971 at age 54 for raping a five-year-old girl.[4] He fled to Fort Lauderdale, Florida, but was apprehended there on May 14 and bought back to Yates County, New York. On May 25, Big Clint, represented in court by public defender Anthony J. Geraci, pleaded not guilty to a first-degree rape charge. He was held on $3,000 bail for his next appearance in court on June 14. At that appearance, before Yates County judge Lyman H. Smith, Big Clint had a new lawyer, Stanley Curtis of Rochester.[5]

Clint Sr.'s son William, then 26, was also arrested for hindering the investigation and endangering the welfare of a child. William was accused of failing to act upon an order from the Yates County district attorney, Fred Hunt.

In the long run, as usual, witnesses were too scared to testify, and the victim was too young to testify. On September 28, Judge Smith allowed Big Clint to plead guilty to a lesser charge of endangering the welfare of a child, and he was placed on three years' probation. The judge further stipulated that Clint was not allowed to see the little girl anymore unless her parents were present[6] (an odd stipulation that only made sense if the accused and the victim were members of the same family and thus were unable to avoid one another). It seemed a miscarriage of justice, but fate handled it: 33 days later, Big Clint died "unexpectedly" in his daughter Bonnie's kitchen.[7] Disbelievers in karma might consider the last months of this monster's life: his secret world of criminal deviance now front-page news in the local paper, made notorious and then sent back out to the streets of his town, exposed and despised. Surely there were family members who already hated his guts, but now it was a sanctioned feeling. He'd lost all control, forbidden fruit at last denied, and pretty soon he was dead.

While surfing a genealogy site, Don Campbell astoundingly found a captioned photo of the Wilson family of Keshequa. Dad was already gone, but Mom was still there sitting in a chair with her family around her, two daughters sitting on either side of her and six sons lined up behind. Judging from Keith's hair, which was long and blow-dried, the photo was from the mid-1970s. Because of the photo, I got my first glimpse of Clint, who looked familiar because for years he'd been our garbage man on Stallman Drive. While good ol' Keith radiated a smile, the other brothers looked like they were trying to intimidate the photographer. Clint looked ready to kill, taut with tension and anger, reddish hair slicked tightly back. His face was round, but his features were small, eyes like icy pinpricks, nose pointy, mouth pursed till minuscule. I couldn't help it. "That's the guy," I thought.

Over time, people gradually recast their stories to make them more interesting, to draw themselves closer to the action. So the reliability of a good ol' country story had to be graded on a curve. Still, when you hear the same thing over and over again, it starts to ring true.

I was impressed by the fact that Philip Albano, Mary Crane, and Richie Barnes all said that the girls invited them to go swimming with them that day. The girls wanted company. Looking at it another way, they perhaps did not want to go back to the swimming hole alone. But none of the invitees could go. Phil had to mow the lawn, Mary was grounded, and Richie had to help set up a graduation party. And they all lived within feet of one another.

Tubman visited a family of Ballantyne Road neighbors (who wished to remain anonymous). They thought "Clint and Keith Wilson were the murderers." Jack Starr might have been the father of George-Ann's baby, although not necessarily. That was the rumor, anyway.

Here was a noteworthy item: Jack Starr's half-sister Carol had been married to Sheriff's Deputy Larry Kane, the guy who told Richie Barnes that Kathy was beheaded. Carol's married name was listed in one obit as "Krane," a typo, so we'd missed the connection. Skip not only lived in the neighborhood, but he'd blabbed crime scene details to his neighbors. "Uterus was missing," he said, a stupid move, tainting the witness pool. Amazing, even then, that Larry could be allowed inside info on a murder when his brother-in-law was a top suspect.

The family solved another mystery. Back in 1966, on Ballantyne Road west of Stallman Drive, there lived an 80-year-old man who stripped off his clothes in the summer and wandered the fields in what appeared to be only a diaper. As he maundered, he sculpted little tee-pees of wood—which would explain the kindling clusters George Mulligan found in my back field when the girls were missing.

"Look how it is even today in Ballantyne," Tubman's informant said. The head of the household still had to show off how well armed he was. The Fear came to Ballantyne Road when those girls were murdered, and it never went away. He, for one, would rather be safe than sorry.

Tubman took over the Burt Braddock file and got some interesting information out of him. Burt admitted that he didn't know for sure who the father of George-Ann's baby was. Could've been Jack Starr, could've been Clint Wilson. He knew one thing for sure. He heard Gina tell Keith that their baby, Dean Keith Wilson, was not his; it was Clint's. He also knew that his daughter and her mother (referring to Dawn and Pauline Putnam) were afraid of George Formicola. "He was wild about women sexually," Braddock said of George-Ann's dad. "They could be 10 or 80!"

On January 24, 2012, Tubman spoke with a 49-year-old man named Roy Wagner who back in the day lived on Ballantyne Road, west of Stallman Drive. Wagner, a friend of Keith and Gina's kid Dean, was an auto parts guy. He didn't personally know anything he considered of value, but he might know someone who did. He'd sold some land off Brighton-Henrietta Town Line Road to a guy named Steve Griffin, an exterminator with his own pesticide business. Griffin told Wagner that he had attended a wild party back by the trestle around the same time as the murders and that "them girls that got killed" were there. Wagner wasn't sure if the guy meant the night of the murders or not long before that night.

17

SCREAMS IN THE NIGHT

On January 17, 2012, Don Tubman made first contact with my old buddy George Mulligan and found out some troubling information. George's sister Nancy had been dead for four years—sad because I liked Nancy very much, but also disappointing because I suspected she was the confidant who told deputies that George-Ann believed that Jack Starr would have married her if her parents had given permission. I assumed at first that Nancy had died of the cancer or emphysema she'd been suffering from when last seen at her mom's funeral. But instead she'd died when she accidentally set her hair on fire.

What did George remember of the night the girls disappeared? Quite a lot. His sister Sue, also now deceased, was having a graduation party behind their house, and music was blaring. Despite the music, everyone heard screaming in the distance. The screams sounded serious: "Help!" The music was turned off out of concern. Then the screams stopped, and everyone shrugged and continued partying.

Later, George's dad, Big George, talked to George Formicola, and he'd said that Clint and Keith Wilson were apparently the last ones to see the girls alive, that they had picked up the girls in a car. (Was this what the witness Bruce Witt had seen?) Tubman said George wanted to talk with me and gave me his number.

Speaking with George was an emotional moment for me, the sound of his voice sending me vividly back to our Huckleberry days. After catching up on each other's lives, George told me about the screams he'd heard. They seemed to come from the northwest. "In that back corner, to the left of your house," he said.

That would put the screams on the Junction Road, between the B& O tracks and our property. Of course the direction could be altered by the wind, and George thought it might have come all the way from Archer Road—which seemed to me unlikely. That would have been almost due west and too far away. There was something immediately bone chilling about a genuine scream of distress. It wasn't someone goofing around. You could feel it, gooseflesh, and everyone did feel it. The screams occurred when the music was playing. By the time the music was turned off to listen, the screams were over. (If the Bensons were on the screened-in porch watching the Glenn Ford movie, we would have had our entire house between us and the source of the screams, which might have been why we didn't hear them. Or maybe we heard but failed to interpret the sound as sinister. We were used to screaming in the night.) That night, after the music was turned off and there were no more screams, the music was turned back on and the party continued. It wasn't until George-Ann and Kathy came up missing that those goose-pimple screams gained significance. The kids at the party waited to be questioned by investigators, but none ever came, so George Sr. went over and told George Formicola what they'd heard that night.

George told me that George-Ann asked his sister Nancy to go swimming in the creek that evening. (Add her name to the list.) Nancy said no. The Mulligans had a pool that made the creek obsolete, and besides, her sister was having a graduation party and she needed to be home. It made no difference, though. Nancy would not have accepted anyway. They hadn't hung out much since seventh grade. Nancy was afraid of the people George-Ann hung around with, bikers and greasers brought into the house by her older sister Gina, like the Wilson brothers. Nancy heard from friends—possibly Mitch Owens or Debby Rockow—that George-Ann was last seen getting into a car with Keith and Clint Wilson. She didn't know for sure the source, just that that info did not come from George Formicola. But Nancy believed it to be true, and when Keith was killed in Henrietta, Nancy said Keith "finally got his." It was simple, Nancy told her brother. "Keith killed George-Ann, so Gina killed Keith."

He asked me if I remembered picking wild strawberries and hanging out in his tree house. I asked him if he remembered riding Benny the pony bareback and jumping ditches. We talked about fishing in the creek. He asked with some concern in his voice if my health had improved since I was a kid, and I told him I was born to live in the city. Animal dander was a problem, but I could breathe soot just fine. We both recalled running the path along the creek for Nancy and George-Ann. I remembered the trap as a string that would trip us. He said the girls told us they'd dug holes and covered them with branches. We were probably both right. Wonderful memories.

He filled me in on the whole Dady Hamilton story. His sister Sue apparently dated the guy briefly in high school but dropped him when she found him scary. He didn't take no for an answer and came over to the Mulligan house. When they wouldn't let him in, he punched his fist through a window in the front door and tried to turn the doorknob from the other side. They called the sheriff's office, and Hamilton ran away. The deputy told them that the next time the kid did something like that, they should drag him inside and shoot him—and then call the state troopers, not the sheriff. This was followed by the already-told incident in which Hamilton lay in wait across the road with a rifle ready to pick off Sue as she got off the school bus. George said they caught Hamilton that time, and he was sent away for years. Once, after he got out, he came back looking for Sue, but she was married and gone.

I drew the conversation back to George-Ann.

George became eloquent: "Nancy and George-Ann were both tomboys at first, but Nancy grew out of it. You know, Mike, we all moved on. We went to school in Scottsville and it was nicer there, so we found excuses to hang out. Sue became a cheerleader. I was into sports. Nancy started dating Scottsville guys, but George-Ann, I don't know . . . she didn't make the switch. Maybe it was because she was a little chunky or something, but while everyone else was stepping up, she began hanging around with Gina's dirtbag friends. Those guys were getting what they wanted from her, so they let her hang around."

For some people, I thought, bad attention was better than being ignored. I also thought that being chunky had nothing to do with it. The Formicola girls may have had to deal with domestic woes and battering rams to their self-esteem. The Mulligans and I did not.

George told me that he'd heard the story that one of those guys drove a garbage truck, and that would have been perfect for moving the bodies because no one would notice the smell.

I told him I'd heard some harsh things about George Formicola, but he didn't know anything about that. "When we hung around over there we'd always talk to Ruth, but that was because George was never around. When he did come home, he was black with soot like he'd spent the whole day and night shoveling coal. He never said much."

On Saturday, February 4, 2012, Don Tubman met for more than an hour with Dawn Putnam over coffee. She offered him a couple of facts that she hadn't told me. He found her to be an attractive, well-kept, and steadily employed woman. But man, where she came from was "fucked up." She said it, and he agreed. She gave him some impossible-to-publish details of her upbringing and then got to the heart of the matter: Clint Wilson *raped* her.

"He came into the house after the doors were locked," she remembered. Maybe he had a key. She didn't know how he got in. He knew there were no adults home. Maybe he'd seen Burt and her mom at the bar. He lay on top of her on her bed. He didn't have a weapon, but he put his hand over her mouth.

"Relax, we're in this for the long haul," he had said.

When he was done, he told her it was simple: if she squealed, she died. She was 12, which made this sometime in 1967, after the murders. She said she didn't even like boys yet.

George Formicola also made moves. She remembered wondering what it was about her that made those men do that. She was seen as an easy target. Because she was small? Was she being set up? Was someone talking behind her back?

Tubman asked about Keith Wilson.

"Keith was always really nice to me," Dawn said.

Despite her troubled childhood, Dawn nonetheless grew into a strong woman who was having a life, some parts still a little messed up but some not. She'd been married three times and had three kids.

Of the Formicolas, Dawn remembered Gina the best. Gina took Dawn out horseback riding with her a couple of times. But it was always the same. They'd get deep into a woods on the horse, and there'd be a boy. Gina would run off with him for a while, leaving Dawn alone with the horse.

She still remembered Keith as a nice guy—but the more she thought about it, the more she was thinking about Clint and the murders.

Tubman and I liked to think about Clint and the murders, too. Clint had allegedly raped a neighbor of George-Ann's (Dawn Putnam) and tried to rape a neighbor of Kathy's (Mary Crane), threatening them both with death, one with a knife. The girls were ages 12 and 10. Gina Formicola had reportedly screamed at Keith one night that their boy was Clint's kid. According to Richie Barnes, Clint particularly enjoyed frightening George-Ann on at least two occasions, once on Halloween and once at the swimming hole.

Jack, on the other hand, was a crazy guy, but there was no indication that he was a sexual sadist. He smacked his women, we learned, but that was a temper issue. Sexual sadists have a philosophy and will lean toward the cruelest thing when given a choice. Jack hit things, but Samantha Sherman gave us no indication of him being anything other than a gentleman and she claimed to have dated him for a year.

On the other hand, Jack was reportedly the one who liked to play with dead things, who couldn't just shoot the woodchuck but had to slit and disembowel it.

Tubman and I had a daily routine, an hour-long conversation during which we discussed scenarios that matched the facts with varying degrees of precision. He did most of the talking, weaving in praises of nature's beauty, small history lessons, and snippets of his autobiography with murder talk. George-Ann was playing dangerous games. She named Jack as the father of her baby, but she told Richie Barnes that she lied. The paternity of her baby may have been up for grabs (a milkshake baby), and she decided to pin it on the unmarried guy with the Corvette whose family had money. When in doubt (and pregnant), seduce a single guy and blame it on him. The actual father perhaps had things to lose, and George-Ann may have been bullied into not telling.

I conjectured that the girls might have been looking to be picked up on Scottsville Road all along. Maybe that was the reason for the whole exercise, why they had to "go back to the swimming hole," why they walked there—and were seen heading there—only to pause for the briefest moment on the stone trestle and move on. From there they most likely walked—George-Ann extremely pigeon-toed—along Junction Road to Scottsville Road, where they wandered up and down the side of the road. They were seen on Scottsville Road between the Castle Inn and Ballantyne Bridge, then on the Ballantyne Bridge returning from Coop's. They were seen all the way south to the Swing—Kathy still in possession of her radio—and then back at the confluence of Black Creek and the Genesee River, where they were summoned with a whistle by an olive-complexioned young man and scampered obediently into a Chevy up on Scottsville Road.

George-Ann was prematurely eroticized and also perhaps influenced by her older sister, who had a wild streak. Gina lived dangerously, dating dangerous men and then playing on the edge of angering them. Did Gina's lifestyle influence George-Ann's fate?

In a span of two years, Gina was married, George-Ann had a baby and was murdered, Dawn Putnam was raped, and two days after the girls disappeared, Gert Tyler got hitched to her sailor. That's a lot of activity for a dirt road with four houses on it.

During that winter, Tubman and I went riding around in his car, looking at locations and shooting the shit, walking along a ridge overlooking the Chili dump site. As we walked that ridge—with a smattering of visible tract houses on either side of the tracks, houses that weren't there then; nothing was there then—I was thinking about the choice of dump site. It must've been very dark, if it was indeed after dark that the bodies were dumped. Also, there was only one way out. If a car had pulled in behind the killer's car, he was screwed.

Tubman told me George Mulligan was the most important witness we'd talked to so far. "I believe he heard the murders," Tubman said.

A few days later Tubman talked to a retired cop named Harry De-Hollander, who started with the MCSO in 1960. DeHollander said he remembered two detectives working the case, and one was Jonathan Smith, who was dead. He recalled that the case had one strong suspect, and when they traced his car, they found that, because of a funky smell, it had been burned and then crushed at Berger Recycles. The thing was, DeHollander didn't remember the name of the suspect.[1]

A few weeks later, Tubman reinterviewed Tom Wiest, who had originally contacted the investigation after Alice and I appeared on TV. It turned out that Tom and Don knew one another and had hunted together. Wiest and Tubman were the same age and had both just graduated from high school—Don from Wheatland-Chili, Tom from Rush-Henrietta—when the girls disappeared.

Wiest had known the Callaghan brothers, who were friends of Jack Starr. Pat died in a Jamaican drug deal gone bad. Dennis died of AIDS, maybe sharing a needle with Jack. Wiest told Tubman, as he'd told me, that his then-girlfriend's sister, Sandy Luke, was one of the last people to talk to the girls, yet no cop ever spoke with her.

He talked about searching for the girls on the Sunday after they disappeared. He said he was familiar with the territory because he'd hunted off of Archer Road, and it was his impression that the bodies were found about an eighth of a mile off Archer.

Plus, Wiest knew Steve Griffin, the man who said he had met the murder victims back by the trestle, but he had never hung out with him.

The name Dady Hamilton came up, the young man who stalked Sue Mulligan. Wiest was of the impression that Hamilton was still alive. "I heard he's in North Carolina or Florida and not in good shape."

"Who were Jack's friends back in 1966?"

"Ed Yaw, Dave Burnetti, Jack Greco. They used to climb trees back behind Greco's and shoot at the trunks of each other's tree, trying to knock each other out of the tree."

Sandra Luke, the Ballantyne Bridge witness, told Tubman that she was walking with Cynthia Kinney across the bridge on their way to Coop's. George-Ann and Kathy were coming the other way, wearing bathing suits. One of the bathing suits was blue and new. The girls said they were heading for the trestle.

"Did you know that George-Ann had been pregnant?" Tubman asked.

"Not at the time," Luke replied.

Steve Griffin was next on Tubman's list. Griffin told Tubman that, even though he was from Henrietta (the Calkins Road area), he often hung around back by the stone trestle when he was a teenager. The reason was that he and his friends could buy beer at the Castle Inn, where they didn't ask for proof of age, and then drive via the dirt road back to

Genesee Junction and the trestle without worrying about running into police.

He and three of his friends were back by the trestle drinking beer sometime in 1966, and the two girls who were later killed came by and talked to them for a while. The three friends were all Henrietta boys: Howard Johnson, who later died of a drug overdose; Bill Wynn, who also OD'd; and Tom Wynn, who Griffin thought might still be alive, although he hadn't seen or heard from him in at least 20 years.

"The girls approached us from the north, sat with us for a while and talked, and when they left, they went back north," Griffin said. "A month later they were dead."

"How can you be sure it was the same girls who were murdered?" Tubman asked.

"Simple. I recognized their pictures in the paper." He didn't remember if the girls told them their names or what any of the conversation was about. He also wasn't sure of the time element, although he thought "a month or two" might've passed between meeting the girls and when he saw their pictures in the paper. He didn't think it was the night they disappeared or the Friday before that. He thought it was earlier. He remembered thinking George-Ann was "pretty." He remembered it being decent weather, sunshiny, maybe late afternoon.

Griffin didn't recall ever taking a girl back in that area. His girlfriend then was still his wife now, so he would ask her if he ever took her back there, but he didn't think so. Even though he and his friends were from Henrietta, he said they never had any trouble from the Ballantyne tough guys. He remembered that he went back to the trestle with different people about a year and a half after the murders and felt a different vibe—a bad vibe.

Griffin believed that the devil came from outside, that the murderer wasn't anyone he knew. Back in 1966, there was something odd about the Junction Road just north of the trestle. There were often guys by themselves sitting in cars, one guy he saw more than once, and others that were different each time. "Weirdo types," he called them. None of the cars were distinctive, and he didn't remember any makes or models. "I always thought one of those guys might be looking to kill girls," he commented.

Tubman wanted to get back to the drugs. Two died of drugs? What kind?

Griffin said he was pretty sure it was heroin. He himself just drank and maybe smoked a little pot, but Johnson and the Wynns did hard stuff. He thought Howard Johnson might've had heroin with him back by the trestle once.

"Ever run into any railroad police back there?"

"No, not any kind of police. That was what made it such a good place," Griffin said.

I verified that HoJo had died from drugs. His remains comprised one of two OD'd bodies discovered late on Thursday, February 18, 1993, on the floor of a bathroom on Chapel Street, Mount Morris. Police responded to a call from that address from a distraught woman. The other dead man was Dale Brew, 33, of Dansville, a lifelong small-time criminal.

I thought about something Griffin said. The girls approached and left to the *north*. They were not coming from home or returning home. Perhaps they had come from Scottsville Road and approached from the north only from Genesee Junction. But if he'd seen them come from a distance in that direction, where would that be? Old maps showed that those tracks led to within feet of the back of the Varsity Inn parking lot, where Klaus Kastenholz claimed to have seen the girls' bodies in the trunk of a car. I consulted our expert, former Varsity Inn bartender Don Campbell. He said, yes, the tracks did go right by the back of the parking lot, only a few feet away, but there was a ditch between the two that was usually filled with water, and there was no road running alongside the tracks. I tended to think the girls came upon Griffin, Johnson, and the Wynns from the direction of Scottsville Road. Maybe the Castle Inn was the only place where Kathy got to see her father.

On a roll now, Tubman spoke with the former Sandy Sage, a Ballantyne girl, Wheatland-Chili class of 1965. She was a familiar face in Ballantyne because of the years she worked at Coop's. When she went to school in Scottsville, she hung out in Scottsville, but she knew both George-Ann and Kathy just as friendly kids in the neighborhood. And she knew Jack Starr, whom she thought to be innocent.

"I was under the impression that Jack took a polygraph and passed," she said. "Jack thought it was *crazy* that this happened. He was *sad* when he talked about it."

Not that he was nice. Jack could be a frightening hothead, fought at the drop of a hat—but not capable of a double homicide.

Asked whom she suspected, she said her favorite suspect back in the day was the weirdo farmer across the street from the Monroe Tree Surgeons (i.e., Russell Hardin*). He was creepy, and he walked around the neighborhood sort of aimlessly. There was also a grown man, a goofy guy, who rode a bike around Ballantyne. She suspected him. Tubman asked about organized man/girl sex, but Sandy knew nothing about that. She thought it amazing that the victims were allowed to parade around the neighborhood in just bathing suits like that. "My parents wouldn't have allowed me to walk around in my bathing suit!"

I'd written two books, *Killer Twins* and *Evil Season*, in which the killer turned out to be a guy referred to by witnesses as "Bikeman." Here was another adult male on a bike—but I had no idea who this one was.

18

WE MAGAZINE

On eBay I acquired a January 16, 1967, copy of *WE*, the triweekly scandal sheet available back then at grocery store checkouts across Rochester. The issue held special interest because it contained full coverage of the Genesee Valley Park rapists' trial[1] and twice referenced the Chili murders: once in a letter to the editor referring to a story in a previous issue in which a man was walking his dogs along a path beside some railroad tracks when the dogs picked up the scent of something and, as a result, certain things perhaps pertaining to the Chili murders were dug up.[2] The other reference was in a report of a rape. The woman claimed that she was drinking in a suburban bar and got into a car with a man who raped her. He reportedly said, "I'm going to kill you and eat you up." For that reason, the victim thought her attacker might be implicated in the Chili murders.[3] It would have been great to know in which suburban bar the victim had been drinking, as well as a location and description of the buried items, but I feared that extant copies of *WE* would be hard to come by. Burt Braddock said he had the issues dealing with Kathy and George-Ann, so I asked his stepdaughter Dawn if we could get copies. A 1951 newspaper article mentioned that *WE* was published by a John Corey. The 1967 issue (vol. 22, no. 24) listed the publisher as George G. Cooper Jr. Under Cooper's editorial thumb, *WE* became increasingly prurient, with smutty stories cloaked in conservative politics. Don Tubman learned that the Coopers lived in Chili, only a mile or so from the Archer Road dump site. Back then you could get a subscription for two dollars annually. It was 15 cents at the store.

My search for other issues proved to be a short one. I learned that the Monroe County Library had a near complete set of *WE* on microfilm. A close friend of the investigation, Amy Minster Hudak, spent a Sunday afternoon in April in downtown Rochester's Rundel Library, in the second-floor Local History Division, on the Genesee River's east bank, sitting atop the city's abandoned subway tunnel. The July 1966 issue was missing, but the others were there, and within days I had copies in my hand. Here's what I "learned" from that bargain basement of pretend journalism:

During the spring of 1966 a pretty white 14-year-old girl, Rita Jancauskas, disappeared in the city of Rochester. She'd been dropped off in front of her school, Franklin High on Norton Street, but never made it inside the building.

In the magazine's breathless style, she had "vanished completely, whisked away by a will-of-the-wisp." Rita's mom, a German immigrant with no money, said she didn't think Rita would run away. There were no problems at home. Rita must be under duress.[4] She was still missing in August, after which Rita was never mentioned again in print.

As was true of many newsstand magazines of the day, *WE* had a cover date weeks in advance of the events it was covering, a minor deception designed to lengthen the paper's rack life. The August 1 issue had a cover story from June: a pack of drug-dealing thugs, led by a badass white teen named Black Chief, was putting Spanish fly in young girls' soft drinks and then taking them to the lower level of the adjacent parking garage for orgies.[5]

WE first mentioned the Chili murders in the August 22, 1966, edition—there are four paragraphs, just to give kudos to Sheriff Skinner for his great job chasing down "the fiend."[6]

It was noted that there was a "scarcity of clues" and that "words cannot describe the horrible mutilation." Police thought the killer was an older man, a woman hater, who lived in the vicinity.

"Logic dictates that nobody but a local resident would have knowledge of the inaccessible and heavily-thicketed area where the decomposed bodies were found. The investigation was hampered, of course, by the Supreme Court's Miranda ruling."

In *WE*'s October 3, 1966, issue, extensive coverage began, and again the theme was that the sheriff would have sewed up the case by then if he didn't have to inform suspects of their rights.[7]

The sheriff's office was "disgusted and alarmed." The real news was that police had a "very prime" suspect. In response to a public plea for tips, the MCSO received a call from a concerned mother reporting her son's bizarre behavior. The young man was "nervous and upset." He'd been "acting peculiarly since the commission of the crime."

The suspect, who lived five minutes from the Archer Road crime scene, "flaunted" his civil rights, telling investigators to charge him with a crime or take a hike. He refused to take a polygraph exam.

As WE noted, these were not the actions of a man who had nothing to hide: "All evidence points to the fact that the murderer hated women, due to the horrible way in which the girls were mutilated. This man is said to be a homosexual, who are noted for their aversion to women." (Modern criminal profiling has determined that the opposite is true. Psycho killers tend to target the gender they are sexually attracted to.)

The coroner had said that the killer was someone familiar with surgical instruments—not expert but familiar. The WE suspect worked as a male nurse at a local hospital and had attended a college in the Midwest where, while he was there, "a murder was committed which was similar in all respects to this one. The murder was never solved."

This fact pattern matched none of the suspects we had investigated. By today's standards, WE was particularly naive when it came to homosexuality. A gay guy in 1966 had plenty to hide, even if he wasn't a murderer. Back then, when cops talked of "sex criminals," half the time they were referring to gay men. The "weirdo" lone males who parked at the Genesee Junction were probably looking for each other. The "sex criminals" sought by the "railroad cop" were likely gay men. It was of course possible that gay men and pedophiles used the same isolated locations for their trysts.

The October 24, 1966, issue of WE announced that, with the slayer on the loose, "the women of Chili" were "scared out of their wits."[8] The situation was aggravated by a continuing campaign of "perverted doings and obscene phone calls."

WE received a phone tip from a man who said he'd been walking his dogs along the railroad tracks near the dump site when they hit upon an odor at a spot with disturbed soil. Nearby, a shovel had been discarded. The man didn't touch anything but called the sheriff's office. Investigators excavated the spot and found two towels, a man's shirt on a hanger, two buckles, and a white T-shirt that appeared to have blood on it.

Investigators said the items appeared to have been buried, dug up, and then buried again. WE theorized that the original cache might have included the murder weapon, which was subsequently removed.

At press time it still hadn't been determined if the stains were human blood. (The location of the site is confused, perhaps purposefully, by the "reporting," at first said to be near the dump site, and later referred to as near the swimming hole.) The story also had no follow-up.

According to WE, the area had been plagued for "over a year" by an obscene phone caller who referred to himself as "Doctor Wild" of Genesee Hospital. He always called between 1:00 and 3:00 in the afternoon, and told his victims that he was taking a poll regarding women's health, which started out innocently enough, then became increasingly vulgar, until he inevitably asked, "How many times a week do you [have sex]?"

The caller, the victims agreed, was conversant with medicine and had a "well-modulated voice." WE theorized that the prime suspect they'd discussed in the previous issue (male nurse, worked in a hospital) might've made these calls. WE then described another prank phone caller, a guy who had "for some time" been calling up teenagers whose names he got out of the newspaper. This guy identified himself as "Mack Belfry" and invited his victims to attend an orgy, which he would describe in "filthy and lurid detail."

The newsmagazine chastised the town of Chili for promising to cut down the brush on all Chili lots when in reality only the Archer Road site had been thoroughly defoliated. The reporter noted, "It was near one of these brush-covered lots that the murdered girls were last seen."

WE ran a report of a young couple who had run screaming from the Grove Place Cemetery at the corner of Marshall Road and Chili Avenue, about two miles from the Archer Road crime scene, "too hysterical to even tell what had happened to them." After calming down, the couple managed to tell police that while cutting through the graveyard on their way to a store, they met a man who grabbed the girl, described as a "beautiful young blonde," and tried to kiss her.

A search for the kissing bandit was fruitless, but one witness said he fled in a dark blue hardtop. The cemetery, it was noted, had long been used as a lovers' lane and teenager party place. The litter problem was comprised of strewn beer cans, whiskey bottles, and used condoms.

The article explained, "Cars and motorcycles were in and out all hours of the day and night. The cars were late models and expensive, not jalopies. Girls could be heard screaming during the night and a tool shed was robbed and equipment taken."

Raw nerves were further rubbed wrong by a "clod" who had been driving slowly up and down Marshall Road, stopping in front of each house for long periods of time, staring intently at the windows. That guy, it said, had been caught by police, sent on his way, and hadn't been seen since.

In the early morning hours of June 26, only hours after the girls were last seen, two "suspicious looking cars" were eyed in the Marshall Road cemetery. One was a tan station wagon, the other a dark blue hardtop.

One driver was said to be slim, fair, and wearing a white shirt. At another time a black car came roaring out of the cemetery at 4:30 a.m., sagging in the back end as if carrying a heavy load.

"Not too long ago," the report continued, "a woman was severely beaten at her home on Chili Avenue and taken to the hospital in serious condition. This occurred on the second floor of her home by an unknown while her husband was out of town. The family has now moved from the neighborhood to a safer place (they hope). Local residents are buying guns in order to protect themselves and their children."

An exposer that haunted Westgate Plaza was caught in the act and turned out to be a "happily married man." Another exposer had flashed a woman on September 14, 1966, through her living room window in Building 14 of the Lee Gardens Apartments near Chili Avenue and Westside Drive. He was described as in his late twenties, 5'9", stocky, wearing dark horn-rimmed glasses, white shirt, and dark trousers.

A prowler had been spotted in a couple of Chili backyards on September 10 on King Road and again on September 15 on Hillary Drive. A woman on Chestnut Ridge Road (the same street on which the publisher of WE lived) reported her doorknob jiggling. A rude state trooper came to her house and snidely asked her if this might be "her boyfriend trying to get in."

WE's September 12 issue included more crime scene detail, indeed detail that our investigation had previously considered outside of public knowledge. It also seemed clear that whoever had given Alice Bernhard her details regarding the crime scene had read this story.

The sheriff's office, the article revealed, had been keeping a secret watch at the dump site. The stakeout lasted "four or five days," but nothing suspicious occurred and it was called off.

"However," WE reported, "on the day the watch had been called off it was discovered that a human being had excreted on the same spot where one of the bodies had been. All indications are that this could have been the murderer because who else would have been so low as to add insult to an already outrageous crime?"

The article reiterated that the murderer had to be a local person just to find the dirt road where the bodies were left. "A person could pass [the road] day after day for years and never know it was there." The defecator also had to be monitoring the police presence at the scene to know when it was safe to deposit the feces.

"Police are also inclined to believe that the crime was committed at a place other than where the bodies were found. No bloodstains were found nor were the bushes and grass disturbed as there would have been had the girls been mutilated and murdered at the place where the decomposed bodies were found.

"Another point of interest is that the girls were found with their bathing suits on. They know that the suits must have been replaced after the murders and mutilation because there were no bloodstains or stab marks on the bathing suits. They must have been replaced after the crime was committed."[9]

It was a point that Alice Bernhard had been dwelling on for 45 years.

The article continued, "There is also an abandoned farm house situated quite a distance back from Ballantyne Road and which overlooks the deserted road where the girls were found.

"People have called in and informed us that lights have been seen blinking inside this house, as if whoever the prowler is is looking for something with a flashlight. Could this possibly be the scene where the murder took place?"

The article concluded by saying that Sheriff Skinner had no intention of letting up.

The July 10, 1967, issue told the story of an "intoxicated woman" who called police and said that her "son killed the two Chili girls." She gave a deputy a towel and claimed it was the one missing from the crime scene. Deputies called the jail and asked for an expert in the case, who arrived at the woman's house shortly thereafter. At that point, she admitted that the towel was not the one missing, but she insisted that her son killed the girls.

"Call it a mother's intuition," she said.[10]

The best story of all came the following summer, in the August 21, 1967, issue, stuff written at about the one-year anniversary of discovering the bodies.[11] The story started by removing all immediacy: "This happened sometime back . . ." But WE had just gotten wind of it, so it was new.

It seems the Chili murder investigators at the sheriff's office received an anonymous phone tip. A man at the airport said a coworker of his had been passing around lewd photographs, which he claimed were of his wife, and showed the woman nude in sexual positions with other men.

The tipster continued: "This man, *and another man closely related to the murdered girls*, just yesterday picked up two young girls in a bar on Monroe Avenue, took them to a secluded spot on Scottsville Road and had them pose in the nude for lewd photographs. He carries the smut in the glove compartment of his car."

Detectives went to the guy's home in a trailer park, and his pretty 14-year-old daughter answered the door. He wasn't home. Could she get a message to him? Sure.

Next day, the guy appeared at the sheriff's station and asked the deputies, "What's up?"

He seemed in a talkative mood at first but clammed up when the deputies mentioned lewd photos of his wife with other men. The deputies asked if they could look in his glove compartment. He said not without a warrant.

"Charge me or I'm walking," the guy said.

He was allowed to leave but not before he told them that he'd had his wife's permission to take those photos.

A few days later, according to WE, "an attractive woman flounced into headquarters." She said that she was the guy's wife, she was cool with the photos, and they made her happy. "I'm glad that he is proud of my body and wants to show me off to others," she said.

The crux of the story was skimmed over lightly: It said an adult male, close to one of the murdered girls, had been accused by an anonymous phone tipster of conspiring to produce pornography in Chili.

The description made me think of a teenage girl we'll call Marlene Dawson,* 14 in 1966, who lived in a trailer on the edge of the airport and was good friends with Kathy Bernhard's neighbor, Melissa Kent, daughter of Fred Kent, the exposer who was on the sheriff's 1966 suspect list. In school, Marlene and Melissa had matching coiffed hairdos, dressed in a sophisticated manner, wore after-dark eye makeup, and sported identical attitudes. They seemed *older*, more *experienced*.

Marlene and Melissa went to vocational school and were taking hairdressing lessons. Melissa had a delicate beauty, an angel with budding horns. Marlene looked harder. She was what the nice girls called a hood.

There was always the chance, of course, that WE made up most of the stories they printed, that the purpose was to titillate the prurient and morbid fascinations of lowbrow people. If they made up the story about the flouncing housewife and the lewd photos, man, it's a lulu.

During the summer of 1967, the so-called Summer of Love out in San Francisco, WE reported, a 24-year-old waitress called the city police and said she'd been raped at knifepoint in Ballantyne.[12]

She told the cops that she could show them where it happened; there might be evidence. Since the alleged attack took place outside the city, the sheriff was called, and county investigators joined the city detective and the victim at a spot 300 feet south of Ballantyne Road, at the railroad tracks, on the dirt road to Scottsville—the same road Samantha Sherman claimed she took when trying to lose her police tail.

The location was searched, and much evidence was located. The woman's panties, girdle, and stockings were found in the bushes on the west side of the lane. The girdle had been cut open with a knife.

Bloodstains were found. Doctors at Strong Memorial Hospital determined that she had suffered an injured nose but was otherwise free of cuts or bruises. The rapists apparently had only had to punch her once, and they'd done it while she was still wearing her white dress, which she'd also turned over to authorities.

The rapists, she said, were regular customers at the southeast Rochester restaurant where she worked. They forced her into their gray truck at knifepoint. They drove her to South Town Plaza, and one went into Dow Drugs to buy condoms.

They stopped at a bar and bought a six-pack to go. Then it was on to Ballantyne Road for the rape. She called the men John and Dave. John was 30, wearing green work clothes, short, with red hair. Dave was about 27, 5'7", 150 pounds, dark hair, crew cut, and wore a "carnival-type hat" with a gold band. She admitted that she left behind in the truck a prescription bottle of cough syrup with codeine that she had.

The day after reporting the incident, the waitress received a threatening phone call: "Press charges and we visit your restaurant." The woman decided not to press charges, citing as reasons a pending divorce case and her previous criminal record.

As far as we could tell, the final mention of the Chili murders in WE came in the May 7, 1968, edition, supplied to us by Dawn Putnam, who got it from the stash saved by her stepfather Burt Braddock.

The tiny item said a man was arrested and charged with assault for "administering drugs." He was known to have advertised for female babysitters. "He takes these girls to a cottage or motel and administers a drug which puts the victims out for ten to twelve hours. However he has never been known to molest them. This man was once a prominent attorney in another state. He is being questioned in regard to the murder of the two Chili girls."[13]

And that was it.

After reading the scandal sheets, my mind was swimming with questions: Was the info reliable? If you pinched and stretched it, you could sort of make it fit some known evidence, but largely the newsmagazine was in its own universe. Credibility was shaky in a variety of ways. If there were "lewd" pictures being taken, wouldn't that mean they were being sold as well? Was someone "close to one of the girls" involved in taking and selling dirty pictures, stuff you couldn't get at Dow Drugs in Playboy?

Where was the buried shirt found? Near the dump site or near the swimming hole? Was the shirt in fact bloody? Who the hell is WE's prime suspect—gay male nurse who went to a Midwest college?

Where was the abandoned house with the mysterious night lights? Far back from Ballantyne Road seemed unlikely, as there were no houses along there from which the dump site could be seen.

And what of the human excrement at the dump site? If it wasn't done by one of the deputies, that seemed to rule out all out-of-town killers. Hmmmm. Of course, the deposit could have been left by someone other than the killer, someone obsessed for another reason with the crime scene, an adolescent perhaps acting on a dare. But, if true, it felt like our guy.

There was also a report of another black car with something in the trunk—shades of Klaus Kastenholz—this time in a cemetery.

I also noticed that the WE reportage was very Chili Center–centric, because that was the side of town where the new publisher lived. Perhaps his sources were all cops he drank with, with fluctuating reliability.

Tubman got excited about WE. The fact that he hadn't previously known the periodical existed astounded him. Our moms wouldn't have allowed that smut in our houses. He decided to find out all he could about the Cooper family, who took over publishing WE only a few months before the Chili murders. He had a feeling in his bones. The "newsmagazine" was odd, downright peculiar, certainly too odd not to mean *something*.

The publisher Cooper and his family had lived on Chestnut Ridge Road near Chili Center. After establishing that they were long gone, Tubman talked to the folks who'd lived on either side of the Coopers, such as Edward Rathbun.

Now legally blind, Rathbun began losing his sight soon after high school. He was living in the house he'd grown up in. It turned out he'd lived until he was five on Chester Avenue in Riverdale and went to kindergarten at Ballantyne School. He thought he remembered the girls who were killed.

At age five he moved to Chili Center and graduated from Gates-Chili High School. He knew the Coopers who published the paper. Both Mr. and Mrs. were dead now. They printed WE out of their basement, very sneaky, and didn't want anyone to know, aware that WE appealed to wackos. If anyone asked Rathbun where the Coopers lived, he was instructed to say that he had never heard of them.

Caught up in the WE spell, I went to work on trying to match a name with WE's story of a male nurse, reported by his mom, who was comfortable around bodies, was a homosexual, and who went to school in the Midwest where another murder had occurred "just like" ours.

There were names on the MCSO suspect list about which I could find nothing at all. This was sometimes because their names were common and it was impossible to distinguish which one was which.

Sometimes the guys who made the list had never made the papers. They were perverts, whose crimes were not reported in the straight press and were reported in *WE* with names removed and perhaps key facts changed to avoid lawsuits.

There was an MCSO suspect that fit the bill better than any of the others by the name of Harold James Shannon,* sometimes known as James Harold Shannon. He grew up in Liecester, New York, but was familiar with the Rochester area because he attended the Rochester Institute of Technology (RIT) at night.

Shannon graduated from RIT in 1964 with a degree in human relations, while simultaneously working, capacity unknown, at a tuberculosis hospital in Mount Morris. The guy was apparently straight, however, and didn't go to school in the Midwest. There was no indication in the public record of how he'd gotten onto the MCSO list.

Totally by accident, I discovered that Klaus Kastenholz and the three Genesee Valley Park rapists were, at least once, all in the same place—and all had gone on to talk to authorities about the Chili murders.

That place was the Monroe County courtroom of the honorable Harry L. Rosenthal on November 14, 1966. Kastenholz was case number 5 on the docket. Green, Green, and Clanton were cases 8 and 9, all prisoners at that time in the county jail. John C. Little Jr. was the prosecutor for all three of those cases. Ward R. Whipple represented James M. Green, and Thomas C. Hartzell defended Clanton. Kastenholz and Andrew Lee Green were apparently without counsel.

19

THE WILSON BOYS

Don Tubman called a phone number in Florida listed to a Gina Wilson. Bingo, it turned out to be the right one. He thought about Gina in school. He could remember how she looked in her gym outfit and those harlequin glasses. She was so quiet in school, aloof—but possibly athletic. Quiet girls, Tubman believed, had a life, but it wasn't in school, a life that made high school dreary, long, and not worth burning a calorie.

The first time he called the number, he left a message. A few days later, Gina's son Dean called back. Dean, we knew, had an arrest record as long as a summer day—theft, assault, sexual battery, drugs.

Gina's son had allegedly stolen cars as recently as 2011. In 2001, he'd been found guilty of sexual battery and coercing the victim by use of retaliation threats. (That sounded familiar.) He had a tattoo of Pegasus on his upper right arm, a skull on his left, stood 5'5", and weighed 160 pounds. He'd been in and out of jail and in trouble with the law his entire adult life.

Dean politely told Tubman his mom was too old and sick to come to the phone—diabetes—but Tubman could hear her in the background, feeding him things to say in a Rochester accent.

Tubman said that he was working with Mike Benson, their old neighbor. Dean said that was impossible. Mike Benson died of an asthma attack 40 years before in his back field.

Tubman explained that wasn't true and asked what happened to the girls in 1966. Dean said "the three Wilson boys" killed them, Clint and his brothers, but they were all dead now.

"Why were the girls killed?" Tubman asked.

Dean answered the question with another question: "Why would anyone outside of this family care about what happened all those years ago?"

"Kathy Bernhard was murdered as well, and her family cares. Mike Benson and I are representing them. Dean, could you put your mother on the phone?"

"No."

"There might be some things she wants to say directly to me."

"I said no."

"I'm looking for William Formicola."

"We're looking for him, too," Dean said. "If you find William, tell us where he is."

Tubman looked at Dean's many mug shots and decided he looked more like Uncle Clint than his dad Keith—and there was that report from the next-door neighbor saying that Gina once screamed at Keith that Dean was Clint's kid, not his.

Tubman asked Dean if he ever considered the possibility that his relationship to William was closer than he thought. Dean became impatient and said that what his family really wanted was to be left alone.

Tubman mentioned that he knew the Wilsons originally came from Keshequa and continued to press for info.

Dean became angry: "Mr. Tubman, if you know we are from Keshequa, then you know that we take care of our own family matters. No disrespect, but I got to get off the phone now."

Tubman's head reeled. Keith died in 1985, Paul in 1991, Clint in 1992. The Wilson boys.

After Don and I stopped hyperventilating over this development, I questioned the "three Wilson brothers, all of them dead" info. The source wasn't the best. After all, Dean thought I was dead.

He had no firsthand knowledge of these events. He only knew what his mother told him. Still, Gina was in an excellent position to know. More research on the Wilson clan was clearly warranted.

Friend of the investigation and research consultant MaryAnne Curry, now a journalist in California, worked some of her Internet magic and learned that Clint's older brother Melvin was shot to death in 1987 in Double Springs, Alabama (population 1,003, 98 percent white, located in the northwest corner of the state, inside a national forest), by a woman named Wilma who was either his wife or his girlfriend.

Francine Wilson had told Don Tubman that spouses had taken out three Wilson brothers. Since Francine believed Gina set up Keith's murder, and Melvin was shot to death, that was two. Who was the third?

On a Sunday afternoon in June 2012, I had a one-hour-plus conversation with the former Anne Werner,* who grew up near the Bernhards. She was eager to help Alice, who was a saint, Anne said, a hardworking single mother who never caught a break from men.

Anne was only six when the murders happened, but she insisted that she had a vivid but isolated memory of Kathy in her bathing suit, walking toward Lester Street—and never coming back.

She knew her mother told a story about the Churchville principal who confessed to his wife and then committed suicide, but she suspected that probably wasn't what happened. She inferred that her mother was not a good source.

I told Anne that her mother did not make that theory up. It appeared to come from a cop who lived on Archer Road and his wife who sold dresses out of the garage. Anne seemed a little relieved.

Still, she told me, she knew a lot of things her mother didn't. As a teenager and young woman, Anne had been quite the party girl. She was in the Castle Inn the night that Johnny Rowe kicked out the light over the pool table. Billy Foster simultaneously tipped the pool table over, and then there was chaos. She ran out of the bar, got in her car, and was pulling out onto Scottsville Road when the police arrived. Everyone was arrested, including Anne, who was charged with crossing a double yellow line. They all had to go to court together, and even the judge got a laugh when he commented that it must have been some night.

She was best friends with Mary Ellen Webster, whose brother Billy was into hard-core drugs along with a crowd that included Jack Starr. I noted that Billy and Jack had once been arrested together for burglary in Caledonia. Anne said, "There was a long time when I just wanted to be where the fun was," but she eventually had to "stop hanging with those people."

It was Anne's impression that Jack did it and had admitted it—although he never admitted it in front of her.

"The only time the subject came up, I was about 13," she said. That made Jack close to 30. Someone mentioned the murders, and Jack, goofed up on drugs, looked at Anne with his "screwed-up Manson eyes" and said, "You probably think I did it, too, right?" (This toying with the notion that he was guilty reminded me of the tone the AIDS-stricken Jack used when talking to state cop Jimmy Newell. The point was never that he did it, but that he was trapped in a world in which everyone thought he did.)

Anne Werner said that there were a number of candidates who might've been present when Jack admitted doing it. One guy who hung with that crowd now had his life together and was on Facebook. (This source later told me he couldn't remember Jack ever mentioning the murders.)

Anne said Billy Webster died of AIDS, also, as did the sister of Jack's wife, who also hung around.

Anne said Mary Ellen Webster was a straight shooter, not a bullshit artist at all, and she said that Jack had admitted doing it. Anne said that Jean Webster might also have heard Jack's admission.

Anne herself had never been in the Starrs' house because they were all so much older than she was. However, a couple of times Nicholas Sr. allowed her to come over and swim.

She sort of remembered Clint and Francine living in the house her brother lived in now but knew nothing about them. Blank. She didn't know Francine, that the Formicolas and the Mortons were cousins, or what Clint did for a living.

Anne's dad was a Hungarian immigrant, very smart, and a talented artist—I mentioned that I'd seen the paintings of Kathy and Patty Bernhard—but he was always being dissed because of his accent, living in a xenophobic world.

Being a so-called suspicious foreigner made her father nuts. He was eventually diagnosed as being schizophrenic and put on Thorazine. He could be scary when he was off his meds and freaking out, but he wasn't the problem.

Then we discussed the Kents, and her tone changed. She had to tell someone. "Fred Kent was a pedophile," she said anxiously. "He got every one of us. He abused boys, girls. He didn't discriminate."

Her own experience with Mr. Kent started when she was six or seven (1966 or 1967) and swimming in the Kents' swimming pool. Mrs. Kent was mentally ill and oblivious. Mr. Kent would be naked at the pool.

One time Anne's mother came over and saw Anne with the naked man, and Anne was punished.

"He would walk around naked, and he would jerk off in front of me." Once he jerked off in a cup and made her look at it as he played with it with his fingers. He would take her into the house, into a room off a room that was always kept locked. In there he would take off her clothes and take photos of her naked, telling her how pretty she was. (That supported my theory that Kent was the taker of lewd photos referred to in the *WE* magazine article.)

"Did he touch you?"

"Hell yes, he touched me."

"What did he do?"

"He stuck stuff up my crotch."

That wasn't the end of the story, though. Anne grew up, got married, got divorced, was dating a bad egg ("crackhead, the works"), and she discovered that he had a kiddie porn collection. She was horrified in general but totally freaked out when she saw that, among the items, was a photo of herself as a child in Fred Kent's secret room.

As for the Kent kids, she could only imagine what they endured. She remembered Melissa very well. She was her babysitter and so pretty.

Tubman finally got through to Jean Owens, Jack Starr's much older half-sister, who'd told her daughter that Jack looked guilty to her, acting crazy after the murders, with his car a mess like he'd driven through a cornfield. Jean had emphysema and could only talk to Tubman for a few minutes. They never got to the condition of Jack's car, but she did say that the primary reason to think he did it was his relationship with George-Ann. As far as Jean knew, Jack never admitted doing it, but his behavior was peculiar afterward. Jean remembered Jack's mom going out of her mind trying to figure out what to do about her troubled son.

As the 46th anniversary of the girls' disappearance approached, I received a phone call from a worried woman, my neighbor formerly known as Gert Tyler. I had found her, still hitched to her sailor. Remembering that she was a friend of Gina Formicola, I wrote her a series of letters explaining my goals. I had inadvertently frightened her. She'd always had trouble spitting out her words, but she now had an extreme stammer.

"I was afraid I was going to get subpoenaed and have to come to Rochester, and I don't have the money for that," she said anxiously. "In your first letter you was asking about George-Ann and in the second letter you wanted to know about Gina, and it don't make no sense."

I calmed her down and asked her what she remembered about living on Stallman Drive. She remembered things as they were in 1960, Gina and kid sister George-Ann, Sue Mulligan (who had a baby brother named George) and Burt Braddock across the street. She didn't remember me. I told her the girls disappeared on her graduation night, and two days later she married the sailor.

She'd moved away and never came back. She got married 48 hours after graduation, not because she had to or was eager to get away, but because that was when her boyfriend could get leave. They had wanted to get married in August, but they moved it up.

"I didn't even know about George-Ann until after I moved away," she said. "I didn't know there was another girl until I got your letter, didn't know Kathy, didn't know any of the Bernhards. I didn't have many friends because my mother was always in and out of mental institutions, and we were known as the Crazy Tylers."

She'd heard that George-Ann was "all cut up." She said she wasn't even living on Stallman Drive in 1966.

"My mom had been put way again, and it was just me and Frankie at home. Dad . . . couldn't take care of us. The Bookmans, Uncle Sid, took me but not Frankie, so Frankie went to live with a family in Egypt, New York."

I thought about that for a beat. The Tyler house had been dark and empty for a while when the girls disappeared.

Gert told me she was having a difficult life. She'd inherited her mother's mental difficulties and was on a list of medicines for depression and other problems. I steered her back toward the Formicolas.

She didn't remember Keith and knew nothing about the men Gina hung out with. Except wait, one thing. Gert didn't remember the year, but she figured it was early 1960s. She and Gina were closest when they were in ninth grade. They used to do homework together sometimes, and once they rode bikes together.

The Tylers only had one bike, her mother's, and the whole Tyler family had to share. There were five Tyler kids, but one died after two weeks. Gert was the youngest.

So she and Gina went riding on Ballantyne Road and stopped at Hardin's farm, where there were horses. Gina *loved* horses. Gert was content to look at the horses from afar, but Gina wanted to get up close.

A Hardin—the "younger one," she didn't remember names—came out of the barn and asked the girls if they wanted to come in the barn and look at more horses. Gina went, Gert didn't.

After a really long while, Gert shouted into the barn that she didn't like this and was going to ride home. Gina didn't answer, and Gert left. Gina was OK after that and all, but she was in that barn for a long time, and Gert had always wondered what she was doing in there.

Gert wanted to know if I was going to call again because she hoped I wouldn't, and she didn't know anything about any murder and couldn't be helpful anyway.

The Gina/Hardin barn story registered on a number of levels. For one, it might explain why Russell Hardin had been on the MCSO suspect list. Hardin's problems, Don Tubman heard, were caused by an incident in a barn with an underage girl, an offense that forced him into the army.

The story of Gina and Hardin also reminded me of Dawn Putnam's tale of riding Gina's horse into the woods, only to be left alone with the horse while Gina ran off with an unknown guy.

How old was Russell Hardin? If he was Old Man Hardin and had been forced into the army because of a tryst with an underage girl in a barn "years ago," did he still have the appeal to attract a ninth-grade Gina Formicola? Would Gert refer to him as the "young one"?

I asked MaryAnne Curry in California, and she again worked her magic, almost instantaneously producing a Hardin family tree. The family had lived in the area since 1865—first in the Scottsville area, then Ballantyne Road sometime before 1920 when a family member married a Curtice, the family that owned most of the land near the old Mosquito Point Road and the B&O Railroad.

The patriarch was James Hardin, 1885–1974, or 81 years old at the time of the murders. His son Russell James Hardin was born in 1919 (died 1999) and would have been 47 in 1966, also an old man in the eyes of children.

The tree didn't extend to the present, so we still didn't know if there was a Russell Jr. Russell was arrested in 1944 at age 24 (the barn incident?), charges unknown, and his mother paid $900 (a huge sum at the time) to bail him out.

Tubman interviewed his former classmate Debby Bookman. They'd graduated together the night the girls disappeared. Of course, she remembered Gert Tyler coming to live with them during senior year.

Dorothy Tyler had a breakdown, and Gert needed a place. Debby had quit talking to Gert, however, because of an incident in gym class in which Gert put a grasshopper down Debby's back.

Debby knew that Gina Formicola liked to visit Hardin's farm, but she thought the attraction was just the horses. Gina loved horses and, before she got her own, Hardin's was where the horses were.

"Russell taught Gina to ride," Bookman said innocently.

Tubman learned that Clint had a friend in the 1960s named Lon David Jr.,* known as Junior. They rode the same garbage truck for a while. I remembered Junior. There was a large brood of Davids—five boys, three girls—who lived on Ballantyne Road, and as far as I knew, Junior was the oldest. Tubman located David at an address in the city of Rochester.

David told Tubman that he was indeed a friend of Clint Wilson's. "I lived with him when I was 14 and 15. There were too many of us Davids, so I went to live with Clint and Francine on Names Road," he said, although later he hinted that problems with his dad might've been involved. That was 1965 and 1966. David was a kid. Clint was a grown-up, in his twenties, married with daughters. He remembered Clint and Francine having only two daughters, Joni and Margaret, and thought it was possible that Clint and Francine separated just before the murders.

After living with him, Junior still saw Clint daily. They worked together picking up trash for Gates-Chili Disposal, a job David had for a couple of years before beginning his ongoing 42-year stint at the Genesee Brewery.

"When you worked on the truck with Clint, what was your route?"

"Buffalo Road, Chili Avenue, Paul Road, Archer Road." That last road caught Tubman's attention.

"What kind of car did you drive back then?"

"When I first got my license I drove a '59 Chevy. Clint taught me to drive."

In 1965–66, Clint was a big-time biker named "Ace," rode a Harley, president of the Hackers, their colors a big wheel with a hatchet in it. Junior was too young to have his own motorcycle, but he remembered Clint giving him rides.

When the Hackers merged with the Hells Angels, Clint's days as a leader were through. Francine had already told us that Clint needed to quit the Angels because they were into hard drugs and he was a beer and reefer man. Now David offered another part of the story: Clint was drinking in a bar called Santa's on Lake Avenue in the Charlotte area of the city, up near the lake, and when he came out, his bike was busted into pieces and spread out in the middle of the street. No longer president, Clint went home in a cab.

David didn't know many of Clint's biker friends, but he did know Bobby "Blackfoot" Turner and Harold "Butcher" Merritt—called Butcher because he'd been Butch as a boy. Tubman knew Butcher, too. Sometime well after the murders, Butcher had laid down his bike and lost a leg. Tubman worked in Genesee Hospital at the time and tended to him. David added that after Butcher got out of the hospital, he moved in with Francine Wilson, who took care of him.

David remembered Clint: "He was just wild, liked to play around. A horny son of a bitch. He was an average guy—well, maybe over-average." One time David and Clint were in the Avon Inn and Junior had to drive the car down a dirt road while Clint in the backseat banged a "sleazy chick" he'd just picked up. (Is it possible he cut off her girdle with a knife and that she left her bottle of codeine in the car?)

"That ever happen again?" Tubman asked.

"Yeah, there was other times. Girl lived off of Genesee Valley Park. Clint took her into her apartment while I stayed in the car." Another incident, the details of which were blurry, involved a road trip to Dansville. Another was in the city, in a bar near Bull's Head.

David remembered Clint making an effort to keep his fooling around and his wife in separate worlds. As far as David knew, Clint didn't do Ballantyne girls, just skanky bar girls.

"How did Clint get along with his wife?"

"They were off and on. He was always fooling around. He'd come home, slap her around, and then go back out. He didn't care."

"Francine says she once tried to run his bike off the road with her car. Any idea when that happened?"

"No. Once, I remember, she went out looking for him and I stayed home."

"Did he act any differently after the girls were murdered?"

"Nope. Same. Same ol' Clint."

David explained that Clint could be hostile toward women. Not just to his wife, but girlfriends too. Once he got into a fight with a girl in the Castle Inn. She ran out to the parking lot and got in her car. Clint followed and reached in her window, and she cut him up the forearm with a box cutter.

David remembered Clint being a regular at the Castle Inn but couldn't remember him ever drinking at Hokie's Place. The great thing about the Castle Inn was they didn't care how old you were. If you knew Big Jim Newell, you could drink there.

David fondly remembered swimming back by the stone trestle. "Swimming naked," he said with a smile. "Drinking beer. We'd throw the empty cans in the crick and shoot 'em with .22s until they sank." No drugs back then. Drugs hadn't come yet. Maybe some pot. He remembered partying back there with the Taggarts, Rowes, and even Barney Wilson, Clint's other little brother.

Tubman asked about Clint's fighting habits, and David explained that Clint fought just about every time he got into an argument. He could be funny, but most of the time he was downright nasty.

Clint wasn't friendly with his neighbors, and he was quick to throw around the N word if he found himself within hearing distance of a black guy.

"He knocked a good number of people on their ass," David concluded. "He once cut a guy with a beer bottle."

Tubman asked flat out, "Who do you think killed the girls?"

Without hesitation, David said, "Keith Wilson. He did it. Keith was the crazy one." When they went hunting with .22s, Keith would shoot at his fellow hunters. Well, maybe not at them, but a few feet from their feet, taking pleasure in scaring the crap out of guys.

Keith was also the one, according to David, who hung around with Jack Starr, which made sense because Starr was "dating" Keith's wife's little sister. He didn't remember Clint and Jack ever hanging out.

"Clint and Keith were both crazy enough to do something like that. Look at 'em wrong, and they'd start a fight. Jack Starr and Keith hung out. They went places by themselves."

Did David know anything about the crime scene?

"Just that the bodies were cut into pieces and put into ziplock bags and left on the girls' doorsteps," he said. Huh?

David explained that not only had Clint married Francine Morton, but also Clint's friend Jake Sailor married Ruth Morton. Jake lived in Riverdale and was another guy that worked on a garbage truck back then.

"What about Barney Wilson?" Tubman asked.

"Barney was around. He had an apartment in the city." He worked on the garbage truck briefly. "He was very quiet, and his brothers didn't like him."

"What do you remember about the night the girls disappeared?" Tubman asked.

"I remember I was at Olympic Bowl (on Scottsville Road), either bowling or playing pool," David said.

"What about the Wilson brothers?"

David didn't know the whereabouts of Barney or Keith. He remembered that Clint was driving around by himself that night.

"In the area?"

"Oh, yeah. Local. Cruising around."

"Deputies talk to you?"

"Afterwards, I spent a half day being questioned by Sheriff Skinner himself. Skinner wanted to know where I was when it happened, how well I knew the girls, and I told him I'd gone out a couple of times with George-*Eeen*."

He glaringly mispronounced her name. What was that about?

"We went back by the trussle together once. Corky Bernhard and me were close friends. I still work at the brewery with Betty Bernhard."

"Ever see anyone suspicious back there?"

"No, no strangers or anything."

"Police talk to Clint?"

"Oh, yeah. Clint was an early suspect."

As far as David could remember, Clint didn't talk about the murders. Clint moved not long after that. Fran gave him the boot, and he moved to Avon or Leroy. David worked for Gates-Chili Disposal until about 1969, when he took a job with Webster Disposal. After that, Genny Brewery—the job he'd had ever since.

David said he never really knew who the father of George-Ann's baby was. He didn't think that Kathy ever dated. Tubman asked what kind of car everyone drove. David remembered Jack Starr in a two-seater sports car, although he thought it was an MG. Clint drove a green or blue 1957 Ford.

Tubman's next stop was the home of Bugsy Yarborough, Jack's best friend as a kid, and his wife Chrissy, who was both Jack's sister and the only Starr that hung out with the Bernhard girls.

The Yarboroughs lived on a nice suburban street in Gates. There was a brand new shiny motorcycle parked at the curb and a junker of a car in the garage. Chrissy answered the door, and when Tubman explained his purpose, she called Bugsy.

They talked on the stoop, and Tubman was not invited in. Bugsy still wore his spectacles and had grown heavy. Bugsy said they'd tried to make a go of it with a pizzeria a few years back, but that went out of business. He gave no other hint as to how they were getting by.

Bugsy had no specific recollections of the night the girls disappeared, but he had never thought his buddy Jack had anything to do with it. "Jack was different, but he wasn't crazy," Bugsy said. "He just did 'wild oats' type stuff." Jack never said he did it to Bugsy, and as far as he knew, Jack never said that to anyone.

"Why did people think he did it?"

Bugsy had a couple of theories. One, the cops were always on Jack's ass, even before the murders, because he drove a Corvette that made policemen jealous. Also, Jack's half-sister Jean seemed to think he did it and had a big mouth about it. "I wouldn't lie for him about something like that," Bugsy added.

"Was Jack much of a hunter?"

Bugsy didn't know. "I've only went deer hunting once, and Jack wasn't with me."

Tubman asked about George-Ann and the baby and the question of paternity. Bugsy knew nothing about that.

"We didn't hang around when it came to girls. We went our separate ways. Jack didn't say much about women."

He didn't know the Wilsons. He remembered Francine and Ruth from Lester Street but had no idea who they married.

"The thing I remember most about the murders was that everyone was scared shitless after that. There were a lot of creeps in the neighborhood, and someone was leaving knives outside girls' bedroom windows."

"Did Jack behave differently after the murders?"

"Not at all. Same before and after."

"Didn't he start taking drugs?"

"That was years later. When Jack started taking drugs, that was it for our friendship."

June turned to July, and Tubman called for the daily shooting of the shit.

"Who you likin'?" he asked.

"I'm likin' Clint and Keith."

"Me too. Same team that attacked Mary," Tubman said.

"Only this time the knife came into play," I added.

Tubman noted that Keith would've had to take a more active role. He served only as alleged lookout and poor tosser of the fish line in the attack on Mary Crane. He wouldn't be able to get away with that kind of passivity with two teenage girls to control.

I said I was always troubled by the relationship between the guys. If it were Clint and Jack, they would have killed each other. They would be attached at the hip by the bad thing they did together. Craziness and much paranoia would ensue. But if the guys were brothers, it was a different story. They were already teammates in a dysfunctional family. Dad was an alleged child raper, so depraved as to clearly be dangerous, even lethal.

The old man, Clint Sr., could've forged some of his sons in his image. Chips off the ol' block. You told the little victim that if she told anyone, she was dead. That kept plenty of mouths shut, maybe mouths that we didn't even know about because they were still shut. There had to be Clint Jr. victims in Ballantyne who never told, who hid away that episode in their lives like a scar. Some may still be afraid to talk because they didn't know Clint and Keith were dead.

"There's already a cloak of secrecy over that family. There must have been family secrets we couldn't even imagine. So double homicide would just-be another secret stuck inside an old dog-eared file," I said.

"And I like Keith because Gina watched Keith die," Tubman added.

"Nancy Mulligan's theory: Gina killed Keith because Keith killed George-Ann."

Seeking more info regarding the discovery of the bodies, Tubman found and talked to Vincent Zuber's nephew Kim, who—along with his younger brother Eric—were 12 and 8 in June 1966. Kim said that a boy named George Peterson was also around the Zuber farm in 1966. Peterson, Zuber said, was easy to find. He'd gone on to become deputy chief of the Rochester Fire Department.

Zuber said the homes that now crowd the dump site both on the north and south sides weren't built until the 1980s. Up until then it was all Zuber farm, at least technically. The land where the bodies were found was adjacent to the land owned by the Zubers, land that was rented by the Zubers for their cows.

Back in the 1960s, Zuber recalled, there was a constant problem with keeping people off the land, because the hunting was fantastic. It looked like our guy might be a hunter. Not only did he carry a hunting knife, but he was very comfortable on that land, choosing it as a place to dump the bodies, then perhaps setting up an observation post where he could watch the police surveillance at the site after the bodies were found and wait until the police were gone before returning to further desecrate the site.

Zuber only remembered the name of one suspect, a guy named Wilcox. There was a Wilcox on the MCSO suspect list, a Ralph Wilcox,* but I knew nothing else about him. (A 1902 map of Chili showed that land at the intersection of Archer and Paul Roads belonged to a family named Wilcox.)

Tubman found Peterson on vacation in the Adirondacks. Peterson said he was only three when the murders occurred and didn't go to work on the Zuber farm until 10 years later. The Zubers never mentioned the murders, and he didn't even know they'd occurred until he was in his twenties and lived on Beaver Road Extension, only a few hundred yards from the dump site. "Vincent never talked about it.

Victor might have mentioned it once, but that would have been many years later."

The firefighter was eager to help and agreed to give Tubman a call back when he returned home. Peterson did call and gave Tubman the lowdown on the Zuber farm during the 1960s. He said the Zuber twins were two old bachelors. "Nothing strange, but inseparable."

"Did they have any trouble keeping hunters off their land?" Tubman asked.

"They wouldn't have cared if hunters used their land," Peterson replied. "Their fear was that someone would burn down one of their barns."

Peterson suggested that Tubman talk to Doris Saile, the widow of Glenn, the first cop to arrive at the crime scene, and that was Tubman's next stop.

Doris said she remembered that horrible day like it was yesterday. She looked out her front window and saw one of the Zuber twins running toward their house—men in their forties don't run that much—screaming something, going cross-lots, taking the beeline, the blood drained from his face. Any other time, Zuber would have just gotten on his tractor and driven to the Sailes' house, but he was so shook he forgot he'd been cutting hay. The police later treated the Zubers like suspects, but she'd seen the look on the man's face moments after he found the crime scene, and he was *not* acting.

"Who did Glenn suspect did it?" Tubman asked.

"People on Ballantyne Road with a horse farm." There was another fellow, too, "a Polish name, a neighbor kid, lived on Beaver Road Extension—Robert, Robert Zablisky, or something like that. Everyone was cleared."

The name was familiar. There was an Alexander Soblosky on the MCSO suspect list, one of the names I'd learned nothing about. I checked Soblosky's location file. I'd looked and found only one Alex Soblosky, and he was 62 in 1966 and died in Cincinnati. Not the guy.

Glenn Saile's widow told Tubman that she didn't know if there were any cop notebooks still in the house. He had a lot of stuff, but she hadn't been through it much.

The horse farm people best ID'd Russell Hardin. I talked to Alice Bernhard later that day. She told me that, according to Betty, there was a man named Russell in the neighborhood back then, and he was a "pest to all the girls."

An MCSO response to my Freedom of Information request revealed many details about the death of Keith Wilson (see appendix D).

One of the witnesses to killer David Young's activities on the night Keith died was Bill David, Junior's brother, who attended a party in Henrietta with his girlfriend that night. Bill didn't know anyone at the party and thought it bizarre when this guy announced that he was going to kill someone, that he needed to pick up his shotgun, and did anyone happen to have a deer slug on them? The guy then left. Later the guy came back to the party and said, "Mission accomplished, the bastard's dead." The next day, when Bill learned that his neighbor Keith Wilson had been killed, he made the connection. He remembered an incident out in front of his house in which David Young tried to run over Keith Wilson, who retaliated by throwing a flashlight at Young's car.

Bill David was recovering from a broken back suffered earlier in the summer when Tubman talked to him in August 2012. "I testified at the trial," he said. He was born in 1962, so he was too young to remember the murders. He repeated brother Junior's version of the crime scene, with the body parts showing up on doorsteps in ziplock bags. After the bodies were found, he'd heard, the Formicolas received phone calls threatening to kill Gina's horse. Bill was young enough to remember Clint and Francine having three daughters—Joni, Margaret, and Rebecca—the third girl being the one Francine was pregnant with at the time of the murders. He knew them because he was the Names Road paperboy for a while. Bill said his brother Robert "Smokey" David was an early suspect because he dated Kathy Bernhard. His dad, Lon Sr., was a suspect, too. Dad worked as a night guard for Monroe County. He remembered Gina, and he knew Keith Wilson—thought he was a pretty nice guy.

Tubman next spoke to Gary Barnes, older brother of Richie Barnes who'd told Tubman that George-Ann lied when she said Jack was the father of her baby. Gary was also a rare individual who knew and had experiences both with the Starrs and the Wilsons. He'd gone to Vietnam with Nicky Starr but came home alone. He had good and bad memories of Jack. Jack Starr, he said, had "emotional issues," but some people liked him. Jack was "somewhat in love" with George-Ann and was probably the father of her baby. Jack worked with his dad at Delco, and Gary couldn't remember him ever being in the service.

Barnes's relationship with the Wilsons was more complicated, and easily stranger.

"Keith Wilson was *impotent*," Barnes said. "So whoever was Dean's father, it wasn't Keith."

Every psychological portrait of the man who mutilated the girls in 1966 had him as impotent, using a knife on the girls' privates because his penis didn't function. Was that Keith? He was a macho man, duck's ass hair, cigarettes inside his T-shirt sleeve, a biker for a brother, multiple brothers who couldn't keep it in their pants, and he couldn't get it up? Keith's voice never lowered, and he must've gotten so mad as he lent his wife out to men who could satisfy her. (And why would Gina, who by all accounts loved sex, marry Keith in the first place? But that was a different subject.) Gary continued: "The father probably wasn't Clint because Clint and Keith were on the outs at that time." Still, memories this old tend to slip in and out of actual chronology, and Tubman recalled Burt Braddock's claim that he'd overheard Keith and Gina having an argument in which she'd screamed that Dean was Clint's kid. Barnes thought Dean's father might be a different Wilson, maybe Melvin. Barnes knew Melvin pretty well. Melvin had once offered him a job down south.

"What kind of falling-out?" Tubman asked.

"They got into a fight after Clint beat up their mother. Once Keith and I were riding around in my car and Clint took a shot at us." He wasn't sure exactly when the shooting incident took place, but it had to be sometime before 1972.

Before the falling out, when Keith and Gina were having trouble, Keith would sleep at Clint and Francine's house.

Barnes knew Clint to be violent with women. Once Clint got into it with a girl at the Castle Inn, and she sliced his arm with a box cutter. Barnes remembered the incident well because he'd been the one who drove Clint to the hospital for stitches.

"Me and Keith shared Gina sexually," Barnes said. "Gina was a nymphomaniac. Man, she was fun to be with."

Keith told Barnes it was okay for him to have sex with Gina, but he didn't want him knocking her up. He wanted one of his brothers to knock her up. Keep it in the family.

"I did Gina for a couple years," Barnes claimed.

The Formicolas, he said, got their horse from Russell Hardin for free because Gina was putting out for him. (This corroborated the incident told by Gert Tyler that Gina went into Hardin's barn with a man and didn't come out for a long time.)

Keith, he remembered, had gotten his railroad job through his father-in-law. Keith was no dummy and had become a union rep for Conrail workers. In the weeks before Keith was killed, he knew something was up. Keith told Barnes that Gina was seeing this guy named David Young and that Young kept trying to make arrangements to meet him in out-of-the-way places. Barnes told him, if it ever came up again, he would go with Keith and have his back. But when the time came, Barnes couldn't go, and Keith was whacked.

Of the Starr brothers, Nicky was Barnes's best friend. Things got strange for Nick during the last months of his life. In December 1967, Nick came home from Vietnam on emergency leave because his wife was trying to sell their kid. Nick tried to talk her out of it but couldn't. After that, Nick returned to Nam and was severely depressed. "I don't think I'm coming home," he told Barnes. He volunteered for the most dangerous missions. He wanted to commit suicide by Viet Cong. Barnes and Nicky had been in the same company. Nick enlisted, but Barnes was drafted.

Barnes said he'd known Samantha Sherman all her life. "I don't even believe she dated Jack Starr!" Barnes said.

Tubman wanted to hear everything Barnes knew about George-Ann's baby.

"George Formicola didn't like Jack Starr, I remember that," Barnes said. If he thought Jack, who was past 20, had knocked up his 13-year-old daughter, trouble, it would seem, would have been inevitable. According to Barnes, that tension was defused a bit when Big Nick Starr agreed to pay George-Ann's medical bills.

Jack wasn't getting along with his dad back then. Fathering children out of wedlock wasn't Jack's only offense. After Nicky was killed in Nam, Jack took his dead brother's driver's license and showed it to cops every time he was pulled over. When he was caught, Big Nick went nuts. Another time Jack got caught cashing his dad's check, but by that time he was probably a guy with a drug problem.

"Who could have killed the girls?" Tubman asked.

"Clint!" Barnes replied enthusiastically. "Clint had issues. He was a weasel, a sucker puncher. He was a suspect at the time." Barnes was on to Clint being a guy with a character flaw from the moment he met him. It was winter, and Clint was playing on a frozen Black Creek, bullying much younger teenagers. Clint was a guy who needed to be in a gang. He needed that backup. And being in a biker gang was no picnic. Barnes knew because Bobby "Blackfoot" Turner had been his best friend and told him that, in a way, it was a sad day when he became a Hacker because he had to give up his family and friends. The Hackers were his family and friends now. Turner and Jimmy Rowe were on the council of bikers and defended the neighborhood from outsiders. Turner didn't like Clint, didn't like that he was a bully and liked to pick on the weak.

Barnes remembered Barney Wilson being around but didn't think Barney capable of hurting anyone. All he remembered was that Barney drove a truck and had a bad back.

Tubman mentioned Dady Hamilton, the guy who stalked Sue Mulligan with a rifle. Barnes remembered Hamilton being a friend, a "tough little bastard, obsessed with Sue Mulligan." He remembered him as "ruthless and cold," a guy who could crack a guy's skull with a tire iron over road rage.

A few days after the Barnes interview, I told my mother that Keith was reportedly allowing other men to have sex with Gina because Gina needed it. She wanted a baby, and if Keith was shooting at all, he was shooting blanks.

My mom said she recalled a time back then when she ran into Gina in a grocery store pushing a baby carriage. She and Keith had taken on a foster child. Soon thereafter, Mom saw Gina again, and Gina explained that they'd had to give the child back because all it did was cry and they couldn't handle it.

20

MULE

The thing about investigations is, just when you've given up on a lead for lack of inertia, zoom, it comes back. Such was the case of MCSO Deputy Steinmiller and the tale of the educator from a nearby school district who confessed to his wife before committing suicide. Some remembered the suspect as a vice principal at either Gates-Chili or Churchville-Chili. Others said he'd dumped the girls off Archer because it was on the way home. The rumors came without names or dates, so the story lay stagnant, overwhelmed by our development of "Wilson boys" leads.

Then one Sunday morning Don Tubman, minding his own business, was bicycling a few miles before church when, in a scene that resembled the original *Invasion of the Body Snatchers*, a wild-eyed pedestrian flagged him down, Mac Symms,* a man he'd known for years.

"I have to tell you something," Symms said. "It's about the murders of those girls." Symms knew all about the teacher/suicide story, and yeah, the guy should *definitely* be a suspect. The dead teacher's name was Tom Armstrong.* Symms had been in the army with his brother, Dick. Tom was a vice principal at a small-town elementary school when he died in May 1970. When he died, he was under investigation by Deputy David Steinmiller (Symms's neighbor and school friend) regarding the Chili murders.

Symms said that, as a child, Tom was crueler than normal. According to brother Dick, Tom learned cruelty the hard way. As boys, Tom and Dick had their fingers clamped in a vise grip before Dad would whip them with a belt in the basement of their home. Symms had also hunted with Tom Armstrong in the fields east of Archer Road, so Armstrong was familiar with the dump site. Tom was nicknamed Mule because he was well endowed. He was also a man to whom bad decisions came easily. One day, in the long-gone Pink Parrot bar on Chili Avenue (immediately north of the little-league fields at Chili Center), two girls asked him why he was named Mule. He turned his back to them, and when he whirled around, his schlong was out. Not good behavior for a teacher. There was also a story, unconfirmed, that he'd knocked up a young girl and had lost his job because of it. He blew his brains out in the spring of 1970 near Weider Bridge over Black Creek on (old) Scottsville-Chili Road. He was buried in Holy Childhood Cemetery off of Chili Avenue. Armstrong's wife, Symms said, was named Mary and lived in Mount Morris. He lived east of Chili Center, and the dump site would have been on Armstrong's way home from Ballantyne.

In a follow-up interview, Tubman established that Armstrong had been known to drink at the Castle Inn and may have driven home via Junction Road when he was drunk to avoid police who might be cruising Scottsville Road. The "back way" was an option back then. You could get from the Castle Inn to Ballantyne Road way down by the Monroe Tree Surgeons without driving on a paved road. Symms admitted that his memory of those days was hazy, not just because it was a long, long time ago, but also because he himself was drinking heavily (he's now long sober). Symms said he thought he remembered the Wilson boys drinking at the Castle Inn, and it was conceivable that Armstrong and the Wilsons drank there at the same time.

Tubman said to me, "It would be interesting to know who was in the Castle Inn when the girls stopped in that afternoon in their bathing suits to get money from Kathy's dad." The girls could have walked the hundred or so yards from the bar to the confluence of Black Creek and the Genesee (where they were seen by the witness Witt) and were picked up by someone from the bar whose interest they'd aroused.

Did the killer make a habit of knowing the vulnerability of young females by knowing which dads were at the bar? Dawn Putnam was raped by Clint Wilson while her mother and step-father drank at a bar. Was Kathy killed when her dad was at the Castle Inn?

I found a story about Armstrong's suicide in a spring 1970 issue of the *Livonia Gazette*. It said Armstrong's body was discovered "in a field

near Black Creek in Chili" the previous Saturday by two boys hunting
crows. The medical examiner ruled the death a suicide by gunshot.
Armstrong was 34 and had left home several weeks before the discovery
of his body. The article gave his address and the details of his last two
jobs, as elementary school vice principal and at another school as fifth-
and sixth-grade teacher. He'd gone to two private high schools in the
city of Rochester and had earned his BA and MA at a local college. He
was a member of a parochial school board around the corner from his
home, a member of the New York State Teacher's Association, and was
survived by his wife, three kids, mom and dad, and six siblings.

Now we knew that Armstrong taught elementary school, making the
"impregnated a student" rumor even more likely to be suicide inducing.
A real estate website suggested that Armstrong's widow was not in
Mount Morris at all, but still at the family home in Chili. She would be
elderly, however, and she wasn't answering the phone. I contacted the
last school that Armstrong had taught at and sent an official request on
Alice's behalf for his resignation papers. I spoke with a school representative who couldn't answer questions. I asked him to answer just one:
Was I barking up the wrong tree? He said no. I did receive the resignation papers, but the cause of Armstrong's quitting was never mentioned.

In February 2014, I followed up on the lead that Tom Armstrong
drank at the Pink Parrot Lounge on Chili Avenue, just north of the Chili
Center ball fields. I asked my social media friends for information on
the bar and received a varied response. It was a good "last stop" before
heading home. It was a pickup bar. It was a gay hangout. There was a
back room where hookers turned tricks. It was a quiet neighborhood
joint. It was a smoky old man's bar. Everybody could have been right.
Bars change clientele over the years and even change atmosphere dra-
matically depending on the hour. An old man's bar in the afternoon
easily became a pickup joint at night.

The most intriguing response was from the former Kim Galipo, a
woman who was in my class and the sister of Ray Morton's wife. She
said that she had worked in the kitchen at the Pink Parrot in the early
1970s, as had her mom, Jeannette. I asked her if she knew Armstrong.
She said that she did, that he'd been a friend of her dad's, and that he'd
committed suicide one field over from her family's land on Scottsville-

Chili Road. He'd shot himself down the cabin road at the old Girl Scout camp.

Unfortunately, Kim's dad had memory problems and wouldn't be helpful regarding Armstrong. She said Armstrong had a muscular build, a neat haircut, and wore black-rimmed glasses.

The newspaper article had implied that Armstrong was missing for weeks when his body was found. Not true, Kim said. Perhaps he'd been kicked out of the house and was floating around during those weeks, but he wasn't *missing*. About a week or so before his death, according to Kim's mom, Armstrong showed up at their house saying that he was "going away" and looking for someone to look after his gray dog Spooky.

Kim said that her brothers saw Armstrong's car as it drove down the cabin road. When they went to investigate, apparently after hours had passed and the car didn't come back out, they were the two boys who discovered the body. Today, Kim noted, there would have been a crime scene set up and CSI people would have looked at everything, but that didn't happen. The body was picked up, hauled away, and that was that.

Kim said one of her siblings passed away recently from a ruptured ulcer, and the other lived in South Carolina.

Astoundingly, though there was no known connection between Armstrong and Clint Wilson other than that they might have had a beer in the same bar, Kim knew them both. She knew Clint because of her relation by marriage to the Mortons. Clint, she said, gave her the creeps—he had a cockhound vibe—and it was uncomfortable at family gatherings both because Clint was a jerk and because he and his wife Francine were always fighting. Tubman talked to Kim's mom and learned that Armstrong had had "some trouble with a woman" before his suicide.

When I filed the request on Alice's behalf for any and all records regarding Mule at the last school where he worked, among the documents I received in return was Mule's resume, which included under "work experience" that he worked at Russer's Meat Market as a "produce cutter."

Sometime after the Tom Armstrong info came in, I was rereading *WE* magazine and came across one item that had meant nothing to me earlier but now smacked of significance. The publisher, George Cooper Jr., who cloaked his prurient content in conservative outrage, had his own column that he called "Rochysteria." It resembled a big-league newspaper's society column, with bold names and short items connected with ellipses. He once complimented a young woman for being able to serve drinks with both hands at a recent motel party. He was constantly giving a plug to his favorite bartenders and would offer thanks in print to anyone who gave him a much-welcomed ride home, thus saving him the price of a cab. In the December 26, 1966, issue, he wrote, "Many thanks to Tom 'Mule' Armstrong from Chili for the recent favor he did for this reporter."[1]

On March 18, 2015, I received a letter from one of Tom Armstrong's sons in response to my repeated efforts to speak to his mother. Given an opportunity to proclaim his dad's innocence and my suspicions unfounded, he chose to instead ask for mercy.

"We have decided we will not speak with you or discuss the events surrounding my father's death. Please do not further contact my mother. We have moved on from this horrible tragedy which occurred many decades past. We now live joyful, responsible lives in which we cherish our time on planet Earth. Please respect our wishes concerning this event," he wrote. Nowhere did the letter express sympathy for Alice's plight.

21

PROFILING

I tried isolating the things that didn't make sense—things that maybe I'd taken for granted but that didn't hold up under scrutiny.

One, there were problems with Alice's story regarding the evening the girls disappeared. She didn't remember that night anymore, but she wasn't going to admit it. A mother is supposed to remember the night her girl is killed. She says the girls return from swimming, eat, and leave again. Alice says be back in an hour, we're having company. Then, presumably, there is a party, either graduation or family or whatever, but a get-together in the backyard, and Kathy isn't there. Alice must have been aware, if she's telling the whole truth, that Kathy was unaccounted for long before the middle of the night when Ruth woke her with a phone call. And every word on the girls' activity that evening, both in the police summary and the newspapers, comes from Alice. Her story *is* the story, and it is oddly incomplete.

Two, the missing crime scene. Why? Why not just leave the girls right where they died and get the hell away from them? It lends credence to the theory that the mutilation is premeditated. Perhaps taking the bodies was part of the killer's plan. Why take the bodies? Because playing with them was fun? Was it because one of the girls screamed, and the guy thought someone might have called the cops? Or was it because the murders' location would tend to implicate the guy? Was the crime scene moved to buy time, to prevent the murders from being discovered right away, and if so, how did the guy know the eventual dump site would not be quickly located as well? If the crime scene was along Black Creek, just (according to George Mulligan's vector) to the west of the Benson property, then wouldn't it have been discovered by search teams that went up and down that road? Those search teams were looking for girls. They were kids and teenagers, some of them. Would they have noticed a lot of blood in the weeds after at least one rain?

Three, Keith and Gina. Why would a lusty woman marry an impotent man? Why was Gina married so young when no baby came until years later? Gina and Keith were both immature, wanting a foster baby and then getting bored quickly once they had one.

Thinking like an FBI profiler, the case was a rather typical lust crime, with some strongly disorganized aspects. The victims were killed rapidly but mutilated slowly. The mutilations were typical: breasts and genitals knifed to dewomanize the victim and make her less frightening. The faces were not slashed, but there had been an attempt to behead one of them. Judging from these disorganized traits, our killer should be a mess. He should be barely able to have a relationship with a woman, perhaps a virgin, unable to hold down a job, and angry and afraid of women because of something that happened in his past, most likely during his childhood. He should be a torturer of animals, perhaps a bed wetter. (He should be more like Shawcross, or Miller in Pennsylvania, masturbating in his room to porno instead of having a social life.) When disorganized lust killers come from a large family, they tend to be among the younger siblings. They are unlikely to have friends who would come to their defense. Yet none of our local suspects fit this profile. Clint, Keith, Jack, and Tom Armstrong were all married and had children. Shawcross was married, although he suffered sexual dysfunction. His marriages were never happy, and his wives were dull, overweight women. Keith fit the profile best because he was a younger sibling and because, according to his friend Gary Barnes, he was impotent and his libidinous wife needed other men for satisfaction and baby making. Plus, Keith was no innocent. Reportedly, Keith at least once functioned as a lookout for his older brother's attempted rape.

If you look at all of Big Nick Starr's kids, Jack is low on the birth order, but he is first among Big Nick's second family. Jack is his mother's oldest child. He may have had sexual problems, although he fathered children. He did have friends who defended him, even those who say he pretended to be crazy as a defense mechanism, a shield for bullies. He lost his friends years later when he became a drug addict, not at the time of the murders.

Clint, on the other hand, was a bully, and such a despicable one that outlaw bikers found his character weak.

All of these men held down a steady job, which made them unlikely necrophiliacs and cannibals.

Yet the Chili murders had some strong aspects of an organized lust killing as well. Either the killer had a plan, or he was very lucky. He had a car, which he used to move the girls from wherever he found them to the spot where he left them. He had something—a tarpaulin or seat covers—to wrap the bodies in so he could carry them and then drive his car without leaving telltale bloodstains. He had a place to clean up and change clothes without anyone asking why he was blood drenched. The location of the actual murders is unknown. Organized lust killers often chose strangers to kill and were far more socially adept than their disorganized counterparts. They might have a job and be capable of having a normal conversation. They might even be superficially charming. Two men on motorcycles could have committed the crime, as long as the girls were taken to Archer Road alive, and the crime scene was near the dump site but never found. If the murder site was in the Archer Road area, a killer would not have needed to protect his car from blood, except for the blood he got on himself during the killing and mutilating—but he would need the power to get the girls into the car with him and keep them calm while driving them two miles to the west. (The scream and the location of the radio were indications of a sudden attack or abduction, so personal charm was probably not a factor.) Or the girls could have been transported dead in a vehicle that was immune to getting messy, such as in the back of a garbage truck, although such a truck might be conspicuous pulling down the dirt road off of Archer. Still, all of these scenarios necessitate an organized killer. Or, one guy on a motorcycle could have committed the crimes. He could have offered the girls rides, one at a time. Put one on the bike, take her somewhere and kill her, then return for the other, take her to the same spot and kill her. Later a car would be needed to locate a site and execute the dump—or the murder scene was in the dump site vicinity.

Unfortunately all killers are unique. Profiling only gets you so far. The combination of organized and disorganized elements seen here wasn't unusual. A killer could be organized, disorganized, or any combination of the two. It could mean that the killer was an organized man most of the time but became disorganized (let himself go) when he was killing or mutilating. Perhaps there were two killers, only one of whom was organized.

Taking a geographical profile of the case, we find a tight cluster of activity, with the distances between things—the homes of the two victims, the homes of the local suspects, the stone trestle, the spot where the radio was found, and the location of the eyewitness sightings of the girls just before they disappeared (including the spot where Witt saw the girls get into a car)—all measurable in yards rather than miles. The dump site, way out on Archer Road, is the thing that doesn't fit, a spot chosen perhaps because it was far from home, not because it was on the way home or in the killer's backyard. The geography supported the notion of a local killer. On the other hand, I thought we were giving too much weight to the dump site defecation immediately following the discontinuation of police surveillance. The sole source was WE magazine, and if it was such a major issue indicating a local killer, why did the police continue to look at Miller in Pennsylvania, months after the defecation incident? If we include the dump site with the other locations, the thing that all sites have in common is that none are more than a quarter mile from the West Shore track of the New York Central (later Conrail) railroad tracks—which was the railroad for which one victim's dad and brother-in-law worked. Again, the finger of suspicion pointed at Keith.

The killer had to have been a mess in another way, too—a bloody mess. Where was the blood? Jean Owens loved to talk about how muddy her half-brother Jack's car was after the girls disappeared. But she saw no blood. Both after the killing and then again after the mutilation, the killer needed to be confident that he could clean himself up and change clothes without being seen. No one at any time that we know of saw suspicious blood after the girls disappeared. The blood from the killings and mutilations was never found, nor were the missing body parts. No one even noticed any blood. Where did these activities take place? We had no clue.

22

THE SIGNATURE

In September 2012, Tubman spoke with Ed Yaw, a step-brother of the Taggarts who'd been reported as one of Jack Starr's friends in 1966. I'd chatted some with Ed on Facebook. He was a musician. I told him I liked a local Rochester band called the Rustix. He told me he used to play with the Rustix. Very cool. Yaw grew up as a river rat in West Brighton but now lived in Scottsville.

Yaw could only be so helpful with Tubman because he was in the service at the time of the murders. He served a year in Vietnam, stationed after his tour at Fort Jackson, South Carolina, discharged June 1969.

Was Jack Starr ever in the military? As usual, the question received a vague response. Yaw couldn't swear to it, but he thought maybe he had been. Jack might have gotten out just as Yaw went in.

No way Jack did it, Yaw said. "I knew his secret," Yaw said. "His persona was as a crazy guy—but he was actually sane."

Yaw had been aware that Jack was a suspect in the murders, but he never asked him about it. It was just a code of Yaw's behavior that you don't ask a dude a question like that. Besides, Yaw didn't believe it was true. He knew it didn't mean everything, but Jack was *always* gentle with women in public.

Tubman asked about the Wilson boys, and Yaw didn't know them. He knew the Morton sisters but had no idea who they married. The member of the Hackers that Yaw knew best was Dady Hamilton, who was still alive. Yaw spoke with Hamilton on the phone in 2010, during a World Cup soccer game.

If Dady Hamilton, the guy who punched through a window in the Mulligans' front door and stalked Sue Mulligan with a rifle, was in the Hackers at the same time that Clint "Ace" Wilson was their leader, that could make for an interesting combination.

I received a summary of Jack Starr's criminal record. He'd been arrested seven times, stood 5'5", and weighed 154 pounds. Not a big guy. Skin tone: light/medium. Not the olive-complexioned man seen by Bruce Witt at the mouth of Black Creek. He'd been charged with 15 crimes, five of which were felonies. But he'd only been convicted of four, all misdemeanors or lower. He had always appeared in court when he was supposed to, and he was not a sex criminal. (George-Ann's pregnancy never became a legal issue.) The crime that was most interesting came on December 1, 1966, when Jack was arrested somewhere in Monroe County for second-degree assault. The charge was lowered to third degree, and Jack pleaded guilty. He was charged with a one-year jail sentence suspended and two years' probation. (The Red Creek incident, perhaps?)

Interestingly, the next arrest was not until February 11, 1980, and his last came on October 24, 1988. There were two crime sprees separated by years of inactivity. That would seem to represent the heroin years. There were three arrests in 1980 (details in appendix F) for burglary, issuing a bad check, and disorderly conduct. He avoided jail time by seeking out drug treatment.

There followed seven years without an arrest. Possibly Starr got off the junk, was in a position where he could maintain his habit without stealing things, or stole but wasn't caught. Then his bad luck started up again. In 1987 and 1988 he was arrested four times for stealing and forging checks. By that time Jack was a truly pathetic man in his forties.

Bottom line: this is not a criminal with *girls* on his mind.

The killer undressed the girls, cut them up, and then put the bathing suits back on. Alice was on it all along. There it is. That's the signature. That's the thing that's sicker than sick. The murder was swift and frenzied, committed by a right-hander. Very common. The mutilations were common. Sex mutilation murders all involve the breasts and genitalia, of course. We could find many mutilation kills that resembled this one, Black Dahlia (slow kill, dump site not the murder scene) and Jack the Ripper (quick kill, bodies left where they were killed) being the famous ones. But this guy (quick kill, dump site not the murder scene) put the bathing suits back on, all except George-Ann's bottoms. *The killer covered up the places where he had removed parts.* Kathy's breasts, covered. Kathy's excised vagina, covered. George-Ann's breast, covered. George-Ann's genitals were stabbed but not removed and didn't need to be covered. Are there any other murders from this time period—anywhere, for that matter—in which the clothes were put back on after the mutilation? If so, that would be a *strong* connection. And if not, what do we learn about the killer's psychology because he did this? Was he suddenly filled with regret? Did he try to cover up the horrible thing he'd done? There's this horrible bloody mess, and he's putting bikini bottoms back on? It reminds me a little bit of mothers who kill their children and then tuck them into bed so it looks as if they are asleep.

I received a phone call from Steve Frazier, the friend of Evie Douglas who'd said Jack and Clint knew one another. Frazier had been a Ballantyne "wild child," wandering the streets at all hours. I remembered him as precociously libidinous, fairly bright, with a nasty mouth that got him in trouble. Later, he was a hippie hood who got into worse kinds of trouble, but he always seemed to me like a guy with redeeming social value. In 1966, he was 11. He was a neighbor of the Mortons on Lester Street, and Clint was married to Francine Morton, so he got to see the guy up close.

"He was a nutcase, a vicious individual," Frazier said. "I don't remember where he came from, down south, somewhere in the boondocks. He roped up with Francine. Greaser. Thought he was a big shot. Thought he was badass."

Clint was quick to anger. He had "spittin' spells." Frazier bragged that the other boys his age were scared of Clint, but Frazier gave him lip, pissed him off. He knew he could outrun him. He was no Alan "Greased Lightning" Myers, but he had wheels.

Clint picked on the weak. He was like a terrorist: fear was his predominant product. He said he knew a woman, a girl at the time (not Mary Crane, but another special-class girl), who had issues with Clint. He knew that Clint "came after her." It was around the time when they were "digging the ditches"—that is, the sewers were being installed, so the houses on Lester Street were saying good riddance to their out-houses. The ditches didn't come to the Bensons because we had a septic tank. Frazier said he didn't know anything about Clint being a biker. I tried to get him to repeat to me what he'd said to Evie Douglas, that Clint and Jack hung out back then, but he wouldn't. He'd had a long talk with Johnny Rowe recently, and he knew all about Johnny's theory that Jack hired two guys to kill the girls for him. When the subject of Clint came up and Frazier said the name first, he kept refer-ring to him as "your theory," that is, the Benson theory, which sounds like it might have been the way Johnny Rowe characterized it. Rowe knew I had pumped him for info about "Ace," and he put two and two together.

I read him the quote as per Evie Douglas and asked him point blank if he'd said it. "Yeah, I put them together," he said. The notion that Clint and Jack could have worked as a team was not well substantiated.

I asked about little girls having problems in Ballantyne back in 1966.

Frazier told me of a girl who grew up on Black Creek Road being raped when she was 12 (1969-ish) by two young men from the neigh-borhood whose names had previously not come up in this context. Two more suspects we didn't need.

What about Jack? Frazier thought Jack was an "idiot nutcase" but basically okay, until he turned into a junkie asshole, but that was later. Jack seemed like a guy who had it together—worked at Delco, drove a Corvette, married Ann who was good looking. Frazier had no idea that George-Ann had a baby, and he certainly didn't know that Jack was supposed to be the father. How could Johnny Rowe leave that out? After Jack "got into the bad stuff," Frazier said, meaning heroin, he became pathetic, always in and out of the VA hospital. (I noted this as further evidence that Jack was indeed in the military.) Once a junky, Jack became a "hustler." The last few times Frazier saw him, Jack hit him up for money. The last time, in the Castle Inn on a quiet Tuesday afternoon, Jack and Steve got into a fight after Jack tried to mooch money.

Frazier remembered that it was "those guys from Henrietta," whose names he either couldn't or wouldn't mention, and Judy Nash* who brought heroin into Ballantyne. "She was the one who tried to entice us into doing it. I remember when Billy Webster did it the first time. I said no thanks, I don't need that shit."

"Beer and a bong," I said.

"That's all you need," Frazier laughed. Judy Nash, he told me, was on methadone just about her entire life and died circa 2009. (I remembered her well. She was older, but we'd had a study hall together and hit it off. I checked, and she'd signed my yearbook the year she graduated, citing our long conversations about nothing and everything.)

Just being friendly, Frazier said that in the whole neighborhood he liked the Benson house the most, because it was "always the same, right down there at the end of the road."

He said that he'd had a conversation about the murders with Roy Gibson, and Roy claimed he'd been the one to find Kathy's radio. (Donna Melideo had previously told me that her foster brothers Roy and Bubby Gibson found the radio. The Gibsons were in the same special class with Mary Crane and very well might have been in the same search party. Phil Albano could have been in that search group as well, anything to be helpful. One found it; all took credit. Mary was the only one brave enough to return the radio to the Bernhards, handing it to Betty. When Roy showed up at the Ballantyne School field to play football, it automatically became a game of two-hand touch, because no one could tackle Roy.) Roy, Frazier said, worked at the time of their conversation "at the Tropicana," but Roy was dead now.

I asked him if there was anyone other than those we'd already talked about who might have been perverted enough to do something like mutilating bodies. The first name to pop out of his mouth was Billy Batrack, but he backed off immediately, finally only conceding to the fact that Batrack was "a greaser."

He told me a story about how he and his friends, when they were still teenagers, were all "goofing up." They had an unfortunate encounter with an ex-junky narc who planted dope on them and got them busted. The judge gave them all the same alternative: jail or army. So the boys enlisted together—and none of them went to the jungle. Frazier ended up in Germany 1972–73 having the time of his life.

Frazier said he wanted to get his mind back to 1966, so he started going up and down the streets, naming who lived where.

Frazier knew Debby Rockow because she was his babysitter. And babysitting him was no picnic because he was on the active side. When

Debby couldn't do it, George-Ann babysat him—but that only happened a couple of times. Frazier said he couldn't imagine the ladylike
Debby hanging out at the trestle, not unless she was escorted by one of
the neighborhood's knights in shining armor, like the Owens brothers
or Billy Hunter.

He remembered that getting from Lester Street to Stallman Drive
in 1966 was a snap, because there was a plank over the runoff and a
path that formed a beeline and went right past the root cellar where
George Mulligan and I had a fort.

Then he remembered Fred Kent, the man alleged by our witnesses
to be a child rapist and pornographer. Frazier said he and girls he knew
would go over to the Kents to swim in the swimming pool. "The old
man was a pervert," Steve said. "He would come out of the house after a
couple of hotty-toddies and get naked. 'Let's go skinny-dipping,' he'd
say. The girls I was with didn't like that. They wanted to go into the
woods and build a bonfire, you know?"

23

GHOSTHUNTERS

On Veteran's Day 2012, Tubman was driving his dad to church in his Mustang, and he took Archer Road, past the dump site. As he passed, he noticed two men out there. They didn't have guns; they weren't hunters—but they did have devices of some sort, maybe metal detectors or divining rods. That night, Tubman received a call from Danny Johnson who said that he'd just conducted a paranormal investigation into the murders with his old friend (and Wheatland-Chili baseball teammate) Tom Zimber. They'd been ghost hunting for about three years, called their organization Ghosts and Paranormal Seekers 3 (GPS3). "We do historical investigations. We've spent a lot of time in Gettysburg," Danny explained. And they'd spent an entire day at the trestle and the dump site with an EMF meter and an Ovilus meter that scans radio frequencies and could translate spiritual energy into words. "You can hear the spirits words through a computer voice."

The next day I talked to Danny and was thoroughly debriefed on GPS3's investigation into the Chili murders. I asked Danny how he got the idea, and he insisted the idea was thrust upon him.

"I was home in my living room when the EMF went off like crazy. I turned on the Ovilus. I asked the spirit if it was a child. Yes. I couldn't think of any children who'd died in the area. Then it occurred to me. Are you George-Ann? I asked. Yes."

A few nights later Danny heard a voice in his head, no equipment involved. It sounded like it was right in his ear, a child giggling. He called up his GPS3 partner, and Zimber said, "Maybe it's the girls who were murdered." Danny hadn't mentioned his earlier contact with George-Ann, so that bit of intuition impressed him.

The men set up their equipment at the swimming hole, and they immediately started getting responses near the trestle.

"Both the spirits of George-Ann and Kathy were at the trestle," Danny said. "George-Ann did most of the talking. Kathy was sort of quiet."

I said that this was probably the way it was in life as well.

Yes, they wanted Danny and Tom to help. Tom and Danny asked about the killer. The Ovilus said "man" or "men" and then "evil." The spirits didn't want to talk about the murder, however.

"I think they were afraid to tell me who did it," Danny suggested.

"Maybe they didn't know their killer, so they can't say who he is," I replied.

"At one point I asked George-Ann if she remembered me from school, and the Ovilus said, 'You were always nice to me,' which is crazy because you seldom get a full sentence like that." Did the killer have a weapon? Yes. A knife? Yes. Then the EMF went off, and I asked, 'Is this George-Ann?' No. 'Is this Kathy?' No. 'Is this the killer?' Yes. 'Are you sorry about what you did?' Yes. 'Will you apologize to George-Ann?' Yes." Danny asked George-Ann if she would accept the apology, and she said no.

The pair then moved their operation to Archer Road, coincidentally as Tubman was driving by, and they walked up and down the railroad tracks there until they found activity about 100 yards east of Archer. There they asked specific questions about the killer's identity. Is it Pat Callaghan? Tom asked. Nope. Is it Gilbert Wellington? Nope. Dady Hamilton? Uh-uh.

Pushing my absolute skepticism aside, I told Danny that, if he had time, he should walk the Junction Road with his equipment and see if he could find any one particular area that made the EMF jump. He said he would.

Since I had him on the phone, I asked him some follow-up questions to those he'd answered weeks before when talking to Tubman.

He'd said there were Peeping Toms back in 1966, and he thought they were Jack or another of the Starr boys. "I went running outside with a baseball bat in my hand," Danny said. "I didn't see the guy, but a neighbor said she thought it was one of the Starr boys."

"There were other things going on, too. One morning my dad found a set of work clothes in our car. We never knew how they got there. There was a break-in a few houses down from us, across the street from the Douglases, and the burglars did weird things inside. Weird sex things. I don't know exactly what. I heard my dad talk about it. Maybe semen on panties that had been pulled out, something like that." Danny couldn't remember the name of the family who lived in that house. (I asked Evie Douglas, but the incident didn't ring a bell.)

Minutes after I hung up with Danny (the last time I would speak with him, as he passed away only weeks later), I called Steve Frazier back to continue our interview. Other than Jack's Corvette, what sorts of cars were parked at the Starr house back then?

"The Starrs always had an assortment of jalopies they were driving around—junkers that they tinkered with." He didn't remember any specific makes or years. '57 Chevy? Probably. He didn't remember.

Frazier had a Dady Hamilton story I hadn't heard before. Years after the Sue Mulligan incidents, Hamilton took up with a girl who lived on Black Creek Road. "When she tried to get rid of him, he stabbed himself repeatedly. I heard he tried to commit hara-kiri." This was perhaps another version of the "tried to emasculate himself" story.

The bum who lived in a shack back by Genesee Junction—previously mentioned by the Grecos—was Ol' Pete. Frazier remembered a couple of buildings back there at the time, all very close to the spot where the two sets of railroad tracks crossed.

"I used to bring Ol' Pete cigarettes. I'd take my dad's Bull Durhams and give a pack to Pete." (I did some research. Ol' Pete was Peter Mangino, who died on September 27, 1965, nine months before the murders. Seriously, Pete's pre–zip code mailing address was Genesee Junction, Rochester, 23, NY.)

Were there ever city people back there?

"All the time," Frazier said. "Black guys fishing for carp. City people were common. I used to find empty liquor bottles back there, used condoms. There was a lot of dirty dealings going on. There were railroad police, but only during the day."

Were there hookers working back there? Probably. And there really were hoboes like my mother had warned me about.

"Just across the creek, straight back from your house, there was a little camp where guys who hopped freight trains would stay for days at a time," Steve said.

Frazier recalled that he and his gang of Ballantyne boys used to have what they called the Caboose Club, because there were cabooses parked back there near the junction that the boys used as clubhouses.

"We smoked cigarettes," Frazier recalled with a laugh. Bad, bad boys.

The club came to a sudden end: "A friend of mine came one day with a bottle of elderberry wine, drank it, and then set a caboose on fire. A big fire. There was a big investigation, and that was it for the Caboose Club."

Another time Frazier broke into a freight car that was filled with boxes of corn flakes. He made a bunch of trips and stole about 100 boxes. "I fed all of Lester Street," he said with a laugh.

In 2013, a man named Joseph Naso was tried in Marin County, California, for the murders of four women—Roxene Roggasch, Carmen Colon, Pamela Parsons, and Tracy Tafoya. The bodies of the victims were all found in rural areas of California, and the killings covered a span of 17 years. Carmen Colon was also the name of the Rochester DIK's first victim. To make his story even more hair raising, Naso was originally from Rochester, New York, and frequently visited the city during the time of Rochester's most notorious killings. Unfortunately, attempts to connect him with the three Rochester victims were in vain. But what about 6/66?

On March 26, I sent a letter to Judith Ellen Naso at her home out west (an address found by Don Campbell). I found a newspaper article about Joseph and Judith's wedding, which included her maiden name and her Rochester address, which rang a bell. I wrote her, saying my dad lived at 16 Rundel Park growing up, and if she wasn't the Judith Weiermiler that was my dad's neighbor, then she should throw the letter away. Then I apologized profusely and told her I had a question about Joseph. I explained about George-Ann and Kathy and my relationship with Alice, and I asked where they lived in 1966. On April 23, 2013, I received a letter from Mrs. Naso in reply. She didn't mention my dad, but wrote, "We moved to Calif. in May of 1965 with a 2-year-old and another baby on the way. Joe would not have been in Rochester—or the Rochester area in 1966. I am sure of this. I am sad for your client's great loss. Sincerely, Judith Naso." What a classy lady. And pretty conclusive.

On August 1, 2013, Burt Braddock told Don Campbell that the Wilson brothers didn't get along with one another and at some point split up into teams: Keith, Barney, and Billy versus Clint, Melvin, and Paul. The rift apparently started when Dean Wilson, Gina and Keith's kid, had a chainsaw accident and needed a blood transfusion. Keith, of course, offered to be the donor and was stunned to learn that his blood was incompatible. When Gina heard about the incompatibility, she said, "Try Clint's blood." Clint's blood was a match, and he gave blood to save his nephew. But the cat was out of the bag. Keith and Clint were at war. There was a period there when the two brothers were taking pot-shots at one another, not verbal, but with guns!

Burt said that Old Man Hardin, the guy who allegedly gave Gina a horse in exchange for some quality time in his barn, died at a very old age, struck by a car as he crossed Ballantyne Road on foot.

Burt made several interesting points:

- George and Ruth Formicola met at a horse stable on Ballantyne Road, but he didn't remember if it was Hardin's or another one.
- Pauline Putnam reportedly was afraid of George Formicola and cited him specifically as a reason why she didn't want to live on Stallman Drive anymore.
- Ruth and her adopted son William moved to Florida first. George continued to live on Stallman Drive until he could retire and get his pension, at which point he joined them in Florida.
- Keith called Burt on the night he was killed and asked if he could borrow a gun. Keith decided to go with the baseball bat, which turned out to be a mistake.
- Gina used to ride her horse while wearing a two-piece bathing suit. (I have to admit, that rang a bell with me too.)
- Gary Barnes was one of Gina's boyfriends while she was married to Keith, which confirmed info we'd been given by Barnes himself.

In November 2013, Don Tubman had a phone conversation with David Young, the man who shot and killed Keith Wilson. Young had his own gutter-cleaning business and was doing well. He said he hadn't seen Gina in 25 years. Keith's killing was a pure case of a love triangle. He was afraid for his own safety, and Gina's, which was why he did what he did. It had nothing to do with the 1966 murders.

"Did you and Gina ever discuss her sister?"

"No, but when I was at the Formicola house, Ruth and Gina talked about George-Ann."

"What did they say?"

"Ruth said Clint killed the girls."

We knew from the MCSO report that Ruth initially suspected Jack. What made her change her mind?

In 2014, I finally spoke with Harold "Dady" Hamilton. He now lived in Florida and spoke with slurred speech. He apologized in advance for his bad memory, saying that he'd been in a motorcycle accident in 1984 and had sustained a serious head injury.

He apologized for not knowing who I was, but remembered Stallman Drive as being "just on the other side of the tracks." He was 19 at the time of the "tragedy." He said he didn't know the Formicolas or the Bernhards.

Dady remembered that George-Ann had a big sister, but not even well enough to say hi to. He just knew who she was, the big sister of the murdered girl. (And probably as the girl who waited at the bus stop with Sue Mulligan.) He didn't know Gina's name or to whom she was married.

Who did it? He said that the name that was going around was Jack Starr. He didn't know why. That was just what everyone said. He didn't know the guy because he was "older," but he knew that Jack died of AIDS. (I'm pretty sure Jack was only one year older than Dady.)

Dady drank "all the time" in the Castle Inn but couldn't remember anyone else who did. He didn't know John Bernhard, who would have been an older man, but he recalled Ajax Auto as the junkyard near the drive-in.

He said the name "Ace" meant nothing to him. He had heard of Clint Wilson, remembered him vaguely. No details, though. Dady claimed to have been a member of the Hackers, even though he didn't have a motorcycle at the time. They let him in as a "wannabe."

Dady did eventually get his own bike and became a member of the Outcasts, a motorcycle club out of Syracuse. Then he "got away from that scene." He'd heard of the Satans Diciples but knew nothing about them.

Other Hackers he remembered were Bobby Turner, aka Blackfoot, and a guy named "Jesus," whose real name might have been Hal or Al Rogers. The Hackers, he said, came from all over Monroe County and had their meetings in a veterans' club on Ames Street in the city. He later described the location as "downtown near Tony's."

To survive in Ballantyne, he said you had to be bad, meaning tough, but he didn't know anybody pervy in a sex killer way. Dady was away from 1963 to 1965 for malicious mischief, i.e., the Sue Mulligan incident. "That deal really screwed up my life," he said.

The murders happened after he got out and he was interviewed one time by a detective, but he doesn't remember the questions he was asked. He said that old Chevys were pretty common in those days because no one had money for a good car. He remembered one green '57 Chevy belonging to a river rat whose younger brother had been in my class.

He came back to the subject of Clint on his own, but only to reiterate that he didn't really remember the guy.

Ed Yaw and Mike Taggart spent some time looking at an aerial photo of Ballantyne in 1966 that I took from a *D&C* news clipping and posted on Facebook, and they got to talking. They eventually decided that they needed to talk to me, and Ed put that together.

They'd both talked to Tubman and liked him, but Mike felt that Tubman didn't believe him and he hoped I was more open-minded. I said I could listen to Shawcross stories all day long.

Ed told me that his jaw dropped when his kid brother Mike Taggart first told him the story of beating up Arthur Shawcross back by Black Creek. (Ed is not sure of the precise location of the incident because he never went past Tacy's bait shop, behind Ballantyne School, and this happened a ways further up the creek. Mike said it was near the aqueduct, but he wasn't sure where that was. I assured him that I knew the spot.)

Mike's point was that they pissed off Shawcross when they beat him up, so it only figures he would come back and get his revenge. Shawcross was big. Mike was 14. Others who were back there when it happened were Richie Barnes and Johnny and Jimmy Rowe. Mike also told him the story about Billy Batrack and faking drowning. "The cute one," meaning George-Ann, jumped in the water to save him.

Ed Yaw then told me about an odd thing that happened to him in 2010 or 2011, when he was technically retired but back working as a security guard part time for Monroe County Parks and he was the night guy in the little house at Northampton Park, the spot where Shawcross dumped a number of his bodies and close to where Shawcross was arrested. This was definitely after Shawcross died (he died in 2008). It was dusk, almost dark, when there was a knock on the door and two guys were out there, both in their mid-forties, maybe younger. Ed asked them what they wanted, and they asked for permission to go bone hunting—that is, looking for deer antlers and the like—on a specific plot of woods near where 590 (actually 531) exits onto Washington Street. Ed told the men that he couldn't give permission because that plot was state not county land. There were plenty of other places to look, of course, but they were only interested in that one spot. Ed asked them who they were, and one of them said that his claim to fame was that his mother had once been Arthur Shawcross's girlfriend. It seemed to Ed that maybe those guys weren't looking for deer antlers but other types of bones. Did Shawcross tell his girlfriend about an undiscovered body, and did she pass along the message to her son? And if that did happen, what interest would the son have in discovering the body?

Ed told me that Jack Starr used to tell him that he'd gone to Nam when he was in the army, but he didn't have any war stories. "I was a cook," was all Jack would say. Ed said Jack wasn't the guy. He didn't start taking heroin until much later in life, and he had a beautiful wife and kids. It wasn't him.

I knew that Shawcross had several girlfriends. He usually had a wife and then something on the side. He would eventually move on, so the girlfriend became the new wife, and it started over. So who was Shawcross's girlfriend referred to by the bone collector? I have no idea.

On April 24, 2014, I talked to Ed's brother Mike Taggart, and he told me about running off the pervert. (The violence had been removed from this version of the story. The pervert was no longer stomped, but merely scared off.)

At the time of the incident, he was with Bryan Davis (last heard to be spending time in a federal prison, current location unknown) swimming at the "stone aqueduct," and Richie Barnes joined them, approaching along the tracks from the south. Billy Batrack was there. They were just hanging out when Billy Foster, who was about 11, and another kid Billy's age came running up saying there was a guy over there without any clothes on.

They were on the west side of the bridge, and Billy said the guy was on the east side, about 30 or 40 feet from the swing rope. Bryan picked up a piece of board and started swinging it menacingly. Billy led the way, and they couldn't see the naked guy until they were right on top of him.

They wanted to beat him up, but he started talking. They were kids. This guy was older, not much older, but a man as opposed to a kid. He was a big guy with big shoulders and sandy colored hair. (Shawcross was 21.) They let him put his clothes on, his clothes were behind a bush, and then ran him off without hurting him.

He ran north, up the Penn tracks toward the airport (and the rear of the Varsity Inn). Mike was the only one who remembered there being an old red pickup truck parked back there that day, and he wondered if it was the naked guy's vehicle. It didn't have to be. It could've been anyone fishing. He didn't see the naked guy go to the truck. He just remembered it being back there.

Mike still insisted that there is a mention in one of the books written about Shawcross that his favorite fishing spot was in Black Creek near the aqueduct, and that he discovered the spot on a trip to Rochester in which he arrived by bus. Mike said he had that section of the book highlighted and showed it to a guy named Tommy, a retired RPD officer who was working at the time for the Boards of Cooperative Educational Services. (All efforts to find this passage in the book have failed.)

On the day the girls disappeared, Mike, some Ballantyne kids, and some fellow West Brighton kids were swimming in the river, just south of the iron trestle, which was odd because they almost always swam north of the bridge, the same side as all of their houses. But, because they were on the south side, they could see the girls as they walked north on Scottsville Road between the Castle Inn and the bridge.

The boys waved, and the girls waved back. Billy Batrack went into action. He swam out into the river and then started to bawl that he was drowning, he was having cramps, he didn't wait an hour after he ate, ahhhh!

The girls were crossing the bridge to come over and say hi. They knew Billy was goofing around and happily jumped into the river to "save" him. They were wearing bathing suits. They came ashore, and the girls joined the boys on the Brighton side.

It was then that Mike realized that Billy and George-Ann had a thing going on. He could tell by the stuff they were saying to each other. Sparks were flying.

The girls stayed about a half hour. When they left, they walked back across the bridge, and instead of turning left they went straight, following the railroad tracks. Somebody told Mike that that was okay, that they could take the beeline to their houses that way.

A couple of days later, Mike and Richie Barnes were in a search party, and Richie says today that they were within 30 feet of the spot where the girls were later found. Mike said years later that he was reading a book about Shawcross when he realized that he was the naked guy they chased away from the swimming hole. Why believe him? Because he's good with faces, that's why. He told me a story about the time he'd been looking at photos of D-Day and saw a young Al Cliff—who worked at our high school—in one of the photos. He called Al and asked him if he was in the war. Al said yes. Was he at the Normandy invasion? He was. Al looked at the photo and was amazed that there was documentation of him being there.

The point was, Mike was a guy who remembered faces, and he remembered Shawcross's face. He said this guy Tommy, the ex-cop, told him the police knew it was Shawcross but didn't do anything since he was already serving life in prison.

Mike said he knew Jack and Clint, and it wasn't them. Jack liked handicapping horses at the Finger Lakes Racetrack and drinking beer. Clint couldn't keep it in his pants, but that didn't make him a mutilator and cannibal. Those were Shawcross traits.

That turned out to be the last chance I had to speak with Mike, who sadly passed away in early 2015.

During September 2014, Don Tubman talked to Mitch Owens, George-Ann's friend and Jack's nephew.

"I always thought Clint did it," Mitch said. "Because he liked to bother all the girls."

I received a call that same month from Joseph Picciotti, former MCSO deputy and chief of police in Fairport who said he worked the case back in the day, and his primary suspect was a meat cutter. He had an interesting story, which had nothing whatsoever to do with any of our known suspects. Sometime following the murders, date unknown, Motorcycle Deputy John Rossman (still alive, younger than Picciotti) came upon a station wagon parked in the parking lot of a shopping mall at Route 31 and 250 in the town of Perinton. The car was filled to the brim with clothes and stuff. The occupant of the car seemed disoriented and hostile, so Rossman called for backup. So up rolled Picciotti in his car. The subject identified himself as Francis Peralta, a man in his forties employed as a meat cutter at a meatpacking plant on Scottsville Road and living in his car. Picciotti went through the car, seeing what he could see, and found a folded piece of paper. He unfolded it, and written on it was

two girls walking. black dog following.

Rossman and Picciotti put Peralta in the backseat of the cruiser. Peralta's vehicle was towed. Picciotti drove Peralta to the sheriff's interrogation area near the jail. On the ride, Peralta said lewd and vicious things about young girls walking on the street. Picciotti was bothered by the things he said. The guy hated women, especially young girls. Peralta was brought in to see Mike Cerretto, who found the note compelling, he said, because one of the girls had a black dog. (This was the first we'd heard of a black dog, a chilling image but with no basis in reality.) Cerretto, Picciotti told me, refused to interview Peralta, who was clearly unstable, because nothing he said could be used anyway. Peralta was taken to the Rochester State Hospital. Sometime later, during a recreational walk around the perimeter of the facility, Peralta wandered off. Investigation revealed that he'd taken a bus to California. It was unknown where he got the money to purchase the ticket, and Picciotti doesn't remember where in California, only that the area had recently experienced a sexual mutilation murder. Tubman and I searched for a Frank Peralta and found a couple of them, but neither interesting.

24

CLINT'S DEMISE

Very late in the investigation, I received a call from MCSO investigator Steven Peglow. He said he was the MCSO cold-case investigator and wanted to know if there were any questions he could answer.

I asked if there was any physical evidence extant from the dump site that could result in DNA analysis, just in case my investigation developed a really good suspect.

He asked if my investigation *had* developed a good suspect. I said I thought we had and gave him a rundown of the case against Clint and Keith Wilson. I mentioned the killing of Keith in Henrietta, and he said that was quite a coincidence as he had recently arrested Keith's killer, David Young, who allegedly had become violent again.

Peglow told me he'd only just looked into Smoyer-King and Double Initials, but not Bernhard-Formicola. His suspicion was that there was no remaining evidence because back in those days, if a case reached a certain age, the thinking was that it didn't matter anymore.

Two weeks later Peglow called me back. He found two boxes of evidence, including the bloody swimsuits and the towel. He strongly doubted that there was any DNA from the killer.

"There's nothing testable. Even if the guy left some sweat behind, blood overtakes everything, and there was a lot of blood, all of it the blood of the victims. We sent all of this stuff to the FBI lab, and they found no sperm or blood from an unknown source," Peglow said.

He did however have info on another investigatory front: Jack's alibi held, he said. Contrary to what Alice now said, in 1966 everyone agreed that Jack had been at the Bernhards' house that evening waiting for the girls to return. When they didn't, he went on his date with Samantha. In addition, Jack admitted to being the father of George-Ann's baby and passed a polygraph, as they say, with flying colors.

This made me think that a lot of what was remembered as cops harassing Jack occurred when the girls were missing, as he was a likely candidate to know their plans and location if they'd run away. Once the bodies were found, they polygraphed him, checked his alibi, and moved on. So then why did Jim Newell *still* think he did it?

Clint's name was in the files multiple times, almost all because George-Ann's family talked about him, but there was no follow-up worth mentioning. Peglow assumed from this that they didn't consider Clint a strong suspect, because when they felt strongly about a guy, they went hard. They never went hard at Clint.

"What did Clint do to get his name on the suspect list?" I asked.

"Well, you know about the August 1965 report, right?"

"I don't think I do."

"Gina Formicola reported that Clint raped her in a house in the city. It was an RPD case. I don't know the outcome."

I scribbled that down with a shaking hand. We no longer had to connect dots to have a motive. There it was. Gina called the cops on Clint and cried rape. That must have made him *so* angry.

Peglow continued, "According to the files, Ruth Formicola doesn't mention Clint until July 23, 1968, but that might be a typo." Peglow was referring to the fact that this was very close to the second anniversary of the bodies' discovery.

"Clint Wilson comes up in a couple of other contexts," Peglow said. "His wife reported that he tried to kill her. There was also a report that he tried to drown someone."

I thought about the reported incident in which Clint held George-Ann's head underwater at the swimming hole. Peglow assured me that George-Ann was not the victim in this incident and that there was nothing in the files directly linking George-Ann and Clint at any time.

There was a report of a girl yelling, "Help!" back by the creek in the vicinity of the swimming hole on June 25, 1966, but the report did not come from the Mulligans. He didn't remember the source.

He also said that, contrary to what I'd said during our first conversation, it appeared that many of George-Ann and Kathy's friends had been interviewed during the initial investigation, and many of the interviews were done with a stenographer present. (Actually, my point had been that children weren't interviewed, and they were allegedly Clint's victims.)

It bothered me that we still had no definitive story as to how Clint Wilson met the grim reaper. One database listed his final address as Leroy, New York, and said he died in Rochester. Gary Barnes told Don Tubman that Clint had moved down to Texas, had been arrested for raping a child, and had died down there.

Clint's daughter Joni became my Facebook friend, and I asked her, through the private channel, if she'd be willing to talk to me about growing up on Names Road. I mentioned that it was possible her friend Tracy had already alerted her that I wanted to speak with her. Apparently Tracy had briefed Joni, because her written response was that I should talk to her mother Francine for any info regarding her "so-called father." She supplied her mother's phone number, perhaps unaware that her mom had already talked to Don Tubman. I asked in return why she called him her "so-called father." A few days went by before she replied that Clint "was a drunk and like to rape 3 yr girls." It was unclear if she was referring to the reported crime in Texas or something else. I decided my best chance of getting an informative response was to assume the worst. I replied simply, "Oh, Joni, I'm so sorry."

"It's all right. He's dead anyway. No loss," she replied.

I asked Joni how her dad died, and she said, "Slowly. He was in with people who don't like his sort."

"Why were you down in Texas, anyway?" I asked. "That's a long way from Names Road."

She said that they went down there for a fresh start.

"It worked for a short time," she said. "Then all this shit happened. But we're all good now. I've been married for 25 years and have awesome grandkids. Ruthie Morton lives down there still."

I asked her if Clint liked to pull a knife on people, and she said sure, he was always threatening people with weapons. I asked if she remembered her Uncle Keith. She said she did and that she always thought he was all right.

Did she remember any of the Hackers who hung around her house?

"Not really," she said. "There was Bear and Crazy Mike. I don't know their real names. I was too small to know."

What about her other aunts and uncles, not the Mortons but the Wilsons?

"William, Melvin, and Barney were all right. They helped their mom. Barney, Melvin, and Bonnie started a nursing home out of their house in Keshequa. We lost touch with them when I was about 12 or 13. Mom or Ruthie would know better."

Tubman did talk to Joni's mom Francine one more time at the trailer where she lived.

"I can't tell you any more than I told you," Francine said. Tubman thought her body language indicated deception.

Don Campbell was hard at work on the question of Clint's demise, and his efforts paid off. Campbell found Clint's Texas criminal record. It said he was a white male, gray hair, blue eyes, 5'8", 150 pounds, and listed as one of his aliases "Ace" Wilson. This was our first corroboration that "Ace" was Clint's biker name, a factoid we had previously only heard from the late Johnny Rowe. It listed his birthday as the summer of 1941.

He had been arrested in Texas once, in spring 1990, by the Eastland County Sheriff's Office. Eastland County was about 100 miles west/southwest of Fort Worth. He was charged with aggravated sexual assault. The age of the victim was not mentioned. He was convicted and sentenced to 75 years in prison.

His custodial agency was the Department of Criminal Justice in Huntsville. His death was not mentioned, but if our info was correct, Clint lived only 10 months after his arrest. If we assume that, even in Texas, a trial would take some time, Clint did not survive in Texas prison for long, and the odds increase that he was incarcerated for raping a child and this led to his quick death. He'd gone to prison, was labeled "short eyes" (i.e., pedo), and died in prison, circumstances unknown. Maybe it was that heart defect that Ray Morton had talked about. Maybe not.

A few days after the Campbell info came in, I received a package from Michelle Honea, the deputy district clerk in Eastland County, which contained Clint's two-page indictment and a two-page summary of the judgment and sentence at his subsequent jury trial. The indictment, passed down by the June 1990 Eastland County Grand Jury, charged that Clint did "intentionally and knowingly cause the penetration of the female sexual organ of Annie Davis,* a female child then and there younger than 14 years of age, by inserting his . . . sexual organ in said female sexual organ." A second charge accused Clint of penetrating the child's sexual organ with his finger. The indictment listed the complaining witness as Terry Simmons.

At his arraignment, Clint stood mute, and the court entered a plea for him of not guilty. Clint's trial was held on July 26 of that year. The prosecutor was William C. Dowell, representing the office of state's attorney Emory C. Walton. Clint's defense attorney was Leslie Vance, and the trial was presided over by Judge Jim R. Wright. The trial was brief and the deliberation equally quick. Jury foreman Alvin Limmer announced that Clint was guilty of both charges of aggravated sexual assault (the aggravating factor being the age of the victim). The jury then determined Clint's punishment to be a fine of $1,000 and 75 years of confinement in the Texas Department of Corrections. Clint was given credit for the 69 days he had already spent in jail.

A quick search of this investigation's accrued knowledge revealed that Annie Davis was Clint's close relative. (It was possible that both Clint Sr.'s and Clint Jr.'s final rapes were incestuous—making Ace a malevolent chip off a nefarious block.). A quick check of our own growing archives revealed that "Annie M. Davis" was born in 1982, age eight at the time of her attack.

The same day I received the package, I spoke to Rebecca McCrary, an Eastland newspaper reporter. With a nose for news, "Becky" was interested in these strange related rapists whose path of destruction ran all the way from the southern shore of Lake Ontario to the Lone Star State.

Becky recalled the sheriff, David Franklin, who took over about that time. I told her that the indictment listed the witness as Terry Simmons.

"Dang!" she said. "I'm going to call him right now. You may be hearing from him." She also mentioned that the prosecutor, Bill Dowell, was a good friend of hers.

Sure enough, within an hour I received an e-mail from Terry Simmons, who explained that he was a deputy for the ECSO in 1990 and was the complaining officer in this case. It was a long time ago, but he recalled that the victim was Wilson's relative, who was eight or nine years old but suffered from a mental handicap that "put her much younger." The crime, he believed, took place in the town of Olden. He recalled the perp having a northern accent. Wilson, he recalled, steadfastly denied raping the girl and "showed no remorse."

Simmons said that cases like this were often hard to prosecute because the victim lacked the ability to articulate the crime. But this case brought a conviction because of the strong case developed by Mr. Dowell with the help of Child Protective Services. He had no knowledge of what became of Wilson after he was sent to prison.

Becky had a contact that vaguely remembered the case and thought that perhaps Wilson had died of a heart attack in prison, but then added that the prison was liable to proclaim Wilson's death as due to natural causes no matter what the real reason was, just to avoid an unnecessary investigation. In other words, what happens in Huntsville stays in Huntsville.

It was as close to *just desserts* as we were going to get.

EPILOGUE

From the time this story began in earnest in 1966 until the point that I write this, in 2015, so much has changed in America. We have gone from a society that thought of mass murder as a foreign thing, a once-in-a-blue-moon thing, to a society that so takes violent and senseless crime for granted that it is the subject of dozens of network TV shows, some of them comedies. Hopefully this particular violent and senseless crime is a little bit less mysterious than it was when I found it. We knew in 2011, when the latest of my investigations began, that it would be hard to prove who killed Kathy and George-Ann. We needed an eyewitness, a confession, or a DNA match, and with multiple generations having passed, all three seemed unlikely. We did get the son of a suspect calling out his dad and his uncles, and doing it in front of his mom, the sister of a victim. Not bad. We had motive, opportunity, and temperament. But with no DNA, there could be no conclusive investigation-ending solution. There is always the hope that the publishing of this book might in itself dislodge the info that seals the deal. But until then, this thing inside me stays, the answer at best a shadow in the fog, grainy and gray, receding, a ghost unshackled of its earthly bonds and lost now perhaps forever in the back crick of eternity. This is not to say that my efforts were all in vain. I did some good. I gave at least some of the other damaged children, the living victims—Mary Crane, Dawn Putnam, Anne Werner, Cathy Carter—an opportunity to lighten their burden. I did all right by Alice. I kept my promises. I was the first to tell her that Kathy had not been tortured to death, and I made a lot of people think about Kathy, who really was forgotten way too soon. Hopefully I reinforced in the Rochester area the notion that Kathy and George-Ann were precious individuals with lives that mattered. I have paid my penance for not waving back at a pregnant George-Ann as she stood in her living room window, for wishing she'd go away because her pregnancy frightened me. I did some harm, too. I probably was responsible for aggravating some cases of posttraumatic stress. I brought the nightmare back for some, and to those people I apologize. I made many innocents worry about their dirty laundry, concerned that they would be embarrassed by what I wrote about them, despite the fact that they'd had nothing to do with the murders. I have done my best to protect those people, and if anyone is embarrassed, I am so sorry. There were times when I felt like a time-traveling giant eye in the sky, pulling the roofs off 1966 Ballantyne homes and peering inside at things best kept private. To those people, I promise, I will always keep my mouth shut.

APPENDIX A

Details of Arthur Shawcross's Known Crime Scenes[1]

Victim Number One:
Jack Blake
Age: 10
Date Disappeared: May 7, 1972
Date Found: September 6, 1972

Only known male victim. Shawcross had previously taken the victim fishing. Murder took place in Watertown, New York, just upstream along Kelsey Creek from Black River, near a bridge and railroad tracks. Shawcross was seen around the time of Blake's disappearance exiting the woods behind a motel/gas station near North Watertown Cemetery. His boots were muddy, and he carried a broken fishing rod he said he'd found beside Kelsey Creek. Four months passed before the body was discovered, and decomposition was nearly complete. The skeleton was naked. Some of the bones were out of order because of animal activity, and several of the boy's teeth had been knocked out during the murder. Police found the victim's clothes 45 feet away. The arms of the boy's green jacket had been tied in a knot. Cinders found on the bottoms of the boy's feet and scratches on his arms indicated that at one point he'd gotten away and had run through thorny brush as far as the railroad tracks, but the killer had caught him and dragged him back into the woods. Dr. Richard S. Lee performed the autopsy and wrote that the boy had been stripped naked before he was killed. Cause of death: most likely asphyxiation and/or strangulation. Years later, following his Rochester arrest, Shawcross told a psychiatrist that he'd cut off the boy's "penis and balls" and eaten them.

Victim Number Two:
Karen Ann Hill
Age: 8
Date Disappeared: September 2, 1972
Date Found: September 2, 1972
Victim was from Rochester and was visiting Watertown, New York. A stranger to Shawcross. Was thought by her mother to be playing in the backyard of 503 Pearl Street in Watertown, just around the corner from Jack Blake's home on Water Street, and a block north of the Black River. Her body was found about 10 hours after her disappearance beside the river, underneath the iron Pearl Street Bridge. The body was at the bottom of an embankment, covered with concrete paving slabs, face down, with a red circle around her neck. There were bruises on her face. She was naked from the waist down. Her red, white, and blue shorts were discovered beside her body, bloodstained. Also bloody and nearby were her blue panties. The medical examiner determined that, when found, the girl had been dead for 8 to 12 hours. She had been punched in the face and stomach, raped, and sodomized so viciously that her skin was torn. There was semen present both in vagina and rectum. Mud was stuffed into the mouth and throat. Shawcross was seen around the time of the murder on the south side of the river, on Factory Street, walking past an old plant and some railroad tracks. Shawcross, police came to believe, had been fishing in Black River near the bridge. Karen was crossing the bridge, having wandered off from the backyard on Pearl Street on her own, and was lured down to Shawcross's location below. Shawcross later said he did it because of a "Vietnam flashback." When later describing this murder, Shawcross called the area "along the creek bed."

Victim Number Three:
Dorothy Blackburn
Age: 27
Date Disappeared: March 15, 1988
Date Found: March 24, 1988

First known Rochester victim. Tiny prostitute with dark curly hair and full lips. Shawcross picked her up off the street in a car on Saratoga Street, just off Lake Avenue in Rochester, and after an attempted trick in a parking lot behind Nick Tahou's Restaurant on West Main Street in Downtown Rochester, he manually strangled her in Northampton Park, off Route 104, west of Rochester. He tore out a portion of her vagina with his teeth and dropped the body off of a bridge into Salmon Creek. Workers cleaning out the culvert discovered her nine days later. The body was face down, covered with a layer of silt and resting against a chunk of concrete that turned out to be the missing home plate from a nearby baseball field. She was clothed in jeans, a hoodie, and sneakers. Her blue shirt was pulled up so that her midriff was bare. Her left eye was closed. The autopsy report read, "Multiple lacerations vaginal area, right labia minora has 3 cm vertical and 1.5 cm horizontal laceration from clitoral area. Lateral to this, laceration labia majora left of clitoris." Also: "Contusions to right supraclavicular area and hemorrhage into right neck strap muscles, consistent with manual strangulation."

Victim Number Four:

Anna Marie Steffen

Age: 28

Date Disappeared: July 9, 1988

Date Found: September 9, 1988

Diminutive (95 pounds), pregnant, and homeless prostitute. Met Shawcross in a bar on Lake Avenue. According to Shawcross, the murder occurred after a trick went bad in the weeds near a construction site at the top of the gorge cliff, on the river's west bank, near the Driving Park Bridge, an impressive structure that spans the gorge just below the Genesee River's final waterfall. However, around the time of Steffen's disappearance, she was seen by a friend, crying, upset as she crossed the Driving Park Bridge, complaining that "someone was after her." According to Shawcross, someone came near their spot, and he was afraid that discovery might result in a parole violation. When she threatened to scream, he "grabbed her by the throat and just held her and squeezed her until she quit." When she was dead, he just "rolled her off the edge of the cliff" until she came to a rest "behind a bush." A man searching for discarded deposit bottles discovered the body two months later alongside the river gorge. He first saw a leg bone protruding and then noticed that it was wearing clothes. The body was hidden in weeds and ferns, partially covered with sticks and slabs of concrete. The victim's white tank top was found bunched around the left wrist bone, and the jeans were inside out and around the skeleton's ankles. Fifteen feet from the body were the victim's flip-flops. Near the body was a large rock. When lifted, police found a hank of hair that had been ripped from the skull. Decomposition had occurred rapidly because of the summer heat. Because the remains were skeletal, a forensic anthropologist (like the titular character on the *Bones* TV show) was called in to identify them. A reconstruction of the victim's face formulated from the skull was so accurate that Steffen's father ID'd her.

Victim Number Five:
   Dorothy Keeler
   Age: 59
   Date Disappeared: July 29, 1989
   Date Found: October 21, 1989

The oldest of Shawcross's victims, Keeler was a destitute woman whom Shawcross had once hired to clean his apartment. On her final day, Keeler came to Shawcross's house appearing filthy and explained that she'd been, in his words, "sleeping over here by the river under the trestle." He allowed her to take a shower. Afterward he took her to Seth Green Island, which was in the Genesee River. He said that they "were having an affair." While there, he claimed, he caught her trying to take money out of his wallet, so he struck her on the side of the head with a log, broke her neck, and killed her. He then carried her body to tall grass where it couldn't be seen. Shawcross stayed with the body for hours before leaving and later visited the body repeatedly. "There was a smell, but no one wanted to check it out," he said. Three months later he used a stick to separate the skull from the rest of the remains and toss it into the river. Three fishermen from Pennsylvania seeking spawner salmon discovered the remains three months later. They said they were "bones in clothes," partially covered with weeds and maple tree branches. The skeleton was in a fetal position and wore jeans that had been pulled down to mid-thigh. A pair of high-heeled shoes were found a few feet away.

Victim Number Six:

Patricia Ives
Age: 25
Date Disappeared: September 29, 1989
Date Found: October 27, 1989

Prostitute picked up by Shawcross in the Princess Diner on Lake Avenue. He murdered her behind the fence at the rear of the YMCA. The spot overlooked the river gorge just south of Driving Park Bridge, on the west bank of the Genesee River. He strangled her while having anal sex with her. It "took her a long time to die," and Shawcross had his "first orgasm in a long while." Shawcross put her body up against the fence and covered her with a large board. He murdered Keeler and Ives exactly two months apart. The two women's remains were found six days apart. A boy who climbed through the fence at the back of the Y to retrieve an errant baseball found Ives's remains. He saw a foot protruding from underneath a large sheet of cardboard. The remains were found face up wearing pants and a sweater, with no underwear.

Victim Number Seven:

June Stotts
Age: 30
Date Disappeared: October 23, 1989
Date Found: November 23, 1989

Stotts was neither a hooker nor a drug addict, but rather a shy, slow, and perhaps slightly schizophrenic woman who had befriended Shawcross and his girlfriend. Shawcross picked her up in his car. She was sitting on a park bench on Bloss Street, in Edgerton Park. He took her to Turning Point Park, on the Genesee's west bank, across and a mile downstream (north) from his previous murder. The river at that spot had been widened so barges could turn around. From there they walked down a "cinder road" to a spot beside the river where a barge was tied up. The location was beneath a cement plant, and the air reeked of standing water. The only way to get there was to follow a dirt path through the foliage off Boxart Street. Stotts was strangled to death. He removed her clothes and hid her body in bushes. He threw her clothes in the water 30 feet from the body. He remained at the site for three hours, presumably molesting the remains. He revisited the body a week later and had sex with her corpse. He used Stotts's own knife on the body and gutted it from throat to crotch, as a hunter might gut a deer. "I cut out her pussy and ate it," he later confessed. When done with her, he dragged her into nearby standing water and threw a discarded rug over her. A man walking his dog discovered her body on Thanksgiving Day. On the ground was a piece of carpet with a human foot sticking out from under it. Crime scene investigators could tell right away that the face-up victim had been moved some time after death. Blood had settled to the front of the corpse, so it was face down at first and then later flipped over. One knee had been pushed up under the body so that the buttocks were raised up in the air. Police found a pocketknife nearby and a bloody towelette. No semen was found on or near the remains.

Victim Number Eight:
Maria Welch
Age: 22
Date Disappeared: November 5, 1989
Date Found: January 5, 1990

Welch was a diminutive, blonde, bespectacled, heroin-addicted prostitute. Shawcross picked her up in a car in front of Mark's Texas Hots hotdog stand at 48 Lake Avenue, just north of Lyell Avenue. She was 5'2", 100 pounds, with brown hair and eyes and tattoos of a unicorn, a marijuana leaf, and the letters L-O-V-E on the knuckles of her left hand. Before she disappeared, she'd been plagued by prank phone calls by a man pretending to be a cop, taunting her about prostitution and threatening death. (Twenty-three years earlier, the Bernhards had to suffer similar prank phone calls in which Kathy was called a whore and Betty was threatened with death.) According to Shawcross's account, the murder took place in a parking lot behind a warehouse somewhere in the Lyell/Lake area. Welch's body was found, after Shawcross's arrest and with the killer's assistance, in a woods near Lake Ontario, not far from June Stott's dump site. The remains—still wearing jeans, underpants, sneakers, and two necklaces—were in a sitting position, head pitched forward almost to the knees.

Victim Number Nine:
Frances Brown
Age: 22
Date Disappeared: November 11, 1989

Date Found: November 15, 1989

Shawcross picked Brown up in a car at the corner of Lake and Ambrose Avenues. He killed her in the car while parked in a parking lot behind a Kodak factory along the east bank of the Genesee River on Seth Green Drive, about a half mile downstream (north) of "the island." He claimed that he asphyxiated Brown by pushing his penis too far into her throat. After she was dead, he said, he French-kissed her and used her body to stay warm for a while and then rolled it off a "cliff" into the gorge near the parking lot. A fisherman who disregarded a "Do Not Enter" sign off Seth Green Drive discovered her body only a few days later. He saw the body first from about 40 feet above on the slope leading down to the river. At first he thought it was a mannequin. The body, naked except for a pair of white go-go boots, was partially covered with uprooted grass, branches, and twigs. The body was face down, on its knees with buttocks raised, arms encircling a concrete block, leaning to one side against a tree. The words "kiss off" were tattooed onto one of her buttocks. Because Brown was discovered so soon after her murder, the medical examiner was able to recreate events more precisely. Pinpoint hemorrhages behind her eyes indicated asphyxiation. Scrapes and bruises on the body revealed that she'd been beaten before she was murdered. There was no semen.

Victim Number Ten:

Elizabeth Gibson

Age: 29

Date Disappeared: November 25, 1989

Date Found: November 27, 1989

Shawcross picked her up in his car from outside Mark's Texas Hots on Lake Avenue. By this time police knew that there was a serial killer at work, but Shawcross gave no indication of changing his methods to avoid detection. He asphyxiated her in a parking lot at the corner of Avenue D and St. Paul Street, just south of the Driving Park Bridge on the east bank of the river gorge. The site was directly across the river from the YMCA where he killed Patricia Ives. Shawcross traveled with the body, then dumped it face down in a creek near a dirt road in Wayne County. He'd parked his car about 60 feet off County Line Road, 12 miles east of the city, and carried the body the remaining "few hundred feet" to the dump site. A hunter discovered her only hours later.

Victim Number Eleven:

Darlene Trippi

Age: 32

Date Disappeared: December 15, 1989

Date Found: January 5, 1990

Streetwalker picked up by Shawcross in a car on Daus Alley, just north of Lyell Avenue. Trippi was asphyxiated in a parking lot off Emerson Street near the back wall of a loading dock, between two tractor trailers. Her body was dumped in a culvert, under a small bridge, off a desolate section of North Redman Road in Brockport, west of the city. The dump site was in the same general direction as Salmon Creek. Both sites would be accessed by leaving the city via Ridge Road West (Route 104). Her clothes were disposed of separately on Shawcross's way home in a clothing box at the Salvation Army near the intersection of Manitou Road and Ridge Road West. Trippi's remains were found after Shawcross was caught, and only with the killer's assistance. The body, when discovered, was frozen in ice, spread-eagle and face up.

Victim Number Twelve:

June Cicero

Age: 34

Date Disappeared: December 17, 1989

Date Found: January 3, 1990

Originally from Brooklyn, Cicero was known as the oldest, toughest, and meanest prostitute working Rochester's streets. She'd been a streetwalker for 15 years. A cocaine addict who worked longer hours than the other women to support her habit, she was no longer a beautiful woman but had managed to keep her body in attractive shape. By the time she disappeared, the murders, fear, and the cold, snowy weather had depleted the number of available street hookers in Rochester to just a few. As with all of Shawcross's victims, she was small, 5'2". He picked her up in a car in front of City Mattress on Lyell Avenue. He dumped the body in Salmon Creek near the Route 31 bridge, not far from Northampton Park and the dump site of Dorothy Blackburn. He kicked snow over the body to hide it. He disposed of some of her clothes in his favorite Salvation Army box at Ridge and Manitou. He returned to the scene "two or three days" later, pulled the body out of the ice, and used a "saber saw" to cut out her vagina. "Bone and all," he explained. He drove around with the vagina in his car for a time. Then, after pulling out the hairs and wrapping it in a bar towel, "I ate it frozen," he later bragged. It was the discovery of Cicero's body—face frozen into the ice, buttocks raised—that coincided with Shawcross's apprehension. She was wearing white kneesocks, a white jacket, and one earring—the mate later found in a vehicle Shawcross had driven. Using black light at the crime scene, investigators discovered orange specks in the snow, which turned out to be human sawdust from the sawing of the victim's crotch.

Victim Number Thirteen
  Felicia Stephens
  Age: 20
  Date Disappeared: December 28, 1989
  Date Found: December 31, 1989
Shawcross's only known African-American victim. She was a slight woman, 5'5", 115 pounds, with black hair, brown skin, and dark brown eyes. It should be noted that many (more than 10) black hookers were murdered in Rochester during this same time period, but, with the exception of Stephens, Shawcross denied involvement in any of those crimes—including that of Kimberly Logan, who is listed in some unofficial sources as a Shawcross victim. (Police believe that at least some of those murders were committed by a black man named John White who lived in the town of Gates, west of the city, and who had been seen behaving peculiarly near one of the dump sites. When police showed White's photo to hookers on the street, he was ID'd as a john who'd been seen with some of the murdered women. White was interrogated, but unlike Shawcross, he refused to talk. He was put under constant surveillance until his 1994 death by heart attack.)

Shawcross encountered Stephens while stopped at a red light at the corner of Plymouth and Main in downtown Rochester. According to him, Stephens stuck her head in his open passenger side window, and he closed the window on her, catching her throat. She began screaming, so he grabbed her head with both hands, pulled her into the car through the window, and choked her to death. Then he took her to

Northampton Park and dumped her. She was found face down, buttocks slightly elevated, near the spot where June Cicero was dumped. Stephens's jeans were discovered on New Year's Eve by a Northampton Park guard who spotted a "dark patch" in a snowbank along the park's border and discovered the frozen pants after parking off of Sweden-Walker Road. Hours later a jogger discovered one of Stephens's boots in the park. Police knew the body might be somewhere nearby but did not release this information. Four days later—on January 3, 1990, when visiting the nearby body of June Cicero—Shawcross was caught.

APPENDIX B

Details Regarding the Murder of Sandra Solie[1]

Sandra Solie was 38 years old and seven months pregnant when she disappeared on May 23, 1994. Her apartment was "down by the canal" on Route 350. Her car was parked in its normal spot outside. She had appointments written on her calendar. The dog dish for her pet poodle was filled. The dog, however, was also missing.

Solie was on disability leave from Kodak because of a head injury. Long after police stopped looking for her, Private Investigator Richard Ingraham was still looking. On the anniversary of her disappearance he would hand out flyers with her photo on them in Macedon. Ingraham thought the person responsible for Sandra's disappearance was someone close to her.

"I always look at the in-laws before the outlaws," he liked to say. It was a piece of advice I took seriously.

She was last seen at 2:30 in the afternoon in an Ames Plaza store at a Macedon shopping center on Route 31 by an elderly friend named Ed Miller for whom she ran errands.

She must have returned home before she disappeared, as her dog disappeared as well. She was reported missing by her landlord on June 2, 1994, after she failed to pay her rent.

During the first days of the investigation into her disappearance, police repeatedly interviewed her ex-husband Ralph Solie Jr., but after a while he lawyered up.

She'd planned to meet her ex-husband on the day she disappeared. Her baby was her ex-husband's, and they were having an affair despite the fact that he had remarried.

Her poodle's tags and her purse were found in a Penfield car wash dumpster, and police said that some of her credit cards had been used. Police caught the parties that ran up a $1,000 bill but learned that the culprits got the cards from a boy who found Sandra's wallet on North Street in the city of Rochester.

A high school teacher remembered her as a pretty girl with a sparkling personality. She was 5'5" and weighed 130 to 140 pounds. Her date of birth was December 19, 1955. She had brown hair and brown eyes. Sandra was not reported missing until she'd been gone for almost two weeks, and then by her landlord rather than by a friend or family member.

This did not look like the work of a serial killer.

APPENDIX C

The Trial of the Genesee Valley Park Rapists

Monroe County district attorney John Little personally prosecuted. Judge John Conway Jr. presided. The victim's boyfriend testified, saying that he, like the victim, was a graduate student. He'd known the victim for two years, and they dated occasionally. On this day they'd had a small picnic in Hamlin Beach Park on Lake Ontario, gone swimming and sunbathed, then gotten dinner at a Chinese restaurant, and decided to cap the evening with a visit to Genesee Valley Park. They drove over a little bridge crossing Red Creek and parked for about an hour, necking and petting. She sat on his lap, and both remained fully clothed. No, he'd never "possessed the victim sexually." They wound up with her behind the wheel and him in the passenger seat. Another young couple was parked about 60 feet away. Then a third car pulled up, facing the couple, and turned out its lights. A black man appeared at the right side of the car, opened the door, and shouted, "Get out of the car." The girl screamed, "Don't do that to me!" The man pulled a knife and ordered the witness into the backseat. Instead of complying, the witness delivered "an uppercut to the groin" and ran, back across the bridge to the main road where he flagged down a passing motorist. By the time they returned to the car, his date and the black man were gone. The witness then went immediately to the Henrietta State Trooper Barracks and reported the incident.[1]

The victim testified, telling the jury that she remembered shouting, "Leave him alone!" Then there was a hand at her throat from behind and a voice saying, "Shut up, or we'll kill you." One of the men chased her boyfriend but couldn't catch him, and he returned to the parking area out of breath. She was forced onto her back in the backseat. Her dress was pulled up and her panties were pulled down. She heard a voice say, "This isn't going to work." She was dragged out of the car and to another, theirs, where she was again forced onto her back in the backseat. They drove for a while and parked next to a building from which loud music was blaring. One man was in the back with her, and two others were in the front seat. Her panties were gone. "Please don't do this to me, I'm a virgin!" she shouted. "You won't be for long!" her attacker replied. She tried to squeeze her legs together but they forced her to open them. The three men took turns raping her, and all three sex acts were completed. One had a temporary problem because the other two men were watching. They had to turn their backs so he could complete the rape. Each attacker offered his own death threat. The car started up again, and they drove. She was forced onto the floor, and the man in the back kept pushing her head down so she couldn't be seen. After a while one of the men said a cop was following them and they sped up. She was bleeding from her torn vagina, and her legs were covered with mud from being dragged across the parking lot.

Deputy Robert F. Falzone took the stand and described the arrest, how the victim's face looked "distorted" and she couldn't stop sobbing, that there was mud on the victim and on the inside of the 1960 Dodge. A knife was found in the pocket of a defendant. In the back of the Dodge was a lurid detective magazine and empty beer cans.

A female ambulance attendant testified that, when she first saw the victim, the young blonde was slumped in the deputy's car in a "state of shock." In the ambulance she cried hysterically and repeatedly needed oxygen. A female physician testified that the victim gazed into space, had an abnormally rapid heartbeat, and "had a condition of wetness over the pubic area." Her hymeneal ring had been perforated by half an inch, and there was five cc's of semen in her vaginal region. "She had blood on her thighs. I gave her a tranquilizer," the doctor said. The following day the victim was further administered "medication and also something to help prevent pregnancy."

A psychiatrist testified that the victim told him she had a thick hymen that would have required surgery before she became a wife.

The three defendants each had their own counsel. Although two defense lawyers kept their clients off the stand, the third allowed his client to testify. The defendant, who came from Virginia, had a wife and four children, said the other two defendants picked him up at his home and the three went to Sea Breeze Amusement Park. They left Sea Breeze around 10:00 and drove to Genesee Valley Park. The witness said they were looking for a secluded place so the other two could teach him how to drive. They came across the girl's car. One of the defendants went over to her car and came back with her, holding her by the hand but not dragging her. She got willingly into their car, and they drove her to Clarissa Street for a drink and then to a bar on Main Street. Sure, they had sex with the girl, but she never made a peep of protest and no one forced her to do anything.

The jury deliberated for only an hour and a half before returning a guilty verdict.

APPENDIX D

The Death of Keith Wilson[1]

Late on Friday night, May 24, 1985, Sergeant Gary Thompson was parked in the lot of the Henrietta town hall, which was adjacent to Henrietta Park, and was close enough to hear the shots and respond to them as an ear witness. After hearing the first shot, Thompson turned down his radio and listened. About 20 seconds passed before he heard a second shot. Thompson reported shots fired in Henrietta Park and called for backup. Soon the park "was surrounded." Thompson was informed by dispatch that a citizen who'd heard both shots and a female scream had already called in the incident. Entering the park, Thompson found one car in the parking lot, a small blue station wagon, unoccupied. The time was four minutes before midnight. Thompson subsequently found a body just off the parking lot at the north side of the playground, a male body, face down and bloody, 25 yards from the station wagon in the grass adjacent to the circle at the end of the road.

Thompson checked and was somewhat surprised to find that the man had a small amount of respiration. A Henrietta ambulance was called, arrived noisily, and took the limp form to Strong Memorial Hospital in Rochester, where he was pronounced dead at 12:35 a.m., May 25, and his body was turned over to the medical examiner's office.

Police, now a mixture of county and state officers, conducted an immediate search of the parking lot area and found the stock of a long gun of some sort, either a rifle or a shotgun, a bloody handkerchief, and an axe handle.

Officers went out into the neighboring streets in search of anyone who might have seen or heard something. Entrances to the park were blocked off. The crime scene was secured with tape. More investigators and technicians arrived. Sergeant Thompson, first to be on the scene, was also present the longest, and the sun was coming up before he was allowed to leave the park. A second search of the area was done in daylight, with negative results.

The victim was identified as Keith Wilson, of Stallman Drive, Chili. There was only one car in the parking lot when police arrived, parked facing west, a 1975 American Motors station wagon registered to the dead man.

Investigators found a witness on nearby Strawberry Hill who heard the shooting. The witnesses—there turned out to be two of them—were Carol Trinchini and her relative Diane Beuge. Trinchini said that five minutes before midnight they were sitting on her living room couch and heard a gunshot in Henrietta Park, which was right across the street. After the shot, there was about 15 seconds of silence, and then a voice screamed, "Help! Help!" six or eight times. It sounded like a woman, but Trinchini couldn't be sure. (Keith's voice, as we know, was very high.) After the screaming stopped, there was a second shot. About a minute later she saw a sheriff's car pull into the park. She didn't see any cars leaving.

Investigators set up surveillance at the victim's house on Stallman Drive. At 7:00 a.m. they saw 16-year-old Dean Wilson walking on Stallman Drive from the direction of Ballantyne Road. He turned at the old Formicola driveway and headed toward the house. Police stopped the teenager, who explained that he'd just spent the night at a friend's house and was returning home. The officers advised the youth to return to his friend's house immediately and to wait for a phone call from his mother.

Parked in the driveway on Stallman was a gold-colored Pontiac Grand Prix with Florida plates. The car had been driven forward into the driveway and placed in park. At police request, the car was put on a hook by Joe Benson's Tow (on Scottsville Road, no author relation) and pulled to the police garage at headquarters, 130 South Plymouth Avenue, for tech work. Investigators took custody of the vehicle.

Sergeant Joseph E. Marhetta received a phone call from Chief Barker at the Formicola house. Seconds later, Marhetta called for two persons of interest to be picked up: David Young, of Rush, and Gina Wilson, the victim's wife. Marhetta himself, along with Sergeant Alex MacKenzie, drove to Young's home and rang the doorbell at 3:40 a.m. Young's sister answered the door and said sure, David was there, he was on the couch.

David greeted the officers with a stretch and a yawn. The trained observers could tell he was faking sleepiness. David's mom came downstairs, and Marhetta took her into the kitchen where she told him that she knew who Keith Wilson was. He was the almost ex of David's girlfriend who had threatened her son in the past. She said that she'd gone to bed at 10:00 p.m. and that David was not home at the time. The sister added that she'd gotten in at 12:45 a.m. and David *was* home at that time. Young told Marhetta he'd been home since 10:00 p.m. Marhetta invited him to criminal investigations headquarters. Young said okay. They arrived at CID, and Young was interrogated by Marhetta and MacKenzie beginning at 4:00 a.m. Young said that before 10:00 p.m. he was with his friend Dan Weissenborn.

There was a phone call for Marhetta. A new piece of info came in. This boyfriend and the wife had just gotten back from Florida, and there were problems over that with the husband. Marhetta advised Young of his rights, made sure he understood them, and stated point-blank that he thought Young was in Henrietta Park the night before and that he was the one who killed Keith Wilson. Young wouldn't budge. Chief Barker entered the room and told Young to smarten up.

"We got your girlfriend Gina, and she says you and her were at the scene."

"Nope," Young said, lips clamped together.

It took 33 minutes, but Young finally sighed and admitted that he was there. He said that Gina and he were parked and Keith drove up. Keith charged the car with a shotgun, and David had to open the door on him. David got out of the car, grabbed the shotgun, and tried to wrestle it away from Keith. He got the shotgun away from him and then shot him twice with it.

Young almost immediately realized his error and winced. That lie wasn't going to hold water, and he knew it. The shotgun had been a single shot. Where did he get the second shell? Young hung his head. They had him.

Eventually the interview was turned into a written deposition. Young said he'd known Gina Wilson for about a year, had met her when they worked together at York Steak House in Market Place Mall. He knew her to have a teenage son named Dean. Gina had been his girlfriend for about six months. He was "in love" with her, and they'd talked marriage. Gina and Keith were getting a divorce. Keith, Young said, had been mistreating Gina the whole time he knew her. In November 1984, Gina and he ran away together, to Ocala, Florida, to get away from Keith and be close to Gina's parents. Gina and he lived together for a time in Ocala and were joined for part of that time by Dean, who'd already been in Ocala for a few months, running away from an abusive Keith to live with his grandmother Ruth.

Three times Keith came down to Florida to take his woman back, the first time in January 1985 when Keith followed Gina to her job and she had to call the cops. It was the same thing on his other two visits. Keith "caused a lot of problems" and made David and Gina "deathly afraid of him."

After Keith's third visit to Florida, David decided they needed protection. He went to Jerry's Pawn Shop in Ocala and purchased a 12-gauge H&R single-shot shotgun. David and Gina had only returned to the Rochester area the previous week because he needed a better job and Gina wanted to "straighten things out with the divorce." David was afraid of Keith ever since he got back. Twice Keith called David's mother's house, where David was staying, to make threats.

At 4:00 p.m. on May 24, David called Gina, and they made plans to meet. She would pick him up on Rush Scottsville Road (Route 251). Gina called him back an hour later at his mother's house and said she'd pick him up at 9:30 p.m. On David's way out the door to their meeting place, he stopped at the garage and dug out the shotgun he'd bought in Florida. He'd had it hidden in his mom's garage ever since he returned north.

Gina pulled her gold Grand Prix onto the shoulder of the road in front of her boyfriend. She greeted him with a kiss and told him to put the gun in the backseat.

David had two red-and-gold shotgun shells in his pocket.

Gina drove to Henrietta Park, the shotgun still in the back.

Then, as if by magic, Keith pulled up. They'd only been there a few minutes, and bam, there he was driving his little blue station wagon. Keith parked his car a couple of car lengths in front of them. As Keith got out of the car, David grabbed the shotgun from the backseat and hurriedly loaded a shell into it. Young said that Keith was carrying something that appeared to be a baseball bat. Keith took a couple of steps and then began to run toward Gina's car. Young jumped out of the Grand Prix holding the shotgun. Young shouted for Keith to stop, but Keith didn't stop. When Keith got to within 10 feet of Young, he lifted the shotgun and shot him in the arm. Keith started to go down, but he came back up and continued moving forward. Young put the second shell, his last, in the gun and fired at Keith again. That dropped him to his knees. Keith tried to get up, but he was in a lot of pain and couldn't. Keith tried to walk forward on his knees, so Young held the shotgun by the barrel and swung it like a baseball bat. He struck Keith with the stock in the side of the head. David admitted that his memory of specifics was a little cloudy from all the adrenaline. He swung at least once and maybe twice more, hitting Keith in the head at least one more time, and stopped swinging because the stock of the pawnshop gun snapped off and fell to the parking lot. Keith had now fallen completely and lay motionless. Young, panting, got back into the car. Gina tore out of the parking lot with no lights, saying they had to get rid of the gun. Gina drove to the pond off West Rush Road, on a dirt road just before the 390 overpass. Young heaved the shotgun into the pond. After that, Gina drove Young home, and they agreed not to tell anyone about the incident.

Gina Wilson was picked up and brought in. During a portion of Young's statement, Gina was brought into the room, and the officers repeatedly caught her trying to signal Young, telling him to shut up. When he wouldn't, she just sat there looking angry.

Young concluded his deposition by admitting that he had lied earlier to police, but now he was telling the truth. With a chilling detachment, Young added that he never had any use for Keith Wilson. He hit him with the gun after shooting him to put him out of his misery. When Young got home and it was over, he didn't have any trouble sleeping. "It doesn't bother me that he is dead," Young said.

Gina subsequently said aloud that Young's statement was true. It was self-defense all the way. One thing, she might've turned on the car lights before exiting the Henrietta Park parking lot.

When investigators began deposing her, however, she changed her tune and said that she hadn't even been in Henrietta Park. She was promptly booked for hindering the prosecution. Now she and her boyfriend could be arraigned together.

At that arraignment in Henrietta Court, David J. Young was formally charged with murder in the second degree. The complainant was Marhetta, who swore that he heard the story of Keith's death from David Young himself, *after* Young had been thoroughly advised of his rights.

While this was going on, the sheriff's scuba divers were in the pond off West Rush Road, where they quickly found both Young's broken shotgun and his bloody shirt. The serial numbers on the shotgun had been filed off, another indication that the killing of Keith Wilson was planned.

Bill David* was one of the partygoers who encountered David Young on the evening of Keith Wilson's death. He was 22 years old, lived on Ballantyne Road, and coincidentally was the kid brother of Clint Wilson's buddy Junior David. Bill told police that he'd never seen Young before, but they were introduced. Bill said Young told the people at the party that he was going "to kill someone tonight." Bill didn't remember who he said he was going to kill. Young asked everyone at the party if anyone had any shotgun shells. Everyone said no. Bill said Young returned to the party at 12:40 a.m., and he was certain of the time because he was just getting ready to leave and go to another party. Someone asked Young if he took care of his business, and he said he did. Bill only later learned that the victim was Keith Wilson, his neighbor. Bill even had a Keith Wilson anecdote. That winter there was a commotion in front of Bill's house. He ran outside and saw Keith Wilson yelling that David Young had just tried to run him over in his car. Keith said he threw a flashlight at Young's car.

On May 27, investigators went to a remote motel to visit Gina Wilson and give her the happy news that the charges brought on her were to be dropped. Gina said thanks and stated emphatically that she was fearful of her brother-in law.

"His name is Clint Wilson," Gina said. "He'll kill me."

Just that day, she'd bought a 20-gauge shotgun for her protection. She said she was returning to Stallman Drive the next day. An investigator told her to give them a call if she saw Clint. She said no way. She was calling before she went there so they would be there when she arrived. She gave the cop Clint's contact info and suggested that, if they spoke to him, they should tell him that she was not directly involved or present at "the murder."

Clint, as it turned out, was not lying in wait for Gina. He was in Keshequa with the rest of the Wilsons, making funeral arrangements.

Nowhere in the police reports was there any indication that authorities were aware that Gina Wilson was George-Ann Formicola's sister and that Keith Wilson was her brother-in-law.

APPENDIX E

Timeline: Clint Wilson Jr.

August 1941, born and lived in Keshequa, New York, later Avon.

1954–57, according to future wife Francine, attended school in Scottsville, New York.

September 6, 1959, 10:00 p.m., while living in Avon, arrested for third-degree burglary. Entered the home of George Rhode, Price Road, on two occasions. He was arrested on the East Lake Road by Undersheriff James Emery and Deputy Sheriff James Dougherty.

1959, Clint's brother Melvin arrested for rape. Witness refused to testify. At one point Clint and Melvin were in court at the same time.

Late 1950s, unconfirmed reports that Clint worked with future wife Francine and victim George-Ann's mother Ruth at Conti Meatpacking, perhaps as a butcher.

1959, married Francine Morton (first cousin, once removed, of victim George-Ann Formicola) and lived temporarily on Lester Street with her parents and brothers. Reportedly beat Francine when drunk.

May 6, 1960, living in Mount Morris, Clint arrested on Route 39 north of Geneseo for reckless driving (with brother Paul). The incident involved "horseplay." At about 11:00 p.m., Clarence Merrill of Avon reported to Sergeant Frank DiFranco of the Geneseo Police Department that he had been traveling on Route 39 when a car with two boys in it passed him, started weaving back and forth across the road in front of him, slowed while one of the occupants started using vulgar language, and then sped away. Merrill obtained the license plate number and gave it to Sergeant DiFranco. Deputies O. T. Anderson and James Dougherty traced the car to the boys, who, upon arraignment before Justice of the Peace Mark Welch, both entered pleas of guilty. Paul Wilson was sentenced to the Livingston County Jail for 30 days on the disorderly conduct charge. The sentence was suspended and was placed on probation to Livingston County probation officer Dean Harrison for three months. Clint Wilson, who admitted operating the motor vehicle, was sentenced to Monroe County Penitentiary for six months, suspended sentence, and was also placed on probation to Mr. Harrison for six months on the reckless driving charge.

1961, involved in two-car crash. Gave his address as the South Road dump in Garbutt, New York.

June 6, 1963, caught speeding in Scottsville, fined $10.

1964–66, member of motorcycle club the Hackers, biker name "Ace."

1961–?, with Junior David, drove garbage truck for Gates-Chili Disposal. His route, according to Junior, included Archer Road.

April 1963, bought home on Names Road, several doors down from victim Kathy Bernhard. Brother Keith married Gina Formicola, George-Ann's older sister.

August 1965, Gina Formicola called the Rochester Police Department to report that Clint had raped her in a house in the city. Disposition of this case unknown.

1965–66, at least twice "bothered" victim George-Ann Formicola, after she soaped his windows on Halloween and at the swimming hole. Soon thereafter George-Ann became pregnant. She tells her mother the father is Jack Starr but tells friend Richard Barnes that she lied when she said that. Clint was believed by George-Ann's uncle Burton Braddock to be the father of George-Ann's baby.

Spring 1966, with brother Keith as lookout, reportedly attempted to rape 10-year-old Mary Crane at knifepoint. The crime was never reported.

Spring 1966, George-Ann Formicola, now 14, gave birth in a home for unwed mothers.

1966, reportedly raped 12-year-old Dawn Putnam, George-Ann's neighbor, in Dawn's home. Entered locked home, method unknown. The crime was never reported to authorities.

June 25, 1966, George-Ann Formicola and Kathy Bernhard, last seen getting into a car on Scottsville Road with a man they seemed to know. According to Junior David, Clint was "driving around" on the evening the girls disappeared.

June 1966, victim's father George Formicola reportedly told neighbor George Mulligan Sr. that Clint and his brother Keith were the last to see the girls alive and had picked them up in a car.

July 20, 1966, victims' mutilated bodies found along the West Shore railroad tracks near Archer and Beaver Roads.

July 1966, according to Francine Morton, her family's dog was found on the Pennsylvania Railroad tracks between Ballantyne Road and the swimming hole, neatly slit down the middle and gutted.

1960s, Clint was kicked out of the Castle Inn for abusing a waitress. Also at Castle Inn, perhaps in a separate incident, suffered cut forearm. Woman cut him with box cutter. Also picked up women in bars and had sex with them while teenager Junior David acted as his chauffeur.

1960s, Francine called the sheriff saying Clint had tried to kill her. Later told this investigation that she tried to kill Clint by running his motorcycle off Scottsville Road near the restaurant then known as Schiano's.

1966, Clint's name appeared on the MCSO suspect list for the Chili murders.

December 5, 1969, the Hackers officially became the Rochester, New York, chapter of the Hells Angels. Bobby Turner, who disliked Clint and found him of poor character, supplanted "Ace" as leader. Clint left the Angels and, according to state cop Jim Newell, joined the Buffalo chapter of the Devils Diciples.

Late 1960s, Keith and Clint fought after Clint reportedly beat up his mother. Clint took a shot at Keith while Keith was driving with Gary Barnes.

May 1971, Clint's dad was arrested for raping a five-year-old girl. Clint's brother William was arrested for hindering an investigation and endangering the welfare of a child (in connection with his father's rape charge).

September 1971, Clint Sr.'s rape victim was too young to testify, so Clint Sr. was given a suspended sentence after pleading guilty to a lesser charge. Judge said he was not allowed to be with his victim anymore unless her parents were present.

November 1, 1971, at age 55, Clint Sr. died "unexpectedly" at his daughter Bonnie's house.

1972, after 13 years of marriage, Clint and Francine were divorced. They had three daughters. Clint moved to Sterling Street on the west side of Rochester.

September 14, 1973, while living in Keshequa, Clint's brother Paul robbed and assaulted a 70-year-old man.

1976, bought a trailer home in Mumford.

May 25, 1985, brother Keith was shotgunned to death in Henrietta Park by wife's boyfriend David Young. Afterward Gina went into hiding and bought a shotgun, claiming she was afraid of retribution from Clint. "He'll kill me," she said.

July 7, 1987, brother Melvin was shot and killed by his wife/girl-friend Wilma in Double Springs, Alabama. She successfully claimed self-defense.

May 17, 1990, was arrested for aggravated sexual assault in connection with an assault on a seven-year-old girl. In a keen example of Texas justice, Clint was speedily tried, convicted, and sentenced to 75 years in Huntsville prison.

January 29, 1991, Clint died in a Texas prison (another source has DOD as January 15, 1991).

December 20, 1995, brother Paul died in Himrod, New York, at age 52.

2012, Clint's nephew Dean Wilson told Don Tubman that according to Gina, "the Wilson boys" killed George-Ann and Kathy, but they "took care of it" inside the family.

APPENDIX F

Timeline: Jack Starr

September 17, 1944, born in the City of Rochester, grew up in a house on Names Road, the same street on which victim Kathy Bernhard lived.

1950s, by all accounts had lifelong behavioral problems. Second-grade teacher Muriel Dech called little Jackie a "naughty boy," one apt to grow up "wild and woolly." According to Don Reichel, Jack "flew off the handle really easy." Dig Taggart said that Jack pulled a knife during a fight with Mike Taggart. Johnny Rowe said Jack was crazy, that he ripped his own hair out when he was angry. As a teenager, Jack broke his brother Jerry's nose with his teeth. According to Dave Burnetti, Jack was a "gory guy." He shot a woodchuck and pulled its guts out. According to Samantha Sherman, Jack suffered from a seizure disorder.

1959, photo last appeared in a Wheatland-Chili yearbook.

Circa 1962–64, in the U.S. Army. There is a strange amnesia about this time of his life. No one recalls Jack being in the army. Info comes from Jack's obit. (Request for Jack's DD214 denied because our investigation lacked affiliation with Jack's next of kin.)

Mid-1960s, Jack worked at Delco, a manufacturing plant in the city of Rochester, with his father. According to victim's mother, Alice Bernhard, her husband John drank with Jack at the Castle Inn.

Summer 1965, 13-year-old George-Ann Formicola became pregnant, told her mother that the father was 20-year-old Jack Starr. George-Ann and Jack reportedly had been seen sneaking into the Lester Street "clubhouse" to listen to music and have sex. George-Ann's father reportedly "didn't like Jack."

Late 1965, George-Ann told her friend Richard Barnes that, although she told her mom that Jack was the father of her baby, she had lied. According to Richie's older brother, Jack was "somewhat in love" with George-Ann.

Spring 1966, George-Ann gave birth in a home for unwed mothers. Jack's dad reportedly agreed to pay for all of George-Ann's medical bills. According to the MCSO report, quoting a friend who was quoting George-Ann, Jack and George-Ann wanted to get married but were forbidden by George-Ann's parents.

1966, Jack's dad was a bigwig in town politics, his mom a director of a local historical society. Jack drove a Corvette.

1960s, Jack reportedly hung around with Clint and Keith Wilson.

Spring 1966, Peeping Toms plague Morrison Avenue and Ballantyne Road. According to Danny Johnson, Jack or some of his brothers were the Peeping Toms.

Last day of school, 1966, witness saw George-Ann and another girl, not Kathy, get into a "sports car" outside the school and drive off.

June 25, 1966, George-Ann Formicola and Kathy Bernhard disappeared. They were seen by Hispanic Black Creek picnickers at 6:30 p.m., talking to and getting into a car with Jack, who apparently drove them from the swimming hole to Kathy's house. According to Jack's alibi, between 7:30 and 9:30 he waited at the Bernard house for the girls to return from the swimming hole. In 2011, Alice and Betty Bernhard said Jack was never at their house. After 9:30, Jack said, he was on a date with Samantha Sherman, who corroborated his statements. Sam claimed that Jack told her he was going to attend her high school graduation ceremony that evening in Scottsville but had not shown up. On their date, they went to the Charlotte section of the city in his Corvette for a hamburger but returned quickly. The date, their last, was cut short at 11:30 p.m. because, Jack said, the car's lights were not working properly.

June 26, 1966, According to Jack's half-sister, Jack's car was muddy, and there was "cornfield stuff" stuck up under it. The girls missing, Jack cleaned his car "inside and out."

July 20, 1966, girls' remains were found along the West Shore railroad tracks near Archer and Beaver Roads.

July 1966, MCSO believed that Jack was the father of George-Ann's baby. Jack was repeatedly picked up and questioned by police. According to the MCSO, Jack took a polygraph and passed. "Jack was sad when he talked about it," Sage said.

August 1966, Jack's brother told police that he and friends were swimming in Black Creek the day the girls disappeared, and he saw a gray 1959 Olds pull quickly out from a path leading from the creek to Scottsville Road on the Junction Road, kicking up dust.

December 1, 1966, Jack was arrested somewhere in Monroe County for second-degree assault. The charge was lowered to third degree, and Jack pleaded guilty. He was sentenced to one year in jail, suspended, and two years' probation. Charges may have stemmed from Jack starting a fight (reportedly at the Red Creek) with a cop, feeling that he was being hounded.

December 1967, according to Gary Barnes, Jack's brother Nicky came home on emergency leave in a vain attempt to keep his wife Mary Lou from selling their baby. Nicky returned to Vietnam feeling depressed. "I'm not coming home," he said.

1968, Jack's brother Nicky was killed in Vietnam. Jack took his dead brother's driver's license and showed it to cops every time he was pulled over. When caught, his father was angry. Former sheriff's deputy Garry Coles said, "I was at the [Starr] house many times, executing numerous arrest warrants."

July 29, 1969, Jack and wife received the deed to a house on Names Road, only a few doors from the Starr family house.

Date unknown. According to Julie Burnetti, her older brother David claimed to have been in Jack's presence when he admitted to killing the girls. "Jack used to brag about it when he was drunk," David reportedly said. To this investigation, David twice denied hearing any confession.

March 1971, Jack, still working at Delco but $35,000 in debt, filed for bankruptcy.

May 1972, Jack and wife had a baby girl.

Circa 1973, according to Julie Burnetti, Jack's wife took karate classes to defend herself against Jack and sometimes came to class visibly bruised.

Late 1970s, when the subject of the murders came up, Jack, with "Manson eyes," reportedly said to Anne Werner, "You probably think I did it, too, right?" Anne said her friend Mary Ellen Webster (deceased) heard Jack confess, but Mary Ellen's sister Jean Webster Hall, still living, might also have heard Jack confess. Attempts to interview Jean were unsuccessful.

February 11, 1980, 36-year-old Jack and friends Billy Webster and Dennis Callaghan were arrested for burglarizing a Caledonia gas station. Pleaded guilty to illegal entry, sentenced to three years' probation.

February 17, 1980, already in jail in the city of Rochester, was arrested again by a sheriff's deputy in Henrietta and charged with third-degree burglary and second-degree grand larceny, regarding a crime that took place in Henrietta on January 7, both felony counts. But the case was dismissed due to "no true bill."

May 24, 1980, arrested by a state cop in Henrietta for issuing a bad check and disorderly conduct. Convicted, he received a conditional discharge to seek drug treatment and was fined $100.

August 18, 1987, arrested in Henrietta by a state cop, charged with attempted petit larceny and harassment with physical contact.

January 19, 1988, arrested by Gates and then Brighton police on February 19, 1988, each time charged with petit larceny. His Brighton case was dismissed after he pleaded guilty to the Gates charge.

May 31, 1988, arrested in Henrietta for trying to pass a bad check and charged with forgery 2, possession of a forged instrument 2, and petit larceny. The case was issued a Henrietta Town Court case number and held for grand jury. If there was an outcome, no one punched it into the database.

1990s, state cop Jim Newell interviewed Jack, who was suffering from AIDS, and asked him what happened to George-Ann and Kathy. "I'll tell you before I go," Jack said, but he never did. Newell came away believing Jack was the killer.

June 26, 1992, age 47, almost 26 years to the day after the murders, Jack died of AIDS. Many of Jack's friends also died of AIDS during this same time period.

APPENDIX G

Details on the Smoyer-King Murders[1]

One of the first things Sheriff Skinner said after the Chili bodies were discovered was that the case reminded him of the unsolved slayings of the double-initialed Shari K. Smoyer, 18, and John King, 17, who were found shot to death in the back with a .45 and bludgeoned, sprawled side by side in front of King's car on a lovers' lane along Irondequoit Creek on July 14, 1963, in the town of Pittsford. The girl was the daughter of a Rochester real estate man and a sophomore at Ithaca College. The boy grew up in Tonawanda near Buffalo and had just graduated from high school in Geneseo. Smoyer had been described in the papers as a "strikingly attractive co-ed."[2] Her family had recently moved to Perinton. The two had gone on a Saturday night date—not their first, but they were not going steady. King drove from his home in Geneseo and picked up Smoyer at her house in Perinton at 8:15 p.m. King was driving his father's green-and-white 1955 Chevy. Smoyer's father told King to get his daughter home by 1:30 a.m. They were going to see *Mutiny on the Bounty* at the Starlite Drive-In in Henrietta (adjacent to the junkyard where Johnny Bernhard worked). It was a long movie, so the date would have to run late if they were to stay for the end. Police had a witness that saw Smoyer and King at the Starlite at 9:30. The movie ended at 1:00 a.m. Another witness saw Smoyer and King at 1:50 a.m. speeding home from the drive-in, already 20 minutes late for Smoyer's curfew. At 7:00 a.m. on Sunday, Smoyer's parents called the sheriff. Only minutes later, a 67-year-old Brighton man who'd been looking for a place to fish discovered the bodies. The site, less than a half mile from Smoyer's home, was on a dirt road that led to a state-owned hunting and fishing area off of "old Route 96." The fisherman drove from the murder scene to a firehouse in nearby Bushnell's Basin, and they called the sheriff. The bodies were close together on the ground near the front of King's car. King was lying on his left side. Neither his slacks nor his short-sleeved sport shirt were in disarray. He was shoeless. His loafers lay nearby. Smoyer was face down, and she was wearing shorts, blouse, and white sneakers. Her clothing also was undisturbed. Police speculated that they had been ordered to lie down before they were shot, and the woman apparently clutched King in fear just before they died. She was shot twice in the back and bludgeoned in the back of the head. He'd been shot once in the back of the head and several times in the lower back. There were no powder burns on the body, suggesting that the shots had been fired from some distance, not point blank. Five shells from a .45 were found near the bodies, and a fifth was found inside King's car. A quarter and a penny lay on the dirt road. There was $15 in King's wallet. Milk shake containers were found in King's car. Smoyer had a small amount of money in her purse. Robbery wasn't the motive. There was a massive search of the hunting and fishing area and scuba divers went into Irondequoit Creek and the Erie Canal, but the gun was never found. The parents of the victims said they didn't think the victims were into heavy petting, as if young people confided in their parents about such things. Friends said they didn't think Smoyer knew about the lovers' lane despite its proximity to her house because her family hadn't lived in Perinton that long, only seven months, and she'd been away at school for most of that. It wasn't King's stomping grounds either. Sheriff Skinner postulated that the couple had been forced or cajoled into giving their killer a lift. The sheriff concluded this because of a fresh set of "sideswipe" scratches on the car, which hadn't been there before the date. Skinner theorized that the killer may have used his car to force the couple off the road. Three days after the murders, the MCSO told United Press International that they had "all kinds of leads and plenty of secondary suspects" but nothing concrete. A witness came forward who said the green-and-white Chevy had been parked on Route 96 at Bushnell's Basin at 2:30 a.m. The witness said two young men were talking behind the car and a girl stood on the edge of the road near the driver's door. Police also learned that, according to one witness, the victims' car was not at the spot where it would be found at 3:30, because the witness had gotten his car stuck in the mud there at 3:30 and he'd been quite alone. The guy called the sheriff's tow truck to pull him out, so there was indisputable evidence that King and Smoyer were not at the spot where they died as much as two hours past Smoyer's curfew. The medical examiner said the victims died at about 4:30 a.m. The girl had been bludgeoned after she was dead. "It's a hard nut to crack," Skinner said at the time. Detectives questioned 10 of Smoyer's college boyfriends, and 25 friends of King were interviewed. Nada. The crime lab in Albany reported that the slugs in the bodies came from a World War II army-issue .45 colt pistol, of a type that could be mail-ordered for $17.50. With an eight-slug clip, the weapon would be heavy and inaccurate beyond 45 feet. (For years the MCSO was collecting .45s, but never got a ballistic match.) On Tuesday, two sheriff's detectives were sent to Buffalo to question a "well-dressed vagrant" who'd been picked up by the New York Central Railroad police for jumping a train in Rochester.[3] After talking to the man, Paul E. Berry, they said his story "seemed to check out." Berry's age and address were unknown. He was sentenced to 30 days in the Erie County Jail on a charge of being a "state tramp"—that is, a guy who hitched rides on trains. In April 1964, a 30-year-old Rochester man named Vernon Hunter ran the Thruway tollbooth in Henrietta, led cops on an hour-long chase, and when captured in Penfield, an army .45 fell out of his car.[4] It was exciting—the man was a former resident at Willard State Hospital, an ancient asylum for the "chronic insane," and told cops he was a "son of God," that "teenagers were bad and needed to be punished." Hunter told the sheriff that he knew the area where the victims were found because he used to ski there. He said he couldn't be sure, but he might've driven by there one Saturday night the previous July. Then the FBI ruined it. The gun was no match. Hunter proved incompetent to stand trial on the weapons charge and was institutionalized at the Matteawan State Hospital for the Criminally Insane. He was released in June 1965.

NOTES

FOREWORD

1. www.churchofsatan.com (accessed December 15, 2014).
2. "2 Missing Girls Are Found Slain: Upstate Victims, 14 and 16 Had Been Swimming," *New York Times*, July 21, 1966.

I. COUNTRY LIFE

1. "Hetenyi as Free Man Creates New Mystery," *Daily News*, June 6, 1966, 1.
2. Alan Jeffry Breslau, *The Time of My Death: A Story of Miraculous Survival* (New York: E. P. Dutton, 1977).
3. http://www.democratandchronicle.com/story/news/2014/07/19/rochester-riots-timeline/12885229 (accessed August 8, 2011).

2. MISSING

1. "Last Day in Lives of Two Slain Girls," *Rochester Times-Union*, July 22, 1966, 1B, 6B.
2. "Summer in the City," song recorded by The Lovin' Spoonful, written by John Sebastian, Mark Sebastian, and Steve Boone.
3. "Hanky Panky," song recorded by Tommy James and the Shondells, written by Jeff Barry and Ellie Greenwich.

4. "Wild Thing," song recorded by The Troggs, written by Chip Taylor.

5. "Li'l Red Riding Hood," song recorded by Sam the Sham and the Pharaohs, written by Ronald Blackwell.

6. "Hungry," song recorded by Paul Revere and the Raiders, written by Barry Mann and Cynthia Weil.

7. "The Pied Piper," song recorded by Crispian St. Peters, written by Steve Duboff and Artie Kornfeld.

8. "Bloodhounds Join Search for 2 Girls," *Rochester Times-Union*, June 29, 1966.

9. "Search Continues for 2 Chili Girls," *Rochester Democrat & Chronicle*, June 29, 1966, 7B.

10. "Deputies Checking Calls about Two Missing Girls," *Rochester Times-Union*, June 30, 1966.

11. "Bloodhounds Join Search for 2 Girls," *Rochester Times-Union*, June 29, 1966.

12. "Missing Girls Puzzle Police," *Rochester Democrat & Chronicle*, July 1, 1966.

13. "House Check Begins for Missing Girls," *Rochester Times-Union*, July 1, 1966, 6B.

14. "2 Chili Girls Still Missing," *Rochester Democrat & Chronicle*, July 4, 1966, 4B.

15. "Beach Towel of Missing Girl Sought," *Rochester Times-Union*, July 12, 1966.

16. Jan Sturdevant, "Crank Callers Plague Missing Girls' Mothers," *Rochester Democrat & Chronicle*, July 15, 1966.

17. "Sheriff's Office Sends Out 'Flyer' on Missing Girls," *Rochester Times-Union*, July 15, 1966.

18. Dennis L. Breo and William J. Martin, *The Crime of the Century* (New York: Bantam, 1993).

19. Bob Secter, "The Richard Speck Case," http://www.chicagotribune.com/news/nationworld/politics/chi-chicagodays-richardspeck-story-story.html (accessed September 3, 2011).

20. http://www.findagrave.com/cgi-bin/fg.cgi?page=gr&GRid=24706855 (accessed February 5, 2015).

21. "Sheriff Asks Help," *Gates-Chili News*, July 21, 1966, 1.

3. FOUND

1. Murray Schumach, "Slain Girls' Town Gripped by Fear: Children Kept from Creek Where Victims Swam," *New York Times*, July 23, 1966, A19.

2. Tom Ryan, "2 Missing Girls Found Murdered," *Rochester Democrat & Chronicle*, July 21, 1966, 1A.

3. Tom Connolly, "Girl Killings 'Fiend' Hunted," *Rochester Times-Union*, July 21, 1966, 1A, 14A.

4. "Bodies of 2 Missing Girls Are Found," *Canandaigua Daily Messenger*, July 21, 1966, 1, UPI dispatch.

5. Tom Connolly and Cliff Smith, "Big Knife Used to Slay Girls," *Rochester Times-Union*, July 22, 1966, 1B, 6B.

6. "Chili Democratic Candidates Call for Police Force Hearing," *Suburban News*, July 26, 1966, 14.

7. Tom Ryan. "Knife Sought in Slaying of Chili Girls," *Rochester Democrat & Chronicle*, July 22, 1966, 1B.

8. "A Tragic Warning: Killer at Large," *Rochester Democrat & Chronicle*, July 22, 1966, 10A.

9. Cliff Smith, "Death Auto Hunted in 2 Chili Slayings," *Rochester Times-Union*, July 23, 1966.

10. "Probers Seek Speck Checkout in Chili Slayings," *Rochester Democrat & Chronicle*, July 23, 1966, 5B.

11. "Psychiatrist's Theory," *Rochester Times-Union*, July 23, 1966.

4. CHRISTINE WATSON AND MARSHA JEAN BEHNEY

1. "No Trace Found of Girl's Slayer," *Erie Daily Times*, July 20, 1966.

2. "Murder Details Kept Quiet," *Erie Daily Times*, July 20, 1966.

3. "Testimony Improper, Killer's Lawyer Says," *The Vindicator*, January 18, 1989.

4. Years later, I learned from NYPD detective Robert Mladinich that the Erie murder was not connected to the Chili murders. In 1989, 26 years after it happened, police arrested Eugene E. Patterson of Waterford, Pennsylvania, the same man that the six-year-old eyewitness had picked out in 1966. A K9 team had picked up Patterson's scent in the vicinity of the murder. But Patterson said he didn't do it, and there wasn't enough evidence to prosecute. If only the eyewitness had been just a little bit older. The kid couldn't stand up under cross-examination. Now police had a witness, a preacher, who could place Patterson in possession of the shiny silver star badge found under Christine's body. Patterson was 20 at the time of the murder, 46 at the time of his arrest, yet he was tried and convicted. Despite this, Patterson always, and to this day, vehemently maintained his innocence. And many people of Erie agreed with him. They felt Patterson was being railroaded. Everyone knew that it had been

a circus worker that killed Christine. The circus, they screamed, was in Millcreek at the time of the murder, with their tent set up at the current site of the Millcreek Mall.

5. Don Knorr, "Lot Cleanup Aims at Clues in Chili Deaths," *Rochester Democrat & Chronicle*, July 28, 1966.

6. "Chili and County Plan War on Underbrush," *Gates-Chili News*, August 4, 1966 (clipping).

7. Gary M. Lavergne, *A Sniper in the Tower: The True Story of the Texas Tower Massacre* (Austin: University of Texas Press, 1997).

8. Tom Connolly, "2nd Call Awaited on Chili Murders," *Rochester Times-Union*, August 10, 1966.

9. "She May Have Seen Killer of Two Girls," *Syracuse Herald-Journal*, August 10, 1966, 2.

10. Clay F. Richards, "'Logical Suspect' Held in Death of 2 Girls," *Canandaigua Daily Messenger*, August 25, 1966, 9.

11. "Texan Cleared in Chili Probe," *Rochester Times-Union*, August 26, 1966.

12. "Woman Charged," *Milwaukee Journal*, March 10, 1984, 2.

13. "Sandra Behney Tells How She Identified Defendant but Didn't See Sister Stabbed," *Reading Eagle*, September 21, 1967, 1, 16.

14. "Murder Charge Possible in Death of Country Girl, 12," *Lebanon Daily News*, September 6, 1966, 1.

15. "Legal Snags May Delay Hearing of Slaying Suspect," *Lebanon Daily News*, February 27, 1967, 1, 2.

16. "Amendment Filed to Miller Plea," *Reading Eagle*, July 19, 1967, 67.

17. "Miller Goes on Trial for Murder," *Reading Eagle*, September 18, 1967, 1.

18. "Found Guilty of Murder in Second Degree: Killer of County Girl Confesses to Deputies after Hearing Verdict," *Lebanon Daily News*, September 25, 1967, 1, 11.

19. "Probe Set in Alleged Confession," *Reading Eagle*, September 25, 1967, 1.

20. Glenn Wall, *Sympathy Vote: A Reinvestigation of the Valerie Percy Murder* (Middletown, DE: self-published, 2014).

21. http://www.tvobscurities.com/articles/cbs_and_psycho (accessed February 23, 2012).

22. Carol Rubright, "Slayings Still Probed," *Rochester Times-Union*, January 9, 1967, 1B, 3B.

23. "Lynda Moore Funeral Wednesday," *Binghamton Press*, July 25, 1966, 3A.

24. http://www.murderpedia.org/male.H/h/herrington-michael.htm (accessed December 16, 2014).

25. "Slaying of 2nd Girl Frightens Milwaukee," *Watertown Daily Times*, October 18, 1966, 10.

26. "Stabbing Victim," *Buffalo Courier-Express*, November 5, 1966, 5.

27. http://www.murderpedia.org/male.H/h/herrington-michael.htm (accessed December 16, 2014).

28. Jack the Stripper was not an invented name but one that had appeared on the news in reference to a London serial killer who murdered possibly eight prostitutes between 1964 and 1965. As was true of Jack the Ripper, the murders seem to have stopped on their own, and the killer was never identified.

29. Tom Connolly, "2 Murder Cases: Files Remain Open," *Rochester Times-Union*, April 13, 1967.

30. "County Girl's Slayer to Be Questioned about N.Y. Deaths," *Lebanon Daily News* (Pennsylvania), September 27, 1967.

31. "Miller Faces New Queries," *Reading Eagle*, September 27, 1967, 1.

32. Tom Ryan, "Did Murderer Stop in Area?" *Rochester Democrat & Chronicle*, October 14, 1967.

33. "Calls Reveal 20 People Saw Miller," *Rochester Democrat & Chronicle*, October 18, 1967.

34. "Girls Frightened in Chili," *WE*, September 11, 1967, 9.

35. "Man Found Slain in Chili Driveway," *Rochester Democrat & Chronicle*, December 21, 1967.

5. THE DOUBLE INITIALS MURDERS

1. Agatha Christie, *The ABC Murders* (New York: Morrow, 2011). Originally published 1936.

2. "Girl Is Slain after Motorists Ignore Her Pleading for Help," *Watertown Daily Times*, November 22, 1971, 1A.

3. "Second Rochester Girl Found Raped, Strangled on an Errand to a Store," *Schenectady Gazette*, April 4, 1973, 16.

4. "Police Find Body of Missing Girl; Murder Linked to Earlier Killings," *Auburn Citizen-Advertiser*, November 29, 1973, 2.

5. Cheri Farnsworth, *Alphabet Killer: The True Story of the Double Initial Murders* (Mechanicsburg, PA: Stackpole Books, 2010).

6. Darcy O'Brien, *Two of a Kind: The Hillside Stranglers* (New York: New American Library, 1985).

7. Ted Schwartz, *The Hillside Strangler: A Murderer's Mind* (New York: Signet, 1982).

8. http://roc.democratandchronicle.com/section/specials84 (accessed December 14, 2013).

9. Fictionalized film: *The Alphabet Killer*, Starz/Anchor Bay, directed by Rob Schmidt, made 2008, released 2009.

6. ZODIAC AND OTHER CONSPIRACY THEORIES

1. Gary M. Lavergne, *A Sniper in the Tower: The True Story of the Texas Tower Massacre* (Austin: University of Texas Press, 1997).

2. "Co-ed Stabbed to Death on Riverside College Campus," *Los Angeles Times*, November 1, 1966, 3.

3. "Evidence Links Zodiac Killer to '66 Death of Riverside Coed," *Los Angeles Times*, November 16, 1970, A1.

4. Philip Carlo, *The Night Stalker: The Life and Crimes of Richard Ramirez* (New York: Pinnacle, 2006).

5. James Ellroy, *My Dark Places* (New York: Vintage, 1997).

6. Julie Tamaki, "'90 Slaying Case Nears Its Final Chapter," *Los Angeles Times*, November 14, 1993.

7. Trish Mehaffey, "Iowa Woman's Testimony, DNA Evidence Leads to Conviction in 21 Year California Cold Case," KCRG.com (accessed December 16, 2014).

8. Maury Terry, *The Ultimate Evil* (New York: Bantam, 1989).

9. Peter Hirschfeld, "Jacques Charged with Murder of Brooke Bennett," *Vermont Press*, October 2, 2008.

10. Lisa Rathke, "Michael Jacques Pleads Guilty to Kidnapping, Killing Brooke Bennett, Niece," HuffingtonPost.com, August 27, 2013 (accessed March 12, 2015).

11. Elyssa East, *Dogtown: Death and Enchantment in a New England Ghost Town* (New York: Free Press, 2009).

7. A GENERATION LATER . . .

1. Jon Hand, "Mother Won't Give Up on Decades-Old Cold Case," *Democrat & Chronicle*, December 16, 2014.

2. Vernon J. Geberth, MS, MPS, former commander, Bronx Homicide, New York Police Department, "Anatomy of a Lust Murder," *Law and Order Magazine*, May 1998.

3. Adriane Raine, *The Anatomy of Violence: The Biological Roots of Crime* (New York: Pantheon, 2013).

4. Geberth, "Anatomy of a Lust Murder."

5. http://www.thewall-usa.com (accessed March 22, 1999).

6. "Local Serviceman Missing in Action," *Scottsville News*, March 7, 1968, 1.

7. "First Boy in Area Loses Life in Vietnam," *Scottsville News*, March 28, 1968, 1.

8. "Posthumous Awards Given," *Scottsville News*, July 4, 1968, 1.

9. Jack Olsen, *The Misbegotten Son: The True Story of Arthur J. Shawcross* (New York: Island Books, 1993); Dr. Joel Norris, *Arthur Shawcross: The Genesee River Killer* (New York: Pinnacle, 1992).

10. Evelyn Dow, "Arrest Made in Homicides," *Suburban News*, January 9, 1990, 1.

11. "Parolee Shawcross Confessed Harassing Another Boy, 6, Just after Jack Blake Disappeared," *Watertown Daily Times*, October 30, 1972, 24.

12. Stafford Mann, "Karen's Corpse Was the Key to Jackie's Grave," *Front Page Detective*, January 1973, 46–49, 66–69.

13. Steve Govoni, "The Kid's Friend Was a Killer," *True Detective*, February 1973, 36.

14. David C. Knowlton, "Society Must Be Protected," *Watertown Daily Times*, July 7, 1976.

15. Marshall Cavendish, *Murder Casebook, Investigations into the Ultimate Crimes*, vol. 6, pt., 82, *Monster of the Rivers, Arthur Shawcross* (Tarrytown, NY: Marshall Cavendish, 1991), 2950.

16. Adam Miller, "New eBlast at eBay as Killer's Art Is Auctioned," *New York Post*, September 11, 1999, 6; Joe Mahoney and Dave Goldiner, "Making a Killing: Inmate Art Show Brings Big Bucks," *Daily News*, April 3, 2001, 5.

17. Dennis Hevesi, "Arthur J. Shawcross, Serial Killer in Rochester, Dies at 63," *New York Times*, November 11, 2008, B19.

9. ALICE AND CORKY

1. Todd Lighty, "Chili Man Killed in Shotgun Attack," *Rochester Times-Union*, May 26, 1985, 1B.

2. "Obituaries: Keith B. [Wilson]," *Finger Lakes Times*, May 28, 1985, 8.

3. http://www.hells-angels-rochester.com/start-lite.htm (accessed September 3, 2011).

10. MAKING PEOPLE REMEMBER

1. Caroline Tucker, "Crime Writer Tries to Dig Up Chili Cold Case," rochesterhomepage.com, posted August 26, 2011 (accessed August 28, 2011).

2. "Miller Murder Case to Go to Jury Today," *Reading Eagle*, September 23, 1967, 1.

3. "Pa. Suspect Faces Quiz in Chili Slaying," *Rochester Democrat & Chronicle*, April 13, 1967.

4. "Man Quizzed in Slayings," *Rochester Times-Union*, October 6, 1967.

5. "Within the Dark Shadow: The Case of John Kelly Given to the Jury," *Rochester Democrat & Chronicle*, March 8, 1883, 6.

6. "Italian in Drunken Frenzy Shoots Companion in Heart—Is Under Arrest," *Rochester Democrat & Chronicle*, June 1, 1915, 1.

7. "20-Year Prison Term Is Started by Pearl Odell," *Auburn Citizen*, June 9, 1920, 6.

11. THE RAGAMUFFINS

1. http://en.wikipedia.org/wiki/Genesee_Junction,_New_York (accessed September 2, 2011).

2. http://gold.mylargescale.com/Scottychaos/GeneseeJunction.html (accessed September 2, 2011).

3. Ibid.

4. *Lathrop Atlas of Monroe County* (New York, 1902).

12. PAT PATTERSON

1. See appendix A.

2. Robert K. Ressler, Ann W. Burgess, and John E. Douglas, *Sexual Homicide: Patterns and Motives* (New York: Free Press, 1992).

13. THE FILES

1. Beck, Iaculli, and investigators R. H. Hampson, J. D. Sarnowski, T. A. Constantine, R. C. Lewandowski, W. C. Sargent, and W. K. Goetschius.

2. "Assault Suspects Quizzed in Chili Girls' Murders," *Rochester Democrat & Chronicle*, July 29, 1966.

3. "One on Critical List in Café Gun Death," *Utica Daily Press*, October 19, 1964, 24.

4. "Stray Bullet Wounds Woman," *Lockport Union-Sun and Journal*, April 28, 1967, 5.

5. "Suspect Held for Jury in Albion Shooting," *Buffalo Courier-Express*, October 24, 1967, 3.

6. Robinson v. Smith, No. CIV-77-300E, United States District Court, February 9, 1982, http://leagle.com/decision/19821916530FSupp1386_11715.xml/ROBINSON%20v.%20SMITH (accessed March 14, 2015).

7. State v. Knott, No. 1520-EX.&C. 302 A.2d 64 (1973), Supreme Court of Rhode Island, March 22, 1973, http://www.leagle.com/decision/1973366302A2d64_1366 (accessed December 24, 2011).

8. Kathy had a total of seven wounds, three in the left breast area, one on the left wrist, one on the left arm, one on the right arm, and one on the right wrist that had cut through part of the bone. There were three holes in the left side of Kathy's swimsuit top. Cerretto wrote, "Both breasts cut off, vagina cut out, uterus pulled out." George-Ann had four knife wounds to the left breast, two on the back of her left forearm, and cuts through the neck both at the front and in back so that the head was "almost severed." He added that the "cut curves to the left on the neck front. There was one knife wound, horizontal, on the left front shoulder. The left breast had been cut off, but the right breast was intact. He wrote, "No scars on stomach, bra has three holes left side, one hole in center, one stab wound right side of vagina high, one stab wound on the left side of vagina low, three knife wounds back of blouse, uterus intact, no fracture of skull." The wounds on both bodies appeared to have been caused by the same 1¼-inch blade.

14. DON TUBMAN

1. "Ambulance Calls for December for Scottsville Fire Department," *Caledonia Advertiser*, January 10, 1963.

15. EVE'S ABDUCTION AND BEATING UP
A PERV

1. See appendix B.

2. Marshall Cavendish, *Murder Casebook, Investigations into the Ultimate Crimes*, vol. 6, pt. 82, *Monster of the Rivers, Arthur Shawcross* (Tarrytown, NY: Marshall Cavendish, 1991), 2950.

16. DEVILS DICIPLES

1. "Caledonia Station Burglarized," *Avon Herald News*, February 12, 1980, 9.

2. "Vital Statistics, Marriage Licenses," *Daily Record* (Rochester), July 27, 1965, 8.

3. "Credit News, Judgments in Supreme and County Courts." *Daily Record* (Rochester), November 6, 1974, 11.

4. "Grand Jury Is Recalled for June 7 on 2 Cases," *Geneva Times*, June 3, 1971, 1.

5. "Rape Case Placed for Pre-trial," *Geneva Times*, June 15, 1971, 20.

6. "Keshequa Man Gets 3 Years Probation," *Geneva Times*, September 28, 1971, 12.

7. Obituary, *Geneva Times*, November 3, 1971.

17. SCREAMS IN THE NIGHT

1. The story most resembled that of Alvin Lynn, the pervert whose Dodge, according to MCSO files, had been sold to a used car dealer in Pennsylvania, then checked out by investigators Iaculli and Clark with "negative results."

18. WE MAGAZINE

1. "Rapists Found Guilty of Assaulting Co-Ed," *WE*, January 16, 1967, 9.

2. "Something Smells," *WE*, January 16, 1967, 15.

3. "Alleged Rape," *WE*, January 16, 1967, 5.

4. "Fourteen-Year-Old Teenage Girl Missing: Mother Near Collapse," *WE*, June 20, 1966, 1, 6.

5. "Drug Peddlers Infest Midtown Plaza; Sexual Stimulants Sneaked into Girls Soft-Drinks," *WE*, August 1, 1966, 5.

6. "Kudos to Sheriffs Office on Chili Murders," *WE*, August 22, 1966, 10.

7. "Chili Murder Suspect Flaunts Supreme Court Decision at Police," *WE*, October 3, 1966, 7.

8. "Chili Women Terrified with Girl Slayer at Large; Bloody Towels, Shirt Unearthed," *WE*, October 24, 1966, 12.

9. "Did Chili Killer Return to Scene?," *WE*, September 12, 1966, 7.

10. "Says Son Killed Girls," *WE*, July 10, 1967, 10.

11. "Lewd Photos of Wife," *WE*, August 21, 1967, 3.

12. "Waitress, 24, Abducted at Knife Point—Attacked in Wooded Area," *WE*, September 11, 1967, 3.

13. "Possible Chili Murder Suspect," *WE*, May 7, 1968, 7.

20. MULE

1. George Cooper Jr., "Rochysteria," *WE*, December 26, 1966, 7.

APPENDIX A

1. Jack Olsen, *The Misbegotten Son* (New York: Island Books, 1993); Dr. Joel Norris, *Arthur Shawcross: The Genesee River Killer* (New York: Pinnacle, 1992); Marshall Cavendish, *Murder Casebook, Investigations into the Ultimate Crimes*, vol. 6, pt. 82, *Monster of the Rivers, Arthur Shawcross* (Tarrytown, NY: Marshall Cavendish, 1991), 2950.

APPENDIX B

1. www.charleyproject.org/cases/s/sollie_sandra.html; https://www.youtube.com/watch?v=5uMBnhcE_cw; https://www.youtube.com/watch?v=5guCLrJ_iu0; http://projectjason.org/forums/topic/291-missing-woman-sandra-sollie-ny-05231994 (all accessed February 5, 2015).

APPENDIX C

1. "Rapists Found Guilty of Assaulting Co-Ed," *WE*, January 16, 1967, 9.

APPENDIX D

1. All information courtesy Monroe County Sheriff's Office in response to a Freedom of Information request.

APPENDIX G

1. Ruth Reynolds, "The Summertime Murders," *Reading Eagle*, November 13, 1966.

2. "Co-ed, Boy Friend Slain in Rochester Lovers' Lane," *Schenectady Gazette*, July 15, 1963, 30.

3. "Man Quizzed in Double Killing Near Rochester," *Tonawanda News*, July 17, 1963, 15.

4. "Suspect Arrested in Smoyer-King Slayings Following Speed Chase," *Livingston County Leader*, April 30, 1964, 3.

BIBLIOGRAPHY

"**A**mendment Filed to Miller Plea." *The Reading Eagle*, July 19, 1967, 67.

"Assault Suspects Quizzed in Chili Girls' Murders." *Rochester Democrat & Chronicle*, July 29, 1966.

"Beach Towel of Missing Girl Sought." *Rochester Times-Union*, July 12, 1966.

"Bloodhounds Join Search for 2 Girls." *Rochester Times-Union*, June 29, 1966.

"Bodies of 2 Missing Girls Are Found." *Canandaigua Daily Messenger*, July 21, 1966, 1. UPI dispatch.

Breo, Dennis L., and William J. Martin. *The Crime of the Century*. New York: Bantam, 1993. Re Richard Speck.

Breslau, Alan Jeffry. *The Time of My Death: A Story of Miraculous Survival*. New York: E. P. Dutton, 1977.

"Brush Cut for Clues in Slaying." *Rochester Times-Union*, August 9, 1966.

"Caledonia Station Burglarized." *Avon Herald News*, February 12, 1980, 9.

"Calls Reveal 20 People Saw Miller." *Rochester Democrat & Chronicle*, October 18, 1967.

Cavendish, Marshall. *Murder Casebook, Investigations into the Ultimate Crimes*. Vol. 6, pt. 82, *Monster of the Rivers, Arthur Shawcross*. Tarrytown, NY: Marshall Cavendish, 1991.

"Chili Democratic Candidates Call for Police Force Hearing." *Suburban News*, July 26, 1966, 14. In light of the "horrible and recent murders," politicians suggest Chili get its own police force.

"Chili Murder Suspect Flaunts Supreme Court Decision at Police." *WE*, October 3, 1966, 7.

"Chili Women Terrified with Girl Slayer at Large; Bloody Towels, Shirt Unearthed." *WE*, October 24, 1966, 12.

"Co-ed, Boy Friend Slain in Rochester Lovers' Lane." *Schenectady Gazette*, July 15, 1963, 30. Re Smoyer-King murders.

"Co-ed Stabbed to Death on Riverside College Campus." *Los Angeles Times*, November 1, 1966, 3. Re murder of Cheri Jo Bates.

Connolly, Tom. "2 Murder Cases: Files Remain Open." *Rochester Times-Union*, April 13, 1967.

———. "2nd Call Awaited on Chili Murders." *Rochester Times-Union*, August 10, 1966.

Connolly, Tom, and Cliff Smith. "Big Knife Used to Slay Girls." *Rochester Times-Union*, July 22, 1966, 1B, 6B.

———. "Girl Killings 'Fiend' Hunted." *Rochester Times-Union*, July 21, 1966, 1A, 14A.

Cooper, George, Jr. "Rochysteria." *WE*, September 26, 1966, 7.

"Coroner Rules Death Suicide." *Livonia Gazette*, June 4, 1970, 6.

"County Girl's Slayer to Be Questioned about N.Y. Deaths," *Lebanon Daily News* (Pennsylvania), September 27, 1967.

Crough, Patrick. *Chronicles of a Rochester Major Crimes Detective*. Charleston, SC: History Press, 2011.

"Deputies Checking Calls about Two Missing Girls." *Rochester Times-Union*, June 30, 1966.

"Did Chili Killer Return to Scene?" *WE*, September 12, 1966, 7.

"Drug Peddlers Infest Midtown Plaza; Sexual Stimulants Sneaked into Girls Soft-Drinks." *WE*, August 1, 1966, 5.

"Evidence Links Zodiac Killer to '66 Death of Riverside Coed." *Los Angeles Times*, November 16, 1970, A1.

"Found Guilty of Murder in Second Degree: Killer of County Girl Confesses to Deputies after Hearing Verdict." *Lebanon Daily News*, September 25, 1967, 1, 11.

"Fourteen-Year-Old Teenage Girl Missing: Mother Near Collapse." *WE*, June 20, 1966, 1, 6.

Geberth, Vernon J., MS, MPS, Former Commander, Bronx Homicide, New York Police Department. "Anatomy of a Lust Murder." *Law and Order Magazine*, May 1998.

"Girl May Have Facts on Murders." *Watertown Daily Times*, August 20, 1966.

"Girls Drugged or Drunk." *WE*, November 14, 1966, 9.

"Girls Frightened in Chili." *WE*, September 11, 1967, 9.

Govoni, Steve. "The Kid's Friend Was a Killer." *True Detective*, February 1973, 36.

"Grand Jury Is Recalled for June 7 on 2 Cases." *Geneva Times*, June 3, 1971, 1.

Hand, Jon. "Mother Won't Give Up on Decades-Old Cold Case." *Democrat & Chronicle*, December 16, 2014.

"Hetenyi as Free Man Creates New Mystery." *Daily News*, June 6, 1966, 1.

"House Check Begins for Missing Girls." *Rochester Times-Union*, July 1, 1966, 6B.

Hughes, Kyle. "Shawcross Worried about Marital State." *Rochester Democrat & Chronicle*, September 1, 1999, A3.

"Italian in Drunken Frenzy Shoots Companion in Heart—Is under Arrest." *Rochester Democrat & Chronicle*, June 1, 1915, 1. Re fatal shooting of 22-year-old man along Penn Railroad, killer hiding in a shanty at Genesee Junction.

"Jury Convicts Man of Murder in Girl's 1966 Slaying." *Vindicator*, January 18, 1989. Re murder of Christine Watson.

"Keshequa Man Gets 3 Years Probation." *Geneva Times*, September 28, 1971, 12.

Knorr, Don. "Lot Cleanup Aims at Clues in Chili Deaths." *Rochester Democrat & Chronicle*, July 28, 1966.

"Kudos to Sheriffs Office on Chili Murders." *WE*, August 22, 1966, 10.

"Last Day in Lives of Two Slain Girls." *Rochester Times-Union*, July 22, 1966, 1B, 6B.

"Latest on Chili Murders." *WE*, December 5, 1966, 2.

Lavergne, Gary M. *A Sniper in the Tower: The True Story of the Texas Tower Massacre*. Austin: University of Texas Press, 1997.

"Legal Snags May Delay Hearing of Slaying Suspect." *Lebanon Daily News*, February 27, 1967, 1, 2.

"Lewd Photos of Wife," *WE*, August 21, 1967, 3.

Lighty, Todd. "Chili Man Killed in Shotgun Attack." *Rochester Times-Union*, May 26, 1985, 1B.

Mahoney, Joe, and Dave Goldiner. "Making a Killing: Inmate Art Show Brings Big Bucks." *Daily News*, April 3, 2001, 5.

"Man Found Slain in Chili Driveway." *Rochester Democrat & Chronicle*, December 21, 1967. The driveway belonged to the Bookmans.

"Man Held in Slaying of Girl, 12." *Reading Eagle*, February 18, 1967, 1, 10.

"Man Quizzed in Double Killing Near Rochester." *Tonawanda News*, July 17, 1963, 15. Re Smoyer-King murders.

"Man Quizzed in Slayings." *Rochester Times-Union*, October 6, 1967. Re John I. Miller.

Mann, Stafford. "Karen's Corpse Was the Key to Jackie's Grave." *Front Page Detective*, January 1973, 46–49, 66–69. Re Arthur Shawcross.

Miller, Adam. "New eBlast at eBay as Killer's Art Is Auctioned." *New York Post*, September 11, 1999, 6.

"Miller Faces New Queries." *Reading Eagle*, September 27, 1967, 1.

"Miller Goes on Trial for Murder." *Reading Eagle*, September 18, 1967, 1.

"Miller Murder Case to Go to Jury Today." *Reading Eagle*, September 23, 1967, 1.

"Missing Girls Puzzle Police." *Rochester Democrat & Chronicle*, July 1, 1966.

"Murder Case Hearing Waived." *Reading Eagle*, July 9, 1967, 6. Re murder of Marsha Jean Behney.

"Murder Charge Possible in Death of Country Girl, 12." *Lebanon Daily News*, September 6, 1966, 1.

"Murder Tip Dwindles." *Rochester Times-Union*, July 26, 1966.

"No Trace Found of Girl's Slayer." *Erie Daily Times*, July 20, 1966. Re Christine Watson.

Norris, Dr. Joel. *Arthur Shawcross: The Genesee River Killer*. New York: Pinnacle, 1992.

Olsen, Jack. *The Misbegotten Son*. New York: Island Books, 1993. Re Arthur Shawcross.

"One on Critical List in Café Death." *Utica Daily Press*, October 19, 1964, 24. Re the Brick Wall nightclub in Albion.

"Pa. Suspect Faces Quiz in Chili Slaying." *Rochester Democrat & Chronicle*, April 13, 1967.

"Possible Chili Murder Suspect." *WE*, May 7, 1968, 7.

"Probe Set in Alleged Confession." *Reading Eagle*, September 25, 1967, 1.

"Probers Seek Speck Checkout in Chili Slayings." *Rochester Democrat & Chronicle*, July 23, 1966, 5B.

"Psychiatrist's Theory." *Rochester Times-Union*, July 23, 1966.

"Rape Case Placed for Pre-trial." *Geneva Times*, June 15, 1971, 20.

"Rapists Found Guilty of Assaulting Co-Ed." *WE*, January 16, 1967, 9.

Ray, Del. "It's 'A Real Mystery.'" *Rochester Times Union*, July 7, 1966.

"Reckless Driving Charge Placed against Young Men." *Mount Morris Enterprise*, May 25, 1960, 7.

Ressler, Robert K., Ann W. Burgess, and John E. Douglas. *Sexual Homicide: Patterns and Motives*. New York: Free Press, 1992.

Reynolds, Ruth. "The Summertime Murders." *Reading Eagle*, November 13, 1966. Article is about both Chili murders and 1963 Smoyer-King killings.

Richards, Clay F. "'Logical Suspect' Held in Death of 2 Girls." *Canandaigua Daily Messenger*, August 25, 1966, 9.

"Robinson v. Smith." http://leagle.com/decision/19821916530FSupp1386_11715.xml/ROBINSON%20v.%20SMITH (accessed March 14, 2015).

Rubright, Carol, "Slayings Still Probed." *Rochester Times-Union*, January 9, 1967, 1B, 3B.

Ryan, Tom. "Did Murderer Stop in Area?" *Rochester Democrat & Chronicle*, October 14, 1967. Re Richard Speck.

———. "Knife Sought in Slaying of Chili Girls." *Rochester Democrat & Chronicle*, July 22, 1966, 1B.

———. "2 Missing Girls Found Murdered." *Rochester Democrat & Chronicle*, July 21, 1966, 1A.

"Sandra Behney Tells How She Identified Defendant but Didn't See Sister Stabbed." *Reading Eagle*, September 21, 1967, 1, 16.

"Says Son Killed Girls," *WE*, July 10, 1967, 10.

Schumach, Murray. "Slain Girls' Town Gripped by Fear: Children Kept from Creek Where Victims Swam," *New York Times*, July 23, 1966, A19.

"Search Continues for 2 Chili Girls," *Rochester Democrat & Chronicle*, June 29, 1966, 7B.

Secter, Bob. "The Richard Speck Case." http://www.chicagotribune.com/news/nationworld/politics/chi-chicagodays-richardspeck-story-story.html (accessed September 3, 2011).

"She May Have Seen Killer of Two Girls." *Syracuse Herald-Journal*, August 10, 1966, 2.

"Sheriff Asks Help," *Gates-Chili News*, July 21, 1966, 1.

"Sheriff's Office Sends Out 'Flyer' on Missing Girls." *Rochester Times-Union*, July 15, 1966.

"Slaying of 2nd Girl Frightens Milwaukee." *Watertown Daily Times*, October 18, 1966, 10. Re murder of Sherryl Thompson.

Smith, Cliff. "Death Auto Hunted in 2 Chili Slayings." *Rochester Times-Union*, July 23, 1966.

"Stabbing Victim." *Buffalo Courier-Express*, November 5, 1966, 5. Re the murder of Diane Olkwitz.

"Stray Bullet Wounds Woman." *Lockport Union-Sun and Journal*, April 28, 1967, 5. Re shooting at the Brick Wall in Albion.

Sturdevant, Jan. "Crank Callers Plague Missing Girls' Mothers." *Rochester Democrat & Chronicle*, July 15, 1966.

"Suspect Arrested in Smoyer-King Slayings Following Speed Chase." *Livingston County Leader*, April 30, 1964, 3.

"Suspect Held for Jury in Albion Shooting." *Buffalo Courier-Express*, October 24, 1967, 3.

"Testimony Improper, Killer's Lawyer Says." *Vindicator*, January 18, 1989. Re murder of Christine Watson.

"Tests Are Continued in Death of 2 Teeners." *Kingston Daily Freeman*, July 22, 1966, 16.

"Texan Cleared in Chili Probe." *Rochester Times-Union*, August 26, 1966.

"Three Plead Innocent in Yates County Court." *Geneva Times*, January 9, 1974, 19.

"3 Rapists Guilty in Assault on Helpless Co-Ed." *WE*, January 16, 1967, 9.

"A Tragic Warning: Killer at Large." *Rochester Democrat & Chronicle*, July 22, 1966, 10A.

Tucker, Caroline. "Crime Writer Tries to Dig Up Chili Cold Case." rochesterhomepage.com, August 26, 2011 (accessed August 28, 2011).

"20-Year Prison Term Is Started by Pearl Odell." *Auburn Citizen*, June 9, 1920, 6. Re murder of Edward J. Knelp, body stashed in 1920 under the stone trestle.

"2 Chili Girls Still Missing." *Rochester Democrat & Chronicle*, July 4, 1966, 4B.

"2 Missing Girls Are Found Slain: Upstate Victims, 14 and 16 Had Been Swimming." *New York Times*, July 21, 1966.

"Waitress, 24, Abducted at Knife Point—Attacked in Wooded Area." *WE*, September 11, 1967, 3.

Wall, Glenn. *Sympathy Vote: A Reinvestigation of the Valerie Percy Murder*. Middletown, DE: self-published, 2014.

"Within the Dark Shadow: The Case of John Kelly Given to the Jury." *Rochester Democrat & Chronicle*, March 8, 1883, 6. Re the murder along the Genesee Valley Canal of Jacob Lutz.

"Woman Charged." *Milwaukee Journal*, March 10, 1984, 2. Re suspect Ellis Kennedy Douthit.

INDEX

ABOUT THE AUTHOR

Michael Benson is originally from the town of Chili, New York, and attended Wheatland-Chili High School. He has a journalism degree from Hofstra University and is the author of many true-crime books, including *Murder in Connecticut*, *The Burn Farm*, and *Killer Twins*. He has appeared on the *CBS Morning News*, *On the Case with Paula Zahn*, *Deadly Sins*, and *Southern-Fried Homicide* programs and is a regular on the Investigation Discovery network's *Evil Twins* and *Evil Kin* series.

I THOUGHT MY
FATHER WAS GOD

G·K
Hall
&Cº.

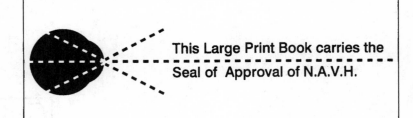
This Large Print Book carries the
Seal of Approval of N.A.V.H.